JHL nur

90   Mesop div. = "magic"

117   div. as subspecies of magical actions
121   def. of divination

233   "pseudo-categories"

258   adumn

JOURNAL FOR THE STUDY OF THE OLD TESTAMENT
SUPPLEMENT SERIES
142

Editors
David J.A. Clines
Philip R. Davies

Executive Editor
John Jarick

Editorial Board
Richard J. Coggins, Alan Cooper, Tamara C. Eskenazi,
J. Cheryl Exum, Robert P. Gordon, Norman K. Gottwald,
Andrew D.H. Mayes, Carol Meyers, Patrick D. Miller

JSOT Press
Sheffield

Divination in Ancient Israel and its Near Eastern Environment

A Socio-Historical Investigation

Frederick H. Cryer

Journal for the Study of the Old Testament
Supplement Series 142

Copyright © 1994 Sheffield Academic Press

Published by JSOT Press
JSOT Press is an imprint of
Sheffield Academic Press Ltd
343 Fulwood Road
Sheffield S10 3BP
England

Typeset by Frederick H. Cryer
and
Printed on acid-free paper in Great Britain
by Bookcraft
Midsomer Norton, Somerset

British Library Cataloguing in Publication Data

Cryer, Frederick H.
    Divination in Ancient Israel and Its
    Near Eastern Environment:
    Socio-historical Investigation.—(JSOT
    Supplement Series, ISSN 0309-0787; No. 142)
    I. Title II. Series
    221.6

ISBN 1-85075-353-9

CONTENTS

PREFACE

For the opportunity to express the ideas in this study I should like to take this occasion to thank my two Doktorväter, Prof. Dr. Benedikt Otzen, of the University of Aarhus, Denmark, and Prof. Dr. Dr. Siegfried Herrmann, of the Ruhr-Universität Bochum. Both have provided me solely with encouragement to complete the study; they are in no wise responsible for any of the ideas here proposed, and no doubt disagree with many of them.

I should also like to thank my friend and former colleague, Prof Dr Rüdiger Liwak, now of the Kirchliche Hochschule/Humboldt Universität, Berlin, for many rich and stimulating hours of discussion of OT themes and issues and, at a more personal level, for making my adjustment to life at the Ruhr-Universität more than tolerable. Many thanks, too, go to my former colleague, Wissenschaftlicher Mitarbeiter (now Pastor) Friedbert Fellert, for countless absorbing theological discussions, and for comradship of great value.

Thanks are also in order to John Van Seters, with whom I have conducted an intermittent dialogue for several years, and who overcame my initial reluctance to see how late are the texts we are dealing with by sheer patience, cogent argument, and much good humour. That he now no doubt regards me as something of a radical is absolutely my own doing, and no fault of his. Thanks also to Jack Sasson for calling my attention to a good deal of interesting literature, and also for continually pointing behind the history of interpretation to the motives which have led scholars to read the texts as they have done.

I should also like to thank several of my Bochumer students, Lars Gehrmann, Armin Rosen, Dirk Schwiderski, Susanne Kosslers, Andreas Kutz . . . I could go on and on. Without the feedback with which talented students supply us, we scholars would have little sense of the significance of what we do.

On a more personal level, I should like to thank Biskop Thyge Kragh and his wife, Rigmor Kragh, for their extraordinary hospitality which I have enjoyed on many visits to their home in Haderslev,

Denmark. It was in the privacy of their guestroom that I originally conceived several of the theses which are presented here.

Thanks are also in order to Bente Kragh, my wife's mother, who is too dear a friend to be called "mother-in-law", or else she has redefined the concept; and to my brother, sinologist and author James Cryer, and his wife Debbie, whose calm certainty that I would, sooner or later, finish this book was of great help to me.

No thanks could sufficiently express my gratitude to my wife, Liselotte Horneman Kragh, both for her forbearance with the irascible figure that a scholar in mid-stride must inevitably cut, and for her unflagging interest and perceptive comments on the book as it developed apace. Quite amazingly, she actually managed to get some work done towards her own degree while keeping our ménage in order.

Finally, love and much more to my mother, Barbara Harris Cryer, who enabled me to study theology, and to whom this study is dedicated; and to the memory of my father, James Magill Cryer, Jr, who was suspicious of theology, but who respected scholarship in all its forms.

Frederick H. Cryer

ABBREVIATIONS

AA	*American Anthropologist*
AEM	*Archives épistolaires de Mari*
AfO	*Archiv für Orientforschung*
AHw	W. von Soden, *Akkadisches Handwörterbuch*
ANET	J.B. Pritchard (ed.), *Ancient Near Eastern Texts*
AOAT	Alter Oreint und Altes Testament
ARM	Archives Royales de Mari
ASTI	*Annual of the Swedish Theological Institute*
ATD	Das Alte Testament Deutsch
BA	*Biblical Archaeologist*
BAR	*Bonner Akademische Reden*
BHS	*Biblia Hebraica Stuttgartensia*
Bib	*Biblica*
BKAT	Biblischer Kommentar: Altes Testament
BN	*Biblische Notizen*
BO	*Bibliotheca orientalis*
BWANT	Beiträge zur Wissenschaft vom Alten und Neuen Testament
BZ	*Biblische Zeitschrift*
BZAW	Beihefte zur ZAW
CAD	*The Assyrian Dictionary of the Oreintal Institute of the University of Chicago*
CBQ	*Catholic Biblical Quarterly*
CSSH	*Comparative Studies in Society and History*
DBAT	*Dielheimer Blätter zum Alten Testament und seiner Rezeption in der Alte Kirche*
DBSup	*Dictionnaire de la Bible, Supplément*
DISO	C.-F. Jean and J. Hoftijzer, *Dictionnaire des inscriptions sémitiques de l'ouest*
DTT	*Dansk teologisk tidsskrift*
EvT	*Evangelische Theologie*
HSM	Harvard Semitic Monographs

HTR	*Harvard Theological Review*
HUCA	*Hebrew Union College Annual*
IDB	G.A. Buttrick (ed.), *Interpreter's Dictionary of the Bible*
IDBSup	*IDB*, Supplementary Volume
IEJ	*Israel Exploration Journal*
JAOS	*Journal of the American Oriental Society*
JBL	*Journal of Biblical Literature*
JCS	*Journal of Cuneiform Studies*
JEA	*Journal of Egyptian Archaeology*
JJS	*Journal of Jewish Studies*
JNES	*Journal of Near Eastern Studies*
JNSL	*Journal of Northwest Semitic Languages*
JQR	*Jewish Quarterly Review*
JRAI	*Journal of the Royal Anthropological Institute*
JRAS	*Journal of the Royal Asiatic Society*
JSJ	*Journal for the Study of Judaism in the Persian, Hellenistic and Roman Period*
JSOT	*Journal for the Study of the Old Testament*
JSOTSup	*JSOT* Supplement Series
JSS	*Journal of Semitic Studies*
JTS	*Journal of Theological Studies*
KAI	H. Donner and W. Röllig, *Kanaanäische und aramäische Inschriften*
KD	*Kerygma und Dogma*
MDOG	Mitteilungen der deutschen Orient-Gesellschaft
OBO	Orbis biblicus et orientalis
OLZ	*Orientalische literaturezeitung*
Or	*Orientalia* (Rome)
OrAnt	*Oriens antiquus*
PAPS	*Papers of the American Philosophical Society*
PEQ	*Palestine Exploration Quarterly*
RA	*Revue d'assyriologie et d'archéologie orientale*
RB	*Revue biblique*
RE	*Realencyklopädie für protestantische Theologie und Kirche*
REg	*Revue d'égyptologie*
RevQ	*Revue de Qumran*
RGG	*Religion in Geschichte und Gegenwart*
RivB	*Rivista biblica*

RLA	*Reallexikon der Assyriologie*
RSO	*Rivista degli studi orientali*
RSV	*Revised Standard Version*
SBLSP	*Society of Biblical Literature Seminar Papers*
SEÅ	*Svensk eksegetisk årsbok*
SJOT	*Scandinavian Journal of the Old Testament*
SR	*Studies in Religion/sciences religieuses*
ST	*Studia theologica*
TAPS	*Transactions of the American Philosophical Society*
ThWAT	G.J. Botterweck and H. Ringgren (eds.), *Theologisches Wörterbuch zum Alten Testament*
ThZ	*Theologische Zeitung*
TLZ	*Theologische Literaturzeitung*
TRE	*Theologische REalenzyklopädie*
UF	*Ugarit-Forschungen*
VT	*Vetus Testamentum*
VTSup	*Vetus Testamentum, Supplements*
WMANT	*Wissenschaftliche Monographien zum Alten und Neuen Testament*
WZKM	*Wiener Zeitschrift für die Kunde des Morgenlandes*
ZA	*Zeitschrift für Assyriologie*
ZAH	*Zeitschrift für Althebraistik*
ZÄS	*Zeitschrift für ägyptologische Studien*
ZAW	*Zeitschrift für die alttestamentliche Wissenschaft*
ZDMG	*Zeitschrift der deutschen morgenländischen Gesellschaft*
ZDPV	*Zeitschrift des deutschen Palästina-Vereins*
ZfE	*Zeitschrift für Ethnographie*
ZRG	*Zeitschrift für Religionsgeschichte*
ZThK	*Zeitschrift für Theologie und Kirche*

Divination in ancient Israel and her Near Eastern environment? A vast topic, and one fraught with difficulties. The two primary difficulties are indicated by the subtitle of this study, "A Socio-historical Introduction". Sociology is, of course, many things. As a discipline, it has existed ever since man began to speculate in a more or less systematic fashion as to the nature of the relationship between the individual and the larger whole(s) of which he is inevitably a part. As a science, it is usual to trace its beginnings back to Auguste Comte and Karl Marx. Unhappily, there is still no unconditional consensus as to either the philosophical basis or the precise subject matter of the young science. Thus there are sociologies of small groups, social psychologies, sociologies of culture, of knowledge, of power, and what have you. Terminology, too, has proliferated to what is for the layman a bewildering degree, a point which is lamented by some, ridiculed by others, and mistrusted by yet more. Thus there is, for example, no firm distinction between ethnology, ethnography, sociology and anthropology, although various "schools" and individuals have various opinions on the subject. By "sociology" or "social anthropology", which are used interchangeably in this work, the writer means the study of man in relation to the social forces which constitute the basis of his existence. Although I am an American by birth, I carry no torch for the conventional American emphasis on "culture", rather than "society". The concept seems to me simply to be too amorphous ever to prove very useful.[1]

---

[1] Note the following definitions of culture which various scholars have offered: E.B. Tylor: "culture may refer to any product of the social life of man, either in the past or in the present". R. Linton: "A culture is the configuration of learned behavior and results of behavior whose component elements are shared and transmitted by the members of a particular society". A.R. Radcliffe-Brown: "learnt ways of thinking, feeling and acting". Cited in F.W. Foget, "The History of Cultural Anthropology," in J.J. Honigmann (ed.), *Handbook of Social and Cultural Anthropology* (Chicago,

Soci-owl-ogy?

An English professor of Old Testament of my acquaintance is fond of reminiscing about a young American graduate student who was once in his charge. This student, so the professor, spoke unceasingly of "soci-owl-ogy", and was so enthusiastic in his advocacy of the science that he once, in discussion, exclaimed that he was convinced that there was "an over-arching theme that undergirds the whole thing!" But, tortured metaphors and mid-western accents apart, sociology has in some cases been over-used, and by persons not properly qualified to use it at all, as a magic wand to make the Biblical and other ancient texts intelligible to us. But we should note that the same professor has written a very perceptive study showing the extent to which the Old Testament researches of the "school" of Alt and Noth were predicated on the sociology of Max Weber, although Weber himself was seldom mentioned in this connexion.[1] His thinking was simply a broadly accepted presupposition for understanding society in the German academic world around 1920.

Now no one, I think, would question the qualifications of an Albrecht Alt or a Martin Noth; the lesson to be learned from this example must then be that, will-we, nil-we, sociological views inform our understanding of society, and hence of history, even in ways we do not ourselves perceive. Thus it is best to be as candid about our socio-historical presuppositions as possible, even though there will always remain a portion of them of which we are unaware. In this sense, complete objectivity in sociological and historical research is impossible, the striving to achieve it the residue of the ancient positivistic dream of

---

1973), p. 2. A.L. Kroeber and C. Kluckhohn ("Culture: A Critical Review of the Concepts and Definitions"; *Papers of the Peabody Museum of American Anthropology and Ethnology* 47 [1952], pp. 1-223) once listed a hundred-thirty-odd definitions of the concept. Culture as defined in linguistic or archaeological studies is another matter, as the criteria seem to be at least somewhat more objectifiable.

   [1] Cf. E.W. Nicholson, *God and his People: Covenant and Theology in the Old Testament* (Oxford, 1986), pp. 37-55; and see already H.F. Hahn, *The Old Testament in Modern Research: With a Survey of Recent Literature* (H.D.Hummel) (Philadelphia, 1966 [1954]), pp. 159-73.

certainty.[1]

The social anthropology of the 19th century was overwhelmingly concerned with the question of the origins of types of human behaviour.[2] In a sense, this was a quest for meaning, since the dominant assumption of the time was evolutionary: we can understand the present if we see how it has grown up out of the past. Hence the countless studies showing this, that, or the other social phenomenon to be "survivals" of earlier types of behaviour. The studies in question were relentlessly comparative in nature; the social context of a phenomenon was unimportant, as it served simply to illustrate the persistence in advanced societies of features also present in "primitive" ones. The drawback of this sort of theorising is that we really have virtually no evidence as to the purported "origins" of social phenomena, and, in the absence of all documentation, how could we be expected to do so?[3]

With the advent of structural functionalist social anthropology, with which we associate the names of Durkheim and Mauss in France and those of Radcliffe-Brown, Malinowski, and Evans-Pritchard in

---

[1] Following on the heels of the social philosophical deliberations of the so-called "Frankfurt School", a furious debate has raged within recent German historiography as to the possibilities of objective socio-historical study. Some go so far as to insist on the deliberate and systematic importation of theoretical frameworks into an historical investigation; others, however, are more hesitant (see, e.g., J. Rusen, "Der Historiker als 'Parteimann des Schicksals': Georg Gotttfried Gervinus und das Konzept der objektiven Parteilichkeit im deutschen Historismus", in R. Koselleck, W.J. Mommsen, J. Rusen (eds.), *Objektivität und Parteilichkeit* (Munich, 1977), pp. 77-125; see further the contributions of K.-G. Faber (pp. 270-319), H.-W. Hedinger (pp. 362-93), K. Acham (pp. 393-425), W.J. Mommsenn (pp. 441-69), and J. Kocka (pp. 469-77) in the same volume.

[2] This was fully in harmony with the major concerns of 19th century historical thought, whose works reveal a plethora of evolutionistic schemes; cf. H.E. Barnes, *A History of Historical Writing* (Toronto and London, 2nd edn 1963), pp. 174-76; further, R.G. Collingwood, *The Idea of History* (Oxford, 1970 [1946]), pp. 86-133.

[3] Thus, for example, Evans-Pritchard on "originistic" studies of "primitive religion": "if they cannot be refuted, they also cannot be sustained, and for the simple reason that there is no evidence about how religious beliefs originated". *Theories of Primitive Religion* (Oxford, 1965), p. 29; similarly, I.M. Lewis: "Origins are certainly often interesting, but they do not necessarily have much to do with the present functioning and meaning of things" (*Social Anthropology in Perspective* [Harmondsworth, 1976], p. 53).

England, the meaning of social phenomena came to be equated with their social use. Thus kinship structures were no longer to be understood as enshrining reminiscences of earlier matriarchal social structures; rather, they were seen to regulate the exchange of women between social groups, thus ensuring social stability. Hugely detailed studies were carried out by generations of serious social anthropologists; they contributed vastly to our understanding of the interplay of the forces active in numerous societies. And yet, structural functionalism, too, has an obvious drawback, namely the fact that the "regulatory" model of social dynamics presupposes that equilibrium is the goal of social behaviour, which does not seem to leave room for the plain fact that societies do develop in time. Moreover, at a deeper level it could be objected that the "function" hypothecated by one or another social scientist for a given social phenomenon is indemonstrable, since we cannot experiment on human societies to discover how they would get on without the function in question. Ultimately, structural functionalism relies on a species of teleological argumentation in which the telos in question is the equilibrium presupposed by the researcher.[1] One is reminded of the old joke in which a passerby, seeing a hippy walking along snapping his fingers, asks him why he does so. "Man, it keeps the vampires away!" he is told; and when he asks if the hippy really believes that finger-snapping repels vampires, the other replies, "You seen any vampires lately, have you?" A further difficulty is that structural functional characterisations of social phenomena were irretrievably anchored in the societies in which they were observed. A phenomenon observed in one society might have a completely different significance, that is, use, in another society. Perhaps the most thought--provoking example of this has been provided by I.M. Lewis:

> In the installation ceremonies of the Divine King of the
> Shilluk tribe of the southern Sudan one of the most cherished
> items in the cermonial regalia is now apparently a Scottish

---

[1] Cf. C.G. Hempel, "The Logic of Functional Analysis", in L. Gross (ed.), *Symposium on Sociological Theory* (Evanston, 1959), pp. 271-307; further, F.W. Foget in Honigmann (ed.), *Handbook*, p. 39. This is not to say, however, that functional explanation is incapable of useful definition and so of playing a significant part in socio-anthropological explanation even today; see A. Bruck, "Neue Überlegungen zum Konzept der Funktion", *ZfE* 113 (1988), pp. 1-20.

international rugby cap-one of the more exotic relics of the British colonial legacy in Africa. This borrowed item, no doubt bequeathed by some burly and well-meaning district commissioner, does not possess quite the same significance in this ambience as it had in its original context.[1]

By implication, we cannot legitimately compare phenomena across social boundaries, a feature of structural functionalistic studies which many have felt vitiates the ultimate usefulness of the functionalist programme. Of what use is a lot of disparate information if we cannot generalise it in some fashion?

Having progressed from comparative studies which understood meaning as genesis to fieldwork analyses which interpreted meaning as the function of social structures, in the mid-1960s in southern Europe, and from the early 1970s in northern Europe and America, social anthropology came under the spell of Claude Lévi-Strauss, and so progressed to what might be termed a cybernetic understanding of social facts. At the same time, however, it moved as by a swing of the pendulum back to a comparative study of societies which had no interest in individual societies and attempted instead to make universal statements about man in general.[2] Virtually no fundamental structuralist tenet has gone unchallenged by very able scholars; particularly the structuralist transferral of de Saussure's famous distinction between langue and parole onto social phenomena has attracted criticism,[3] as has Lévi-Strauss' adherence to the now outmoded distinctive-feature binary

[1] Lewis, *Social Anthropology*, p. 63.

[2] Cf. E. Leach, *Claude Lévi-Strauss* (New York, 1970), p. 2; Leach's book is by far the best informed of the numerous partisan studies of Lévi-Strauss's accomplishments.

[3] See, e.g., G.S. Kirk, *Myth: Its Meaning and Functions* (London, 1970), p. 43: "The linguistic analogy, so heavily used in structural studies in general and by Lévi-Strauss in particular, is ambivalent and confusing in its application to myth. The function of language is to convey content, not to convey its own grammatical and syntactical rules—its own structure, that is".

(linguistic) analysis of Roman Jakobsen.[1] In general, it may be said that structuralism has had more success with texts than it has had with societies; certainly in conjunction with the analysis of myth it has made a lasting contribution to sociology.[2] Moreover, in demonstrating the sophistication of native systems of classification,[3]

Lévi-Strauss went a long way towards rehabilitating "primitives" in the eyes of social anthropologists, who had perhaps relied over-long on condescending theories of "primitive mentality".

From the 1970s and onwards, social anthropology has posed the question of meaning in a variety of ways independent of the structuralist approach. Under the rubric of "cognitive anthropology", scholars have attempted to study the ways in which men define their interrelationships through communicative acts, be they verbal or non-verbal.[4] Closely related to this have been a number of investigations devoted to the study of the symbolism(s) inherent in ritual and ritual-like social behaviour.[5] Other studies have attempted to define the ways in which perception of

---

[1] Cf. Leach, *Lévi-Strauss*, p. 23, who, however, predictably defends Lévi-Strauss (p. 23 n. 3). Even strong adherents of Jakobson's linguistics acknowledge the difficulties Jacobson's binary linguistics have encountered; cf. e.g. E. Holenstein, *Roman Jakobsons phänomenologischer Strukturalismus* (Frankfurt am Main, 1975), pp. 131-32. For a very learned discussion of the critical reception structuralism received in America, see B. Sholte, "The Structural Anthropology of Claude Lévi-Strauss", in Honigmann, *Handbook*, pp. 637-716, with an extensive bibliography on pp. 704-16. A list of critics versus supporters is supplied by Sholte on p. 693.

[2] Besides the *Mythologiques* of Lévi-Strauss himself, see such studies as G.S. Kirk's previously-mentioned study.

[3] In *La Pensée Sauvage* (Paris, 1962).

[4] Cf. e.g. A.V. Cicourel, *Cognitive Sociology: Language and Meaning in Social Interaction* (New York, 1974).

[5] Cf. N.D. Munn, "Symbolism in a Ritual Context", in Honigmann, *Handbook*, pp. 579-612; further, J.L. Dolgin, et al. (eds.), *Symbolic Anthropology* (New York, 1977); Steven Lukes, "Political Ritual and Social Integration", *Sociology* 9 (1975), pp. 289-308; the survey by V. Turner, "Symbolic Studies" *Annual Review of Anthropology* 4 (1975), pp. 145-161, as well as his earlier study in depth, *The Forest of Symbols: Aspects of Ndembu Ritual* (Ithaca [NY], 1967).

reality is socially presented to the individual,[1] while still still others have attempted to explore the ways in which the beliefs of given cultures, often so impenetrable to outside observers, can be seen to be intelligible in terms of the internal logic of the beliefs themselves and the institutions of the society in question.[2] Some recent investigations have returned to the question of the mental performances of "primitives" in a variety of fashions. Thus J. Goody and others have studied the interrelationships between savage society and literacy,[3] while a number of studies have explored the logic of primitives;[4] a few have even ventured onto the treacherous terrain of discussing the performance--competence of primitives, with predictably controversial results.[5] Finally, adding profoundly to the confusion of the layman interested in sociology is a recent study which proposes to conduct social study without reference to such structured "system" models as the notion of "society".[6]

[1] Cf. P. Berger and T. Luckmann, *The Social Construction of Reality* (New York, 1967); the same, "Sociology of Religion and Sociology of Knowledge", in R. Robertson (ed.), *Sociology of Religion* (Harmondsworth, 1976 [1969]), pp. 61-73.

[2] Cf. e.g. M.B. Black, "Belief Systems", in Honigmann, *Handbook*, pp. 509-77; see above all the study by F.A. Hanson, *Meaning in Culture* (London, 1975), which attempts in a serious fashion to grapple with the philosophical issues involved.

[3] Cf. J. Goody (ed.), *Literacy in Traditional Societies* (Cambridge, 1968); *idem*, *The Domestication of the Savage Mind* (Cambridge, 1977).

[4] Cf. e.g. D.E. Cooper, "Alternative Logic in 'Primitive Thought'", *Man* N.S. 10 (1975), pp. 238-56; see the reply by M.H. Salmon, "Do Azande and Nuer use a Non-Standard Logic?", *Man* N.S. 13 (1978), pp. 444-54; further, from the point of view of post-Wittgenstein "game theory", E.M. Ahern, "Rules in Oracles and Games", *Man* N.S. 17 (1982), pp. 302-13.

[5] See especially C.R. Hallpike, "Is There a Primitive Mentality?" *Man* 11 (1976), pp. 253-70; the same, *The Foundations of Primitive Thought* (Oxford, 1979), and the spate of articles this work has provoked, including R.A. Shweder, "Has Piaget been Upstaged? A Reply to Hallpike". *AA* 87 (1985), pp. 138-44; Hallpike's own rejoinder in the same issue, pp. 144-46; further, C.O. Frake, "Cognitive Maps of Time and Tide Among Medieval Seafarers", *Man* 20 (1985), pp. 254-70; A. Gell, "How to Read a Map: Remarks on the Practical Logic of Navigation", *Man* 20 (1985), pp. 271-86.

[6] M. Mann, *The Sources of Social Power. Vol I. A History of Power from the Beginning to A.D. 1760* (Cambridge; 3rd edn, 1988 [1986]).

Exciting as the present ferment in sociology may be, it should be evident from this all too cursory review that no single set of assumptions has won for itself anything like a general consensus of opinion among scholars. The outsider, desirous to utilise sociological insights to illuminate his own area of competence, is accordingly well advised to exercise extreme care.

History?

The second problematical topic, again, as suggested by the title of this study, has to do with history. History is itself problematical. Where historians of, particularly, the late 19th century were largely concerned to study political events on the more or less positivistic assumption that "the facts" of history were discoverable,[1] historians of the 20th century have been mainly interested in writing social history, and to speak more in terms of relations than of "facts". Moreover, particularly in recent times, they have become aware of the "fictionalising" quality of historical reconstructions.[2] To put it briefly, there is no formal characteristic that distinguishes narratives in the past tense which have to do with figures who once existed and events that really happened from narratives dealing with invented actors and events. Conversely, an historian who attempts to explain past events necessarily utilises canons

[1] See Barnes, *Historical Writing*, pp. 239-76, esp. pp. 266-75; Collingwood, *Idea*, pp. 126-33 (on "positivism"). However, it is important to acknowledge that the so-called "scientific historians" were as much influenced by idealism as by positivism; cf. e.g. R.A.Oden, Jr, "Hermeneutics and Historiography: Germany and America," *SBLSP* (1980), pp. 135-57, esp. pp. 139-40; R. Vierhaus ("Rankes Begriff der historischen Objektivität", in R. Koselleck, W.J. Mommsen and J. Rüsen [eds], *Objektivität*, pp. 63-77) explains the "fact-transcending" aspects of von Ranke's historiography as the results of religious belief (esp. p. 69). Oden has understood the tradition more deeply.

[2] On social history, see already Barnes, *Historical Writing*, pp. 330-92; F. Braudel, "History and Sociology" in *On History* (Chicago, 1980), pp. 64-82 (a slightly expanded version of Braudel's contribution to G. Gurvitch [ed.], *Traité du sociologie* [Paris, 1958-60]). On the "fictionalisation" of history, see H. White, "The Question of Narrative in Contemporary Historical Theory", *History and Theory* 23 (1984), pp. 1-33; and the works cited in F.H. Cryer, "To the One of Fictive Music: OT Chronology and History", *SJOT* 2 (1987), pp. 3-4, n. 5.

of plausibility, probability, verisimilitude, and so on: all features which figure prominently in the repertoire of the novelist, dramatist, or scriptwriter. This has led contemporary historians to attempt the critical study of historical narrative, even to the extent of trying to compose a new *Historik*.[1] Obviously, this does not mean that the discipline of historiography is lost in the wilderness; a great deal of fine historical studies manage to appear across the spectrum of historical provinces. But it does mean that no particular theory of historical interpretation can be said to dominate the field so completely as to offer the outsider a convenient point of departure.

Ancient History and Sociology?

If the situation in contemporary sociology can be characterised as being in flux, the situation in contemporary historiography is no less so. We are accordingly justified in being hesitant in the extreme about asserting of any historical society that it was thus and so; the gap between text and social reality seems ever-widening. Thus it is hardly surprising that well qualified scholars wonder whether historical sociology is at all feasible.[2] This question becomes all the more poignant when we

---

[1] See above all J. Rüsen, *Für eine erneuerte Historik: Studien zur Theorie der Geschichtswissenschaft* (Bad Canstadt, 1976); the same, *Historische Vernunft: Grundzüge einer Historik. I: Die Grundlagen der Geschichtswissenschaft* (Göttingen, 1983); the same, *Rekonstruktion der Vergangenheit: Grundzüge einer Historik II: Die Prinzipien der historischen Forschung* (Göttingen, 1986); *contra*: G. Mann, "Plädoyer für die historische Erzählung", in J. Kocka and T. Nipperdey (eds.), *Theorie und Erzählung in der Geschichte* (Munich, 1979), pp. 40-57. The most prominent Anglo-Saxon opponent of the "narrative historiography" approach remains W.H. Dray, *On History and Philosophers of History* (Leiden, 1989), esp. "On the Nature and Role of Narrative in History", pp. 111-30.

[2] Cf. e.g. E.E. Evans-Pritchard, *Anthropology and History: A Lecture delivered in the University of Manchester with the support of the Simon Fund for the Social Sciences* (Manchester, 1971 [1961]), pp. 1-22. See further for a thorough treatment of the problems involved M.Szalay, *Ethnologie und Geschichte: Zur Grundlegung einer ethnologischen Geschichtsschreibung* (Berlin, 1983), esp. pp. 15-64. In connexion with the ancient Near East, see G. Feeley-Harnik, "Is Historical Anthropology Possible?" in (eds.) G.M. Tucker and D.A. Knight, *Humanizing America's Iconic Book*. (Society of Biblical Literature Centennial Addresses 1980; [Chico, CA, 1982]), pp. 95-126.

consider developments that have taken place in the field of ancient history in recent times. There are four major difficulties, and some subsidiary aspects.

One of the main problems should be obvious: ancient historians have not the abundance of source material available to them which their colleagues, the historians of the modern periods, enjoy. One has merely to consider that when H. and P. Charnu attempted to chronicle the economic contacts between Spain and the Spanish posessions in the New World between 1504 and 1650 (which, strictly speaking, preceeds the modern period), the statistical material alone available to them extended to six volumes![1] By way of contrast, when the Danish Assyriologist M.T. Larsen attempted to describe the Old Assyrian city-states and their relations to their Anatolian colonies (in the process utilising virtually every relevant document in existence), the result was a single volume, and one which could not satisfy the original intentions of its author.[2] Thus it is not surprising that ancient historians have traditionally stretched their sources to the limit in order to wrest what relevant information from them they could. One of the earliest developed means of doing so was what we would today call the discipline of tradition history. To quote Hermann Bengtson, the late doyen of recent German ancient historical research, "Modern scholarship generally takes the middle view: the narratives are not regarded as free inventions; rather, they were written down on the basis of historical traditions which contain some authentic historical features".[3] As the best example of the agreement of ancient historians on this point, Bengtson instances H.Schliemann's excavations of Troy and Mycenae and asserts confidently that "Nowadays no one would deny any more that the (Iliad) contains an historical nucleus".[4] It is worth juxtaposing alongside of this quotation the following remarks of the late M.I. Finley, himself no mean

[1] *Séville et l'Atlantique* (Paris, 1955—1956); cf. the review in Braudel, *On History*, pp. 91-104.

[2] Cf. *The Old Assyrian City-State and its Colonies* (Copenhagen, 1976); and note Larsen's prefatory remarks, p.9.

[3] H. Bengtson, *Einführung in die Alte Geschichte* (Munich, 8th edn, 1979), p. 114.

[4] *Einführung*, p. 114.

historian of antiquity:

> Schliemann's achievements were epoch-making. Nevertheless, despite
> the claims, the unassailable fact is that nothing he or his successors
> have found, not a single scrap, links the destruction of Troy VIIa
> with Mycenaean Greece, or with an invasion from any other source.
> Nor does anything known from the archaeology of Greece and Asia
> Minor or from the Linear B tablets fit with the Homeric tale of a
> great coalition sailing against Troy from Greece . . . Troy VIIa turns
> out to have been a pitiful poverty-stricken little place, with no
> treasure, without any large or imposing buildings, with nothing
> remotely resembling a palace. It is not mentioned in any contempo-
> rary document in Hittite or any other language, nor is a 'Trojan War'.
> And there are other archaeological difficulties with the tale, notably
> in the chronology."[1]

Finley's argumentation for his point of view is both meticulous and
scathing towards his opponents—perhaps to such a degree that he
rhetorically compelled them to stick to their guns. In reality, as he was
himself aware, he was merely adhering to a tradition of careful
historiography which demanded compelling objective evidence for the
supposition that a legendary source contains historical information, a
tradition which, in this instance, goes back to Eduard Meyer.[2]

Once a powerful force in Biblical studies, particularly in
Scandinavia, tradition history at present enjoys little status;[3] Prof. N.P.

---

[1] M.I. Finley, *The World of Odysseus* (Harmondsworth, 2nd rev edn 1978
[1954]), p. 43; see also his remarks in "Lost: the Trojan War", in the same, *Aspects
of Antiquity* (Harmondsworth, 1977 [1968]), pp. 31-42.

[2] See *Aspects*, Appendix II, pp. 159-77, and note that Bengtson, *Einführung*, p.
113 cites Meyer for "a. . . direction which strives to be just from an historical
viewpoint to both myth and popular tradition".

[3] Although the tenor of K. Jeppesen's and B. Otzen's summary of the
Scandinavian retrospective on tradition history (*The Productions of Time: Tradition
History in Old Testament Scholarship*, [trans. F.H. Cryer] [Sheffield, 1984], pp.
127-33) held at Sandbjerg Manor in south Jutland in May of 1982 is hardly elegiac,
it is nevertheless clear that the Scandinavians are coming back to the fold.
Particularly the failure of the congress participants to respond to the methodological
assault of T. Veijola ("Remarks of an Outsider Concerning Scandinavian Tradition
History with Emphasis on the Davidic Traditions", pp. 29-53) on the heritage of I.
Engnell allows us to suppose that, as far as "the Scandinavian approach" to tradition
history is concerned, the cupboard is bare.

Lemche, of the University of Copenhagen, notes quite simply that,"the method suffers from the lack of objective controls, since we ordinarily do not possess other sources which could show that the results arrived at by the method are correct".[1]

Thus the number of sources available to the critically-minded ancient historian is to be carefully restricted. Finley spoke with characteristic contempt, in his last-published work, of "the widespread sentiment that anything written in Greek or Latin is somehow privileged, exempt from the normal canons of evaluation".[2] No doubt, were he here today, he would be perfectly willing to extend his statement to cover Hebrew and other Semitic languages as well.

The second major problem facing the ancient historian has to do with the kinds of sources available to him, rather than with their number and distribution. Finley speaks of the "paucity and . . . the rudimentary state of the (Greek and Roman) archives"[3] as one of the reasons Greek and Roman history writers rarely refer to documents. They referred to sagas, legends, oral traditions, and so forth, of whatever nature and quality, for the good reason that they had no other sources available. Finley was namely at heart an adherent of the "scientific historians" of the 19th century, at least to the extent that he insisted on the indispensableness of narrative sources that are more or less contemporary with the events they describe.[4] Thus he could well have agreed with, or even have paraphrased, J.G. Droysen:

> That which one might or should technically term the first source is

---

[1] N.P. Lemche, *Ancient Israel* (trans. F.H. Cryer; [Sheffield, 1988]), p. 67; and see Lemche's criticisms of tradition history in his *Early Israel: Anthropological and Historical Studies on the Israelite Society Before the Monarchy* (trans. F.H. Cryer; [Leiden, 1985]), pp. 380-83.

[2] In his *Ancient History: Evidence and Models* (New York, 1986), p. 10; note that Finley was also firmly aware of the problem of the "fictionality" of historical writing: "I am unaware of any stigmata that automatically distinguish fiction from fact (p. 18)"; he also stressed the fact that "The ability of the ancients to invent and their capacity to believe are persistently underestimated" (p. 9).

[3] *Ancient History*, p. 21.

[4] See above all *Ancient History*, p. 11: "Unless something is captured in a more or less contempoary historical account, the narrative is lost for all time regardless of how many inscriptions or papyri may be discovered".

> not the mass of swirling rumours, opinions or views. Indeed, not
> even all the individual diplomatic accounts of a negotiation, taken
> together, comprise the history of that negotiation . . . It is not the
> sum, the addition of all the particulars, but rather the first summary
> of it all as a whole . . . that is the first source.[1]

On this issue the ancient historian faces thorny ground, indeed. If one
adheres to the time-honoured definition of a "source", then we have no
better ancient sources than whatever ancient narrative reconstructions
have survived to us, riddled though they may be with all manner of
tendentious or suppositious "traditions". We can then criticise these
sources as best we may and, on Finley's view, if they prove to be bad
sources, then so be it. The only alternative he offers is the interpretation
of the sources via the cross-examination of them by various interpretative "models".[2] Unfortunately, Finley had no suggestions to make as to
the nature of the appropriate models.

Alternatively, if criticism of the ancient source reveals its
inadequacies, then it may be held that we are obliged to patch together
our own reconstruction as well as we can on the basis of whatever
archaeological and epigraphic (but non-narrative) information is
available. The latter course seems to be the position N.P. Lemche has
arrived at. After having laboriously and with great learning striven to
show how poorly informed and tendentious is the Old Testament
account of the formation of the Israelite people,[3] he proffers instead a
model based on modern sociological studies of nomadism, ethnicity, and
the like. In so doing, Lemche is in reality composing a new "source",
in Droysen and Finley's terms; that is, he proposes for our consideration
a narrative of his own devising. Admittedly, Lemche's narrative no
longer has intrepid Joshua leading hordes of Yahweh-inspired Israelites
into the possession of the promised land; instead we find rather more

---

[1] *Historik: Vorlesungen über Enzyklopädie und Methodologie der Geschichte*;
originally published in a shorter form in Jena, 1858; here quoted from *ibid.*, R.
Hübner (ed.), (Munich, 8th edn, 1977), p.137.

[2] Finley, *Ancient History*, p.18.

[3] Cf. *Early Israel*, *passim*; for Lemche's rejection of the OT text in toto, note:
"once one has dismissed the OT recollection of Israel's immigration into Palestine
as ahistorical and late, one is also thereby compelled to ignore the narratives
concerning the origins of Israelite religion" (p. 413).

anonymous retribalised peasants establishing their small holdings in the Palestinian highlands, having fled the collapse of the Bronze Age city-states.[1] But this is and remains a narrative, no matter how abstract its author has laboured to make its theme, as Golo Mann has recently argued must be true of all historical reconstructions.[2] The question presents itself then, as to just why we should prefer Prof. Lemche's "source", composed some 3,200 years after the events they purport to describe, to the Biblical version, which, tendencies, ideologies, myths, legends, and all, nevertheless at least came into being rather more proximately to the period in question.[3] I offer this merely as an example of the daunting theoretical difficulties confronting the ancient historian; I should hasten to add that there is much to be said for Prof. Lemche's position.

In passing, we may consider a philosophical problem which arises out of the contemporary preoccupation with the problem of narrative versus "historical" discourse. Earlier students of semantics were convinced that the basic element of meaning was the word; hence the countless works from the 19th century and well into this one attempting to detail historically the possible meanings of words, as an aid to interpreting texts. In recent times, however, the unit of meaning has come to be considered either the sentence or even longer units of text.[4] Thus the narratologists insist that the semantic unit is the story, of which

---

[1] Cf. *Early Israel*, pp. 410-35; *Ancient Israel*, pp. 77-118.

[2] "Plaidoyer für die historische Erzählung", in *Theorie und Erzählung*, pp. 40-57.

[3] Lemche maintains that "The real problem is that the narratives (scil., of the conquest and settlement) are much later than the events which form their themes. . . we must stress the fact that this implies that they are of no use as historical sources without a critical pruning" (cited in N.P.Lemche, "Rachel and Lea. Or: On the Survival of Outdated Paradigms in the Study of the Origin of Israel-I", *SJOT* 2(1987), p.152. But not all historians share his disdain for secondary sources; members of the Annales school were notably sceptical of narratives written near the time of the events themselves (cf. Braudel, *On History*, p. 4: "We must beware of that history which still simmers with the passions of the contemporaries who felt it, described it, lived it. . . It has the dimensions of their anger, their dreams, and their illusions").

[4] On the development from lexical semantics to the semantics of sentences and larger units (including ultimate contexts, like culture), see J. Lyons, *Introduction to Theoretical Linguistics* (Cambridge, 1971), pp. 403-42.

the individual words and sentences are only parts, and from which they derive their significance in some sort of reciprocal relationship. But then, one notes, in Joshua 8 we have a description of the conquest of Ai by the Israelites under Joshua. Various historical-critical (including archaeological) reasons persuade us that the story is of very late date, compared to the event it attempts to describe. Accordingly, on the view of Lemche and scholars who are on his wavelength, the narrative in Joshua 8 is a good source for the theology and ideology of the 7th century and later, and is irrelevant to the Early Iron I period. But this means that all individual statements contained within Joshua 8 do not mean what they appear to mean; they cease to become statements about the settlement of Palestine, and become something else instead. Yet, somehow, it seems odd to claim that the statement "Joshua burned Ai, and made it for ever a heap of ruins" (Josh 8.28) in reality means something quite different. The formal similarity of the statement to "Nelson won the battle of Trafalgar", which we would not be inclined so to question, is inescapable.[1] Some sort of coherent explanation of this is required.[2]

---

[1] In any case, there is no question of accepting the statement as a simple declarative sentence; there is no earthly reason to suppose that the "historical Joshua" ever existed; and, archaeology has shown that the only site that comes in question as that of Ai had lain in ruins for about 1,000 to 1,300 years by the time usually assigned to the Israelite invasion/immigration (cf. Lemche, *Ancient Israel*, p. 111).

[2] Of course, if one chooses a purely narratological approach to the understanding of texts, the problem does not arise, as the individual components of a narrative are only considered to be meaningful in relation to the rest of the narrative. But traditional exegesis has a strong bias in favour of straighforward linguistic approaches, so that individual statements have to be considered as such. I have no solution to offer to this problem, although modern linguistics offers a few possibilities. One might consider Josh 8.28 in reality to be a performative, that is a member of the class of statements first identified by J.L. Austin (*How to Do Things with Words* [Cambridge, MA, 1962]) and since elaborated by J.R. Ross ("On Declarative Sentences", in R.A. Jacobs and P.S. Rosenbaum (eds.), *Readings in English Transformational Grammar* [Waltham, MA, 1970], pp. 222-72), of utterances which, declarative in form, in reality perform one or another socially-pro- grammed action (like "I do", in the context of a wedding ceremony). Ross argued that performatives need not have the "I (hereby pronounce/ do/ promise/ recom- mend/ command/ declare...etc.)" introduction, so that virtually all utterances could

The third challenge to the ancient historian today is the so-called "New Archaeology". Difficult to set a date to, one of the formative events in the inception of the new movement was the publication of V. Gordon Childe's famous *What Happened in History*.[1] Making only cursory reference to written sources, Childe applied the methods of cultural anthropology to the archaeological study of prehistory and extended this focus all the way to the decline of the Roman empire. This was very much a socio-cultural history; even in the periods of the great civilisations which have left literary records behind them, Childe mentioned the names of individual historical figures only incidentally. For Childe ancient "history" consisted of man's cultural achievements, instead of the who-defeated-whom-when of conventional early history (such data being often all that was written down).[2] Naturally, ancient historians of the Greco-Roman period, prehistorians, Assyriologists, and Biblical scholars have reacted variously to this new tendency. The "New Archaeological" understanding of the past entails allowing the archaeological materials, illuminated by appropriate sociological models, to

be regarded as performatives. Of course, this trivialises the concept (cf. e.g. G. Leech, *Semantics* [Harmondsworth, 2nd ed. 1987], p. 325) to the point of uselessness. Moreover, Josh 8.28 would only poorly answer the formal criteria of a performative utterance. Alternatively, following the insight that "The meaning of an utterance includes, but is not exhausted by, the meaning of the sentence that is uttered. The rest of the meaning is contributed by a variety of factors that may be referred to, loosely, as contextual" (J. Lyons, *Language and Linguistics* [New York, 1981], p.140), we might claim that, in the context of the 7th century or later, Josh 8.28 as an utterance is irrelevant to considerations of truth or falsehood. Its meaning could, for example, be claimed to be phatic, that is, fellowship-creating (or -sustaining): "Yahweh did thus and so through Joshua", implying "and is still prepared to do so for us". But whatever option scholars urging the radical redating of OT past-referring statements should happen to choose, they do owe us some sort of explanation of the relation of sentence to "text" or "narrative".

[1] (Harmondsworth, 1982 [1942]); see also Childe's programmatic work, *Social Evolution* (London, 1951).

[2] This is not to suggest that Childes' assault on traditional archaeological history was entirely successful; virtually all of his major claims were stood on their head by the publication of C. Renfrew's *Before Civilization* (Harmondsworth, 1976 [1973]); see also Renfrew's recent and controversial approach to European prehistory, *Archaeology and Language. The Puzzle of Indo-European Origins*, (London, 1987).

speak for themselves, instead of, as has often been the case, using material finds to "illustrate" one or another ancient text.[1]

A.L. Oppenheim, whose inspirational *Ancient Mesopotamia* has blazed a trail for the study of ancient Mesopotamia,[2] never mentioned Childe in his work. And yet, for all Oppenheim's well known concern to write a history of Mesopotamian society,[3] it is notable that he devoted impressive sections of his work to precisely the written materials which Childe only mentioned in passing. And, of course, classical scholars and classical archaeologists have been hesitant, as well.[4] In the field of Old Testament studies, there is no doubt but that archaeologists of Palestine have been champing at the bit for some time in reaction to what some have felt to be the domination exercised by the Biblical version of the history of the region. The shadow of William Foxwell Albright has loomed large indeed. As late as in Kathleen Kenyon's *Archaeology of the Holy Land* we find a fairly traditional examination of all periods which in the "historical" periods follows not merely the Biblical narrative, but even to some extent the interpretations of that narrative by modern Biblical scholars.[5] In the intervening years there has been considerable debate as to the legitimacy of such a procedure.[6] Helga Weippert's *Palästina in Vorhellenistischer Zeit*,[7] the

---

[1] See further L. Binford, "Contemporary Model Building: Paradigms and the Current State of Palaeolithic Research", in D. Clarke (ed.), *Models in Archaeology* (London, 1972), pp.109-66; the same, and S.R. Binford (eds.), *New Perspectives in Archeology* (Aldine, 1968); and, more popularly, D. Wilson, *The New Archaeology* (New York, 1975); on parallel developments in German cultural archaeology/ancient history, see J. Bergmann, *Die metallzeitliche Revolution. Zur Entstehung von Herschaft, Krieg und Umweltzerstörung* (Berlin, 1987), pp. 16-27.

[2] 1st edn Chicago, 1964; repr. with notes by E. Reiner, (Chicago, 1977).

[3] A well-known Sumerologist who shall here remain nameless once groused to me that it seems as if the only history emerging from the Chicago school since Oppenheim has been social history.

[4] Cf. Finley, *Ancient History*, pp. 18-19.

[5] (New York and London, 1979 [1960]); note in this connexion especially Kenyon's version of the exodus, pp. 204-5.

[6] See the survey by E. Noort, *Biblisch-archäologische Hermeneutik und alttestamentliche Exegese* (Kampen, 1979).

[7] (Munich, 1988).

most recent large-scale study of the archaeology of Palestine, differs from Kenyon's approach almost as night from day, so reduced a rôle does the Biblical text play in the elucidation of the archaeological materials. We may say at present, that, as far as the archaeology of the Syro-Palestinian region is concerned; the "archaeological data and the text of the Bible cannot be brought together directly; each needs to be interpreted. In the process it has emerged that only on very rare occasions do archaeological data shed direct light on the text of the Bible or vice versa. Thus archaeological data (like the text of the Bible) remain independent sources for conditions (and on occasions also events) relevant to the history of culture, society, economics and religion".[1]

Objections to the "New Archaeology", as one might expect, have been mainly from traditional Biblical scholars and classicists who are loath to see one of their few sources of confirmation, however limited, taken away from them.[2] A more pertinent objection, and one which I feel focuses the discussion on substantive issues, is that of Finley. As a professional gadfly, one might have expected Finley to throw in his lot with the New Archaeologists. But instead, in his last work he pointed out that the discussion has seduced ancient historians to believe that

---

[1] D. Conrad, "An Introduction to the Archaeology of Syria and Palestine on the Basis of the Israelite Settlement"; Appendix 1 in J.A. Soggin, *A History of Ancient Israel* (Philadelphia, 1984), p. 360. On this point, there is no theoretical disagreement even from I. Finkelstein, who represents the new breed of Israeli archaeologists who are not primarily concerned to conduct "Biblical archaeology", i.e., archaeology on Biblical premises. With its express disdain for the Albright-school's "conquest theory" and the adherents of the Mendenhall-Gottwald "sociological approach", Finkelstein's fine recent study (*The Archaeology of the Israelite Settlement* [Jerusalem, 1988]) in reality offers cold comfort for those seeking any sort of rapprochement between the archaeological evidence and the Biblical text.

[2] Israeli historians are particularly typical in this connexion; cf. e.g. A. Malamat, "Die Frühgeschichte Israels-eine methodologische Studie", *ThZ* 39 (1983), pp. 1-16. Note, however, the more thoughtful objections of S. Herrmann, "Israels Frühgeschichte im Spannungsfeld neuer Hypothesen", *Rheinisch-Westfälische Akademie der Wissenschaften*, Abh. 78, "Studien zur Ethnogenese", Bd. 2 (1988), pp. 43-95; and J. Strange, "The Transition from the Bronze Age to the Iron Age in the Eastern Mediterranean and the Emergence of the Israelite State", *SJOT* 1 (1987), pp. 1-19, both of whom find the archaeological situation in Palestine in the period in question too complicated for the use of oversimplified sociological models.

the most insistent historical question one can put to an archaeological find is, Does it support or falsify the literary tradition? That approach gives automatic priority to literary evidence . . . [1]

This objection is just; the job of the historian is to ask questions about the past, and the information at his disposal is either relevant to those questions or it is not, in which case it is not information (although it may be with respect to other questions). Finley says emphatically,

At issue are not two qualitively distinct disciplines but two kinds of evidence about the past . . . There can thus be no question of the priority in general or of the superiority of one type of evidence over the other . . . . [2]

The fourth difficulty which presents itself to the ancient historian who wishes to reconstruct an archaic society is one which receives frequent lip-service,[3] but little actual attention. This is the fact that *the ancient world had no historical writing*. This sounds like a bold statement, and naturally requires some clarification. In a provocative article which appeared quite some time ago,[4] J.G.A. Pocock pointed out that societies relate *at all levels* to the past, and in a variety of ways. From a structural functionalist perspective, he holds that

Since all societies are organised consciously or unconsciously to ensure their own continuity, we may suppose that the preservation of statements about the past has in various ways the function of ensuring continuity, and that awareness of the past is in fact society's awareness of its continuity . . . [5]

---

[1] Finley, *Ancient History*, p. 21.

[2] *Ancient History*, p. 20.

[3] Cf. e.g. H.H. Rowley, *The Growth of the Old Testament* (rev. edn, New York and Evanston, 1963 [1950]), p. 49: ". . . the ancient author was not really interested in history from the modern point of view. Nor did he think of these (scil., the Biblical) books as primarily historical".

[4] "The Origins of Study of the Past: A Comparative Approach", *CSSH* 4 (1961-1962), pp. 209-46; on the varying social perceptions of time, see also the seminal article of E.R. Leach, "Two Essays Concerning the Symbolic Representation of Time", in E.R. Leach (ed.), *Rethinking Anthropology* (London, 1961), pp. 124-36; further, M.W. Helms, *Ulysses' Sail: An Ethnographic Odyssey of Power, Knowledge, and Geographical Distance* (Princeton, 1988), pp. 33-35.

[5] *CSSH* 4 (1961-62), p. 211.

Pocock then further maintains that

> Since a society's structure is perhaps the most important single
> element in its continuity, it is often the continuity of the structure that
> the past is designed to ensure, and awareness of the past is awareness
> of the past of the structure.[1]

To explain briefly, there are many structures in any society which
reinforce the present stability of the society and which do so by, among
other things, maintaining continuity with the past. An example which
Pocock does not mention, but which is intuitively clear, is that of
kinship structures and terms. The regulative functions of kinship
structures have been exhaustively explored by socio-anthropologists
since the nineteenth century, and so should require no further mention.
But we should consider that terms like "father", "mother", "son",
"daughter" are also what A.C. Danto has described as "past-referring
predicates"; that is, if, as Bertrand Russell once semi-facetiously
suggested, the world was in reality created five minutes ago, then all
such terms, which occur in ordinary language, would be quite
inappropriate.[2] Thus kinship terminology organises past experience; this
is even more clearly the case if we consider such terms as
"mother-in-law", "father-in-law", "ex-wife/husband", "divorcé/divorcée",
and so on, all of which refer, not to determinate biological relationships,
but to past socially-established procedures. And if this is true of such
social structures as kinship, it is also true of other social phenomena,
such as law (which, among other things, has to do with how one has
resolved conflicts in the past), cult (dealing with how the relation to the
divine has traditionally been maintained), and so forth. In short, to
return to Pocock, "any society may have as many pasts as it has
elements of continuity . . . ."[3] In the rest of his article, Pocock is
concerned to argue that societies become concerned with the past, that
is, engage in reflection about it, when the continuity of traditional
structures has been cast in doubt, as may occur more or less naturally,

---

[1] *CSSH* 4 (1961-62), p. 212; see also E. Shils, "Tradition", in *CSSH* 13 (1971),
pp. 122-59, esp. pp. 125-29.

[2] Cf. A.C. Danto, *Narration and Knowledge: Including the Integral Text of
Analytical Philosophy of History* (New York, 1985), pp. 70-75.

[3] Pocock, *CSSH* 4 (1961-62), p. 212.

when the scholars of a cultic tradition examine its roots, or brutally (an example Pocock does not use), when a new social order is imposed on a society from without. Pocock is concerned to show by his study that

> If we once study the history of men's awareness that they have pasts which are important in various ways to their presents, we discover that historiography produced by this awareness . . . was appearing in Western Europe before the historicist revolution (scil., of the 18th-19th centuries).[1]

This is where I part company with him, because I feel it is important for our purposes to acknowledge that, since consciousness of the past is a result of confrontation with changes in social structure, also that type of consciousness which we associate with the so-called "historicist revolution", and which is reflected in what we term "historiography", is a product of such processes. There is accordingly a chasmic distinction which must be drawn between the types of reflection about the past which obtained before the "historicist revolution" and those which have obtained since.

To make explicit the differences in question, it will suffice to concentrate on two factors which are so much a part of modern historiography that we take them for granted, yet whose fundamental significance for obtaining knowledge of the past was never fully acknowledged in antiquity, whether Mesopotamian, Israelite, or Greco-Roman. The first of these differences has to do with *description*. In order to be able to distinguish (past) event A from (past) event B, it is essential that both events be sufficiently described. This was notably not the case in Mesopotamian historical inscriptions, in which only the names of the foreign powers involved are recorded; numbers, and even such actions as the payment of tribute, were frequently merely the results of scribal convention. The Old Testament, too, delights in this sort of inaccuracy; but we would be making a serious error to imagine that the imprecision in these matters is the result of mere ideological concerns. It is instead the result of the fact that the nature and quality of the actual historical encounters in question were not felt to be significant. In spite of all the painstaking astronomical studies of Mesopotamian civilisation, the learned observations of a Hippocrates,

---

[1] *CSSH* 4 (1961-62), pp. 210f.

and even the minutely detailed anatomical studies of a Leonardo or a
Paracelsus, the duty of exact observation and systematic description as
a precursor to obtaining knowledge of the phenomenonal world was not
fully realised before the seventeenth century.[1]

The second distinction applies to *time*, for, without a concern to
determine the temporal priority of A or B, judgements as to whether A
caused B, B caused A, or whether both were caused by a prior third
factor, C, are impossible. Again, these facts are today so much a part of
even the dullest schoolboy's understanding of his world that we tend to
disregard them. Thus we are inclined to be "tolerant" of the self-contradictory Israelite chronology,[2] and assume that clumsy "secondary
hands" have spoiled what must once have been a good broth. Assyriologists, not quite so naive, merely lament that Mesopotamian scribes did
not attempt seriously to rectify lacunae in the various kinglist traditions.
This failure is symptomatic; copies of dated contracts were deposited in
Babylonian temples for safe-keeping from the Old Babylonian period

---

[1] Note that even in astronomy, the most "exact" of the sciences of ancient
Mesopotamia, the local scholars did not hesitate to amend their observational
protocols with data which were not observed and which were not even observable,
as in some notations of the heliacal rising times of various stars. It was not before
this fictive aspect of Babylonian astronomical tables was acknowledged by O.
Neugebauer and others that it even became possible to make sense of them. As
Neugebauer has remarked, "Ancient astronomy tends far more to mathematical
schematisation than one is willing to assume on the basis of our modern background" (*A History of Ancient Mathematical Astronomy*, Pt.1 [Berlin, Heidelberg,
New York, 1975], p. 366; further, F. Rochberg-Halton ("Stellar Distances in Early
Babylonian Astronomy: A New Perspective on the Hilprecht Text (HS 229)", *JNES*
42 (1983), pp. 209-17) remarks that, "It remains characteristic for Babylonian
astronomy that from the earliest examples, astronomical texts deal with numerical
schemata (p. 209)"; ultimately, she finds the stellar distances implied in HS 229 to
be meaningless, that is, non-observational.

[2] Cf. my previously-mentioned article, "Fictive Music", with extensive notes on
the various scholarly attempts to "balance the checkbook" of the Israelite chronogra-
phers; see further N. Na'aman, "Historical and Chronological Notes on the
Kingdoms of Israel and Judah in the Eighth Century B.C.", *VT* 36 (1986), pp. 71-92,
which shows, if nothing else, how complicated is the actual state of Israelite
chronology. See further the recent and very learned, if not entirely successful study
by J. Hughes, *Secrets of the Times. Myth and History in Biblical Chronology*
(Sheffield, 1990).

on; yet there is no indication that any Babylonian scribe ever attempted to make use of such "empirical" materials to correct a chronology. Likewise, Middle Assyrian archival documents were usually dated and sometimes, for no obvious reason, they were supplied in their conclusions with brief references to then-current important military, political, or cultic matters; but, although such tags are useful to us in our attempts to reconstruct Middle Assyrian history, I know of no evidence that any Assyrian scribe ever availed himself of the same opportunity.[1] Egyptologists, it might be mentioned, work out newer and ever more ingenious ways the Egyptian scribes may have used at various times in order to bequeath to us the jumbled chronological tradition now in our possession.[2] No one seems as yet to have grasped the essential point that the insight that chronology is an essential, if banal, presupposition of historical knowledge was not reached in antiquity. Moreover, these comments apply as much to classical Greco-Roman culture as to the ancient Near East.[3] We may find this comical, absurd, or strange, especially when it was the case in cultures which had actually developed very accurate measures of long time periods, like the Egyptian Sothis

---

[1] Cf. A. Harrak, "Historical Statements in Middle Assyrian Archival Sources", *JAOS* 109 (1989), pp. 205-9.

[2] Cf. e.g. W. Barta, "Zur Entwicklung des ägyptischen Kalenderwesens", *ZÄS* 110 (1983), pp. 16-26, who lists all of eight possible Egyptian calendars. This does not, however, mean that the Egyptians actually employed eight calendars, but only that we must assume at least eight differing ways of reckoning time in order to make sense of the way the Egyptians recorded dates in the periods covered by Barta.

[3] Note the famous remark of F. Jacoby in his fundamental study of Greek historiography: "a delimited, rigorous and independent science based on the investigation and depiction of historical events of the distant or recent past, and which corresponds to our 'history', never existed in antiquity". (*Klio* 9 [1909], p. 83.) I agree with Jacoby's conclusion, though not with his reasons for arriving at it, since all he seems to demand of historiography is that it be systematic, a discipline in its own right. While such fine modern studies as those of K.J. Dover (*The Greeks and Their Legacy* [Oxford, 1988]) and C.W. Fornara (*The Nature of History in Ancient Greece and Rome* [Berkeley, Los Angeles and London, 1988]) powerfully (and rightly) emphasise the achievements of classical "historians" in characterisation, narration, description and so on, they do not seem to have grasped the fact that all of these features are merely adjuncts of verisimilitude, not tools which are essential to the pursuit of knowledge.

calendar; or of short time periods, as measured by the klepsydra, or waterclock. But it would be a serious misunderstanding of the societies in question to assume that these pragmatic adaptations, which were introduced to regulate the affairs of court and temple or to aid the calculations of the astronomers, respectively, actually point to an awareness of the historical significance of time. Societies, as we have seen, have many different ways of relating to the past, and the one we associate with "historical" thought was a very late arrival on the world scene. Consider, for example, the simple fact that until the second half of the eighteenth century, the German word "Geschichte" designated the many narratives about the past, rather than a single unified phenomenon; thus *Jablonski's Allgemeinem Lexikon der Künste und Wissenschaften* was able to note, in 1748, that "History are (Ger: Die Geschichte sind) a mirror of those virtues and vices in which one may learn through foreign experience".[1] Accordingly, when scholars speak blithely of plotting past events on "the x and y co-ordinate axes" (i.e, of space and time), or refer to "Cartesian co-ordinates", or the like, they are, in connexion with ancient societies, proposing to introduce utterly anachronistic criteria of only slight relevance to the past-relations of the societies in question.[2]

Conclusion

Having described all the features above, the new ground-breaking in contemporary social anthropological and historical studies, as well as the difficulties facing ancient historical research, what justifies an undertaking of this kind at this time? The answer is that the situation in research has never been any different; scholars have invariably found themselves caught in the transition between one set of assumptions and the adoption

---

[1] Cited by R. Koselleck, *Vergangene Zukunft: Zur Semantik geschichtlicher Zeiten* (Frankfurt am Main, 1979), p. 50.

[2] Perhaps it would be best not to mention any names here, although some recent contributors to *JSOT* do come to mind. Note that the concept of time, too, has had a lengthy, curious, and quite uneven development in various cultures: G.J. Whitrow, *Time in History* (Oxford, 1988); and, in connexion with ancient Israel, see P. Steensgaard, "Time and Religion in Judaism" in A.N. Balslev and J.N. Mohanty (eds.), *Time and Religion* (Leiden, 1991), for a very sophisticated and differentiated understanding of the Israelite relationship to time and history.

of new ones. The manifest weaknesses of, for example, the early comparative sociological studies, ought not to obscure the fact that many of the observations of Tylor, Frazer, Robertson-Smith and others retain their usefulness today; as do tremendous amounts of careful observation by the structural functionalists; many functionalist theories, too, still have a part to play (the functionalists were better theorisers than is often acknowledged); nor should we ignore the brilliant hypotheses of the structuralists and post-structuralists. The contemporary historical uncertainties about narrative historiography should likewise not blind us to the fact that a very great deal of excellent historiographical study nevertheless manages to get written. Finally, the problems of ancient history in particular ought to caution us not, for one thing, to expect too much from our sources (material or written); and, for another, to be extremely precise in the application to the data of whatever hypotheses we shall find appropriate.

Two Cautionary Notes about Old Testament Social History

All of us remember the halcyon days of M. Noth's amphictyony hypothesis. Literally dozens of works, ranging from major monographs to articles and entries in various lexica appeared in the years after the publication of *Das System der zwölf Stämme Israels.*[1] Many of these works attempted to trace one or another group of OT texts back to some "amphictyonic institution" of the period of the judges. Thus we experienced debates as to the respective rôles of the major and minor judges, the activities of the prophets as covenant mediators, the establishment of the Israelite monarchy as a further development (in the Weberian sense of "rationalisation of the charisma") of the authority of the judges, and much besides. Discussion of these positions would be superfluous, as scholarship has dealt with them at great length, and in any case it is not my intention here to canonise saints or excoriate sinners. The vast majority of these studies are today quite irrelevant to the historical study of Israelite society (I cannot recall the last time anyone proposed to interpret a text on the basis of its employment in a —presumably amphictyonic—festival of covenant renewal, or the like),

---

[1] *BWANT* IV/1, Stuttgart, 1930.

and I think we can point to at least two reasons why this is the case. First, scholars were previously prone to accept theories which were highly conjectural (like the amphictyony, or the impressive rôle assigned to oral tradition by the "Scandinavian school") and only slightly susceptible to testing. Testability, in the sense that a theory must, at least in principle, be empirically falsifiable, made its entry into the theory of theory formation thanks to the efforts of Sir Karl Popper, who has argued unceasingly for his views since the 1930s,[1] and, to a lesser extent, thanks to the insights of C.G. Hempel.[2]

To provide an example of the failure by OT scholars to offer falsifiable theories, it is difficult to imagine just what could count as evidence that Judg 5 does not reflect an amphictyonic struggle (whether 10- or twelve-tribe is irrelevant) against Israel's enemies. Similarly, in the conclusion to his *Early Israel*, Lemche was forced to acknowledge that

> if one takes one's point of departure in Israel's stage of social development (i.e., if one claims that the Israelites were pastoral nomads), one could then claim that they have left no remains behind them, since it is characteristic of nomadic cultures that they neither possess goods nor property which would be available to later archeologists. This would make it possible to sustain the concept of Israel's peaceful immigration into the land of Canaan as sketched out by Alt, no matter how often and vociferously the adherents of the "sociological" revolution theory should happen to protest.[3]

In short, it is the duty of any scholar attempting to reconstruct an ancient society to formulate his hypotheses so sharply that they may, at least conceivably, be falsified.

---

[1] Popper's first statement of the concept was in his *Die Logik der Forschung*, Vienna, 1934; reissued in revised form in countless English (under the title *The Logic of Scientific Discovery*) and German editions since 1959; see also *Conjectures and Refutations*, London, 1963; *Objective Knowledge*, Oxford, 1972; and Popper's intellectual autobiography, *Unended Quest*, London, 1976 (4th edn 1978).

[2] *Aspects of Scientific Explanation and Other Essays in the Philosophy of Science* (New York, 1965); *The Philosophy of Natural Science* (Englewood Cliffs [NJ], 1966); See also E. Nagel, *The Structure of Science* (New York, 1961).

[3] *Early Israel*, p. 412. I note to my dismay that I. Finkelstein, *Archaeology*, p. 338, offers a similar sort of "hedge" against the expectation of signs of cultural discontinuity in connexion with the emergence of Israelite culture.

The second error which I feel OT scholars have tended to commit has been to assume that if you can describe one period well, you can deduce the subsequent periods from this description, or the reverse. Hence, for example, the concept of "charismatic" judges being supplanted by "institutional" kings. This represents a fundamental misunderstanding of the function of social and historical theory (moreover, in this particular case it represents a misunderstanding of what Weber meant by social history).[1] Social theories, pace Karl Marx and the historians and sociologists who attempted to delineate laws of social development, are not nomothetic, that is, law-making; they are descriptive, and predictive only in a statistical sense at best. Once again we have Sir Karl Popper to thank for devoting many years to establishing that this is the case.[2] An American historian has noted, apropos of the sort of error in question, that it is "very common in historical writing. It is psychologically gratifying, for it supplies a sense of completeness and it encourages a sense of certainty. But these are illusions which an empiricist must learn to live without".[3]

---

[1] Cf. P. Rossi, *Vom Historismus zur historischen Sozialwissenschaft* (Frankfurt am Main, 1987), p. 9: "The liberation (i.e., Weber's) from both economic and psychologistic historicism is in reality only the external aspect of a much more radical break, namely the release from the stance of the historistic school and its heritage"; p. 10: "he (Weber) dismisses the understanding of history as a unified process...and also the claim that the lives of the peoples may be traced back to a common development with its own 'laws'".

[2] See especially *The Poverty of Historicism* (London, 1957 and later editions); *The Open Society and Its Enemies* (London, 12th edn, 1977); and note the exchanges, or the lack of them, between Popper and T. Adorno in T.W. Adorno et al. (eds.), *Der Positivismusstreit in der deutschen Soziologie* (Darmstadt and Neuwied, 1969; repr. 1972); Popper: pp. 103-25; Adorno: pp. 7-81; 81-103 and 125-45. Note, however, that Adorno's first two (polemical) articles played no part in the congress proceedings, but were added subsequently by Adorno in conjunction with the book publication, so that Popper had no opportunity to reply (cf. Karl R. Popper, *Auf der Suche nach einer besseren Welt. Vorträge und Aufsätze aus dreißig Jahren* (Munich and Zurich, 1984), p. 79, n.). Cf. also C.G. Hempel, "The Function of General Laws in History", *The Journal of Philosophy* 39 (1942), pp. 35-48 = *Aspects*, pp. 231-43, for a critical statement of the sorts of "laws" that may legitimately be employed.

[3] D.H. Fischer, *Historians' Fallacies: Toward a Logic of Historical Thought* (New York, 1970), p. 69.

In consequence, when our knowledge of a given period is limited, we must simply admit that this is the case, rather than try to abstract from other periods. As Lemche has said, "our most important duty is to acknowledge our ignorance".[1] In practice, this means that I shall be most most reluctant to attempt to attach the phenomena under study to particular periods or events. It should be evident from the preceding remarks that I do not feel we can confidently reconstruct Israelite history at present. What we have seen in recent years has been a growing disenchantment with any OT information pertaining to the pre-monarchical period;[2] but there is little reason to think that the materials in the Books of the Kings are any more reliable.[3] Old

---

[1] *Early Israel*, p. 414.

[2] Cf. e.g. the notes in my article, "On the Relationship Between the Yahwistic and the Deuteronomistic Histories", *BN* 29 (1985), pp. 58-73; further, G.W. Ramsey, *The Quest for the Historical Israel: Reconstructing Israel's Early History* (London, 1981), esp. pp. 25-104; see also the previously-mentioned articles by Lemche (i.e., "Rachel and Lea").

[3] The pendulum-swing from a lack of faith in the pre-monarchical traditions (Wellhausen, Duhm, Stade, et al.), in favour of the traditions of the period of the monarchy, then back to the pre-monarchical period, and now once more to "the time of David and Solomon, at the earliest", has been well chronicled by J.A. Soggin in the jubilee issue of *ZAW* (Supp.) (100 [1988], pp. 255-267). Soggin counts among the "radical revisionists" such figures as N.P. Lemche, G. Garbini, J. Van Seters, T.L. Thompson, R. Rendtorff, H. Donner, and B.J. Diebner, and indicates that he himself has moved somewhat in their direction since the English publication of his own history of Israel. Soggin himself can hardly be considered a "radical"; yet, as far as the question of when to place our faith in the Israelite account of Israel's history is concerned, he says: "Would we then be forced to begin only towards the end of the 9th century, with the divided monarchies, when Israel and Judah first appear in ancient Near Eastern historiography? Or perhaps even with the Deuteronomistic History? Judging from the current state of our science, I would not dare to offer an affirmative answer to either of these questions" (p. 260). The situation south of the Alps (a new Ultramontanism?) is today such that one would be hard put to find a scholar who regards the Biblical account of Israel's pre-monarchical history as in any way useful. Cf. G. Garbini, *Storia e Ideologia Nell'Israele Antico* (Brescia, 1986) (English trans. [John Bowden] *History and Ideology in Ancient Israel* (New York, 1988), who represents the "radical" wing (see below); and M. Liverani, *Antico Oriente. Storia - Società - Economia* (Roma-Bari, 1988), pp. 661-92, who, somewhat surprisingly, assumes the rôle of a "moderate" in that he assumes reliable tradition to begin with the time of the monarchy (cf. esp. pp. 666-72).

Testament scholars have for some years been aware of the need for a re-examination of the principles of OT historical interpretation;[1] this is very much an on-going enterprise, though it is too early to tell whether a new synthesis will emerge from the discussion, or whether, as the writer feels, the time for syntheses is past.

In the following pages we shall, hopefully, be able to keep most of the above depicted cautions in mind. Our first task in the study of Israelite and Near Eastern divination will be to consider the category of magic, as it has been studied by social anthropologists. From this we shall attempt to derive some guidelines to apply to the various traditions in question, after paying due heed to the past study of these areas. These guidelines will, hopefully, not be uncritically forced onto the materials; they will be modified where and as the facts demand. Finally, a few conclusions will be drawn and suggestions for further research will be made.

---

[1] As I once noted to my surprise about ten years ago, it is possible to read through practically any of the histories of Israel which emerged between Noth's *Geschichte Israels* (Göttingen, 1950) and G. Fohrer's work of the same name (2nd rev. edn Heidelberg, 1979) without finding either theoretical discussion or any reference to historiographical works from fields extraneous to OT study. Dissatisfaction with this state of affairs set in already towards the close of the 1970s, when S. Herrmann, himself a student of an immensely careful ancient historian (A. Alt), found it necessary in *Zeit und Geschichte* (Stuttgart, Berlin, Köln, Mainz, 1977) to offer a general discussion of the principles of the ancient historical study of the Old and New Testaments. Since Herrmann's work appeared, of course, the theoretical discussion has become hugely more complicated, but it is interesting to note that Herrmann's student R. Liwak ("Die Rettung Jerusalems im Jahr 701 v. Chr. Zum Verhältnis und Verständnis historischer und theologischer Aussagen", *ZThK* 83 [1986], pp. 137-166; the same, *Der Prophet und die Geschichte. Eine literar-historische Untersuchung zum Jeremiabuch* (Stuttgart, Berlin, Köln, Mainz, 1987), esp. pp. 9-58) has continued this necessary task in exemplary fashion. Most recently, G. Garbini (*Storia e ideologia*) has been severely critical of the tradition leading from Alt to the present and has offered an "ideological" interpretation of the OT based on the assumption that the documents are very much later than has been assumed. While Garbini may well be right, he is not as radical as he supposes; already Alt and Noth were *critical* as to the period from which we may presume to possess reliable information. The difference is more of emphasis than of substance.

CHAPTER 1

WHY MAGIC?

Actually, it requires little argumentation to justify a concern with magic in the context of a discussion of the phenomenon of divination in the ancient Near East. After all, the phenomenon was assigned to the realm of magic already in antiquity (cf. the "Magi" of Matt 2.1,7, etc., who are clearly presented as astrologers), and has since then consistently been discussed under such headings as "magic", "Magie", "Mantik" and the like. Although magic is notoriously difficult to define, and although we do make mistakes in the matter, we usually know magic when we see it. My second reason for choosing to apply the category of "magic" to the phenomenon of divination is that it is the more inclusive category. At least since the 19th century there have been numerous attempts to understand magic, whereas studies of Near Eastern and classical divination have tended to concentrate on the minutiae, that is, on the who, how and when, on the terminology, relationship to cult and pantheon, and so forth, without ultimately attempting to come to grips with the meaning of the practice.

However, as I indicated in the introduction to this work, sociology does not offer us a passe-partout to historical study. Thus I shall have to examine, however briefly, and with all the limitations of the non-specialist, the main sociological contributions to the understanding of magic. The studies which shall concern us here are those of E.B. Tylor,[1] J.G. Frazer,[2] M. Mauss-H. Hubert,[3] B. Malinowski,[4] and

---

[1] *The Origins of Culture: Part I of Primitive Culture* (New York, 1958 [1871]); hereafter *Origins*.

[2] *The Golden Bough: A Study in Magic and Religion*, Vols.1-2 (London; 3rd edn, 1911 [1890]); hereafter *Golden Bough*. Unless otherwise indicated, all relevant citations here are from the first volume.

[3] *Esquisse d'une théorie générale de la magie*. Reprinted from *L'Année Sociologique* 1902-03 by C. Lévi-Strauss (ed.) / Presses Universitaires de France, in *Marcel Mauss: Sociologie et Anthropologie* (Paris, 1966); hereafter *Esquisse*.

D.L. O'Keefe.[1] Regrettably, only cursory reference can be made here to the famous studies of E. Durkheim,[2] A.R. Radcliffe-Brown,[3] and M. Weber.[4] While all three refer to magic and magical practices extensively, they fail to offer any comprehensive attempt to define or explain the phenomenon. Other studies certainly could have deserved inclusion here; yet at some point one must draw the line.[5] In conjunction with this effort, we shall in the next chapter investigate the modern social-anthropological study of divination. Here our primary focus will be developments since the decisive contribution of E.E. Evans-Pritchard.[6]

E.B.TYLOR

As I indicated in the introduction to this work, most socio-historical study in the 19th century was evolutionistic, that is, there was a pronounced tendency to attempt to describe the diversity of social forms

[4] *Magic, Science and Religion and Other Essays* (London, 1974 [1948]); hereafter *MSR*.

[1] *Stolen Lightning. The Social Theory of Magic* (Oxford, 1982); hereafter *Lightning*.

[2] *Les formes élémentaires de la vie religieuse* (Paris, 1912). As it has become established usage in international sociology, reference here will be made to the English translation of J. Swain (Robert Nisbet, ed.), *The Elementary Forms of the Religious Life* (London, 2nd edn, 1976); hereafter *Forms*. The English translation of Mauss-Hubert's *Esquisse* while also frequently referred to in the literature, has more the status of an odd sort of editorial revision-cum-targum, and will not be referred to here.

[3] *The Andaman Islanders: An investigation of the physical characteristics, language, culture, and technology of a primitive society* (Cambridge, 1964 [1922]); hereafter *Islanders*.

[4] *Gesammelte Aufsätze zur Religionssoziologie*, Vols.I-III (Tübingen, 1920--1921); hereafter *Aufsätze*.

[5] See particularly K. Beth, "Das Verhältnis von Religion und Magie" in L. Petzoldt (ed.), *Magie und Religion* (Darmstadt, 1978 [1914]), pp. 27-47; and, in the same work: T.W. Danzel, "Die psychologische Bedeutung magischer Bräuche" (orig. pub. 1922), pp. 79-84; T. Preuß, "Das Irrationale in der Magie" (orig. pub. 1938/39), pp. 223-48.

[6] *Witchcraft, Oracles and Magic among the Azande* (Oxford, 1937); hereafter referred to as *Witchcraft*; references will follow the abridged edition (Oxford, 1980 [1976]).

both chronologically and hierarchically, from antiquity to the present and from simpler to more complex forms of social organisation. This effort naturally prompted the question as to how then-contemporary non-industrialised societies (what we today would call "savage", "primitive" or "traditional" societies) were to be understood. The evolutionistic solution was to regard them as pseudo-Darwinian "survivals" of earlier social forms, on the analogy of biologically primitive animals which have persisted because local conditions have left a niche in the ecology which has enabled their survival (like the shark, crocodile, coelocanth or South American lungfish). Thus 19th century traditional societies could be held to be societies which had missed the decisive epistemological turning which led to empirical science, industrialisation, and the modern (Western) highly stratified social picture.[1] This was a very comfortable view to hold for 19th century white Christian Europeans, and was understandably popular among scholars, as it allowed the armchair satisfaction of looking complacently down upon virtually the entire panorama of historical and then-existing societies. Moreover, in addition to societies which had failed to evolve, there remained features also in modern societies which were reminiscent of those to be found in "primitive" ones; these, too, were "survivals". It might be held that for E.B.Tylor, the doctrine of survivals was a necessary outgrowth of his evolutionistic methodology. At the very beginning of The Origins of Culture Tylor states that

> the uniformity which so largely pervades civilization may be as-
> cribed . . . to the uniform action of uniform causes: while on the
> other hand its various grades may be regarded as stages of growth of
> development or evolution, each the outcome of previous history, and
> about to do its proper part in shaping the history of the future.[2]

If historical development is everywhere the result of rational response to empirical stimuli, then aberrations in that development are necessarily irrational manifestations. Thus when we turn to Tylor's explanation of magic we are told that "The nobler tendency of advancing culture, and above all of scientific culture, is to honour the dead without grovelling before them . . . Yet . . . an unprejudiced survey may lead us to judge

---

[1] Further on "survivals", see J.W. Rogerson, *Anthropology and the Old Testament* (Oxford, 1978), pp. 1-22.

[2] *Origins*, p.1.

how many of our ideas and customs exist rather by being old than by being good".[1]

Magic, then, asserts itself also in modern cultures by simple virtue of the authority acquired by great age.[2] In cognitive terms, Tylor characterised it as an "elaborate and systematic pseudo- science".[3] He asked almost rhetorically, "is there in the whole monstrous farrago no truth or value whatever? It appears that there is practically none, and that the world has been enthralled for ages by a blind belief in processes wholly irrelevant to their supposed results".[4]

All of this sits rather oddly with Tylor's secondary claim that magic is a "sincere but fallacious system of philosophy".[5] As far as the practitioner of magic is concerned, Tylor is equally ambivalent. On the one hand the magician is a charlatan who avoids confrontation with empirical disappointments by means of "rhetorical shift and brazen impudence";[6] on the other, however, he notes in passing that the sorceror "generally learns his time-honoured profession in good faith, and retains his belief in it more or less from first to last; at once dupe and cheat, he combines the energy of the believer with the cunning of a hypocrite".[7]

If I seem to be hard on Tylor in condemning his assumption of the superiority of the Western "empirical" worldview, I do not do so for the arid satisfaction of lampooning Victorian self-centredness. Nor do I do so for the pleasure of whacking away at evolutionistic theorists, though that has been a popular enough sport in recent years. The reason is simply that Tylor considered himself an "ethnographer",[8] and was therefore committed, at least in principle, to a degree of openness

---

[1] *Origins*, p. 157.

[2] Cf. *Origins*, p. 136: "A once-established opinion. . . can hold its own from age to age, for belief can propagate itself without reference to its reasonable origin, as plants are propagated from slips without fresh raising from the seed".

[3] *Origins*, p. 134; cf. pp. 130-31.

[4] *Origins*, p. 133.

[5] *Origins*, p. 134.

[6] *Origins*, p. 135.

[7] *Origins*, p. 134.

[8] Cf. e.g. *Origins*, p. 158.

towards the phenomena he attempted to study. When he refers at the beginning of his investigation to "one of the most pernicious delusions that ever vexed mankind, the belief in Magic",[1] it is evident that he was not adequate to the task. More to the point is the fact that Tylor's overarching concern with the "origins" of social phenomena, plus his subsidiary concept of inner-cultural "survivals", left no room for the question as to just why a given "survival" managed to assert itself for generation after generation. The claim that great age causes a society to respect a tradition is in reality an ad hoc postulate which explains nothing. After all, it is demonstrable that literally millions of beliefs which were held in society A a hundred years ago are not held today, so the task of social anthropology is to show why any one of them should continue to be held.[2] Furthermore, the claim that the magician is at once both dupe and charlatan points up the fatal weakness of Tylor's position. It is so ethnocentric that the possibility of respecting the magician's intelligence sufficiently to suppose that he might have what are to him good reasons for his beliefs never occurred to the ethnographer. The entire problem of the rationality of magic, which has exercised so many scholars today,[3] never occurred to him. As we shall see, the problem of ethnocentricity was to continue to dog the sociological study of magic for years to come.

Having said this, attention must be paid to Tylor's concrete achievements. As virtually the first scholar to have done so, Tylor observed that magical practices are frequently attributed to peripheral social groups.[4] Furthermore, he attempted to provide a cognitive

---

[1] *Origins*, p. 112.

[2] Note that already in antiquity Marcus Tullius Cicero acknowledged that the practice of divination had the strength of an "ancient belief" (*vetus opinio*), and that it had long been practised by the Assyrians, Chaldaeans, Egyptians and Greeks. But even this did not stop him from dismissing the practice (*De Divinatione*, text and ET by W.A. Falconer [London and 1964], Bk.I,1-3).

[3] Cf. the essays in B.R. Wilson (ed.), *Rationality* (Oxford, 1970), esp. I.C. Jarvie and J. Agassi, "The Problem of the Rationality of Magic", pp. 172-93.

[4] *Origins*, p.113: "In any country an isolated or outlying race, the lingering survivor of an older nationality, is liable to the reputation of sorcery". See also pp.114-15.

explanatory model for magical practices; thus he held that primitive man,

> having come to associate in thought those things which he found by experience to be connected in fact, proceeded erroneously to invert this action, and to conclude that association in thought must involve similar connexion in reality.[1]

As Tylor also noted, this process of "Association of Ideas", as he put it, "lies at the very foundation of human reason".[2] Thus magic is a mistaken species of science, or "pseudo-science", as was indicated earlier. More reflection along these lines might have led Tylor to investigate the logic employed in magic, with a view to determining its inner coherence, but the ethnographer's obvious contempt for his subject matter ruled this out.

Tylor's insights into the phenomenology of magic include his acknowledgement of the fact that some magical practitioners claim to be connected "sympathetically" to individuals via objects that had once been in contact with them.[3] Finally, he noted that both analogy and symbolism play a major part in magical practices.[4]

J.G. FRAZER

Frazer's attempt to understand the phenomenon of magic is essentially a reductionist-intellectualist approach, that is, one which tries to explain the entire gamut of magical phenomena through the application of a limited number of (in actuality only two) principles. The first of these is the so-called "Law of Similarity", which manifests itself in charms and spells which Frazer indifferently termed expressions of "Homeo-pathic" or "Imitative" magic, and which are predicated on the assumption that "like produces like, or that an effect resembles its cause".[5] The second was the "Law of Contact or Contagion", based on the assumption that "things which have once been in contact with each other continue to act on each other at a distance after the physical contact has

---

[1] *Origins*, p.116.

[2] *Origins*, p. 116.

[3] *Origins*, p. 117.

[4] *Origins*, pp. 117-18.

[5] *Golden Bough*, p. 52.

been severed".[1] Frazer's magician is accordingly a mistaken natural scientist, one who "assumes that the Laws of Similarity and Contact are of universal application . . . ."[2] Thus he can also claim that "magic is a spurious system of natural law as well as a fallacious guide of conduct; it is a false science as well as an abortive art".[3] If we seem to hear echoes on this point of Tylor's view, this is hardly fortuitous; Frazer in fact cites him and criticizes him only for not having analysed the "associations of ideas" which he thought to uncover.[4] Frazer went on to subsume both types of magic and their attendant "laws" under the general rubric of "Sympathetic Magic", "since both assume that things act on each other at a distance through a secret sympathy . . . .";[5] again, as we have seen, there are echoes of Tylor's observations. The next two sections of Frazer's investigation[6] contain displays of massive erudition, ranging as they do from references to magical practices in ancient India, Babylon, and Egypt to similar ones in the highlands of Scotland or the Australian outback, all of which have been selected to illustrate the applicability of Frazer's two "laws" of magic. Frazer's collecto-mania has incurred much censure,[7] though in reality we ought to be duly grateful that someone took the trouble—for whatever reason—to show just how extensive magical behaviour and practices really are, and in what a wide variety of social contexts they occur. But in terms of proving his twin theses as to the roots of magical practice, even the twelve volumes which *The Golden Bough* eventually achieved are inadequate. The very act of formulating an hypothesis indicates that at least some observation has preceded the formulation, so that once we

[1] *Golden Bough,* p. 52.

[2] *Golden Bough*, p. 53.

[3] *Golden Bough,* p. 53.

[4] *Golden Bough,* p. 53, n. 1.

[5] *Golden Bough,* p. 54.

[6] Entitled "Homeopathic or Imitative Magic" (pp. 55-174) and "Contagious Magic" (pp. 174-214), respectively.

[7] Similar amassing of data was brutally addressed by Malinowski when he referred to "the lengthy litanies of threaded statement, which make us anthropologists feel silly and the savage look ridiculous" (cited in E.E. Evans-Pritchard *Theories of Primitive Religion* [Oxford, 1965], p. 9).

have been assured that some minimum requirement is satisfied, any surplus information offered has at best only illustrative value. It would have been more to the point to seek examples where Frazer's definitions do not apply, or where they do so only with difficulty.[1]

Magic, then, on Frazer's view, is the "bastard sister of science".[2] It arises out of the illegitimate application of principles of association which are correctly applied only in science.[3] This leads to an interesting understanding of the magician in Frazer's work, since the latter cannot avoid seeing the inadequacies of his efforts, and therefore the failure of magic. For this reason Frazer's magician is a huckster almost by definition:

> the ablest members of the profession must tend to be more or less conscious deceivers . . . it must always be remembered that every single profession and claim put forward by the magician as such is false; not one of them can be maintained without deception, conscious or unconscious. Accordingly, the sorcerer who sincerely believes in his own extravagant pretensions is in far greater peril and is much more likely to be cut short in his career than the deliberate impostor.[4]

Unlike Tylor, however, Frazer sees the imposture of the magician as essentially a good thing, one which enables a shrewd magician to attain high prestige and considerable influence, on the assumption that he generally uses this influence for the good of his community. Moreover, the ascension to power of the magician is described as a step on the way to monarchy, itself "an essential condition of the emergence of mankind from savagery".[5] From here we are only a single remove from the divine priest-magician-kings who are the real subject of the rest of *The Golden Bough*. As Frazer says,

---

[1] Mauss-Hubert, *Esquisse*, p. 4-5, accordingly criticise Frazer for casting his net too wide; they conclude (p. 6) that Frazer and a like-minded scholar "have chosen so-called 'typical' facts; they have believed in the existence of a pure magic which they have completely reduced to matters of sympathy; but they have not demonstrated the legitimacy of their choice".

[2] *Golden Bough*, p. 222.

[3] *Golden Bough*, p. 222.

[4] *Golden Bough*, p. 215.

[5] *Golden Bough*, p. 217.

> Nor. . . is it an accident that all the first great strides towards civilisa-
> tion have been made under despotic and theocratic governments. . . -
> where the supreme ruler claimed and received the servile allegiance
> of his subjects in the double character of a king and a god.[1]

One cannot help but note a parallel here to Weber's subsequent notion of semi-magical"charisma".[2]

Virtually the same objection seems to present itself to Frazer's understanding of magic as we previously raised to Tylor's. But where Tylor's ad hoc principle which ensures the perpetuation of magic is traditional authority (plus human gullibility, it should be added), Frazer's is the cunning of the magician and his skill at slight-of-hand. One wonders if people really could be taken in for thousands of years by the same few old tricks, and whether magicians could be satisfied to do so. After all, having, as Frazer suggests, been confronted with the inadequacy of magic, why would they not just abandon it immediately for something better (Frazer's "science")? Moreover, Frazer's insistence that magicians are normally among the most talented in their society actually counts against his theory, because if they are truly intelligent, why do they fail to get out of their epistemological prison and try another "association of ideas"?

Once again, the problem of ethnocentrism raises its head: in specifying magic as mistaken science, Frazer is comparing a phenomenon in traditional society to one in ours, to the detriment of the former. Curiously, "science" is taken for granted in the process, as if the word and the procedures and concepts associated with it are universally understood throughout Western societies, while savage magical behaviour is studied in all its multiplicity. Nevertheless, the acknowledgement that the practitioners of magic may well be highly talented individuals is a step beyond simply regarding them as benighted heathen from whom little better could be expected. With the advent of fieldwork,

---

[1] *Golden Bough*, p. 218.

[2] Weber speaks, for example, (*Aufsätze*, Vol.I, p. 397) of the "Charisma of magical energy"; and also of the (Vol. I, p. 408) "charismatic chastisement of the old magical asceticism"; but it can also be the end-result of an educational process for government functionaries (p.416); in this sense Weber speaks of the "popular magico-charismatic understanding of the officially tested institutional qualification", p. 323).

anthropologists were confronted face to face with such figures, and the new respect personal encounter entailed compelled them to wonder just what magic was really all about.

M. MAUSS-H. HUBERT

The *Esquisse d'une théorie générale de la magie* of M. Mauss and H. Hubert[1] may be said to be the first structural-functionalist study of the phenomenon of magic. Against the "grab-bag" comparative approach of Tylor and Frazer, Mauss-Hubert maintain that, "For us, only those things may be termed magical which have truly been so for the whole of a society, rather than those things which have been thus qualified by a mere fraction of the society".[2] By implication, then, the social anthropologist has no license to swoop down on one or another phenomenon, pronounce it "magical", and ignore its concrete social context. Mauss and Hubert proceed nevertheless to assemble a cross-cultural picture of magic, but they do so with the confidence that the phenomena in question really are so regarded in their respective cultures. Moreover, throughout their study they attempt to see the various phenomena of magic in relation to such social distinctions as class, status, sex, and so on. This is a study of astounding methodological maturity, for all its brevity, and for this reason it will be necessary to discuss the contribution of Mauss and Hubert at some length. The only drawback to their procedure is that it stands or falls on the assertion of generalisability; if a phenomenon can be shown not to apply to all societies, then their model must be seen to be only partial, like those that preceded it.

For Mauss-Hubert, magic consists of 1) agents 2) acts 3) "représentations", where the "agents" are the performers of magic, the acts are magical rites, while the "représentations" are the ideas and beliefs pertaining to the rites.[3]

---

[1] For no obvious reason, the work is frequently referred to in the literature as if Marcel Mauss were its sole author (e.g., Lévi-Strauss in his. "Introduction à l'oeuvre de M. Mauss", in C. Lévi-Strauss (ed.), *Marcel Mauss*, pp. XLI-LII, passim).

[2] *Esquisse*, p. 10.

[3] *Esquisse*, p. 10.

As far as the rites of magic are concerned, the authors note that they are traditional, and that they are sanctioned by social opinion.[1] They further observe that possibility of confusion exists between the magical, "technical" (in the sense of arts and crafts), and religious spheres.[2] They seek to distinguish magic from the technical sphere by noting that the artisan assumes that effect follows cause "mechanically", and, furthermore, by the claim that in technical practice "the tradition is ceaselessly controlled by experience, which constantly the value of technical beliefs to the test."[3] Already at this point we encounter *in nuce* a difficulty which was to plague subsequent social anthropologists, among them Evans-Pritchard.[4] As we shall see, no member of a traditional society is in any doubt that magic works; therefore it is by definition "confirmed by experience". We might suggest paradoxically that while magical acts are invariably "empirically" confirmed, "technical" ones—what we might be inclined to call rational-empirical actions—may at best only be deconfirmed. But it is obviously not easy to distinguish between a slow-witted potter whose method, perhaps sanctioned by the tradition of his guild, or whatever, happens to be fallacious, and a sorceror who is likewise disinclined to see the disconfirmation of his efforts because his orientation explains away failure with ease.

To distinguish magic from religion, Hubert and Mauss contend that magic and religion ultimately tend towards different poles: "the pole of sacrifice and the pole of malevolence"; between them, they add, "there extends a confused mass of facts whose specific character is not immediately apparent"[5] One wonders if this is necessarily true, or is it merely the consequence of the limited selection of literature available to Mauss and Hubert. After all, in ancient cultures, at least, the main religious cult could itself be quite malefic towards the enemies of the

---

[1] *Esquisse*, p. 11.

[2] *Esquisse*, p. 11.

[3] *Esquisse*, p. 12.

[4] See the next chapter.

[5] *Esquisse*, p. 14.

society.[1] They also subscribe provisionally to Grimm's definition of magic as the religion of the lesser needs of domestic life.[2] As far as the actors appropriate to magical and religious phenomena are concerned, the authors hold that there are different personnel for each sphere, or that, in cases where the priest performs magic, he does so in ways which differ markedly from his performance of priestly duties.[3] Yet another distinction is the tendency of the magician to isolate himself, and to pass on his knowledge as a sort of arcana: "both the act and the actor are surround by mystery".[4] While one must admit that this is certainly usually true in savage societies, one wonders if the "strangeness" of magic were not worthy a study in its own right to determine the reasons for it.

The latent malevolence of magic, as well as its tendency to remove itself from the ordinary world, lead Mauss and Hubert to conclude that magic is fundamentally *antinomial*; they speak of "the irreligiousness of the magical rite; it is, and its practitioner wants it to be, anti-religious".[5] it is "invariably considered to be irregular, abnormal, or in some manner contemptible".[6] Thus they finally define magic as "any rite which is not part of an organized cult; it is privative, secret, mysterious and tends, as its limit, towards the proscribed rite".[7] As we shall see, this view of the essential opposition between magic and religion was to prove enormously influential in the socio-anthropological study of magic down to our day. Accordingly, one wishes that Mauss and Hubert had provided some evidence of their claim.

In contradistinction to the earlier efforts of Tylor and Frazer, the authors are careful to point out that their theory is not based on the superficial form of the various rites, but on the social conditions in

[1] See G. Widengren's remarks on the impossibility of drawing this distinction in *Religionsphänomenologie* (Berlin, 1969), pp. 8-10; on the problem posed by the ancient "high cultures", see below.

[2] *Esquisse*, pp. 14-15.

[3] *Esquisse*, p. 15.

[4] *Esquisse*, p. 15.

[5] *Esquisse*, p. 15.

[6] *Esquisse*, p. 16.

[7] *Esquisse*, p. 16.

which they occur;[1] theirs is very much a *social* theory. Mauss-Hubert's approach to the difficult problem of the actors involved seems to confound native reports of "witches" with anthropological observations of "witch-doctors" and "sorcerors". They do not note that "witches" mainly exist only by report, whereas the other categories are often observable. This leads to a confusion which was first corrected to some extent, by Evans-Pritchard some thirty-five years later.[2] Thus they hold that the magician is frequently distinguished from his fellows by some physical or abnormal behavioural traits;[3] they also reveal a tendency towards a shamanistic bias in claiming that the magician "falls into ecstasies, sometimes real ones, in general voluntarily produced . . . the audience observes attentively and anxiously, as in our time in connexion with hypnotic seances".[4] But the *signum diaboli*, beloved of the 17th century European witch-hunters, characterises what we would today call a "witch", rather than a "magician". Objective marks enable people to be singled out from their fellows, which makes their bearers easy targets in societies suffering from witch fears.[5] Nevertheless, even confounding the phenomena, as they do, Mauss and Hubert do not hesitate to affirm that people so afflicted in reality form social classes; which explains, given the ambigious situation of women in many societies (based on the mysteries of menses, childbirth, and so on), why women, too, "are the objects, sometimes, of superstitions, sometimes of juridical and religious sanctions which clearly distinguish them as a class within society".[6]

---

[1] *Esquisse*, p. 16.

[2] See the next chapter; the distinction is fundamental to the modern study of witchcraft; cf. e.g. the various essays in J. Middleton and E.H. Winter (eds), *Witchcraft and Sorcery in East Africa*, (London, 1978 [1963]); further O'Keefe, *Lightning*, p. 2 and p. 16 n. 6-12. However, far from all societies in which witch behaviour is observable permit such simplistic analysis as the witchcraft-sorcery duality; cf. V. Turner, *The Forest of Symbols*, pp. 118-19; further, see I.M. Lewis, *Religion in Context*, pp. 10-11.

[3] *Esquisse*, pp. 17-19.

[4] *Esquisse*, p. 19; cf. also p. 17.

[5] E.g., among the Azande, witches are supposed to be recognizable by their red eyes; cf. Evans-Pritchard, *Witchcraft*, p.2.

[6] *Esquisse*, p. 20.

Other groups frequently associated with magical powers are the artisans, since, as suggested previously, the boundary line between the arts and magic is thin indeed.[1] But more important than this is the fact that some societies accord considerable political power to magicians ("Thus the social situation which they occupy predestines them to exercize magic and, conversely, the exercize of magic predestines them to their social situation").[2] Just how this observation coheres with Mauss-Hubert's previously-mentioned postulate that magic tends towards the malevolent, and with magic's supposedly anti-religious character, when one considers that religion usually underpins social order, is not clear.

Mauss-Hubert further note, as Tylor had already done, that minority groups are frequently held to be magicians, be they adherents of an earlier religion or ethnic groups like the Laps or gypsies.[3]

A brief section on the legendary features which are ascribed to magicians notes that their common denominator is "the ease with which the magician realizes all of his desires".[4] Thus he is held to be able to exhale his spirit, which, as Doppelgänger, carries out his will while his body remains at home.[5] Alternatively, he may change into some animal form, generally those having totemic significance in his own culture. Or, he may possess a familiar spirit.[6] The magician's purported movable spirit leads to a discussion of the magician as "possessed"; once again showing that the authors regard shamanistic behaviour as the basic model of magical action, Mauss-Hubert claim that "belief in the possession of the magician is universal. . . there are magical systems in

---

[1] *Esquisse*, p. 21.

[2] *Esquisse*, p. 22.

[3] *Esquisse*, pp. 22-23; cf. p. 24: "One might offer the general hypothesis that the individuals to whom the exercize of magic is attributed already enjoy. . . a distinct condition internal to the society which treats them as magicians".

[4] *Esquisse*, p. 26.

[5] *Esquisse*, pp. 26-27.

[6] *Esquisse*, pp. 28-30.

which possession is the essential presupposition of magical activity".[1]

According to Mauss-Hubert, one becomes a magician by a threefold process of revelation, consecration, and tradition.[2] Often the initiation takes the form of a symbolic death and rebirth,[3] although it may be virtually identical with initiation into the local cult, or simply be a function of the tradition.[4] Membership of a magical society conveys special knowledge; the magician considers himself elect, and is so regarded by society at large. Magical groups are indistinguishable in most respects from religious ones.[5]

Mauss-Hubert place especial emphasis on the rite. They note that "Whenever we are in the presence of true rituals, of liturgical agenda, the precise enumeration of the circumstances is never absent".[6] Thus the time a rite is to be performed is invariably significant: midnight, sunrise, sunset, etc. The place where the rite takes place is likewise circumscribed, whether in the shrines normally used by the cult, or in more exotic locales; and finally "In the absence of any other locus, the magician sketches out a magical circle or square, a *templum*, around himself, and it is there that he performs his task".[7] This is an important insight; we shall later have cause to note that this insistence on temporality and spatiality is reflected in the ways magic is thought to control access to time and space as well.

The materials employed in magical rites are frequently the rejects of sacrifice or of the human body itself (fingernails, excrement, hair, etc.): "everything which is normally rejected and has no ordinary use".[8]

---

[1] *Esquisse*, p. 31; by "shamanistic" I do not intend the universalising Americanism which embraces all forms of spirit mediumship and possession behaviour (cf., on the confusion in Anglo-Saxon ranks, I.M. Lewis, *Religion in Context*, pp. 10-11, but simply "enthusiastic" or "charismatic" behaviour.

[2] *Esquisse*, p. 33.

[3] *Esquisse*, pp. 33-34.

[4] *Esquisse*, p. 35.

[5] *Esquisse*, pp. 35-36.

[6] *Esquisse*, p. 38.

[7] *Esquisse*, p. 39.

[8] *Esquisse*, p. 40.

Preliminary to the magical rite, due attention must be paid to certain tabus or other restrictions; likewise, the rites prefacing the rite itself have virtually the same character as the "entrance rites" of normal sacrifice, and it is not unusual for exit rites to be employed as well.[1] Mauss-Hubert observe that magic has in fact a tendency to multiply the number and complexity of its rituals:

> It is not without reason that it is only the herbs of Saint John, Saint-Martin, Christmas, Long Friday or the new moon which are employed. These are things which are out of the ordinary, and it is ultimately a question of endowing the ceremony with its abnormal character; and it is to this end that all magical ritual tends.[2]

Rites are categorised as either manual or oral. Manual rites make extensive use of sympathetic and symbolic "codes", the number of which is, however, surprisingly limited. But there are also purificatory and sacrificial rites. However, sacrifice plays by no means so extensive a rôle in magic as in religion. Moreover, if sacrifice is absent from the cult, it will also be absent from the local magics.[3] An additional feature of magic, its tendency to rely on the preparation of special ointments, unguents, brews, serums, and so forth, is perceptively seen by Mauss-Hubert as being, itself, enacted ritual. What they fail to point out, and which would have strengthened their case that magic is occasional, while religion is normative, is that the cult usually has such paraphernalia at hand: the magician has to make his.

Oral rites correspond to those found in religious usage, though with a disproportion between elevated means and low object. The magical liturgies are frequently borrowed, above all from abolished or foreign rituals.[4] The authors point out that myth plays an important part in magical incantations: "One assimilates the present case to the case described as to a prototype . . . . "[5] They maintain further that all oral rites have the same function, namely to evoke a presence and to specialise a rite: "One invokes, one summons, one makes the spiritual

---

[1] *Esquisse*, pp. 41-42.

[2] *Esquisse*, p. 43.

[3] *Esquisse*, pp. 44-45.

[4] *Esquisse*, pp. 47-48.

[5] *Esquisse*, p. 49.

force present which is to make the rite efficacious . . . . "[1] The highly
formulaic character of oral rites corresponds to the formalistic nature of
magic. Furthermore, magical rituals frequently import oral rites from
foreign or archaic religious sources.[2] Considerable use is made of metre
and special rhythms; gesture, too, is carefully regulated and prescribed.[3]
The magician, as specialist, is above all the *knower* of the rites
applicable to various cases.[4] As far as the "représentations" are
concerned, Mauss-Hubert point to "a confusion of images without which
the rite itself would be inconceivable".[5] They classify them for the sake
of convenience as impersonal and personal concepts. The former are the
law-like concepts uncovered by Frazer and others; Mauss-Hubert
summarise them under the headings of contiguity, similarity, and
contrast.[6] Having met them already, it will not be necessary to expand
on them further. What is important is that Mauss-Hubert assign them a
more than merely cognitive significance; they maintain that a magical
ceremony is not only based on a given idea, but also on an appropriate
feeling, that is, a "property", "which provides both the sense and the
tone, and which in reality directs and commands all the associations of
ideas".[7] A very perceptive study of the "laws" of contagion and
similarity attempts to plumb the logic of their use; ultimately, it is
pointed out, as Frazer had suggested before them, that the two principles
virtually coincide.

Mauss-Hubert argue that magical thought cannot live on abstrac-
tion alone, but that it is a question of the "properties" "concerning
which both the actions and reactions are known in advance".[8] They
sense that the individual engaged in magic either does not reason or is
unconscious of his reasoning, that is, of the processes by which he

---

[1] *Esquisse*, p. 49.

[2] *Esquisse*, p. 48.

[3] *Esquisse*, pp. 50-51.

[4] *Esquisse*, p. 53.

[5], *Esquisse,* p. 55.

[6] *Esquisse*, p. 57.

[7] *Esquisse*, p. 59.

[8] *Esquisse*, pp. 67-68.

apprehends magical symbolism. Thus, for example, "When one throws the pothook out to ensure good weather, one ascribes virtues of a certain type to the pothook. But one does not retrace the chain of associations of ideas by means of which the founders of the rites in question arrived at these notions".[1] One wonders, of course, whether this is not simply a quality inherent in all symbolisation, i.e., that symbols are super-charged with meaning.[2] After all, how many Englishmen who use the curse "Sod it!" pause to consider that "sod" is a shortened form of "sodomite", and further relate the term to Genesis 18-19? But in Mauss-Hubert's (and later Evans-Pritchard's) view, it will be recalled, the magical symbols alone do not convey meaning; rather, the emotive "properties", together with the symbols, form "virtual rudiments of scientific laws, that is, of necessary and positive connexions which are thought to exist between these determinate things".[3] Lurking behind this view is yet another problem which had already provoked Tylor and Frazer, and which continues to rear its head even today, namely the relationship between magic and science. We shall defer discussion of this problem—which the writer feels to be a pseudo-problem—until later; at present it is sufficient to note that Mauss-Hubert hold that the "properties" which are held to inhere in the various objects of sympathetic-analogical thought are the products of social convention.[4] The authors pursue this line of enquiry by pointing to the fact that classification into at least the categories of good and bad is fundamental to all magic, and that classification is itself a social phenomenon.[5]

Under the heading of "personal representations", Mauss-Hubert address themselves to the fact that the magician's world does not consist of abstract ideas, as the talk of "properties" and "pseudo-laws" might seem to suggest. Rather, "All the magical representations may be expressed in personal representations".[6] The magician's mode of action is, as we have seen, through his detached spirit, or through his familiar

---

[1] *Esquisse*, p. 68.

[2] Cf.e.g. Turner, *The Forest of Symbols*, pp. 27-30.

[3] *Esquisse*, p. 69.

[4] *Esquisse*, pp. 70-71.

[5] *Esquisse*, p. 71.

[6] *Esquisse*, p. 73.

spirit or a demon or the like. Even when composing his salves and unguents he addresses them as were they in some sense personified. The idea underlying a rite may be abstract and mechanical; but the spirit addressed is "an autonomous servant and represents . . . the role of chance. Ultimately the magician admits that his science is not infallible and that his desire may not be accomplished".[1] Here the authors are on uncertain ground. As was noted earlier, one of the primary characteristics of magical acts is that they cannot be empirically falsified. Biblical scholars have, for example, noted in recent years, that what constitutes the "failure" of a prophecy is a very moot point indeed.[2] Nevertheless, Mauss-Hubert conclude that the magician's acknowledgement of failure resulting from a refractory spirit is one of the "antinomial" aspects of magic.[3] The main categories of spirits dealt with by the authors are the spirits of the dead, followed by demons, then the non-specialised spirits which people the magico-religious worlds of many peoples. They conclude that belief in such spirits is the result of collective experience: "their existence is never verified except posteriorly to the belief which imposes them".[4] And beliefs, it should go without saying, are social possessions.

Under the heading of "general observations", Mauss-Hubert return to the question of the status of magic vis à vis religion and science, respectively. Among other things, they note that whereas the sciences and handicrafts are frequently concerned with the theory underlying their undertakings, practitioners of magic almost never are; rather, the theorisation of magic is undertaken by esoterical philosophers.[5] They also observe that the process of transmission and formulation of "technical" ideas is collective, that is, traditional, whereas magical

[1] *Esquisse*, p. 74.

[2] A psychological theory accounting for this has been developed by L. Festinger, *A Theory of Cognitive Dissonance* (Evanston, IL 1957). It has played a rôle in Biblical studies in R.P. Carroll's *When Prophecy Failed: Reactions and Responses to Failure in the Old Testament Prophetic Traditions* (London, 1979); and in T.N.D. Mettinger's *The Dethronement of Sabaoth: Studies in the Shem and Kabod Theologies* (trans. F.H. Cryer) (Lund, 1982).

[3] *Esquisse*, p. 74.

[4] *Esquisse*, p. 79.

[5] *Esquisse*, p. 80.

tradition goes from individual to individual. Moreover, whereas the "technical disciplines" are implicitly creative and self-renewing, magic is not.[1] On the other side of the divide, the distinction between magic and religion, the authors hold that religion "is essentially a collective phenomenon in all its parts . . . Its beliefs and practices are by their very nature obligatory".[2] But, being so strongly collective, religion is essentially anti-individualistic.[3] We may schematise these conclusions in the following manner:

religion—collective—socially integrating
magic—individualistic—asocial (antinomial)

art-science—propagated by collective tradition—creative
magic—propagated by individual tradition—non-creative/ conservative/archaising

ANALYSIS

Mauss-Hubert maintain that belief in the efficacity of magic is one of the keys to its right understanding, and that all such belief is inevitably a priori: "one only goes to visit the magician because one believes in him; one does not cast a spell without confidence in it".[4] As was the case with Tylor and Frazer, this necessarily leads to the question of the magician's good faith; on this issue the authors are more willing to acknowledge the purity of the magician's motives, but are nevertheless puzzled by his evident readiness to claim abilities which are plainly contradicted by experience.[5] This is in part explained by the psychological states into which the magician works himself, so that he believes in what he is doing,[6] and in part by the fact that his public demands to be shown the illusion of power: "The magician dissimulates because it is

---

[1] *Esquisse*, pp. 82-83.

[2] *Esquisse*, p. 83.

[3] *Esquisse*, p. 83.

[4] *Esquisse*, p. 85.

[5] *Esquisse*, pp. 87-88.

[6] *Esquisse*, p. 88.

required of him that he dissimulate; people go in search of him, and they impose on him the necessity to act. He is not free . . . "[1]

This explanation is a wonderful example of an explanatory stratagem which characterises the entire "Durkheim school", namely the attempt to explain social phenomena via an interface of psychological and social forces. The magician is pictured as being in a particular state of psychological excitation, while at the same time social forces act upon him and dictate his actions. As far as its adequacy is concerned, however, there is room for doubt.[2] I have repeatedly referred to the "shamanistic bias" of Mauss-Hubert, meaning that they frequently emphasise the ecstatic or trance-like states of the magician. However, such states are far from universal in magical behaviour; it is by no means unusual for a practitioner of magic to perform his conjuration in conversational, or even quite bored tones.[3] There is therefore no reason to expect that he is invariably self-deluded by his "rapture", thus enabling him the more easily to delude others. Mauss-Hubert are forgetting the extent to which the practitioner's behaviour is, like religious behaviour, a function of tradition. One dispells, for example, the "miasma" of a bad dream by spitting betel juice to the four corners of the world and saying "avert", or "may it not be so", or whatever, not because one is in a particular state, but because father and grandfather did it that way, and so it must be done today.[4]

Mauss and Hubert offer an extensive analysis of the ideas employed by both anthropologists and primitives to account for magical rites. Their main point is that "no magician, nor even an anthropologist, has ever expressly claimed to be able to reduce the whole of magic to

---

[1] *Esquisse*, p. 89.

[2] Cf. E.E. Evans-Pritchard, *Theories*, p. 44: "It is absurd to put priest and atheist into the same category . . . and it would be yet more absurd to say that, when a priest is saying Mass, he is not performing a religious act unless he is in a certain emotional state. . . If we were to classify and explain social behaviour by supposed psychological states, we would indeed get some strange results".

[3] E.g., Evans-Pritchard, *Witchcraft*, pp. 177-78.

[4] Cf. *Theories*, p. 44: "A great many rites which surely almost anyone would accept as religious in character. . . are certainly not performed in situations in which there is any possible cause for emotional unrest or feelings of mystery and awe. They are routine, and also standardized and obligatory rites".

one or another of these ideas".[1] Their analysis of ceremonies of sympathetic magic shows that the symbols employed in them cannot by themselves explain the ceremonies; there is always a "residue" which must be explained in some other way.[2] The formulas employed in sympathetic rites are merely "abstract translations of very general concepts . . . ."[3]

The notion of "property" is likewise unable to explain the belief in "magical facts"; moreover, a "property" is never conceived as inherent in the thing, but as extrinsic, hence conferred upon it.[4] Finally, the belief in "properties" easily generalises to some more general notion of force inherent in nature. "Behind the notion of 'property' there yet remains the concept of milieu".[5] Here, too, a "residue" of meaning is left over when the concept of property has had its say. Belief in demons and other spiritual agents proves to be even worse suited as an explanatory model; it expresses at best some underlying notion of latent power. Mauss-Hubert do not hesitate to identify this power with ancient Assyrian *mamîtu* (Incidentally quite wrongly), Algonquin *manitou*, and Iroquois *orenda*.[6]

The common denominator of the various sorts of surplus meaning pointed to by Mauss-Hubert is the idea of *mana*, a generalized notion originally discovered in Melanesia by R.H. Codrington.[7] According to Mauss-Hubert, mana expresses such things as the "ability to work magic, the magical quality of a thing, a magical thing, a magical being, to have magical power, to be under a spell . . . ." Therefore, it ultimately "realizes this confusion of the agent, the rite and the things which seems to us to be fundamental to all magic".[8]

---

[1] *Esquisse*, p. 91.

[2] *Esquisse*, pp. 91-95.

[3] *Esquisse*, p. 95.

[4] *Esquisse*, p. 95.

[5] *Esquisse*, p. 97.

[6] *Esquisse*, p. 99.

[7] *The Melanesians* (Oxford, 1891); cf. e.g. pp. 118-120 et passim.

[8] *Esquisse*, pp. 101-102.

The authors insist that an important quality of mana is that it cannot be identified with demons or spirits, that it does not function mechanically, and that it functions like an environment ("milieu"), that is, like the "aether" of pre-relativistic physics.[1] They go on to claim that the concept of this "magical forcefield" is in reality universal; it is therefore also present even in societies which have never formulated it precisely: "a has no more need to formulate such an idea than it has to express the rules of its grammar".[2] It is not hard to see that for Mauss and Hubert, mana makes up the "residue" of meaning for which the various facts of magical behaviour were unable to account.

The question which then arises has to do with the precise nature of mana, that is, what sort of fact is it? Mauss-Hubert have no doubt that it is "a category of collective thought".[3] As such, it is more general than the notion of the sacred; in one revealing comment they affirm that

> It is not adequate . . . for us to say that the quality of mana attaches
> to certain things because of their relative position in the society; we
> must add that the idea of mana is nothing else but the idea of these
> values, of these differences of potential.[4]

They are very close to claiming that mana is a sort of thought that precedes thought, one which enables other discriminations to be made. What might be difficult for us is to recognise just who entertains the particular idea that mana happens to be. Mauss-Hubert have no doubt that it belongs to the category of collective thought; thus it is able to serve as a basis for the judgements undertaken by individuals in society.[5]

The authors devote the rest of their study to determining the nature of magical judgements, and conclude that they are synthetic a priori,[6] which is to say that they are complexes of conceptual associations which precede our perception and determine it. A notable feature of this pre-established perceptual "set", as Piaget might express it, is its

---

[1] *Esquisse*, pp. 104-6.

[2] *Esquisse*, p. 109.

[3] *Esquisse*, p. 112.

[4] *Esquisse*, p. 114.

[5] *Esquisse*, esp. p. 115.

[6] *Esquisse*, pp. 115-20.

emotional component: " . . . at the very root of magic are affective states . . . but these states are not those of individuals; rather, they result from the mixture of feelings proper to the individual with those of the whole of society".[1] They accordingly insist that magic is very much a social phenomenon; the magician cannot produce the states in which he works magic by himself. As they very beautifully express the idea, "Behind Moses, who strikes the rock, there is all Israel; and, if Moses doubts, Israel does not".[2]

Thus we return to Mauss-Hubert's shamanistic bias by a perceptual-philosophical route that verges on being a group-psychological solution to the problem of magic. For the authors, the notion of mana sort of floats in the air, a convenient rabbit pulled out of a hat to unify all the various aspects of magic which their very perceptive study has uncovered. Every aspect is explained; the relationship of individual magician to his wider society, the coherence of the various ideas and symbolisations employed in magical rites, even the magician's own perceptual and emotive "set". Moreover, Mauss-Hubert have rendered their concept of mana safe from criticism by the assertion of its de facto universality. The argument of the universality of mana sparked a prodigious search in socio-anthropological studies for parallels to the phenomenon.[3] Needless to say, mana-equivalents are not everywhere in evidence, leaving the mana-enthusiast the options of claiming that the society in question once knew the phenomenon, but has forgotten it; has not yet developed it; or else (the structural-functionalist variation) it has been suppressed or was rendered unnecessary in the first place by some phenomenon already present in the society (i.e., a "functional equivalent"). None of these positions can be seriously maintained today. From the point of view of the theory of theory formation, it makes about as much sense to claim that the manifold phenomena of magic are to be explained by the machinations of—indemonstrable—little green men as to hold that some—equally indemonstrable—all-encompassing psychosocial phenomenon is responsible.

[1] *Esquisse*, p. 123.

[2] *Esquisse*, p. 124.

[3] Cf. G. Widengren, *Phänomenologie*, pp. 10-13; O'Keefe, *Lightning*, p. 166 and p. 174 n. 54-58 (somewhat more positively).

This is not to say, however, that the study of Mauss-Hubert has nothing to tell us today. Quite a number of their observations still count as valid generalisations of magical behaviour, or at least as widely-accepted ones, even if we should be inclined to be more critical as to their theoretical basis than was once the case. And whether we agree with them or not, their observations have very much influenced subsequent research, as we shall see. In this context it will be sufficient to concentrate on the the following points: 1) that Mauss and Hubert disregard intellectualistic explanations of magic; magic is, to them, not a behaviour which takes place because of one or another idea the magician might happen to hold. Magical action is not so much the result of "belief" as of "conviction"; that is, the magician knows (and not merely believes) that y will follow x. Furthermore, 2) he knows this because his perception of the world has already been, so to say, pre-emptively determined before he encounters the situation in question. Also, 3) the authors hold that a particular emotional state accompanies the magician's performance, and that this emotional state characterises the interaction between the magician and his environment. 4) Magic is in every way an "outsider" phenomenon; it uses a wealth of gesture, archaic language, and superabundant detail which distinguishes magical acts from all other actions of normal life. In addition, it is practised by individuals who are themselves outsiders (spirit-possessed "shamanistic" practitioners, ethnic (e.g., gypsies) or social (e.g., women) outsiders, or else—exceptionally—the leadership of the society). 5) Magic itself is latently, if not actually, antinomial, anti-authoritarian, anti-religious, anti-social.

EMILE DURKHEIM

The last point was regarded as crucial by E.Durkheim, who famously maintained that "Magic takes a sort of professional pleasure in profaning holy things",[1] although the example he has in mind is that of the purported European witch-cult.[2] Durkheim is mainly concerned to distinguish magic from religion; to this end he emphasises the antipathy expressed by religions towards magic. Moreover, as he claims,

---

[1] *Forms*, p. 43.

[2] Cf. Durkheim, *Forms*, p. 43 n. 3: "For example, the host is profaned in the black mass".

"Religion . . . is inseparable from the idea of a Church",[1] where, by "Church" Durkheim understands "an eminently collective thing".[2] By way of contrast, magic centres on the individual practitioner; even where there are magical associations the relation between magical specialist and "layman" resembles nothing so much as that between doctor and patient.[3] Otherwise, however, Durkheim is concerned to emphasise the socially integrative function of magical ritual. Specifically, he points to a feature of "imitative" magic which had been overlooked by Tylor and Frazer, namely that, for example, in making an image of his totem animal, the sorceror is asserting, that is, creating, a connexion where none previously existed.[4] Accordingly, the connexion between "signifier" and "signified", as it were, is socially created in the context of the imitative rite; in performing it, men strengthen their consciousness of belonging to the group: "The moral efficacy of the rite, which is real, leads to the belief in its physical efficacy, which is imaginary . . . ."[5] This is a vast improvement on the contempt expressed by Tylor and, to some extent, by Frazer, for magical practice.[6] To the extent that magic utilises ritual, it must, on Durkheim's view, serve a socially-integrative function, which is a far cry from simply dismissing it as an aberration of "primitives".

B. MALINOWSKI

For Malinowski, magic is "an entirely sober, prosaic, even clumsy art, enacted for purely practical reasons, governed by crude and shallow beliefs, carried out in a simple and monotonous technique". We should note that this conflicts to some extent with Mauss-Hubert's claims about the exclusivity and arcane character of magic. In contradistinction to religion, magic is "a body of purely practical acts, performed as a means

---

[1] *Forms*, p. 45.

[2] *Forms*, p. 47.

[3] *Forms*, p. 44.

[4] *Forms*, p. 357.

[5] *Forms*, p. 359.

[6] Unfortunately, Durkheim also followed the lead of Mauss and Hubert and adopted the concept of mana as an explanation for the "force" underlying magico-religious beliefs and practices (*Forms*, pp. 188-204).

to an end".[1] Once again we note the tendency of structural-functional studies to depreciate the cognitive aspects of social phenomena; the converse of this is an emphasis on the emotive aspect of magical behaviour. Thus Malinowski stresses as "of the greatest importance" such features as the "emotional setting" and "gestures and expressions" of the sorceror; he holds that "the dramatic expression of emotion is the essence of this (magical) act".[2] Where all previous scholars had to a greater or lesser degree accepted Frazer's notion of "imitative magic", as we have seen, Malinowski adds to magical rites what he calls "an immediate application of magical virtue";[3] in this connexion the "performer" simply commands the desired result. "Charms" are accomplished by transferring such magical virtue to an object; the main vehicle of this and most other magical activities is the spell. The spell itself consists of 1) phonetic effects 2) words of invocation, statement, or command 3) mythological allusions.[4]

Like Tylor and Frazer, Malinowski powerfully stresses the fact that magic is a tradition-sanctioned activity: "the belief in the primeval natural existence of magic is universal"; more important than this facet of the phenomenon is its corollary, which partially explains the conservatism and archaism noted by Mauss and Hubert: "the conviction that only by an absolutely unmodified immaculate transmission does magic retain its efficiency".[5] Very much against Mauss-Hubert and even Durkheim is Malinowski's claim that the force of magic is always conceived of as inhabiting the performer himself: "It is thus never conceived as a force of nature, residing in things, acting independently of man".[6] Malinowski accordingly distinguishes sharply between "concepts of the mana type" and "the special virtue of magical spell and rite".[7]

---

[1] *MSR*, p. 70.

[2] *MSR*, p. 71.

[3] *MSR*, p. 73.

[4] *MSR*, pp. 73-74.

[5] *MSR*, p. 75.

[6] *MSR*, p. 76.

[7] *MSR*, p. 77.

Malinowski's ultimate explanation of magic is psychological; magical behaviour is born to counter man's awareness of his impotence to deal with his "anxiety, his fears and hopes;" he adds that "his (man's) organism reproduces the acts suggested by the anticipations of hope, dictated by the emotion of passion so strongly felt".[1] Here Evans-Pritchard's objection is once again a propos: it is useless to attempt to define the quality of ritual acts, magical or otherwise, on the basis of some purported emotional feeling that is supposed to motivate them. Where Malinowski's view is exciting is his acknowledgement that magic is an on-going enterprise; that in spite of its apparent (and ideologically motivated) conservatism a magician gathers around him a "current mythology" of success-stories which serve the purposes of legitimation; thus "the running chronicle of magical miracles establishes its claims beyond any doubt or cavil . . . Magic moves in the glory of past tradition, but it also creates its atmosphere of ever-nascent myth".[2] This is an interesting reversal of the position of Mauss and Hubert who, as we saw, thought that magical myth simply assimilates the present (magical) undertaking to a primordial mythical pattern; Malinowski insists instead that this is hardly an intellectual effort; rather, its thrust is "not to explain but to vouch for, not to satisfy curiosity but to give confidence in power".[3] It is therefore an entirely present activity.

Otherwise, Malinowski responds to the time-honoured apparent duty of the sociologist to attempt to distinguish magic from science and religion. While noting, like Mauss-Hubert, that both magic and science have theoretical components and that both concern themselves with certain techniques, he emphasizes that

> Science . . . is based on the normal universal experience of everyday life . . . founded on observation, fixed by reason. Magic is based on on specific experience of emotional states in which man observes not nature but himself.[4]

He finds it more difficult to delimit magic from religion, as both, on his view, arise from "situations of emotional stress"; they are "escapes"

---

[1] *MSR*, pp. 79-82.

[2] *MSR*, p. 83.

[3] *MSR*, p. 84.

[4] *MSR*, p.87.

from the vicissitudes of life; they are both based on the mythological tradition; both stress the miraculous and are hedged about with tabus and other practices which distinguish their acts from profane ones.[1] Thus the main differences between the two phenomena reside in the fact that magic serves the social function of reinforcing the belief in man's power, while its apparent ends are utilitarian. Religion, by way of contrast, "has no such simple technique, and its unity can be seen . . . in the function which it fulfills and in the value of its belief and ritual".[2] The social function of religious faith is that it

> establishes, fixes, and enhances all valuable mental attitudes, such as reverence for tradition, harmony with environment, courage and confidence in the struggle with difficulties and at the prospect of death.[3]

Reading between the lines, it is obvious that Malinowski holds that magical acts strengthen the individual in the concrete contexts in which he seeks magical assistance, whereas religion reinforces broadly collective attitudes. The distance between his view and that of Mauss-Hubert is not so great after all, even though Malinowski nowhere suggests that magic is anti-religious or antinomial.

D.L. O'KEEFE

O'Keefe's *Stolen Lightning* is the first serious attempt to present a detailed general explanatory theory of magic, rather than just a "sketch" ("esquisse") like that of Mauss and Hubert or the cursory, rather reductive attempts of Tylor, Frazer, Durkheim and Malinowski. As such, the work is capacious (581 pages) and extremely learned; we shall hardly be able to go into it in detail here. Nevertheless, a critical account of O'Keefe's work, seen in the retrospect provided by the preceding studies, will roughly bring us to the "state of the art" of current socio-anthropological studies of magic.

Fundamental to O'Keefe's investigation is his acknowledgement that magic is real, that is, that whether or not one believes that witches send their doubles out to devour the flesh of their enemies, it is a fact

---

[1] *MSR*, p. 88.

[2] *MSR*, p. 88.

[3] *MSR*, p. 89.

that many societies believe this, or something similar, to be the case.[1] Since shared belief is a social phenomenon, the job of the socio-anthropologist is to examine such belief in its social context. He does not start from one or two principles, like Tylor and Frazer; instead, he offers "empirical propositions" of general character, but grounded—as already those of Mauss and Hubert were—in actual observation.[2] The study remains nonetheless admittedly positivistic, which puts it squarely in the centre of the Anglo-Saxon socio-anthropological tradition. To go to the other side of the divide, that is, to studies which either more or less critically embrace the worldview under consideration, one would have to go to the many works of Carlos Castaneda, or to the theosophies of Mme. Blavatsky, I.Gurdjieff, I.Shah, or the like.[3] By "positivistic" is meant that the author does not hesitate to say when a phenomenon reported in one or another society does not "really" occur, but is instead only reported. Ultimately, O'Keefe does not even find the phenomenon of magic attractive, but only interesting for theoretical reasons.[4]

The first problem confronted by the author is the difficulty of arriving at a suitable definition of magic. As he points out, previous studies were aprioristic and reductive, trying to subsume the complex phenomena under a very few rubrics: a procedure which inevitably leaves quite a bit out of account. As a self-acknowledged positivist, he

---

[1] O'Keefe further points out (*Lightning*, p. 1) that the institutions of magic fulfil Durkheim's three criteria of social "facticity": externality (to the individual), coerciveness (they compel behaviour), and generality (magic is found virtually everywhere). Moreover, they are also "patterned"; there are typical features from society to society, although not all features are equally present everywhere.

[2] *Lightning*, p. xvi.

[3] In her excellent *Traditions of Belief: Women and the Supernatural* (London, 1987), G. Bennett points out that in addition to the social traditions which conventionally legitimate belief in survival after death, there is a second strain in the West, at least, which she tellingly labels "traditions of disbelief" (p. 16). These traditions seek to explain reports of the supernatural away; as Bennett notes, they are themselves entirely stereotyped and predictable, which emphasises their wholly conventional character. It should be evident that the positivism of many social anthropol-ogists in reality merely follows and mirrors the second of these two traditions, and its ramifications. Navigating between these traditions is a fine art which no one has managed successfully as yet.

[4] *Lightning*, p. xvii.

cannot follow Weber's procedure of proposing an "ideal type" abstracted from experience, as abstractions cannot be verified or disconfirmed. Accordingly, O'Keefe offers two definitions, one "in the weak sense", and one "in the strict sense". The former encompasses the "sympathetic" character of language, the likewise "sympathetic" nature of religious ritual, certain tendencies of the human mind to control its environment, some symbolic aspects of social action, and metaphorical usage of ordinary language in which we label things magical which are not (like calling a woman "bewitching").[1] O'Keefe's "strict" definition accepts that magic is too amorphous to be simply catalogued. He suggests instead that we list those elements that empirically "tend" to be present, but need not be in all cases. These elements include the following observations: 1) the magician tends to have a professional relationship to an individual client or client-group 2) magic derives from religion 3) new religions arise from the conflict between emergent magic and religion 4) magic and religion are mutually antagonistic 5) the Freudian postulate that magic defends the ego against the encroachments of society. All of this leads to the conclusion that "Magic is the expropriation of religious collective representations for individual or subgroup purposes—to enable the individual ego to resist psychic extinction or the subgroup to resist cognitive collapse".[2]

This is a sophisticated thesis; learned, well and cogently argued, and its conclusions represent a synthesis of the main methodological elements of the English and Continental (especially French) socio-anthropological traditions. I disagree with it precisely where the influence from the Durkheim school makes itself noticeable, namely in O'Keefe's insistence on the idea (above, point 2) that magic derives from religion, and on the "Freudian" claim (above, point 5) that magic defends the ego. The psyche, that is, the "ego", is a psychological, not a sociological category. Magic is notably a social undertaking, not an individual one, as its prevalence in a wide range of societies shows. Thus a social explanation of the phenomenon is required, however

[1] *Lightning*, pp. 2-12.

[2] *Lightning*, p. 14.

interesting the psychological aspects of the matter may be.[1] As for
O'Keefe's fourth point, the purported mutual antagonism between magic
and religion, we have seen that it is an old chestnut of socio- anthropological theory; it was, to the best of my knowledge, first advanced by
Robertson-Smith,[2] and we have seen that it recurs in the thought of
most of the early students of magic, under the guise of magic's
supposed "antinomial" character, or whatever. It is not, however, true,

---

[1] Obviously, we cannot go into this too deeply here. At all events, O'Keefe is
not arguing, as scholars in the 1960s and 1970s sometimes did (under the rubric of
"methodological individualism versus methodological holism"; cf. e.g. G.C. Homans,
"Bringing Men Back in", in A. Ryan (ed.), *The Philosophy of Social Explanation*
(Oxford, 1978 [1973]), pp. 50-65; and see the literature cited by S. Lukes in
"Methodological Individualism Reconsidered", in the same work, p. 120, n. 12.), that
the social is reducible to the psychological. But I remain sceptical of the possibility
of eludicidating psychological motives from sociological observations. F.A. Hanson
(*Meaning in Culture* [London, 1975], pp. 3-6) makes the point that as a questioning
activity, psychological and sociological questions address themselves to the same
reality, but from radically different perspectives, viz. "individual" versus "institutional", each of which has its own appropriate logic. We saw above that already
Mauss and Hubert attempted to provide something like a group- psychological
characterisation of the relationship of magical ritual to society. This idea emerges
full-blown in the work of Durkheim, who sees society as energised by the "efferves-
cence" created by participation in ritual (Durkheim, *Forms*, pp. 299-414; cf. E.E.
Evans-Pritchard, *Theories*, p. 63). Now no one would deny that affectual states may
arise in the course of ritual, though, as mentioned above, they need not do so.
However, there is the difficulty that the participants in rituals are groups, not
societies; so an explanation is still required as to how emotively energized "groups"
manage to influence society (as sharply pointed out by A.A. Goldenweiser in his
review of *Les Formes élémentaires de la vie religieuse.*). (orig. pub. in *AA* 17 (1915)
719-35; reprinted in W.S.F. Pickering (ed.), *Durkheim on Religion: A selection of
readings with bibliographies* (London, 1975), pp. 209-27, esp. pp. 218-19). And the
relation of the group to its wider society is indubitably social, so that a social
explanation is the obvious desideratum.

[2] *Lectures on the Religion of the Semites* (New York; 3rd edn, 1959 [1889]);
p. 264: "There was. . .a whole region of possible needs and desires for which
religion could and would do nothing; and if supernatural help was sought in such
things it had to be sought through magical ceremonies . . . Not only did these
magical superstitions lie outside religion, but in all well-ordered states they were
regarded as illicit". Note again already Tylor's observation that magical phenomena
are frequently associated with "outsider" groups, *Origins*, pp. 113-15.

as we shall see below, and represents yet another unfortunate fruit of anthropological ethnocentricism.

The rest of O'Keefe's study consists of his advancement of thirteen "empirical propositions", which he then proceeds to defend. They are, as follows: 1) "magic is a form of social action"[1] 2)"magical social action consists of symbolic performances—and linguistic symbolism is central to magic"[2] 3) "magical symbolic action is rigidly scripted"[3] 4) "magical scripts achieve their social effects largely by pre- existing or pre-figured agreements"[4] 5) "magic borrows symbolism from religion and uses it to argue with religion in a dialectic that renews religion"[5] 6) "logically, and in some observable historical sequences, magic derives from religion rather than vice versa"[6] 7) "magic is a byproduct of the projection of society in religion"[7] 8) "religion is the institution that creates or models magic for society"[8] 9) "magic tries to protect the self"[9] 10) "magic helped develop the institution of the individual"[10] 11) "magic—especially Black Magic—is an index of social pressures on selves and individuals"[11] 12) "magic persists as an expression of certain aspects of civilization"[12] 13) "magical symbolism travels easily and accumulates a history".[13]

In his first section, O'Keefe attempts to determine what kind of social action magic is. He points out, against intellectualist arguments which regard magic as an attempt to comprehend the world through a

---

[1] *Lightning*, pp. 25–38.

[2] *Lightning*, pp. 39-61.

[3] *Lightning*, pp. 62-78.

[4] *Lightning*, pp. 79-118.

[5] *Lightning*, pp. 121-57.

[6] *Lightning*, pp. 158-75.

[7] *Lightning*, pp. 175-209.

[8] *Lightning*, pp. 210-59.

[9] *Lightning*, pp. 263-347.

[10] *Lightning*, pp. 349-413.

[11] *Lightning*, pp. 414-57.

[12] *Lightning*, pp. 458-519.

[13] *Lightning*, pp. 523-69.

symbol system, and against "rational-purposive" understandings of magic, which see it as (mistaken) causal attempts to influence the world directly, that it in fact does both.[1] Against individualist-psychological interpretations, which see magic as a purely passive phenomenon affecting the individual's emotional "set", he points out that even such behaviour is communicative, hence acts on others, hence social.[2]

O'Keefe's second section deals with magical symbolic language. Here it is noted that magic language uses "powerful collective symbols"; it "manipulates" them so as to realise the desired end at an abstract level.[3] Adopting an intellectualist stance, he holds that such symbolisation is central to magic;[4] thus he says that many of the words used in magic "refer to abstract entities or classes, and they are ideas that light up experience and generate thought".[5] Finally, with Mauss and Hubert, O'Keefe adds to the verbal forms of "sympathy" the notion that many of the associations of words used in magic are established by social convention, that is, are traditional.[6] Ultimately, he holds,

> sympathetic magic comes down to links between words provided by primitive classification systems, which are used for the transfer of qualities between concepts in suggestive statements aimed at affecting these entities, which in turn affect their physical referents.[7]

Primitive classification enables us to apprehend the world, but the reciprocal interactions of the classficatory categories which arise in magical speech repattern the world the categories describe. Although few linguists have any faith in our ability to trace the cognitive categories of language back so far, few would deny that language does pattern the reality we perceive.[8] The sentences employed in magical

---

[1] *Lightning*, p. 27.

[2] *Lightning*, pp. 30-34.

[3] *Lightning*, pp. 40-41.

[4] *Lightning*, p. 42.

[5] *Lightning*, p. 45.

[6] *Lightning*, p. 49.

[7] *Lightning*, p. 51.

[8] See the volume of essays entitled *Magie, Grazer Linguistische Studien* 23/24 (1985); also the earlier but excellent study by E.M. Ahern, "The Problem of Efficacy: Strong and Weak Illocutionary Acts", *Man* 14 (1979), pp. 1-17.

language (i.e., in incantations, spells, etc.) utilise the full panoply of effects available to religious language, particularly speech acts, which "really do 'psych out' the other person, induce altered states of consciousness . . . (and) renew faith in the propositions of the religious worldview".[1]

In reviewing the odd, archaising, stilted, ridigly formal and sometimes outré language of magic, O'Keefe attempts to relate it in his third section to "sacred praxis in general",[2] and cites Mauss and Hubert for having shown that magic "expropriates many of its scripts wholesale and ready-made from religion".[3] Now, while Mauss and Hubert do note that magic frequently borrows for its incantations and the like texts from virtually any religious tradition, and the more obscure the better, this is not the same as claiming that behavioural "scripts"—which prescribe certain courses of action—are also so derived. In fact, it is often the case that a foreign text is simply adopted by a wizard entirely a-contextually and brought into relation to some wholly different purpose than was intended in its original situation. Or are we to suppose that the use of the Tetragrammaton or of fragments of the Torah by medieval alchemists or Hellenistic magicians was intended to commend Jewish religious observances? Clearly, the point of adopting materials from foreign traditions is that, being foreign, they are exotic,[4] and, being exotic, can be held to be authoritative for the peculiar purposes of magic. Being foreign, they are unknowns, blank slates; thus materials so extracted from foreign religious traditions are hardly the object of the religious interest of the magician and his clientele, so it is a bit much to claim that "religion" provides the "scripts". An adequate parallel would be the Zande fascination with foreign medicines, on the grounds that "Azande believe that foreigners know much more about magic than they

---

[1] *Lightning*, p. 55.

[2] *Lightning*, p. 64.

[3] *Lightning*, p. 64.

[4] Cf. M.W. Helms, *Ulysses' Sail,* p. 119: "focusing only on material goods, we can see from the ethnographic literature that sheer distance and the magical or symbolic potency associated with distance or with distant places and polities can be important factors in the value assigned to some resources".

do".[1] Obviously, like the Scottish Rugby Union cap, anything can be imported for the purposes of ritual, and will be if 1) an adequate legitimating ideology is available (e.g. "foreign magic is stronger than ours"), and provided that 2) the social coding enables, rather than opposes such imports.

In his fourth section, O'Keefe points out that magic can have quite drastic social effects; he asks, "How . . . is it able to induce altered states of consciousness, cure illness, actually kill people and do other remarkable things"?[2] In searching for an answer, he considers the possibilities offered by symbolic interaction theory and rhetorical studies, and adopts the model of Aristotle's "enthymene", which persuades the audience by use of formulations which are "close enough to the unorganized consensus as to gain unreflected assent";[3] in line with the previous postulate, he finds the premise of such a consensus to derive from the religious sphere. O'Keefe further defines the operation as "a first person singular speaking in the first person plural";[4] he maintains that both institutional magic and science make use of such tacit means of building consensus. However, magic "in the strict sense" cannot be adequately explained by rhetoric or persuasion.[5] A brief review of the type of logic implicit in magical thought shares Lévi--Strauss' view that primitive myth "is mere sustained apposition of contradictories . . . whereas Western logic profanely settles the contradiction—with negation. Hence deduction . . . is possible".[6] He goes so far as to identify this "negativising" tendency of Western logic as an "institutionalized protection" for the ego from the supernatural, one which obviates the need of magic.[7] Without noticing it, we are in the murky waters of ethnocentrist argumentation again, with a cognitive twist: myth affirms the polarities of existence, "Western" logic (whose? Frege's? Riemann's? Aristotle's?) severs the Gordian knots by negation;

---

[1] E.E. Evans-Pritchard, *Witchcraft*, p. 203.

[2] *Lightning*, p. 79.

[3] *Lightning*, p. 82.

[4] *Lightning*, p. 83.

[5] *Lightning*, p. 84.

[6] *Lightning*, p. 90.

[7] *Lightning*, p. 91.

therefore "they" are prey to the terrors of magic, while "we" are able to reject the entire category of magical experience. In any comparison of quantities, it is clearly meaningless, as I suggested in my criticism of Frazer, to describe one quantity extensively and compare it with a non-analysed quantity, or with one that has not been analysed according to the same procedures. This is what makes discussions of magic versus science or magic versus religion, or the like, pointless, and even, on occasion, silly.[1]

In addressing the way magic actually works (in societies where it does work), O'Keefe notes that magic applies to marginal states and experiences.[2] It does so by utilising the "symbolism of sacred drama", which differentiates it from other activities, by illicit or anti-religious activities, by cultivating alternative mental states, and possibly by addressing "some real spiritual experience".[3] He rejects purely psycho-social explanations of the efficacity of magic in favour of a consensual explanation: magic works because its participants agree that it does so.[4] O'Keefe's explicitly sociological explanation of this phenomenon is based on the sociology of knowledge; the cognitive framework through which we experience the world is socially presented to us. Accordingly, even small disturbances of this framework provoke different states of consciousness.[5] The author regards it as one of the functions of religion to provide the normative "patterning" of our experiences; thus he claims that "Part of the tension between magic and religion is due to the comparatively greater use that magic deliberately makes of frame-relaxing phenomena which religion attempts to control".[6] We should note that this line of argumentation already presupposes a sharp distinction between magic and religion, as well as an antithetical relationship between both spheres of activity. This is a bit premature, as the author

---

[1]　R. Horton and R. Finnegan (eds.), *Modes of Thought: Essays on Thinking in Western and Non-Western Societies* (London, 1973).

[2]　*Lightning*, p. 93.

[3]　*Lightning*, p. 93.

[4]　*Lightning*, pp. 95-96.

[5]　*Lightning*, p. 96.

[6]　*Lightning*, p. 98.

first attempts to prove this claim somewhat later.[1] For all that O'Keefe attempts in the subsequent section[2] to describe various forms of social behaviour which form our "reality orientation" in general, his is not a "sociological" presentation in the sense of linking social behaviour to social structures and institutions. Nevertheless, I think we can agree with O'Keefe that where magical experience is synonymous with "paranormal" experience—here the basic "shamanistic bias" of Mauss and Hubert manifests itself again—the magical rite does first elicit the experience (through invocation, drugs, manic dancing, etc.— which, it might be admitted, constitute "relaxing the frame") and then proceed to pattern it.[3] However, the extent to which this can actually be termed "agreeing to agree", or whatever, is not obvious. The notion of "agreement" conveys a sense of assenting to a proposition or a course of action; the spontaneous trance which manifests itself in shamanistic or other "possession" behaviour seems anything but consensual—often enough, those threatened by "spirit possession" resist the notion fiercely.[4] Whatever "agreement" may take place either does so only implicity—that is, at the level of the social scientist's smug "but in reality . . . ", or by a redefinition of the notion of "agreement" as giving expression to socially patterned expectations as to paranormal behaviour—expectations which in any case leave quite a bit of room for individual expression.[5]

---

[1] *Lightning*, pp. 159-209.

[2] *Lightning*, pp. 99-110.

[3] *Lightning*, p. 102.

[4] Cf. e.g. I.M. Lewis, *Ecstatic Religion* (Harmondsworth, 1978 [1971]), p. 66: "The initial experience of possession...is often a distubing, even traumatic experience..."; p. 71: "(in some societies exhibiting possession phenomena). . . the connection between suffering and possession is so overwhelming that at first sight it seems to constitute an end in itself. . . Here, ostensibly at least, posession connotes misfortunes and sickness. . . ."; see also p. 187: "Not only have the personal tastes of the individual theoretically no part in this decision to make himself a shaman, but they are also strongly denied. . . ." (cited by Lewis from an article by G. Moréchand).

[5] Note both the vast range of means of evoking shamanic possession trances recorded in J. Halifax (ed.), *Shamanic Voices: The Shaman as Seer, Poet and Healer* (Harmondsworth, 1979).

Postulate 5, dealing with the magical use of symbolism, again simply presupposes that magic and religion are clearly distinct, and even that religion is logically prior to magic: "both symbolism and agreements that make it work (are) largely borrowed from religion, which is the traditional symbolic projection of the community".[1] Examples are drawn from the Church in the Middle Ages, which "modeled" magic for the people by selling miracles, claiming the efficacity of the Eucharist against illness, to promote fertility, and so on.[2] Other magical borrowings included the use of the Koran in North African magic and the use of primitive agricultural religion in the oriental mystery cults.[3] O'Keefe says that

> the limit of magic is black which reverses every value of religion and appears utterly hostile to it. But this tendency is present in all magic; all the provinces of magic have an antinomian thrust.[4]

Oddly, though, he cites virtually no evidence, and merely repeats the familiar saw from Durkheim (who, as we noted, had the Black Mass of the quasi-mythical witchcraft cult of the Middle Ages in mind),[5] plus

---

[1] *Lightning*, p. 121.

[2] *Lightning*, p. 121.

[3] *Lightning*, p. 123.

[4] *Lightning*, p. 124.

[5] Contemporary "witch-cults" in Great Britain and elsewhere do practice "Black Masses", as the popular media delight to inform us; but there is some question as to what extent there ever were European witch-cults. Margaret Murray (*The God of the Witches* [London, 1952]) held that historical witchcults all over medieval Europe were remnants of earlier pagan fertility cults; H.R. Trevor-Roper, whose *The European Witch-Craze of the Sixteenth and Seventeenth Centuries* (Harmondsworth, 1967) signalled the academic revival of interest in medieval magic, has no doubt that the "witches" existed only in the minds of the inquisitors; K. Thomas (*Religion and the Decline of Magic* [London, 1973], pp. 513-17) finds no evidence of Murray's cult. Magical practices were, however, quite common during the Middle Ages on two social levels: in a broadly-based "common tradition", which was the intellectual property of both high and low; and in an esoteric, highly learned tradition, many of whose practitioners were clerics. See R. Kieckhefer, *European Witch Trials: Their Fouundations in Popular and Learned Culture, 1300-1500* (London, 1976); the same, *Magic in the Middle Ages* (Cambridge, 1990 [1989]). It is unsurprising that the early Durkheimians, coming as they did from a southern European Roman Catholic milieu, should have adopted the Church's uncompromis-

divination does not

a homily or two from W.H. Auden (not a notable social scientist).

Be this as it may, O'Keefe sees the relation between religion and magic as dialectical: magic implicitly challenges the religiously-sanctioned worldview;[1] religion retaliates by expelling magical practices or by banning their importation, even though some magical practices may revivify the religion;[2] new sects emerge as magical protest sects,[3] some of which are "patterned" by the old religion, while others are incorporated within it.[4] O'Keefe has no doubt that what such protest sects mainly protest against is religion itself.[5]

so is it ?

The author acknowledges that the "ethical" world religions present a special problem. However, he argues steadfastly that "many of the world religions are also magical protest sects";[6] as such, they also borrow material from other religions, challenge the existing religion and are patterned by it, and, among other things, protest against the inadequacy of existing magic.[7] He further claims that the world religions have frequently become more rather than less magical with the years, which is certainly true, although one wonders if this is not simply the inevitable result of their socio-historical success: having gained the allegiance of great numbers of followers of disparate backgrounds, some adulteration of original principles may have been a foregone conclusion. But in connexion with Christianity O'Keefe goes overboard and follows the theories of Morton Smith and others who have claimed that Jesus was a "magician" or wonder-worker, and that the early Church was accordingly a magical protest sect.[8] Now this is an odd position; O'Keefe is himself aware that early Christianity was but one of very

---

ing mythology of the reality of European witchcraft, and its antipathy towards the Church. But it would be quite an irony if there never really were any such cults, so that a fiction has managed to become determinative for later theorizing.

[1] *Lightning*, pp. 125-26.

[2] *Lightning*, pp. 126-27.

[3] *Lightning*, pp. 128-30.

[4] *Lightning*, pp. 130-31.

[5] *Lightning*, p. 132.

[6] *Lightning*, p. 135.

[7] *Lightning*, p. 135.

[8] *Lightning*, pp. 138-41.

many sects which practised magic, among other things. Quite apart from the hoary old discussion as to whether Jesus himself did so, one has simply to note that far more "magical" sects were around which failed to win acceptance, like Gnosticism, Mithraism, the Serapis cult, and so forth. Accordingly, magic was clearly not the reason for Christianity's eventual triumph, but only an incidental feature which it had in common with other, competing sects. It is correspondingly difficult to claim that it played any decisive rôle at Christianity's inception. O'Keefe's understanding of Judaism is equally peculiar, although he admits himself that his "magical protest" view is hardly applicable to its origins.[1]

The "dialectic" of magic and religion leads directly to postulate 6, having to do with the priority of religion over magic. Discussions of origins are generally senseless, as we noted in the introduction to this study; we neither have, nor could ever get any relevant evidence. O'Keefe nevertheless attempts to argue backwards: analysis of magical rites and concepts always shows them to contain borrowed elements; moreover, "throughout the third world we have a vast laboratory in which we can see new magics arising by expropriating religious material".[2] Once again, though, they also import the Scottish rugby cap, so the importation argument is less impressive than it might be. The entire discussion is ingenious and well informed (particularly in O'Keefe's astute remarks on the irrelevance of mana),[3] but its only purpose is to undergird the already presupposed razor-sharp (though curiously undrawable) distinction between magic and religion, their mutual antagonism, and the dialectic between them.

Postulate 7, the notion that "magic is a byproduct of the projection of society in religion", depends on the Durkheimian idea that religion is a projection of social structure. The postulate is virtually a tautology, since O'Keefe thinks to have shown already that magic emerges from religion, and not vice versa. The Durkheim position is widely held, as O'Keefe notes.[4] One still wonders, though, just what sort of projective mechanism allows the Azande, who dwell in small

[1] *Lightning*, p. 147.

[2] *Lightning*, p. 164.

[3] *Lightning*, p. 174, n 57.

[4] *Lightning*, p. 176.

villages and have a hierarchical social organisation, to have virtually no religion at all,[1] but only (alongside of a great deal of magic) a very hazy conception of a "Supreme Being" which has practically no consequences for their behaviour, while the not so vastly differently organised Nuer have an extensively developed theology and cosmology (and practically no magic).[2]

Postulate 8, dealing with the way religion models magic, in reality addresses itself to the problem of how to tell both phenomena apart. Thus O'Keefe examines the theories that magic and religion are identical,[3] that they can only be distinguished as participating in a spectrum of phenomena,[4] as well as a variety of "class inclusion theories";[5] ultimately, he opts for his own solution—itself a sort of inclusion theory—namely the idea that religion models magic (i.e., the generative theory we have encountered previously).[6] In chicken-before-egg sociological terms, he says that

> the ceremonialization of social customs which constitutes initial religious rites immediately enhances their sympathetic reverberations; and as the rite is used more instrumentally, the sympathetic magic potential of rites and of symbolism becomes more obvious.[7]

This emphasis on the importance of ritual for social (cognitive) development re-echos Durkheim's insistence on communal ritual as the "dynamo" of society. O'Keefe even goes so far as to tell us an evolutionary "Just-So Story"[8] illustrating the above-mentioned process. [9]

---

[1] Evans-Pritchard, *Witchcraft*, p. 51.

[2] Cf. E.E. Evans-Pritchard, *Nuer Religion*, (New York, 1974 [1956]), esp. p. 313.

[3] *Lightning*, p. 231.

[4] *Lightning*, pp. 231-33.

[5] *Lightning*, pp. 233-35.

[6] *Lightning*, pp. 235-40.

[7] *Lightning*, p. 235.

[8] For non-anglophone readers: the title of Rudyard Kipling's marvelous children's stories of the same name; all are playful aetiologies of the sort "How the Elephant Got His Trunk" (the baby elephant went down to the river to drink; a crocodile grabbed him by the nose and tried to pull him in; a benevolent rock python grabbed his tail and pulled the other way. . ."just so" did the elephant get his

He stresses that

> The sympathy effects of religious rites are part of what is sustaining
> and miraculous and full of hope in religion. When this element
> atrophies, the institution may become sterile and offer no
> efficacy . . . [1]

But if one wonders just why religious sympathy effects should grow
cold, no social answer is produced or even proposed; I conclude that
this process only exists for the purposes of providing a dynamic for
O'Keefe's developmental hypothesis.

The point O'Keefe wants to make is that magic emerges from
"calcified" religion (like medieval Catholicism),[2] continually opposes
religion, whether explicitly or implicitly, and, as magical protest
movement, provides the ground for the emergence of new religion [3].
This is "magic" at the social level; at the individual level, O'Keefe
holds,[4] magic "gives us the courage to act spontaneously in the
dangerous real world. Magic, therefore is the very beginning of action;
action begins in the magic protoaction of fantasy, delusion, dream and
magical thinking".[5] This thesis is extensively developed in studies of
magic's struggle with religion-as-superego,[6] of current psycho-analytical
ego-theory,[7] and of the various threats which religion, as reflection of
the social superego, represents to the self.[8]

Both the threat and the individual's "magical" response to it are
perhaps best illustrated by O'Keefe's own scenario. Here, the individual
(living, apparently, on O'Keefe's model, in a village system, consisting

---

long nose stretched into a trunk. Originally used by Evans-Pritchard to characterize
similar "evolutionary" tales told in the absence of all historical evidence.

[9] *Lightning*, pp. 235-36.

[1] *Lightning*, p. 236.

[2] *Lightning*, pp. 159-72.

[3] The various routes leading to this sequel are depicted in *Lightning*, p. 237.

[4] Following G. Róheim; cf. *Lightning*, pp. 271-75.

[5] *Lightning*, p. 273.

[6] *Lightning*, pp. 275-77.

[7] *LIghtning*, pp. 277-94.

[8] "Voodoo death", "soul loss", suicide; cf. *Lightning*, pp. 294-314.

of what he calls "face-to-face communities",[1] is exposed to the intense pressure to conform exerted by the society as a whole, whose worldview is, as we have seen, contained in the religious representations of the community. The religious worldview includes the concept that witches permeate society and continually threaten it.[2] If one steps out of line, one incurs censure at the hands of some "moral entrepreneur", acting on behalf of the group. Fear of the other's moralising becomes identified with one's witchfear; in retaliation and self-defence, the individual accuses the "entrepreneur" of witchcraft. In this context, O'Keefe does not hesitate to affirm that "Witch accusations are defenses against witch fears, which are religious; hence they are defenses against religion".[3] And, since he has already determined magic as opposed to religion, witch accusations are consequently magical. Accordingly, magic can be seen to support the individual against his society, which leads O'Keefe to conclude that magic was originally responsible for the emergence of the individual, and that it functions in any given society to protect the individual self against the encroachments of the social superego, whose vehicle is religion.

The conclusion that witch fears are religious, whereas witchcraft accusations are magical is a surprising reversal of expectations which requires a little thought, although it has much in its favour. One might point out that it is common to employ the diviner to test accusations of witchcraft (at least in most African societies), so it is empirically legitimate to point to the combination of plaintiff-plus-diviner as "magical", over against the accused. The status of the accused in this equation, however, is not so certain. Qua "moral entrepreneur" who speaks on behalf of society, he obviously represents the integrity of the community, which is, at least implicitly, guaranteed by every religious system known to man. On the other hand, such an "entrepreneur" is equally clearly attempting to assert his status (in this case, his right to speak on behalf of the community) at the expense of someone else—an action which asserts his individuality every bit as much as the witchcraft accusation asserts that of his opponent. So it might be claimed with

---

[1] *Lightning*, p. 415.

[2] *Lightning*; cf. esp. pp. 416-17.

[3] *Lightning*, p. 417.

equal justice that the "moral entrepreneur" makes a bid to achieve social eminence, that is, in Weberian terms, to manifest charisma, essentially a "magical" action, and that the only appropriate defense is likewise "magical"—a witchcraft accusation. O'Keefe's scenario may equally well be claimed to represent a contest between magic and magic, rather than between magic and religion. Moreover, O'Keefe's argumentation does not stand up under closer examination. The premise that moral censure (= religious sanction) is negated by its opposite, that is, magic, on O'Keefe's hypothesis, only works if the antithesis between religion and magic can be seriously maintained. But since the action of censuring is a social activity, any number of "functionally equivalent" social behaviours may exist which are capable of canceling it out. Therefore the witchcraft accusation need not be magical at all; nor, for that matter, need the censuring activity necessarily reflect the religiously-sanctioned worldview (it would do so if the religious worldview were "the only game in town", that is, the sole knowledge-framework of the society, but even in primitive societies this need not be the case). Finally, as I have repeatedly noted, the opposition between magic and religion is not as self-evident as O'Keefe imagines.

Postulate 10, which stresses O'Keefe's view that "magic helped develop the institution of the individual", is frankly and disarmingly speculative. Here the author follows the evolutionary theorists of the early days of socio-anthropology and holds that religion evolved during the Palaeolithic epoch, whereas magic differentiated out from it in the Neolithic.[1] One notes reverberations of G. Childe's theory of the "Neolithic revolution". The social course of development in this period was the transition from "bands" to "tribes",[2] when the increasing demands of social solidarity necessitated the development of magic to protect the individual against its claims, in the process helping to constitute the individual himself. "The Neolithic revolution of magic still haunts the myths of man. It is remembered in stories of the fall, of an exile from a Paleolithic Eden where society was a sacred family . . . ".[3] Again we have an evolutionary "Just-So" story, but one told with vast

---

[1] *Lightning*, pp. 349-96.

[2] *Lightning*, pp. 353-64.

[3] *Lightning*, p. 363.

erudition and a certain degree of plausibility, even if magic's rôle in this evolution is not as clear as O'Keefe maintains.

Postulate 11, the notion that harmful or "black" magic is a useful index of the amount of social pressure on selves and individuals, is as true as it is banal. It has long been known that magic flourishes in situations of acculturation,[1] but then, one supposes, dramatic changes in any social institutional behaviour, like, topically, that of English football fans since the Second World War, are equally indicative.

Postulate 12, the persistence of magic in civilisation, follows the Durkheimian notion of modern society as integrated by the "organic solidarity" of complex socio-economic intercourse,[2] as opposed to the "mechanical solidarity" of savage society, which depends on powerful adherence to religious belief for its integration. But the increasing anonymity of the individual in modern secular society—a consequence of secularisation—deprives him of his sense of identity;[3] the rationality of society is no longer grounded in its individuals, but in its systems. Here the "vague, equivocal and confused"[4] character of religious ideas enables the existing religions to accomodate themselves to the state of society; furthermore,

> The diverse subcults help express the dissatisfactions and conflicts of subgroups within these civilizations. Through dialectic reabsorption of magical protest sects, the world religions become increasingly magical and incoherent, thereby reflecting the increasingly incoherent civilizations.[5]

Religion persists in part by becoming more magical. Conversely, some

---

[1] Cf. already Evans-Pritchard, *Witchcraft*, p. 205, notes that the newly-emergent "magical associations" which had sprung up in Zandeland "are of foreign origin and none formed part of Zande culture in the Sudan forty years ago . . .They are indicative of wide and deep social change"; further, C. Kluckhohn, *Navaho Witchcraft* (Cambridge, MA, 1944), pp. 64-71; C. Kluckhohn and D. Leighton, *The Navaho* (Cambridge MA, 1974 [1946]), pp. 240-52. See also L.S. Spindler's early study of "Witchcraft in Menomini Acculturation", *AA* 54 (1952), pp. 593-602.

[2] *Lightning*, p. 459.

[3] *Lightning*, pp. 461-64.

[4] *Lightning*, p. 464.

[5] *Lightning*, p. 465.

magics, like spiritualism, become religious cults.[1] Thus today

> traditional magic itself is experienced religiously, just as traditional
> religion is experienced magically . . . In a society where consensus
> is no longer often required and community is not always experienced,
> the typical shaman-to-client, one-to-one relationship of magic is
> enough for some people . . . There is a theurgic element in
> contemporary magic and many have remarked on it.[2]

Finally, in his 13th postulate the author offers a sketch of the ways
magic is exported and imported into societies throughout history. As an
essentially exotic phenomenon, he notes that magic "is a bookish
business and always has been since writing was invented".[3] Therefore
it is easily able to "go underground" when confronted with anti-magical
ideologies, but, having been preserved, it always reappears. One of the
modern versions of such "occult revivals" is the splintering-off of
pseudo-scientific sects: "Magic does not evolve into science as Frazer
thought; it evolves into pseudo-science — but so do some sciences
themselves".[4] There follows a review in bird's-eye perspective of
various occult revivals from classical antiquity to the present.[5] O'-
Keefe's concluding note is somber, and recalls Tylor's remark about the
"perniciousness" of magic:

> Every rigid script wrenched from a past religion, every device for
> relaxing the objective frame through agreement to agree, every
> magical defense of timorous selves is potentially transmissible and
> immortal. The magical heritage accumulates as a growing burden in
> cosmopolitan civilizations . . . The magical heritage that man creates
> out of his daring and his weakness casts a threatening and possibly
> permanent shadow over all his other creations . . . there is always a
> limited but real danger that this unshakeable occult heritage might
> overwhelm civilized cultures and change their nature.[6]

To return to our original point of departure, O'Keefe's definition of

---

[1] *Lightning*, p. 468.

[2] *Lightning*, pp. 468-69.

[3] *Lightning*, p. 525.

[4] *Lightning*, p. 528.

[5] *Lightning*, pp. 530-69.

[6] *Lightning*, pp. 569-70.

magic "in the strict sense":"Magic is the expropriation of religious collective representations for individual or subgroup purposes—to enable the individual ego to resist psychic extinction or the subgroup to resist cognitive collapse". I have noted that when the magician borrows something from another society, such as, for example, the divine name YHWH, and incorporates it into a ritual, the name clearly does not have religious meaning for him. In the religious tradition from which it comes, the Name is, after all, not assumed to possess any magical virtue: one cannot command Yahweh by pronouncing his name according to any historical version of Jewish belief. Obviously, such borrowing takes place under the exercise of a sophisticated revaluation of the contents of the religious system in question. As I have argued, it is the foreignness, the exotic quality, the psycho-social distance from the magician's society of the object to be borrowed which endows it with the quality of "blankness" that makes it suitable for borrowing and incorporation. Furthermore, virtually anything is susceptible to "importation" for the purposes of magic, from bits of the Torah or Koran to herbs, spices, or . . . Scottish rugby caps. The magic is in the ideology and imagination of the borrower, not the thing itself. We shall return to this presently.

The rest of O'Keefe's definition is in reality dependent on two polarities which we have examined in some detail. The opposition between religion and magic was, as we have seen, adopted by O'Keefe from Mauss-Hubert and Durkheim. But as I have tried to show, they offer virtually no evidence for the claim, and seem instead simply to presuppose the traditional antipathy of the Roman Catholic Church for magic. Moreover, the supposed blasphemic, parodic witchcult assumed by the Church may in reality never have existed, or, if it did, it is in any case too much a specifically regional and temporal phenomenon to be able to form the basis for a definition of a worldwide pattern of behaviour. O'Keefe himself notes that some world civilizations

> are so magical that we might also seriously consider a catalogue of civilizations based on different kinds of magic. In China . . . we perhaps see a great civilization built on the beneficent white magic of shamanism . . . In India we see another civilization based on the ceremonial magic of the Brahmins.[1]

---

[1] *Lightning*, p. 465.

In addition to these observations—both of which, incidentally, are well supported at least by Weber's studies of the societies in question—we must consider the fact that, historically, magic was the pre-eminent intellectual and spiritual activity of the whole of Mesopotamian civilisation. It was almost no less prominent in ancient Egypt; for example, one of Pharaoh's essential functions "was that of a medicine man, whose magic ensured good crops".[2] Already around the turn of the century, E.A. Wallis Budge declared that

> A study of the remains of the native religious literature of ancient Egypt which have come down to us has revealed the fact that the belief in magic . . . and in the performance of ceremonies accompanied by the utterance of words of power . . .formed a large and important part of the Egyptian religion.[3]

India, China, Mesopotamia, Egypt: in short, in all the great pre-classical

---

[1] This has long been known by assyriologists, though their evaluations of the fact have varied widely. See already e.g. A. Ungnad, *Die Deutung der Zukunft bei den Babyloniern und Assyrern* (Leipzig, 1909), p. 36: "All the viewpoints which represent the area of soothsaying move within a circle of conceptions which is entirely co-extensive with the religious views of the Babylonians: they do not contradict them, but rather stand and...fall with them". A.L. Oppenheim called attention forcefully to this fact in *Ancient Mesopotamia: Portrait of a Dead Civilization* (Chicago, 1977 [1964]) in pointing out that the usual translations of Mesopotamian literary products are entirely unrepresentative of the literary tradition, since, as he remarked, "the cuneiform literature which the Mesopotamians themselves considered essential and worthy of being handed down, concerned, directly, the activities of the diviner and of the priests specializing in exorcistic techniques". J. Nougayrol (*La Divination en Mésopotamie Ancienne* [Paris, 1966], p.16) remarked: "I ask myself whether, far from being an adventitious or relatively secondary element, divination did not constitute the very centre of Babylonian religion, the only living religion". Against this, H.W.F. Saggs (*The Encounter With the Divine in Mesopotamia and Israel* [London, 1978], pp. 129-38) asserts a peculiarly "a-deistic" interpretation of Oppenheim's views.

[2] J.A. Wilson, in H. Frankfort, Mrs. H.A. Frankfort, J.A. Wilson, T. Jakobsen, *Before Philosophy: The Intellectual Adventure of Ancient Man* (Harmondsworth, 1971 [1946]), p.89.

[3] *Egyptian Magic* (New York, 1971 [1901]), p. vii; cf. H. Brunner, *Altägyptische Religion: Grundzüge* (Darmstadt; 2nd edn, 1989), p.101: "God made magic for man as a weapon to defend against that blow of disaster against which people keep watch day and night" (trans. of Pharaoh Aktho's advice to his son).

"high-cultural" civilisations of antiquity, magic was the central religious phenomenon. In Egypt, Mesopotamia, and India, at least, this tradition survived for millennia, which rather suggests that it should be accorded a bit more respect in assessing the relationship between magic and religion than O'Keefe has done. Clearly, we cannot speak of any fundamental "antinomy".

On the other side of the divide, that is, at the personal level, O'Keefe's argument is also faulty, as I have tried to show. Although vastly learned, his argument does not provide compelling reasons to suppose that magic was the specific institution which evolved to defend the human ego against the inroads of social pressure to conform. Parenthetically, I have no doubt that magic practices can and do provide such protections; but it should be clear that other social mechanisms can as well. Thus O'Keefe's huge undertaking fails finally to convince. Of the five main intuitions which guided his formation of the "strict sense" of magic, we have left only his notion, derived from Mauss and Hubert, and reiterated (but not demonstrated) by Durkheim, that the relationship between the magician and his public is that of professional and client or doctor and patient.

Since anthropological theory has not been based on appropriate models (since they do not exist), and since, as we have seen, the existing studies are inadequate, we do not have an adequate theoretical base for our undertaking. Accordingly, I can do no better than to offer some rule-of-thumb observations which will have to serve in lieu of a unified theory. First, there is plainly little point in attempting sharply to distinguish magic from religion. That it was at all possible for Mauss-Hubert, Durkheim and O'Keefe to do so was because their various theories presupposed a polar relationship between both quantities which in reality only applies to Western societies and to a smattering of "savage" ones (O'Keefe himself is repeatedly forced to acknowledge that one or another form of magic in existing societies is largely "theurgic", i.e., religious, in character). The proposed antinomial character of magic in fact breaks down entirely if we once more consider the two schemes previously extracted from Mauss-Hubert's *Esquisse*:

religion—collective—socially integrating
magic—individualistic—asocial (antinomial)

If we regard this scheme in social and institutional terms, it is clear that two *actors* are required to fill it out: the priest, as the agent of the socially collective and integrating forces (as already Durkheim's reference to a "Church" testifies); and the sorceror, at the opposite end of the scale. Yet, for all the misdeeds of the sorceror which, as O'Keefe points out, range from simple murder to black magic,[1] his is not an a-social calling, that is, an act of the promethean psyche in total isolation from society. A psychotic personality substitutes his delusional structures for the mass of values, behavioural models, rôles, concepts, attitudes and so forth with which his society has nurtured him; but the participant in magic is no psychotic.[2] J. Beatty has, for example, noted concerning the Nyoro of Bunyoro that "burogo (sorcery) . . . is a technique; people do it because they so choose and it is learnt, not inborn. . . most sorcerors are simply ordinary people who have learnt how to practise burogo".[3] It should be evident that, if sorcery is learned and patterned behaviour, then it is as "social" as other social acts, even though it may not be popularly approved of or "officially" countenanced (analogous with, say, safecracking or data-"hacking" in our culture). Moreover, the society's own attitudes towards magic may range all the way from a degree of acceptance or even advocacy (consider the status of voudon under the Duvalier régime in Haiti) to persecution.

Thus the rule-of-thumb that applies to magic is in each case to attempt to determine the relationship of the type of magic in question to the society in which it takes place.

The next observation is that if it is in vain that we attempt to oppose religion to magic, it is likewise pointless to impose on magical practices our distinction between "rational-empirical" acts and "faith-de-

---

[1] *Lightning*, p. 4: ". . . only in fairy tales do sorcerors stick to non-physical magic alone. . . It is only in modern civilization that we clearly distinguish physical from psychological agencies".

[2] Thus I.M. Lewis (*Ecstatic Religion*, p. 186) notes that "the majority of participants (in possession cults) . . . have no difficulty at all in communicating their problems. They operate within a culturally standardized medium of communication. Nor, in contrast to the true self-insulated psychotic, do they miss their 'cues'. They respond in the expected way, and others react equally predictably".

[3] "Sorcery in Bunyoro", in J. Middleton and E.H. Winter (eds.), *Witchcraft and Sorcery*, pp. 29-30.

pendent" ones. As O'Keefe and others before him have noted, the societies under study do not know the difference. Admittedly, sometimes we cannot help but do so; but the assumption that we can in every case legitimately so distinguish all too easily falls back into the familiar posture of the Western social scientist who invariably knows what "in reality" goes on in a given society. This is a sophisticated variant of ethnocentrism; it is one in which, instead of merely presupposing the superiority of "science" or "revealed religion", the analyst "compares" the phenomena under examination with "empirical reality", as if the latter were somehow at his beck and call. A Marxist version of this, known as the "ideologiekritische" approach, was fashionable in the 1970s in historiographic and sociological study in northern Europe, thanks to the influence of J. Habermas and others. But the simple point is that the analyst has no privileged position from which to evaluate the phenomena he observes. There is no "wie es eigentlich gewesen ist" which the *Ideologiekritiker* can use as a basis to determine how conventional historiography has distorted the past. He has only his own reconstruction of that past; the social anthropologist finds himself in a similar situation. These considerations suggest that interpretation of magical behaviour has to be based on features internal to the society in question, such as native symbolic actions and utterances, statements of native belief and exegesis of their own behaviour, and so on.

This leads to the next rule-of-thumb, namely the conjecture that magical practice is always logically intelligible when seen "from within". The only societies which fail to apprehend their world as meaningful are those which have become riddled with "anomie" as a result of acculturation, headlong social change, or whatever: situations in which social institutions have simply had no opportunity to adapt, and so to present the new reality to the members of the society in a patterned and intelligible manner. A primary goal of analysis must then be to lay bare the logics implicit in a given social configuration.

Another point is the question of tradition. All of the writers studied were aware that magic is to a large extent a traditional activity, though they rated this fact rather differently. For Tylor, tradition was a guarantee of the obdurate non-rationalism of magical behaviour. Mauss-Hubert and Durkheim mainly registered the fact that magical tradition runs from individual to individual, rather than through collective channels (which need not be correct; even magic knows of guilds, "men's associations", and the like), and that it is pedantic in the extreme. Malinowski to some extent and also O'Keefe have pointed to the creative aspects of tradition: Malinowski in his discussion of the creative function of mythology (as legitimizing the present), and O'Keefe in heavily emphasising magic's propensity to borrow material from elsewhere and, so to say, elsewhen. To this I added the point that just what is borrowed seems to be fully irrelevant, as almost anything can be adapted for the purposes of the magico-religious cult: a point for which we have, in the last instance, Lévi-Strauss to thank.

Finally, there is a point which is related to the previous one, and difficult to formulate. I have emphasized that the requisites used in magical ritual have to have a curious quality of what I have called "blankness": if they come from parts unknown or societies never encountered, they are tabulae rasae. The quality of "distance" which guarantees this "blankness" is realisable within the society itself: the special herbs whose magical use only the magician is privy to; the tabus and other restrictions which set off magical ritual from the other rituals which characterise ordinary life; the special sites; and, as Mauss-Hubert argued, the special times when magical ritual is appropriate. The magician is pre-eminently "the one who knows", that is, the rites, times, herbs, et al. All these features make it correspondingly easier for the magician/priest to "change the frame" of his client or client-group (as we have seen, the only issue where I disagree with O'Keefe in this connexion is his notion of "agreeing to agree", since the consensuality of the process is not always entirely obvious)—he or they being, of course, by definition those who do not know—so that the magical-religious act may achieve its desired effect.

As to the nature of the "effects" in question, I have been repeatedly critical of the stress placed by all of the scholars from Mauss-Hubert to O'Keefe on the subjective emotional states of the participants in magical practices. This I have termed a persistent "shamanistic bias", which is admittedly a bit strong when applied to O'Keefe's highly differentiated account. In addition to Evans-Pritchard's very good point that a social ritual act remains a social ritual act whether performed at a high or low emotional pitch, there are a number of other possible objections to this stance. For one thing, it undervalues the cognitive features of magical symbolism; "sympathetic associations", for example, are things of which the participants in magical acts may well be aware.[1] Likewise, the rôle of myth in magical practice as a cognitive aid to re-presenting the world of the participant to him in a new light seems unquestionable. For another thing, much magical ritual just does not call for elevated emotional states of any kind; this is particularly the case in the more "objective" practices, over which the participants have little or no control, and which external factors decide for them. One has got to acknowledge the complexity of the phenomena; in a single society, magical ritual behaviour may range from strongly interactive and emotionally demanding to the equivalent of tossing a coin.

In our subsequent study, we shall accordingly have to take a good, long look at the phenomenology of Near Eastern divination, noting common features and differences. We shall then attempt to formulate some general statements about the phenomena. It might be appropriate to point out that modern anthropological studies of magic have been conducted entirely in the context of savage societies in the period since contact with the West was established. No one has attempted a socio-anthropological study of magical practices in urban, imperial, socially differentiated, and, above all, literate societies which have remained free of Western contacts—for the good reason that all such happen to be dead societies. I therefore propose to study just a single magical phenomenon, that of divination, as it manifested itself in the ancient Near East, and particularly in ancient Israel. Fortunately, as far as the study of divination itself is concerned, anthropology has been well served by the tradition since E.E. Evans-Pritchard's famous study of the Azande. As a prelude to our investigation of ancient divination, we shall accordingly turn briefly to Evans-Pritchard's study and to the conclusions scholars have drawn since then, in the hopes that they may offer some more specific straws to cling to than my pragmatic observations above.

---

[1] So Evans-Pritchard (*Witchcraft*, p. 177): "The homoeopathic element is so evident in many magical rites and in much of the materia medica that there is no need to give examples. It is recognized by the Azande themselves. They say, 'We use such-and-such a plant because it is like such-and-such a thing'. . ."

CHAPTER 2

E.E. EVANS-PRITCHARD AND THE AZANDE: A MAGIC SOCIETY

As I mentioned in the previous chapter, Evans-Pritchard's study *Witchcraft, Oracles and Magic among the Azande* was of paramount importance for the socio-anthropological investigation of magic, and, indeed, for the study of savage thought in general. Here we shall focus our interest on the rôle played by divination in Zande society. My reasons for choosing the example of the Azande are two-fold. First, the Azande are one of the few peoples among whom divination plays an extremely prominent rôle, which provides at least a basis for comparison with ancient Near Eastern societies. Second, Evans-Pritchard's account of the Azande has won so much acknowledgement and general, though not uncritical, acceptance that D.L. O'Keefe found it possible to describe the Azande as "a natural ideal type".[1] Thus Zande society also provides us a point of departure for understanding the phenomenon of divination per se. The insights gained here will be supplemented by a cursory review of subsequent investigations. After a few theoretical remarks we shall then proceed to the ancient Near East.

Following anthropological convention, I shall use the "ethnographic present" in what follows, even if, as Eva Gillies, who abridged and wrote an introduction to Evans-Pritchard's work, remarks, it feels "a trifle uncomfortable" to do so, so many years after the work first appeared.[2] The Azande of the Sudan (they are also to be found in

---

[1] D.L. O'Keefe, *Lightning*, p. 2 *et passim*. There is a certain irony in this ascription, however, since, as we have seen, O'Keefe is concerned to maintain the antithesis between magic and religion, whereas Zande magic is so omnipresent as virtually to play the part which religion enjoys in other societies.

[2] E.E. Evans-Pritchard, *Witchcraft*, p.vii.

Zaire and central Africa) live in small farming communities[1] and produce nuts, maize, fruit, tubers; they also hunt, fish, raise poultry, and supplement these other efforts by gathering roots, berries, and so forth. They are "sedentary, but not established", as they move their small communities when soil depletion dictates. Social organisation, as mentioned in the previous chapter, is hierarchical, even feudal. Kings and chiefs[2] are recruited from among the leading clan of the Avongara. Families consist of husband, wife or wives, and children dwelling in a single homestead; near neighbours are patrilineal kinfolk.

Among the Azande we find the commonly-held African belief that many people in their society are witches. The Zande distinguish sharply between witches, whose mode of activity is psychic, and whose witchcraft-spirits devour the spiritual flesh of the organs of their victims, and sorcerors, who utilise magical rites and a variety of harmful "medicines" to attack their prey. Witchcraft is what we would call a "sex-linked" inherited trait, which is to say that the male children of a male witch inherit their father's propensity, while the daughters of a female witch inherit their mother's witchcraft. The power of the witch's inheritance grows all his/her life; children are not suspected of the crime, while the witchcraft of elderly people may be greatly feared. Men may be attacked by witches of either sex, while women are normally attacked only by felons of their own sex. This makes good sense in a polygamous society: a husband may be attacked by a social rival or a slighted wife, while a wife's strongest enemy is likely to be her greatest competitor. Kinsmen practically never bewitch each other; moreover, members of the Avongara (the ruling royal class) are never accused of witchcraft. Even powerful commoners are only very rarely the object of witchcraft suspicions.

Beliefs about the activity of witchcraft are manifold. As we have seen, it is not the witch himself who devours the flesh of his victim, but the "soul of witchcraft" which he emits at night, while others sleep, that does so. The "soul of witchcraft" is thought to be visible to non-witches;

[1] For details, see E.E. Evans-Pritchard, *The Azande: History and Political Institutions* (Oxford, 1971), pp. 1-63.

[2] For details, see E.E. Evans-Pritchard, "Zande Kings and Princes" in: *Social Anthropology and Other Essays* (New York, 1966 [1962]), pp. 213-43.

it must be directed to find its target (making it possible to evade witchcraft by secretly changing one's residence); its efficacy diminishes with distance; and its effects are slow and protracted. Witches are also thought to use an ointment which renders them invisible for their forays; a notion which does not accord well with the alleged "psychic" mode of action. They are also held to congregate in gatherings presided over by older members of the species; they are only allowed to kill on the approval of the assembly. This means that witches are held morally accountable for their actions, even though individuals accused of witchcraft almost invariably claim that while it may be possible that they have bewitched someone, they are not aware of having done so. There are indications that some Azande believe that dead witches become evil ghosts.[1]

It is to be noted that all Azande practise magic to some extent, whether for help in hunting, planting, discovering the identities of witches, securing adherents at court, or whatever. As Evans-Pritchard says, "every Zande, except small children, whether old or young, whether man or woman, is to some extent a magician" (p. 187). Magic involves the use of "medicines" which are derived from trees, plants, or herbs, plus some relatively simple techniques and entirely unelaborate verbal formulations of one's intent. Sorcery, however, is regarded as morally evil magic which uses essentially the same or similar materials and procedures for socially unacceptable purposes (pp. 176-77; p. 194). In contrast with magic, sorcery is altogether a more shadowy affair, as far as Evans-Pritchard's respondents are concerned; he notes that "You will never meet a Zande who professes himself a sorcerer, and they do not like even to discuss the subject lest it be thought that the knowledge they have of it comes from practice" (p. 190). This is intelligible, as few people in any society are willing to proclaim themselves morally evil. The sorcerer is held to visit the house of his victim, where he buries his potent "medicine", incants over it, and departs. He may simply kill, but he may also use his magic in non-lethal ways to subvert the legal procedure, to affect a man's happiness or interfere with his marital relationships. Sorcery can also be used to frustrate the efficacy of the poison oracle (pp. 190-91; cf. pp. 156-57; 161).

Interestingly, witchcraft accusations apply almost exclusively to

---

[1] The preceding description is from *Witchcraft*, pp. 1-15.

non-nobles, whereas sorcery can strike down virtually anyone, which in practice means that nobles may suspect (and accuse) each other of sorcery, but only rarely of witchcraft (p. 10; cf. pp. 191-92). Presumably, a commoner would not be so foolish as to attack someone of superiour social standing and concomitant power. Finally, the effects of sorcery are very quick, while, as we have seen, witchcraft only slowly devours its victims (pp. 13-14; cf. p. 184; p. 193).

Evans-Pritchard's evaluation of the phenomena of witchcraft and sorcery is famous; for him, "The difference between witchcraft and sorcery is the difference between an alleged act that is impossible and an alleged act that is possible" (p. 193). Cognitively, both concepts serve the purposes of *theodicy*; if something is wrong with one's life, witchcraft or sorcery may lie at the root of the matter, alongside other possibilities such as the non-observance of tabus (pp. 27-28). Socially, however, a man searches for the causes of his misfortune among his rivals and enemies.[1] The Azande affirm a curious *sic et non* as far as the witch's accountability is concerned; we have seen that witches are held responsible for their actions by the prevailing ideology. At the same time, though, resolution of a witchcraft incident is carefully channeled to minimise unfortunate consequences (pp. 39-48). Ultimately, one suspects, this is because one cannot pick one's parents, and hence one's genetic inheritance, and since witchcraft is held to be heritable, a witch is merely "running according to programme". Thus Evans-Pritchard observes that, "So long as injured party and witch observe the correct forms of behaviour the incident will be closed without any hard words, far less blows, passing between them, and even without relations becoming embittered" (p. 34). Sorcery is clearly another matter, as the author mentions that "it is performed at dead of night, for if the act is witnessed the sorcerer will probably be slain" (p. 188), indicating the seriousness of the offence. By the same token, however, he notes that informants are "unable to produce many instances of persons being punished for sorcery. . . ."(pp. 192-93), and, elsewhere, that "in the old

---

[1] Evans-Pritchard's demonstration that social rivalries and petty jealousies lie at the heart of witchcraft phenomena has been amply supported by such studies as Kluckhohn's *Nahavo Witchcraft*; cf. also Lewis, *Religion in Context*, p.16.

days", according to the Azande, "sorcerers were rare" (p. 195). On balance, Evans-Pritchard finds it unlikely that sorcery is an actual practice among the Azande (p. 192), which, of course, does not prevent occasional accusations. In the event that someone dies and witchcraft or sorcery is suspected, the suspicion is first confirmed by divination, which is very definitely legal magic (the ultimate court of appeal is the prince's own poison oracle). Following this is a lengthy bout of vengeance magic, accompanied by the observance of extensive tabus, which terminates when the oracles reveal that the unknown culprit has died. Vengeance magic, is not, however, sorcery; in fact, the prevailing ideology maintains that it will rebound onto its user, if employed against an innocent man (pp. 221-25).

There are some fascinating features to the inner workings of the witchcraft-sorcery complex as described by Evans-Pritchard. If someone dies an untimely death, it is either as a result of witchcraft or sorcery; his kinfolk therefore avenge themselves on the presumed—but anonymous—witch or sorcerer by performing lethal vengeance magic. They do this until the oracles have assured them that the unknown murderer of their kinsman is now dead. However, the family of the deceased miscreant either do not know, or are not willing to acknowledge that their own deceased was a malefactor (if witchcraft is suspected, that would be tantamount to admitting that they, too, are witches, because of the hereditary conception of the phenomenon), and so they, too, are obliged to enter upon a round of vengeance magic. . . and so on, *ad infinitum*. In principle, only the deaths of babies from some diseases are ascribed to the agency of the "Supreme Being" (p. 29), so the cycle of unreflective vengeance has enormous scope. This would inevitably lead to the conclusion that virtually everyone is a witch: an interesting paradox, since no Zande will own up to it; nor do any Azande draw this conclusion.

Evans-Pritchard devoted great care to the elucidation of Zande notions of causality, and to describing how they differ from our own (pp. 25-32, *et passim*). However, one aspect of this analysis which was probably unavoidable, given the extremely logical positivist orientation of British science in the 1930s,[1] is Evans-Pritchard's thorough-going

---

[1] Note that A.J.Ayer's famous *Language, Truth and Logic* appeared a year before *Witchcraft* (i.e., Oxford, 1936).

distinction between the empirical "facts" and the Zande ideologies which account for them. He notes, for example, that when termites eat away the foundations of a granary, so that it collapses and injures a number of people, the Azande seem to invoke dual notions of causality. One of these is empirical: materials do not last for ever, and if termites graw on wooden beams, they will weaken. On the other hand, though, they would be inclined to say that the reason this particular granary collapsed on top of these particular people was witchcraft directed at one or more of them (pp. 22-23). The metaphor used by the Azande to describe this type of over-determination is that of the "double spear": when hunting an animal, the bag is divided between the thrower of the first spear and the thrower of the second spear. Magic, then, is always the "second spear" (p. 25). Evans-Pritchard likewise maintains that the Azande themselves distinguish between "empirical" and what he calls "mystical" causes. Thus, for example, he argues that,

> when a potter's creations break in firing witchcraft is not the only cause of the calamity. Inexperience and bad workmanship may also be reasons for failure. . . The potter himself will attribute his failure to witchcraft, but others may not be of the same opinion (p.28).

In a similar vein, the author holds that,

> Incompetence, laziness, and ignorance may be selected as causes. . — The mistakes of children are due to carelessness or ignorance and they are taught to avoid them while they are still young. People do not say that they are effects of witchcraft, or if they are prepared to concede the possibility of witchcraft they consider stupidity the main cause (p.29).

These and similar arguments are offered as indications of the Zande propensity for a species of philosophical "over-determination" due to multi-causality (cf. esp. p. 26). But as I argued previously, this tidy distinction is not really an option; nor is Evans-Pritchard really taking the metaphor of the "two spears" seriously. In hunting a large animal, the first spear immobilises or distracts the animal, while the second kills it; but the kill could not take place without *both* spears. Thus, both spears are "the cause" of the death of the animal. By implication, when the Azande claim that magic is involved in an event, they are merely uttering what for them is a truism: that every "significant" (a criterion which is obviously subjectively determined) event has a magico-empirical (though they would surely not use the term) cause. The pot in the example above is not a Platonically "pure" pot baked by robots at ideal means of temperature and pressure, but a Zande pot, one of thousands turned out by a social being under real conditions. The potter may have selected his clay with extreme care, and heated his oven with the best and most uniform grade of charcoal available to him. Even so, some elements in the hardening clay may rigidify faster than others (the selection of clays is a skill, that is, socially acquired), just as local temperature irregularities may occur in any far from perfect oven (also built to traditional, i.e., socially determined specifications), and, of course, the design of the pot (which accords with social, not material, expectations) may overtax the available materials: pots do break, even when a skilled potter has done his level best. The potter attributes such an event to magic; the fact that others may attribute the cause to carelessness or lack of skill merely shows what we already trivially know: that social events are susceptible of multiple interpretations. It should be clear that there is no "empirical" pot, but only a "social" one; and, since magic is a primary factor in Zande perceptions, it cannot be divorced from the pot in the manner Evans-Pritchard supposes. What requires to be demonstrated is that the Azande mean the same thing by saying "unskilled" or "careless" as "we" do. And it would be quite remarkable if they did so, when we consider that the Azande do have a generalised notion that extreme success in anything has something magical about it (cf. p. 187), so that a good potter, and those who know him to be good, would have reasons for thinking his "positive magic" had deserted him—possibly as the result of malign forces. Therefore, as I argued in the conclusion of the previous section, the socio-anthropo-logist does not have the "facts" in his hip pocket—and will never do so; the author's distinction between "empirical reality" and "Zande explanations" of the same cannot ultimately be maintained.

Just how meaningless the distinction in question can be may be illustrated by an event in the course of Carlos Castaneda's initiation at the hands of the Yaqui indian "man of power", Don Juan.[1] Having been taught how to prepare the datura plant for a psychic excursion, Castaneda has an experience of being transformed into a bird and

[1] *The Teachings of Don Juan: A Yaqui Way of Knowledge* (Harmondsworth, 1973 [1972]), pp. 120-28)

soaring above and away from his mentor. After returning to his normal state, he asks Don Juan the "sensible" question as to the "empirical" nature of his experience,

> . . . did my body fly? Did I take off like a bird?" To which the other can only answer "What you want to know makes no sense. Birds fly like birds and a man who has taken the devil's weed flies as such. . . [1]

Of course, it is difficult to take Don Juan's statements entirely seriously, as Castaneda is himself an anthropologist with an axe to grind (O'Keefe rightly lists his works among the numerous popular "theosophies" which are current in the West): he is namely concerned to provide us an "internal" guide to savage magical thought, so the statements of Don Juan sound suspiciously as if they were designed to trounce Western "materialist" arguments. But this is unimportant. The point is that, as the "sociology of knowledge" insists, our very perceptions of the world are socially mediated, so that it is impossible, in a society in which "magic" is a fundamental postulate (as already Mauss and Hubert argued), to distinguish between magical and non-magical perceptions, no matter what seemingly "empiricist" statements may be elicited from individual respondents.

In fact, Evans-Pritchard's insistance on the point is symptomatic. He is aware, as we have seen, that Azande perceptions of witchcraft, magic, divination, and so forth, are pervasive, yet unconnected (cf. e.g., p. 31); they have an *ad hoc* character and are invoked without relation to their mutual implications (if this were not the case, they could scarcely avoid coming to the conclusion, as we have seen, that all Azande are witches). It should be noted that the examples which Evans-Pritchard cites in which various Azande offer "rational" or "empirical" explanations of phenomena are no less *ad hoc*. The unlucky hunter claims that his failure to bag his prey is the result of witchcraft, while others claim he is not much of a hunter, for example. In short, Zande "empiricism" is also only evident in connexion with particular situations, and the various "explanations" arising from it also lack all elaboration of their logical implications. Yet, as Evans-Pritchard everywhere stresses, the magic-witchcraft complex is without question the dominant theme in Zande

[1] *Don Juan*, p. 128.

society:

> I had no difficulty in discovering what Azande think about witch-
> craft, nor in observing what they do to combat it. These ideas and
> actions are on the surface of their life and are accessible to anyone
> who lives for a few weeks in their homesteads. Every Zande is an
> authority on witchcraft (p.1).

Accordingly, it can be argued that the phenomena in Zande society
which require explanation are not magic and its ramifications, but the
contexts in which non-magical explanations of phenomena occur, and
their relations to "magical" explanations of the same phenomena.

A further difficulty with Evans-Pritchard's critique, though implied
rather than stated, is the one I pointed to in the previous chapter in
connexion with the magic vs. science discussion: that sociologists rarely
take the trouble to define both sides of the equation. Evans-Pritchard is
arguing that the Zande differ significantly from "us" in that they
advocate multi-causal explanations of phenomena. We do as well;
frequently in fact. For example, there is an entire medical-health
"theosophy" (as O'Keefe would call it) in the West, eagerly abetted by
numerous doctors, natural scientists, and nutritionists, which tells us that
we can avoid cancer if we 1) stop smoking 2) eat more fibrous food 3)
avoid certain fats, plus x-number of other topical items. Just which of
the above factors, one wonders, is actually being adduced as the "cause"
of cancer?[1]

Azande Divination

The third component of the Zande magical complex is divination. As
mentioned above, this is entirely within the sphere of legal magic, and
all Zande are familiar with various forms of it. The main forms used in
Zande society are 1) the poison oracle 2) the termites oracle 3) the
mapingo oracle 4) the rubbing-board and 5) witch-doctors. We shall
examine these in succession.

---

[1] Cf. L. Thomas, "On Magic in Medicine", in the same, *The Medusa and the
Snail: More Notes of a Biology Watcher* (New York, 1980 [1979]), pp. 16-21.

The Poison Oracle

The poison oracle is the most authoritative oracle known to the Azande; as mentioned previously, the prince's poison oracle is traditionally the source of revelation of last resort (cf. e.g., p. 162). A powerful alkali, called *benge* by the Azande, is derived from a forest creeper under the strict observance of tabus and ritual prescriptions: "Properly speaking, it is only this manufactured *benge* which is *benge* at all in Zande opinion" (p. 147). The poisonous paste alone has no significance for the Azande: "no one has ever conceived of a man using benge as a means of murder, and if you suggest it to him a Zande will tell you that benge would not be any good for the purpose" (p. 148). The substance is alleged by the Azande to possess a *mbismo*, which Evans-Pritchard renders "soul"; they hold that it is this soul that "sees" the things that are inquired of (p. 151). The Azande keep fowls for the purposes of oracular consultation. The consultation itself is relatively straightforward; having observed a number of preliminary tabus, one administers one or more doses of *benge* to a fowl and then addresses the oracle in an ordinary, conversational way: "if X is the case, poison oracle, kill the fowl. If X is not the case, poison oracle, spare the fowl". A single test is insufficient, particularly in important matters, so that the test will be repeated with another fowl as insurance (pp. 159-60). Questions asked of the oracle have to do with "witchcraft, sickness, death, lengthy journeys, mourning and vengeance, changing of homestead sites, lengthy agricultural and hunting enterprises, and so forth" (p. 160). One consults the other oracles about lesser matters, but not the poison oracle.

The Termites Oracle

The termites oracle, or *dakpa*, as it is called, is valued by the Azande next to the poison oracle. As the poison oracle is relatively expensive, both in terms of fowls and the preparation of the benge, the termites oracle is ordinarily used to obtain a preliminary opinion, that is, to "narrow the field", for subsequent confirmation or disconfirmation by the poison oracle (p. 164). Again, certain tabus must first be observed. Towards evening, one approaches a termite mound with two branches, *dakpa* and *kpoyo*. One places them in alternative termite runs in the same mound and poses one's question as follows: "Oh termites, X will happen, eat *dakpa*, X will not happen, eat *kpoyo*" (p. 165). If the termites fail to eat either branch, one seeks another mound; if both branches are eaten, this is regarded as a partial answer (p. 166), depending on which branch has been more consumed. If both have been equally consumed, the Azande conclude that the termites were simply hungry, and that no consultation has taken place. In theory, it would be possible to make a corroborative termites-consultation, but the Azande generally proceed directly to the poison oracle instead.

The Mapingo Oracle

The *mapingo* oracle is the only one used by both sexes and all age groups, although adult males mainly consult it when choosing a dwelling-site. Tabus "should" be, but are not observed in connexion with it. Two short (half an inch long) cylinders of wood are placed in parallel on the ground, with a third perched upon them, and left to stand overnight. The form of the question is simply, "X will happen/is the case. . . *mapingo* you scatter. . . X will not happen/is not the case. . . let me come to examine you and find you in position. . . . " (p. 167). Displacement of the sticks is usually inauspicious, while their remaining in place is propitious. As we might expect, since the socially disenfranchised (i.e., women and children) use it, the *mapingo* oracle is not considered authoritative enough to prosecute a case for witchcraft; in spite of this, it is considered very reliable (p. 167).

The Rubbing-Board Oracle

The rubbing-board is a small (portable) table-like contrivance with a "lid" attached to it; the assemblage has to be extensively treated with various oils and juices, under the observance of the proper tabus, then buried for two days, in order to receive its "virtue" (pp. 167-70). To operate the oracle, tabus must be observed for two or three days, though it is possible to get around this (p. 171), and people are lax about this in any case (p. 172). The "table" and "lid" surfaces are treated with juices and/or wood-shavings, plus water. One addresses the oracle and works the "lid" back and forth across it. The "answer" consists in either the smooth sliding across or in the sticking of the "lid" to the surface of the "table". (pp. 169-70). The desired answer is, then, binary, as in the other forms of divination. As with the termites oracle, it would be theoretically possible to make a confirmatory test, but if the issues in question are important, one goes instead directly to the poison oracle (p. 171). The rubbing-board may be consulted only by middle-aged or old men (p. 172); its accuracy is rated low, on a par with the witch-doctor (p. 168). Since not everyone can use this oracle, those who do so demand a small fee from inquirers who are non-kinsmen (p. 173). Some operators have been known to cheat in the use of the rubbing-board, which perhaps accounts for its low authority (p. 173), though Evans-Pritchard rightly observes that most such "cheating" may well be unconscious.

Zande Witch-Doctors

Azande witch-doctors form a semi-closed "corporation" of magical personnel. They are not only diviners, but also magicians charged with the duty to ward off witchcraft and sorcery for their clients. Initiation into the sodality consists of a period of apprenticeship during which the apprentice is introduced to the vast pharmacopoeia of Zande "medicines" and taught their use, a privilege for which he must pay, and for which he continues to pay after his initiation (pp. 68-70; cf. pp. 102-105). As Evans-Pritchard puts it, "The Zande witch-doctor exercises supernatural powers solely because he knows the right medicines and has eaten them in the right manner" (p. 73; pp. 90-97). The final ceremony of initiation culminates in the—for anthropologists—familiar rite in which the apprentice is symbolically buried and reborn (pp. 99-101; pp. 109-110). Old women may be witch-doctors, but in the event their practice is restricted to leechcraft (p. 72).

We should note that it is possible to be a better or worse witch-doctor; furthermore,

> Fame is not. . . based solely on restricted professional knowledge of the witch-doctor's art, in its aspects of divination and leechcraft, but also on the fact that a noted witch-doctor is generally also a noted magician in other respects. . . such as bagbuduma, vengeance-magic, and iwa, the rubbing-board oracle (p. 112).

This should serve to illustrate the extent to which the various provinces of magic are interlinked in Zande thought and practice; one and the same specialist may both divine and conjure. Socially, it is interesting to see that the witch-doctor has two contact-surfaces: at court, and in consultation with the general public. At court, a visiting witch-doctor modifies his behaviour to correspond to the official gravitas of sophisticated intercourse. He advises princes on magical matters, and also provides information as to the state of the province (p. 81; p. 115). When employed on private commission, general consultation takes place in the vehicle of the seance. Here the witch-doctor's behaviour ranges from "truculent" and "overbearing" to dissociated and trance-like (pp. 81-82).

The "seances" of the witch-doctor may involve several professionals at one time. They utilise dance accompanied by gongs, bells, rattles, and drums to achieve trance-like states (pp. 87-88). Evans-Pritchard emphasises that the "seance" is anything but highly solemn: "everyone is jovial and amused, talking to each other and making jokes" (p. 88). Interaction with the audience is a complex demonstration of innuendo, calculation, cross-examination of the client and unconscious association (pp. 84-87). Hiring a witch-doctor is expensive, although doing so confers social benefits, as a seance is public entertainment, and hence status-giving (p. 77). On the other hand, the Azande are in no doubt that witch-doctors are frequently to some extent swindlers: "Absence of formal and coercive doctrines permit Azande to state that many, even most, witch-doctors are frauds" (p. 107). This applies above all to the practice (otherwise attested throughout Africa) of removing "objects of witchcraft" from the bodies of patients; patients know that the removed "objects" are fakes, but conclude that they have been cured anyway for other reasons (esp. p. 107; p. 112). Ultimately, the reliability of witch-doctors as oracles is rated about that of the rubbing-board (p. 114), which, as we have seen, is manipulable, and hence less confidence-inspiring than the more "objective" oracles, that is, the termites oracle and the poison oracle.

Interpretations

There is no need here to go into the Zande oracles in more detail, nor to attempt to explain their relationship to Western perceptions of causality. After all, these matters have been the subject of intensive inquiry by Evans-Pritchard and those who have followed in his

2. A Magic Society

footsteps.[1] For our purposes, it will suffice to discuss the meaning of magic and divination in Zande and other societies. In this connexion, it will be necessary to return to Evans-Pritchard's attempt to show that the Azande themselves distinguish between "natural" and "supernatural" explanations of various phenomena. As I have suggested, there is reason to doubt the adequacy of this claim. It would be quite remarkable if the Azande—or any other savage folk—maintained two entirely separate and mutually exclusive interpretations of the world (a point which, incidentally, makes all discussions of "sacred and profane" in conjunction with savage societies problematical).[2] H.G. Kippenberg has grasped

---

[1] See, among other things, A. Singer and B.V. Street (eds.), *Zande Themes* (Oxford, 1972), for more on the Azande. R. Horton has discussed causality and its problems in Africa as a whole in "African Traditional Thought and Western Science", *Africa* 37 (1967), pp. 50-71; pp. 155-87; in general, however, Horton emphasises too strongly the "failure" of African belief systems to deal with falsifications of magical practices. Underlying this, one hears echoes of Tylorean and Frazerian condemnations of magic as "pseudo-" or "failed" science. A more appropriate conclusion might be to wonder why the inability of a magical act to bring about the desired effect (e.g., a cure) never leads to disenchantment with magic as such, or even with the particular ritual in question. Cf. A. Young, "Some Implications of Medical Beliefs and Practices for Social Anthropology", *AA* 78 (1976), pp. 4-24. I.C. Jarvie and J. Agassi ("The Problem of the Rationality of Magic" in *The British Journal of Anthropology* 18 [1967], pp. 55-74 = B. Wilson (ed.), *Rationality* (Oxford, 1970), pp. 172-93) have attempted to distinguish between rational-purposive actions, like hunting, fishing and other features of the daily life of primitives, as rational "in the weak sense", a notion revived, as we have seen, by O'Keefe, and actions undertaken on the basis of rational views, as rational "in the strong sense". They accordingly claim that magical action is only rational "in the weak sense", as opposed to (Western) scientific actions, which are, naturally, rational "in the strong sense". It is hard to see the point of investing so much ingenuity in attempting to maintain, in one guise or another, the duality in question. See also I.M. Lewis' pertinent question (*Religion in Context*, p. 19 n. 6), "Why do people go on believing in individual instances of (let us say) witchcraft when in general they know that witchcraft is not quite what it seems?"

[2] Durkheim *Forms*, pp. 37-38) placed great emphasis on the absolute nature of the distinction between sacred and profane in primitive societies; the distinction was eagerly absorbed into social anthropological and history of religions theory (cf. M. Eliade, *The Sacred and the Profane* [New York, 1961]). But already Evans-Pritchard (*Theories* noted that the sacred things may be regarded as such only "in certain contexts and on certain occasions" (p. 65). Note that this is also true of some

this point and concluded

> that the Zande do not know the concept of a single instance underly-
> ing reality on which the two types of causality may be evaluated.
> Both explanations, that is, as stemming from natural or from mystical
> causes, respectively, are only true in correspondence with situations,
> but not through agreement with objective reality.[1]

This suggestion even has the merit of agreeing with Evans-Pritchard's own observation that the Azande do not generalise their various views and opinions about magic, and hence fail to see the numerous contradictions implicit in them.[2] It is accordingly probable that we have to do with ritual acts which are, so to speak, ends in themselves; it would be a misrepresentation to abstract from them to a wider symbolic whole. There nevertheless remains the question as to the meaning of the ritual acts performed by the Zande in their magic, even if they do not regard these as having wider implications.

One of the more popular approaches to this problem in recent social anthropology has been to seize on the notion of "performative utterance" as originally proposed by J.L. Austin and developed by J.R. Ross and J.R. Searle,[3] and to which reference was made in the intro-

---

Western conceptions of the sacred. For example, the holy of holies of an Orthodox church is separated from the rest of the church by the iconostasis. Orthodox congregations are segregated by sex, as is well known; moreover, only men are permitted to enter by the gate in the iconostasis to participate in the Eucharist. Of course, this does not prevent the charwoman from doing the same on cleaning-day. Here, too, sacrality is related to function and intention.

[1] *Magie. Die sozialwissenschaftliche Kontroverse über das Verstehen fremden Denkens* (Frankfurt am Main, 1987 [1978]), p.37.

[2] Thus, as we have seen, Zande affirm that witches are conscious agents of ill, but, when accused of witchcraft, claim that it must be an unconscious process; similarly, they have any number of rationalisations at hand to explain why a given magical process did not have the desired effect. I do not say "did not work": a point ignored by most of the tradition from Tylor to Evans-Pritchard is that magic is always perceived to have "worked". If the answer to an oracle is inconclusive, it is because somebody else's magic has worked better, and so obstructed my oracle, or because I failed to observe the proper tabus, etc.; the efficacy of magic itself is not in doubt.

[3] In addition to the works mentioned in my introduction, see J.R. Searle, *Speech Acts: An Essay in the Philosophy of Language* (London and New York, 1969).

duction to this work. It was there pointed out that the notion of the "performative" has a tendency to become entirely too broad, and so embraces virtually all language. However, the concept is capable of use in a more restricted sense in which its presuppositions are carefully delimited. As the idea has been developed by social anthropologists, magical charms, spells, incantations, and so forth are a type of speech *sui generis*; what they attempt to achieve is actually done when they are pronounced or enacted. Scholars proposing such an approach include R. Finnegan, J. Tambiah, and E.M. Ahern.[1]

Of these efforts, Tambiah's is the most daring, if not entirely successful; he attempts to classify all magical acts as "ritual acts", and goes on to define the latter as

> performative acts whose positive and creative meaning is missed and whose persuasive validity is misjudged if they are subjected to that kind of empirical verification associated with scientific activity.[2]

Tambiah's definition has the virtue of taking account of, in addition to the various rhetorical devices, also the countless non-verbal aspects of ritual, magical or otherwise (he does not distinguish). Moreover, such a "performative" concept of ritual revives Durkheim's insight that magical ritual can be creative. It also makes it possible to include the "sympathetic", "homeopathic" and other symbolisms which figure in ritual within the compass of language. This is surely legitimate in terms of "utterance"-theory, which, as was also noted in the introduction to this study, stresses a very broad conception of "context". On the other hand, to my way of thinking, it is an oxymoron to claim that a performative utterance is "persuasive". A performative is a yes-or-no sort of act, not a diatribe, exhortation, peroration, or whatever. To offer a modest example, promising is a simple type of performative. Unless someone says "I promise", no promise has been given; but if it has been said, whatever items follow (if not inappropriate to the notion of

---

[1] R. Finnegan, "How to do things with words: performative utterances among the Limba of Sierra Leone", *Man* 4 (1969), pp. 537-53; S.J. Tambiah, "Form and Meaning of Magical Acts: A Point of View", in R. Horton and R. Finnegan (eds.), *Modes of Thought: Essays on Thinking in Western and Non-Western Societies* (London, 1973), pp. 199-229; E.M. Ahern, "The Problem of Efficacy: Strong and Weak Illocutionary Acts", *Man* 14 (1979), pp. 1-17.

[2] Tambiah, "Form and Meaning", p. 199.

promising) are merely the terms of the promise. The same is clearly true of an incantation or some extended ritual act, if understood as performatives. Their contents are not performatives, but merely more or less appropriate rhetorical and symbolic complements. Take, for example, the marriage ceremony; it includes a question posed to the respective parties ("do you, X, take Y to be your. . . ."), which must be answered in the affirmative. But the question, which is part of what I have called the complement, is dependent for its significance on the social situation within which the ceremony takes place. The performative consists of the socially pre-established situation, that is, the contracting of a marriage, plus the affirmative, and without these no marriage takes place. The secondary and subordinate nature of the complement is shown by the fact that the text of the marriage ritual may be quite variously phrased, and does vary, both within one and the same confession and interconfessionally. It may even be read aloud under non-performative circumstances (e.g., in the absence of priest and congregation, and without a license; or under inappropriate circumstances, as in Kierkegaard's suggestion the Luther ought to have married an ironing-board), and no marriage takes place. All this tends to suggest that what is actually said in the text of a performative is of secondary importance. A possible analogy is provided by the standardised legal forms for making out rent contracts, powers of attourney, last-will-and-testaments, and so forth which may be purchased in stationery shops in many Western countries. Such documents conform by design to the legal specifications of local law and custom; as such, they are performatives. Yet one may fill them out in any way whatsoever, and as long as the legal stipulations concerning witnesses, notarisation, and so on have been observed, they must be considered proper legal instruments. Of course, this does not mean that a man can rent out property he does not own, will the planet Mars to his widow, or whatever. But it does mean that the documents would have the status of legal instruments, and would be treated by the courts as such. This is not farfetched; nor is it without social consequences, as numerous court cases take place each year in which relatives of the deceased who had once been confident of inheriting attempt to contest a privately-composed later bequest to Mrs. Jensen's Home For Masterless Cats, or the like. This analogy underlines the secondary and inessential character of the complements of performatives.

Nevertheless, the idea of magical acts as performatives has merit;

it points to the fact that they invariably presuppose prior social tacit agreements, and that these should be the proper objects of study. Moreover, as Tambiah says, the empirical criterion wielded by, for example, Evans-Pritchard, is irrelevant to performatives since, as I have indicated, the content of a performative is either appropriate or inappropriate—but not true or false. It is inappropriate to "curse" someone with fecundity and great wealth, or to "bless" them with a lingering illness; but it is not "false" to do so. Furthermore, there need be no logical interrelations between one or more performatives, that is, they need not form a logically integral system. This might help to explain the apparent lack of coherence between the magical acts practised in a society like the Azande.[1]

A not unrelated emphasis has been placed on the complement part of magical ritual by G. Lienhardt. Although Tambiah's "performative" approach is not shared by Lienhardt, Lienhardt's view is that magical ritual enables the individual to make "a model of his desires and hopes, upon which to base renewed practical endeavour";[2] this harmonises well with Tambiah's conception, for, according to Lienhardt, the ritual is in a fashion an end in itself. It provides cognitive and emotive models on which the individual can base his future behaviour. The question of the meaning of magical actions would in this sense have to do with the analysis of the models enshrined in ritual, which would necessarily lead to investigation of the symbolisations otherwise employed in the society in question.

The performative idea therefore directs our attention back to the social conventions surrounding magical ritual (in this case, the use of oracles in Zande society), as they are the presuppositions of the

---

[1] Evans-Pritchard notes that Zande claims about their various magical practices are not integrated, which is to say, rationalised. The understanding of performatives offered above will doubtless not particularly please adherents of a purely formalistic linguistics, that is, those who resist the idea that language can take its significance from something outside of language (i.e., man's total social existence). I am unrepentant.

[2] Cf. G. Lienhardt, *Divinity and Experience: The Religion of the Dinka* (Oxford, 1961), p. 283; for Lienhardt's understanding of divination see the same, pp. 56-74. For a fine survey of symbolic-ritualist approaches see N.D. Munn, "Symbolism", pp. 579-612.

performatives employed, while the symbolic action theory of Lienhardt directs us to the analysis of the symbols employed in the oracular procedure. However, an objection to the performative view of magical ritual, and to Lienhardt's symbolic action view has been voiced by E.M. Ahern, in her previously-mentioned article. Ahern feels that reducing magical actions to social conventions of speech and non-verbal communication, the "modeling" of hopes and expectations, and so forth, do not do justice to the intentions of such rituals. She holds that it is undeniable that people engaging in some magic rituals "sometimes explicitly intend them to have an effect on the exterior world".[1] Thus she feels that we are obliged to distinguish between "strong" and "weak" ritual acts, that is, respectively, between those which are "intended" to change the world, and those which are "intended" to affect the mental states of their actors and participants (i.e., and so are "performatives" or "affective models").

Ahern's objection does not really touch Tambiah's position (in the modified form in which I have proposed it), since, as we have seen, a performative remains a performative almost regardless of the content of its complement. Thus, a "complement" may "intend" or not "intend" to affect "the exterior world", but this would not affect its rôle as (more or less appropriate) complement to a performative. Moreover, ever since social anthropologists began to study magic in the 19th century, no one has ever really seriously doubted that much magic attempts to change "the exterior world". Scholars following Evans-Pritchard's "empirical" lead, which Ahern seems to, at least in distinguishing between the words of a spell and "the world", would no doubt point out that magical addresses are framed in language, and that "the world" does not speak; nor does it hear; people, however, do. They would accordingly hold that there is no question as to the identity of the "real" addressee of a magical act. In other words, the strict separation between the subjective sphere of magical acts and "empirical reality" inevitably leads to the conclusion that magical acts only affect their performers and other actors. This would of necessity support the views of Tambiah and Lienhardt. If, however, one acknowledges that, from the point of view of magic-ritual acts, there is no "external" world, which the observer is somehow outside of, but only a "social" world (like the Zande "social"

[1] Ahern, "Illocutionary Acts", p. 2.

pot mentioned above) which it is appropriate to address as one would other social beings, then there is no problem with the assumption that magic addresses it as if it obeyed the conventions established by society. If this point be granted, however, we must then confront the problem of native "non-magical" or "empirical" explanations, since, as we have seen in the case of causality, any number of native interpretations of phenomena may be elicited by questioning (native intentions are usually only derived by questioning, so they are inevitably interpretations, that is, native exegesis), and their relevance to the phenomena under study is itself an interesting problem. But Ahern's objection nevertheless serves to focus attention on the contents of the magical rituals in use in a given society.

Perhaps a more serious objection to the notion of ritual acts as performatives would be to ask just what constitutes the "performative" aspect of a ritual act, if it is not the words that are spoken in the rite itself. The analogy of promising, marrying, or willing one's fortune are, after all, fairly straightforward performatives. How would it be meaningful to characterise the spontaneous trance of a shaman (it need not always be the result of intensive preparations) or the absolutely unsolicited outbursts of some of the Israelite prophets as legitimate parallels? I think the answer resides in an understanding of the extent to which prophetic-shamanistic behaviour is actually, all appearances to the contrary notwithstanding, closely patterned and even to some extent socially coerced. It may on occasion have surprised the Israelites that a given prophet spoke out on a given occasion; but the fact *that* he spoke out cannot have surprised anyone—unless there was some uncertainty as to the social warrant of the person in question (e.g., "Is Saul also among the prophets?"). Thus the "performative situation" consists in this instance simply of the co-incidence of appropriate personnel with appropriate behaviour.

Ahern's interest in magical ritual led her in a later study to compare the rules governing Zande oracle-divining with those employed in games.[1] Ultimately, though mediated by J.R. Searle, the idea goes back to L. Wittgenstein's well-known insight that many linguistic phenomena may be understood on the analogy of games. That is to say, if one observes a game with sufficient attention, even without being able

---

[1] E.M. Ahern, "Rules in Oracles and Games", *Man* 17 (1982), pp. 302-13.

to play it and without having its rules explained to one, it is still possible to derive the rules being observed by the players. Wittgenstein held the same to be true of the study of linguistic "rules", a suggestion which has had considerable influence on modern linguistics.[1]

This idea has been refined by Searle,[2] who distinguishes two different sorts of "rules" in connexion with language games: regulative rules and constitutive rules. The former apply to a variety of external forms, like a code of dress for diplomats, while the latter, like the rules of a game of chess, simply "are" the game. If a diplomat forgets his black tie, he does not cease being an accredited representative of his country, though he may be regarded as a gauche or unconventional one; but if one moves one's knight in a straight line, one is not playing chess. Applying this distinction to puzzling aspects of Azande statements to Evans-Pritchard about the use of the poison oracle, Ahern manages to show that the anthropologist's questions did not "abide by the rules". For example, it was noted above that Azande hold that the benge oracle-poison would not be any good for the purposes of murder. Naturally not, since the "rules" governing the use of *benge* stipulate that it is to be prepared under close observance of tabus, and that it is to be administered to chickens, rather than men. To do otherwise would be do break the "rules"; it would be meaningless. Thus Evans-Pritchard's respondents could not answer him meaningfully; nor could a chess-player do so, one suspects, if one asked him why he does not jump over interposing pieces with his queen. This idea is very useful, particularly as it points to at least one answer to the question of the meaning of magical acts as the identification of the regulative and constitutive rules which govern them. Practically speaking, though, one must recall that magical phenomena are extremely sophisticated, that societies which use magic borrow from others at the drop of a hat, and that their own magic is constantly changing and evolving to meet present and anticipated

---

[1] Cf. e.g. J. Lyons, *Language and Linguistics. An Introduction*, (Cambridge; 5th edn, 1985 [1981]); pp. 140-41: "Wittgenstein's emphasis upon this connection and upon the multiplicity of purposes that languages fulfil had the salutary effect of encouraging both philosophers and linguists. . .to question, if not always to abandon, the traditional assumption that the rôle of basic function of language is that of communicating propositional, or factual, information".

[2] Cf. *Speech Acts*, pp. 39-42; Ahern, "Rules", p. 303.

demands. Thus the "constitutive rules" of magic in any given society are apt to be in constant development, and need not necessarily be susceptible to precise empirical analysis. Finally, and of great pertinence to this study, is the probability that the lack of existing native informants would rule out the search for the constitutive rules of archaic civilisations.

To summarise briefly, then: magical actions, of which divination is a subspecies, are performative "utterances", which I take to mean both verbal and non-verbal situational contexts which define particular conventional social acts (like commanding, requesting, promising, marrying, etc.). Magical performatives include such phenomena as conjuring, healing, divining, cursing, and so forth. Since, as we have seen, the performatives in use in a given society have no necessary logical inter-relations, any definition of them which can be offered must be extremely general (see below); otherwise, one can only characterise them empirically. The "complements" or contents of these performatives, as implied by Tambiah and Lienhardt, respectively, may be either—in the broadest sense—rhetorical, or symbolic. It should be evident that the analysis of performative complements will be of a piece with the study of other aspects of cognition within a given society. The magical actions themselves are constituted by specific rules which it is possible to identify by inspection, though they will naturally vary from procedure to procedure.

A further consideration is that, as we have seen to be the case with the Azande, divination is usually binary in character;[1] it provides either a yes or a no to a stated question. The exception to this in Zande society is the witch-doctor, who, however, usually tries to limit the number of possibilities on which he is expected to pronounce to either confirming or denying; nevertheless, he clearly sometimes has to evaluate numerous variables at the same time. The same is true of the at least superficially complex systems employed in Nupe *eba*-divining,

---

[1] As is also mainly the case in Lugbara divination; cf. J. Middleton, *Lugbara Religion* (Oxford, 1960), pp. 79-85; and cf. pp. 238-50 on the moral continuum within which Lugbara witchcraft, sorcery and divination operate.

Moslim-Nupe *hatí*-divining, and the related Yoruba *ifa* method.[1] The entire "performative context" of divination-performatives is, like the marriage ceremony, the actual social event. This context necessarily varies from case to case.

The study of the social function of the various divination-performatives in a given society naturally pertains to such features as the sex, social status, rôles, and institutional affiliations of the participants and actors in a given form of divination.[2] Among the Azande, the pre-eminent use of divination has to do with the resolution of social conflicts; witches are usually either social competitors or disgruntled wives, and a sorceror may be anyone with a grudge. The use of the poison and other oracles thus objectifies social tensions in a form carefully prescribed by the society, and links up with other prescribed procedures for reducing them. As performatives need not be logically inter-related, though, there is no necessary relationship between one form of divination employed in a society and any other. Thus, for example, we note that among the Azande there are also many rather trivial uses of divination, such as consultation about journeys, one's health, the weather, and so on. Here it is hard to avoid Lienhardt's conclusion that magic can model one's hopes and projects (which, I should like to point out, it can also do negatively by modeling one's fears and terrors—in order to overcome them), and so infuse confidence in the future into the believer. Here, too, divination contributes to resolve tension. On first consideration, the tension in question might seem to be more psychological than social. However, it is in reality

---

[1] For Nupe divination see S.F. Nadel, *Nupe Religion* (London, 1970 [1954]) pp. 38-67; for the *Ifa* of the Yoruba, see W. Bascom, *Ifa Divination: Communication Between Gods and Men in West Africa* (Bloomington and London, 1969), pp. 26-120. The similarities with such familiar systems as the Tarot and the I'Ching should not be overlooked.

[2] On the social determinants of divination see G.K. Park, "Divination and its Social Contexts", *JRAI* 93 (1963), pp. 195-209. Park sees the diviner as largely legitimating social processes of decision which would otherwise be difficult to enforce (esp. pp. 197-99); thus he remarks that "divinatory procedure, whether 'objective' in quality or merely inter-subjective, constitutes a technique for establishing an effective consensus upon a rather peculiar project" (p. 199).

ultimately social, since the concerns dealt with are social stereotypes, as is shown by the fact that socially-developed means of dealing with these "private" concerns exist, namely divination and magic. As is the case with other provinces of ritual, divination can be seen to function as an interface between the private and the social spheres.[1]

One might be tempted to think that a warning of impending ill heath, bewitchment, or whatever, is socially or psychologically dysfunctional, that is, that they render the inquirer incapable of social action. In actuality, though, negative answers, at least among the Azande, do not have this effect. This led Evans-Pritchard, empiricist to his fingertips, to conclude that the Azande must understand the future differently than we do:

> I have often noticed that Azande on being informed that sickness lies ahead of them do not even proceed to discover the name of the witch whose influence is going to cause them sickness. . . (they) merely wait for a few days and then consult the oracle again to find out whether their health will be good for the coming month, hoping that by the time of the second consultation the evil influence which hung over their future at the time of the first consultation will no longer be there (p. 161).

However, as we have seen, magical acts do not necessarily relate to others unless so stipulated by social convention. Such relations are, for example, evident in the progression from private oracle to the prince's poison oracle among the Azande to determine the ultimate truth in cases of witchcraft or sorcery. But in Azande oracular practice a negative answer requires no confirmatory tests, whereas, as noted above, a positive one must still be further investigated. Thus it seems that in matters of personal fortune no similar convention links a bad prognosis with yet another oracular act, so that individual oracles remain independent of each other. Therefore, if one waits a bit and tries again, the answer may be different, and the "temporal" contradiction in question exists only in the mind of an empiricist who expects all such acts to

---

[1] Thus, for example, as Park ("Divination and its Social Contexts", pp. 196-97) points out, divination to determine where to place one's house might seem at first sight to be a private matter. It is not, however, as dwelling arrangements usually follows the lines of sept, clan, lineage, patri- or matrilocality, or the like, so that any decision to change one's residence inevitably has social features.

generalise to universal concepts.

The acknowledgement that divination is an operative procedure with no inherent meaning, that is, that it derives its meaning from prior social agreements, is an important insight. In this context it shows that oracles really have nothing to do with "predicting the future" in our sense.[1]

There is also the question of the *actors* who engage in divination. Among the Azande, as we have seen, anyone and everyone can practise divination in one or another form, although there are certain restrictions as to age, sex, and political power (e.g., no one may question the validity of the prince's poison oracle; also, and notably, the respectable forms of divination are not immediately accessible to women). It should go without saying that these restrictions reflect existing status distinctions in Zande society. Interestingly, the reliability of an oracle is no guarantee of its prestige; thus, for example, the *mapingo* oracle may be consulted by anyone (actor status plays no importance), it is regarded as extremely reliable, and yet it does not carry sufficient weight to base a legal accusation. Contrariwise, the witch-doctor, who is the only professional diviner in Zande society, is known and acknowledged to be a swindler on occasion, and yet his accusations may be taken to the poison oracle. Moreover, although the court officially despises much of the magic that the common people practise, the witch-doctor may receive the accolade of royal invitation. Thus neither social status nor juridical practice is necessarily related to what are held to be the "empirical" outcomes of divination. Obviously, the extent to which divination expresses itself in any society as an independent institution with its own personnel is dependent on such factors as social structure, political structure, and, not least, pure economics (note, for example, that the oracle poison *benge* is expensive in terms of time and materials,

---

[1] The fact that many societies possess well developed ideologies of "fate" (concerning such notions, see the volume of essays H. Ringgren (ed.), *Fatalistic Beliefs in Religion Folklore, and Literature: Papers read at the Symposium on Fatalistic Beliefs held at Åbo on the 7th-9th of September, 1964* (Uppsala, 1967) does not contradict this. Ideologies, too, are social products, and hence have their social uses, such as, for example, enjoining and encouraging acceptance of the status quo. This does not necessarily entail that the societies in question ever confront or have confronted their understandings of "fate" with other social behaviours, such as divination.

whereas termites are free; thus it is unsurprising that the termites oracle is frequently resorted to, while the poison oracle is reserved for special and important events).

It will not have escaped the reader's attention that Zande divination is entirely non-theistic. This is intelligible when we consider the remote rôle played by the divine in Azande society,[1] and when we further consider that, as I have suggested, divination performatives are not logically related to one another in any sort of system. They merely are, and do as social guidelines prescribe. Therefore whatever relations exist between various divinatory practices will be determined by the social, judicial, and theological cognitions in a given culture.

A point which needs stressing is that, seen from within any given society that practises divination, there is no question but that it works, which is to say, that the members of the society regard it as giving valid information. Thus divination is at least notionally a source of knowledge. This point may be hard for Westerners to grasp, because we are inclined to set the phenomenon of divination within Husserlian "parentheses"; we study the claims that are made about the phenomenon rather than the attitudes behind those claims, for the simple reason that we are dismissive of the claims themselves. But divining societies manifestly do hold that divination produces knowledge, and, since societies regard knowledge as they do any other scarce commodity, the phenomenon is frequently regulated so as to accord with the power and status relationships present in society.[2] We shall hardly be able fully to appreciate this without at least making some attempt to accept the social premises themselves. Thus, as we have seen, no one is allowed to question the prince's poison oracle among the Azande; his oracle is accordingly the ultimate source of knowledge, just as the prince himself is the ultimate source of power. Conversely, the *mapingo* oracle, being open to all comers, enjoys the least prestige and has the least authority.

The above observations allow us to formulate a *purely formal definition of divination as a set of socially defined and structured*

---

[1] Cf. E.E.Evans-Pritchard, "Zande Theology", in *Social Anthropology*, pp. 288-330.

[2] Access to knowledge is always restricted in societies, and its possession grants both status and material benefits;cf.e.g. L. Lindstrom, "Doctor, Lawyer, Wise Man, Priest: Big-Men and Knowledge in Melanesia", in *Man* NS 19 (1984), pp. 291-309.

procedures for producing (notional) knowledge in a society from what
are presumed to be extra-human sources. Social definition and patterning account for the performative quality of divinatory acts; furthermore,
defining the phenomenon as a "set" of "procedures" emphasises the
mutual independence of the various divinatory acts from each other. The
fact that the "knowledge" arrived at is "notional" means that it is
regarded as true or at least highly significant in the society in question;
this says nothing about the actual epistemological status of such
"knowledge". Moreover, it avoids the silly—but widely held—belief that
divination has to do with "predicting the future". Finally, the sources
from which this "knowledge" is derived are held to be external to man:
among the Azande, as we have seen, the source is the oracle itself, but
other societies rationalise the procedure differently, e.g., as deriving
from ghosts, demons, gods, the ancestors, or whatever.[1]

As our last point, it should be observed that divination belongs to
what is by far the the largest province within magic. The phenomenon
is so consistent and has been so extensively studied by now that
O'Keefe labels this province "medical magic" and notes that

> many anthropologists in Africa (and other continents) have confirmed
> his (i.e., Evans-Pritchard's) patterns. Almost everywhere they find
> oracles and diviners as diagnosticians, and witchdoctors or shamans

---

[1] In his excellent article in *The Encyclopedia of Religion* (M. Eliade [ed], [New
York and London, 1987], Vol. 4, pp. 375-82), E.M. Zuesse proposes a "typology of
divination" consisting of three main groups of phenomena (p. 376): 1) "Intuitive
divination (in which the diviner spontaneously 'sees' or 'knows' reality or the
future)". . . 2) "Possession divination (in which spiritual beings are said to
communicate through intermediary agents)". . . 3) "Wisdom divination (in which the
diviner decodes impersonal patterns of reality)". All three fall within the compass
of my admittedly very general definition. If anyone should care to argue that the
Western scientist who attempts to refine or falsify his theories by ceaselessly testing
them against the (to him imperceptible) fabric of the world (a very Popperian
description of the programme of scientific activity) is also a diviner, according to
my definition, I would not be disposed to dispute the point. H. Swoboda (*Propheten
und Prognosen. Hellseher und Schwarzseher von Delphi bis zum Club of Rome*
[Munich and Zurich, 1979]), following Popper very closely (esp. pp. 167-202), has
explicitly drawn the parallel. The distinction, as should be obvious from my remarks
in this chapter and previously, is that the diviner's prognostics in principle cannot
be falsified, while those of the "empirical scientist" in principle must be falsifiable.

or medical cults as healers, providing magic as a defense. . . .[1]

Of course, it would be well to consider that the lion's share of research into divination has been conducted in Africa, and, as has been indicated previously, one may not automatically assume that African phenomena may be unquestioningly generalised to cover all social phenomena. With these considerations in mind, we shall now turn to the examination of divination in a number of ancient Near Eastern societies, after which we shall proceed to its use in ancient Israel.

---

[1] Cf. D.L. O'Keefe, *Lightning*, p. 2. O'Keefe's statement can be allowed to stand, with the reservation that the close connexion of the diviner with medical magic and attendant witchcraft countermeasures seems to be a predominently African phenomenon, and it is becoming increasingly clear today that African phenomena are merely better studied than so many others: it would be risky to generalise as sweepingly as O'Keefe does.

CHAPTER 3

BETWEEN THE RIVERS — AND ELSEWHERE

It is tempting to try to describe the phenomenon of divination in ancient
Mesopotamia through the convenient fiction of the ethnographic present,
as we did with Evans-Pritchard's Azande in the previous chapter, but in
this case, where virtually every characterisation of the society requires
at least some degree of qualification, this would feel very strange
indeed. To be strictly honest, from Eduard Meyer's *Geschichte des
Altertums*[1] to Mario Liverani's *Antico Oriente. Storia - Società -
Economia*,[2] histories of the ancient orient have appeared which contain
only those sociological insights which historians inevitably, whether
consciously or unconsciously, import into their work; they have not had
much in the way of "sociological" data to offer.[3] Speaking of modern

---

[1] Vols. 1-5 (Stuttgart, 1884-1902).

[2] (Roma-Bari, 1988); hereafter *AO*.

[3] I would include in this characterisation such classics as A.T. Olmstead, *A
History of Assyria* (New York, 1923); B. Meissner's *Könige Babyloniens und
Assyriens* (Leipzig, 1926); A. Moortgat's *Geschichte Vorderasiens bis zum
Hellenismus* (Hildesheim, 1984 [1950], which includes A. Scharff's contribution
under the title *Ägypten und Vorderasien im Altertum*); and E. Cassin, J. Bottéro, J.
Vercoutter (eds.), *Die Altorientalischen Reiche*, Bd. I-III (Frankfurt am Main,
1980-1984 [1965-1967]). I should like to emphasise that there is nothing wrong with
these studies; they represent pretty much what historiography could achieve, given
the data available at the time. Where I would fault them — as do Oppenheim and
Liverani — is in their virtually unflinching commitment to writing political history
alone, or where "social" characterisations are proffered, they are largely of an
anecdotal and impressionistic nature. I would even extend this criticism, however
reluctantly, to A. Goetze's famous *Kulturgeschichte Kleinasiens* (Munich; 2nd rev
edn, 1974 [1933]). The social studies of the Soviet school, judging by the little that
has appeared in translation, tend towards the doctrinaire (cf. e.g. I.M. Diakonoff
(ed.), *Ancient Mesopotamia, Socio-Economic History. A Collection of Studies by
Soviet Scholars* (Moscow, 1981 [1969]). The same could certainly be said of efforts
emerging from the sometime Soviet bloc; see e.g. J. Herrmann / H. Klengel (eds.),
Kulturgeschichte des alten Vorderasien (Berlin, 1989). A conspicuous exception to

efforts, Liverani even goes so far as to claim that

> The main part of studies dealing with the ancient orient have to do
> with the examination or publication of new materials: they thus deal
> with archaeology and philology. History, properly considered, that is,
> as distinct from the other two categories, is virtually non-existent.[1]

Naturally, Liverani feels that recent Italian scholarship presents an
exception to this pattern, but in reality even his very learned study, over
a thousand pages long (counting the indices), could not satisfy the
demands of even the most modest sociologist.

Back in 1964 A.L. Oppenheim had noted in his now famous
Ancient Mesopotamia[2] that the region was characterised throughout its
history by centripetal forces tending towards urbanisation and by
centrifugal forces among "certain strata of the population", which made
"definite and often effective resistance not only against living in
settlements of greater complexity than the village but also against the
power—be it political, military, or fiscal—that an urban center was
bound to exercise over them."[3] It is essentially this single insight which
Liverani has elevated to his main principle in discussing 3,000 years of
Mesopotamian history;[4] and plainly, this will not do, even if it is the
best we have at the moment. We still know virtually nothing about
family and kinship structures in Mesopotamia, for the good reason that
the vast majority of our documents are legal materials in which women,
that is, half the ancient population, seldom figure. Also, since, as we
have seen, a great deal of the ancient population of Mesopotamia was
either rural-sedentary or semi-nomadic, they have left very little in the
way of written record. We have no idea what sort of power and

---

this characterisation is M.A. Dandamaev's (trans. V.A. Powell; idem and D.B.Weis-
berg, eds.) *Slavery in Babylonia. From Nabopolassar to Alexander the Great
(626-331 BC)* (DeKalb, IL; 2nd edn, 1984).

[1] *AO*, p. 11.

[2] (Chicago, 1977 [1964]); with notes by E. Reiner; hereafter *AM*.

[3] *AM*, p. 110.

[4] Liverani, *AO*, p. 15: "for all this long period (i.e., three millennia: from 3500
to 500 BCE) may be considered to have possessed a fundamental continuity and
solidity deriving above all from the progressive affirmation and penetration of the
urban model and the palatine state".

hornfurge

authority structures obtained in Mesopotamian villages, and we are unlikely ever to know more about this except by social anthropological analogy.[1] Moreover, since legal and administrative documents are our main witnesses, it should be noted that these are both technical, stereotyped, and massively dull; and most Assyriologists have had better things to do than to spend the excruciating amounts of time it would take to extract the few nuggets of prosopographical and demographical information available in them.[2] Of course, this situation is improving, as there have been some exciting studies of urbanisation,[3] nomadic modes of life,[4] emergent ethnic groups,[5] and so on. But it should be

---

[1] Even the question of public administration and the ancient Near Eastern courts is difficult of access, in spite — and in some cases because of — the number and types of sources available. For example, as far as I know the only published list of personnel in a Mesopotamian court remains that of Nebuchadnezzar, first published by E. Unger in *Babylon. Die heilige Stadt nach der Beschreibung der Babylonier* (Berlin and Leipzig, 1931), pp. 282-94.

[2] Note the remarks of M.A. Dandamayev in "About Life Expectancy in the First Millennium B.C.", in B. Alster (ed.), *Death in Mesopotamia. XXVIe Rencontre assyriologique internationale* (Copenhagen, 1980), pp. 183-87.

[3] Cf. e.g., G. Buccellati, *Cities and Nations of Ancient Syria* (Rome, 1967); M.T. Larsen, *The Old Assyrian City-State and its Colonies* (Copenhagen, 1976); R. Harris, *Ancient Sippar* (Istanbul, 1975). Unavailable to me was: M. Liverani, *L'origine delle città* (Roma, 1986).

[4] See R. Giveon on the shasu "nomads" in *Les bedouins Shosou des documents égyptiens* (Leiden, 1971); and, on ancient nomadism in general, the discussion in: N.P. Lemche (trans. F.H.Cryer), *Early Israel* (Leiden, 1985), pp. 84-163, with copious literature.

[5] E.g., on the old "Hebrew problem": N.P. Lemche, "'Hebrew' as a National Name for Israel", in *Studia Theologica* 33 (1979), pp. 1-23; the same, *Early Israel, passim*; O. Loretz, *Habiru — Hebräer: Eine sozio-linguistische Studie über die Herkunft des Gentiliziums 'ibrî vom Appelativum habiru* (Berlin and New York, 1984); M. Heltzer, *The Suteans. With a contribution by S. Arbeli* (Naples, 1981); J.F.A. Sawyer and D.J.A. Clines (eds.), *Midian, Moab and Edom: The History and Archaeology of Late Bronze and Iron Age Jordan and North-West Arabia* (Sheffield, 1983); on the Ishmaelites: E.A. Knauf, *Ismael: Untersuchungen zur Geschichte Palästinas und Nordarabiens im 1. Jahrtausend v. Chr.* (Wiesbaden, 1984); plus the same author's many contributions in *Biblische Notizen* on the theme of "Supplementa Ismaelitica"; on the Midianites: the same, *Midian: Untersuchungen zur Geschichte Palästinas und Nordarabiens am Ende des 2. Jahrtausends v. Chr.*

recalled that we are dealing with an enormous region over a vast period of time, so in reality we lack all basis for speaking of "social history". This has not prevented a few brave souls from attempting to do so, more or less on the "tell all you know" basis so despised by the late Moses Finley,[1] but it is really rather difficult to see what else one could do: only by synthesising what we know can we derive theories which may be tested.

Our most difficult problem, in dealing with Mesopotamian divination is that we are perforce compelled to deal with written sources alone, which means in practice that we have information stemming from only the diviners themselves or from their correspondence with other literati, who were rather thin on the ground for most of Mesopotamian history. That being the case, any inferences we may make about the rôle of the phenomenon among the non-literate citizenry will necessarily be speculative and analogical.

The analysis of the literary sources of Mesopotamian divination began virtually simultaneously with the decipherment of cuneiform literature, which may be dated to the famous "simultaneous translation" exercise in London in 1857.[2] Within twenty years the first major study of Babylonian divination appeared;[3] and more or less comprehensive investigations had been published by Assyriologists, their knowledge of

(Wiesbaden, 1988); J.R. Bartlett, *Edom and the Edomites* (Sheffield, 1989).

[1] By "tell all you know", Finley means simply rattling off all manner of spurious detail about a given civilisation (spurious, because we cannot possibly develop a sufficiently differentiated picture in most cases to be able to see such statistics in perspective) see "How it really was" in *Ancient History: Evidence and Models* (New York, 1985), pp. 47-66, esp. p. 63. Liverani comes periously close to this in his discussion of towns and villages in *AO*, p. 542; M.A. Dandamaev and V.G. Lukonin's *The Culture and Social Institutions of Ancient Iran* (Cambridge, 1989) certainly falls under this rubric.

[2] Cf. B. Meißner and K. Oberhuber, *Die Keilschrift* (Berlin, 1967), pp. 15-17; E. Leichty, *The Omen Series Šumma Izbu* (Locust Valley, NY, 1970 (= *TCS* 4)), p. 1.

[3] F. Lenormant, *La Divination et la science des présages chez les Chaldéens* (Paris, 1875); see also A.H. Sayce, "The Astronomy and Astrology of the Babylonians" in *Transactions of the Society of Biblical Archaeology* 3 (1874), pp. 145-79; the same, "Babylonian Augury by Means of Geometrical Figures", in *Transactions of the Society of Biblical Archaeology* 4 (1876), pp. 302-14.

Babylonian and Assyrian hugely improved, by shortly after the turn of the century.[1]

This may be termed the first phase in the study of the phenomenon; at this time Assyriologists were commendably concerned mainly to make sense of the texts, rather than to evaluate the phenomenon as such, although a fair amount of speculation, much of it based on the classics, was also in evidence. Some, like Jastrow, even referred to such social anthropological literature as was available to them to bring divination into perspective.[2] Nevertheless, the use of the term "Zukunftsdeutung" by German scholars, and of "présage" by French ones, indicates that the general point of departure for understanding the phenomenon was based on the notion of divination as prediction; nor were English-language scholars different in this respect.[3] As we have seen in the previous chapter, however, it would be a mistake to assume that divination performatives actually do relate to "the future". But the notion was characteristic, as we have seen, of the 19th century—and even more recent—sociological study of magic and divination; so it is naturally both understandable and pardonable that Assyriologists

---

[1] Cf. R.C. Thompson, *The Reports of the Magicians and Astrologers of Nineveh and Babylon*, Vols. 1-2 (London, 1900); H. Zimmern, *Beiträge zur Kenntnis der Babylonischen Religion* (Leipzig, 1901), esp. pp. 82-91; C. Fossey, *Textes assyriens et babyloniens relatifs à la Divination* (Paris, 1905); A. Ungnad, *Die Deutung der Zukunft bei den Babyloniern und Assyrern* (Leipzig, 1909). M. Jastrow, *Die Religion Babyloniens und Assyriens*, Vol. 2 (Gießen, rev edn, 1912), pp. 174-415 deals mainly with extispicy (which Jastrow, following contemporary tradition, calls "Leberschau"); other divinatory phenomena are treated on pp. 138-73 and, in Vol. 3, pp. 416-970); see also M. Jastrow, *Aspects of Religious Belief and Practice in Babylonia and Assyria* (New York, 1971 [1911]), pp. 143-265; all of which represents only a fraction of the intense production of Assyriological works on divination which appeared in this period; the latest of these introductory studies were the brief contributions by A. Boissier, *Mantique Babylonienne et Mantique Hittite* (Paris, 1935), which presented what was known of the Hititte divinatory practices at a level accessible to non-specialists (pp. 25-44); and by E. Dhorme, *Les Religions de Babylone et d'Assyrie* (Paris, 1949), pp. 258-98.

[2] Cf. e.g. *Die Religion*, Vol. 2, p. 214.

[3] Cf. e.g. Jastrow, *Aspects*, p. 144: "The cult of Babylonia and Assyria. . . revolves to a large extent around methods for divining the future. . ."

embraced it. However, it did have the practical effect of assimilating the phenomenon of ancient divination in Mesopotamia to modern contacts with palm-readers, tea-leaf readers, "astrologers" (here in inverted commas to distinguish them from their ancient and medieval predecessors), and the like.[1]

The second phase of Assyriological study may be said to have begun with an article by A.L. Oppenheim which appeared in 1936, and in which he argued that,

> Where inscriptions and legal documents remain silent, the interpretations of the omen collections are informative. Here the little man, in all his wretched daily existence, steps forth to meet us; exposed to sickness, poverty, hunger, and with no rights in the face of the arbitrary wielders of power in his country, he lives his life as best he can, and his wishes aspire no higher than to nourishment and descendants.[2]

Rightly or wrongly, Oppenheim here maintains that the Mesopotamian collections of omina preserve the private fears and hopes of the individual, and offer us one of the few chances we have of seeing the "inside" of the Mesopotamian social experience.[3] He adhered to this

---

[1] One should note, however, that this was not the only Assyriological perception of the phenomenon; Ungnad, for example, called it a "Wissenschaft" (*Die Deutung der Zukunft*, p. 13) although in doing so he was careful to bracket the word with inverted commas; as he went on to say, "The observation of the heavens by the Babylonian had no scientific importance in our sense of the word, but only a purely practical purpose which he took to be scientific, as the same was then true in the ancient orient as in the Middle Ages, namely that the examination of deity was the ultimate goal of all study" (p.19). Here we note a recurrence of the problem that had bedevilled Tylor, Frazer, Mauss-Hubert and other social anthropologists (even as late as Evans-Pritchard in 1937, as we have seen), namely the relation of divination to "science". Moreover, however superficially attractive Ungnad's suggestion might seem, in reality it proposes the doubtful interpretive programme of illuminating an unknown X by assimilating it to an only slightly better known Y.

[2] "Zur keilschriftlichen Omenliteratur", *Orientalia*, N.S. 5 (1936), pp. 199-228; here p. 202.

[3] Ungnad, by contrast (*Die Deutung der Zukunft*, p. 12), claims that at least in connexion with extispical omina "private affairs are only quite rarely examined".

doyes?

view throughout his career,[1] though, sadly, no one has as yet attempted to realise his programme. This contribution signalled the entrance of social anthropological concerns into the study of divination in a serious way.

As if in response to Oppenheim's challenge, already in 1940 G. Contenau published a full-fledged phenomenological study of Mesopotamian divination[2] which explored all the major types of divination and their literary genres. Contenau located divination solidly in the context of Babylonian religion—an important acknowledgement of the religious or "theurgic" (D.L. O'Keefe) character of Mesopotamian divination; attempted to describe the actors involved[3]; and defined it sociologically as consisting of both a popular and an élite tradition,[4] one which was both cognitively a sort of "science" and (like Jastrow and R.C. Thompson before him) an institution of the Mesopotamian apparatus of government.[5] Contenau's work was followed up by countless extraordinary studies by J. Nougayrol[6] and others, making the French contribution to the study of the subject at least as important as those

---

[1] Cf. A.L. Oppenheim, "Perspectives on Mesopotamian Divination", in: Centre d'Etudes Supérieures Spécialisé d'Histoire des Religions de Strasbourg (ed.), *La Divination en Mésopotamie Ancienne et dans les Régions Voisines* (= *XIVe Rencontre Assyriologique Internationale*) (Paris, 1966), p. 38. Hereafter *DM*.

[2] *La Divination chez les Assyriens et les Babyloniens* (Paris, 1940).

[3] *La Divination chez les Assyriens*, pp. 63-107.

[4] *La Divination chez les Assyriens*, pp. 359-60.

[5] *La Divination chez les Assyriens*, p. 361.

[6] E.g. "Textes hépatoscopiques d'époque ancienne conservés au musée du Louvre", *RA* 38 (1939-1941), pp. 67-88; "Textes hépatoscopiques d'époque ancienne au musée du Louvre", *RA* 40 (1945-1946), pp. 56-97; "Textes hépatoscopiques d'époque ancienne au musée du Louvre", *RA* 44 (1950), pp. 1-44; "Présages médicaux de l'haruspicine babylonienne", *Semitica* 6 (1956), pp. 5-14; "Rapports paléo-babyloniennes d'haruspices", *JCS* 21 (1967), pp. 219-35; "Le foie d'orientation BM 50494", *RA* 62 (1968), pp. 31-50; (with J. Aro) "Trois Nouveaux Recueils d'haruspicine Ancienne", *RA* 67 (1973) 41-56; "Les 'silhouettes de référence' de l'haruspicine", in: B.L. Eichler, et al. (eds), *Kramer Anniversary Volume. Cuneiform Studies in Honor of Samuel Noah Kramer*, (Neukirchen-Vluyn, 1976), pp. 343-50.

appearing in English and German.[1]

The third phase of the study of Mesopotamian divination may be said to have begun in 1964, with the publication of Oppenheim's *Ancient Mesopotamia*, closely followed by the fourteenth "Rencontre Assyriologique Internationale" (July 2nd - 6th, 1965) which led to the publication of *La Divination en Mésopotamie Ancienne et dans les Regions Voisines*. The latter was followed by the publication in France of *La Divination. Etudes Recueillies par André Caquot et Marcel Leibovici* in 1968,[2] which included Egypt, Babylon, and Israel within its compass.

Oppenheim's work stresses divination in the context of an impressionistic but extremely knowledgeable interpretation of Mesopotamian society—political history is only peripherally discussed in the work. The chapter in which divination is discussed deals with religion, although Oppenheim is clearly uncomfortable with the juxtaposition of the two phenomena. Thus he presents divination as "a major *intellectual* (emphasis mine) achievement in Mesopotamia and surrounding countries" (p. 206). He accordingly underlines the copying and collection of ominous texts and handbooks over the millennia; he also sees the collection of observations about ominous happenings as a step in divination's removal "from the realm of folklore to the level of a scientific activity" (p. 210). On this issue, some familiarity with the social anthropological study of divination and magic would have been useful. The pseudo-problem of magic versus science continues to rear its head. Unapologetically "pan-Babylonian" in his approach, Oppenheim stresses the influence he thinks Mesopotamian divination demonstrably exercised on the rest of the ancient Near East (pp. 205-28, *passim*). He also argues that divining presupposes the willingness of "supernatural forces" to communicate with men to help them evade disaster (p. 207).

Oppenheim's powerful emphasis on divination as an intellectual

---

[1] We shall meet Nougayrol's studies below; the question of divination and "science" was raised by R. Berthelot, *La Pensée de l'Asie et l'Astrobiologie:* Les origines des sciences et des religions supérieures (Paris, 1949); cf. esp. pp. 41-76, and see p. 41, n 1-2, where the author refers explicitly to Tylor and other social anthropologists.

[2] Vol. 1 (Paris, 1968). Hereafter *La Divination*.

achievement bore with it an intensified interest in the diviner, who is now seen as a cultured, multi-lingual figure (able to read and write at least Akkadian and Sumerian), rather than as a purveyor of primitive superstition:

> the Mesopotamian diviner is not a priest, but an expert technician and, first of all, a scholar. . .in a rather modern sense, not a Greek teacher-philosopher-scholar, nor a Chinese scholar-official. . .His is not the knowledge based on intuition: he has to undergo a strict training with examinations and his livelihood depends. . .on his fame, that is, on his successes in divination.[1]

Ultimately, the writer feels,

> the Assyriologist may. . .be in a position to throw more light on the conditions and circumstances which foster or hamper. . .the rise of that cultural manifestation which we call today 'science'.[2]

It should almost go without saying that Oppenheim's argument, which demands increased respect for both the diviner and the tradition he represents, at the same time leads him to the absurd impasse already arrived at long before by Frazer in particular. To put it simply, if the diviner collects observations of significant events and correlates them with other, subsequently-observed events, thus coupling a "protasis" (if-clause) to an "apodosis" (then-clause), so as to determine which regularly-recurring phenomena herald what sort of outcomes, why does he not abandon the system when his "predictions" are not fulfilled? Exactly as is the case with Frazer's argument that magicians are ordinarily very talented individuals, Oppenheim's insistence on the diviner's intellectual callibre in reality only makes the "failure" of the diviner to abandon his "fallacious" system even more paradoxical. This "failure" becomes positively perverse when we consider that Oppenheim shows that the Mesopotamian divinatory tradition persisted from Sumerian times until the Seleucid period, that is, for over two millennia. Any Assyriologist or historical social anthropologist who takes this approach puts himself, figuratively speaking, in the position of a maiden aunt who is trying to work up some enthusiasm about her adored little nephew's brilliant collection of pickled spiders. As we saw in the

---

[1] *DM*, p. 40.

[2] *DM*, p. 43.

previous chapter, though, these problems do not arise if it is assumed that the diviner in reality is attempting to do something else than to "predict the future".

The two contributions by J. Nougayrol[1] comprise a retrospect far more detailed than I have been able to present here of research into Babylonian divination and its ramifications in the rest of the ancient Near East. Here we shall content ourselves to note a single revealing statement:

> In reality, what characterises Babylonian thought, in contradistinction to our own, is not so much the fact that (Babylonians) made use of supernatural explanations or procedures, as that the supernatural and the natural shared equal regard, they ceaselessly mixed. . .both 'mystical' thought and experience as we understand it. One might furthermore add that they probably held the former to be superiour to the latter.[2]

In short, like others before him, Nougayrol held that Babylonian thought distinguished between the categories of the natural and the supernatural; thus for him, while he regards divination as a species of "science", it is a science of the supernatural. The example he instances in the above cited context makes this completely clear:

> In Mesopotamia, the conjuring-doctor enjoyed greater prestige than did the simple practitioner, and, rather than diminishing, his status only increased over the centuries.[3]

We find ourselves confronted with the same antithesis Evans-Pritchard had proposed in 1937, namely that between "magic" and "empiricism", and, as I have repeatedly emphasised, this is a false antithesis which

---

[1] In *DM*, pp. 5-19 and *La Divination*, pp. 25-81.

[2] *La Divination*, p. 58.

[3] *La Divination*, p. 58. Nougayrol's distinction between the "exorcist" or "conjurer", considered as a religio-magical functionary, and the "doctor" or "surgeon", considered as a profane one, is well known in Assyriology; it was, for example, asserted by A. Ungnad already in "Besprechungskunst und Astrologie in Babylonien", *AfO* 14 (1941-1944), p. 252, and recurs in Oppenheim's *AM*, pp. 290-305, where the author distinguishes between the "scientific" medical practitioner (actually Nougayrol's exorcist, since this figure was educated to observed the physical "signs" of illness) and the "practical" variety, who lanced boils and administered herbal remedies.

cannot make the magical phenomena intelligible. This problem is still quite general in Assyriology, and it has consequences which are tangible even in very recent work.

To take a prominent example: J.J. Finkelstein held, in a learned contribution which appeared in 1963,[1] that the presence in Mesopotamian chronographic literature of phrases and vocabulary deriving from the genre of omina indicate that omina provided source material and an ideological point of departure for Mesopotamian historiography. A.K. Grayson has apparently felt that a close relationship of the chronographic texts to "magic" would jeopardize the "historical" and "scientific" character of Mesopotamian historical thinking. He has accordingly repeatedly been dismissive of Finkelstein's claim,[2] and has in general attempted to minimise the importance of the omen literature for Mesopotamian past-relating texts. In this he has been followed by J. Van Seters, in his recent study of ancient Near Eastern and Israelite historical writing.[3] Van Seters seems to echo Grayson's antipathy to divination in the following statement:

> . . .it was actually the gods who wrote the sign on the viscera of animals at the moment of sacrifice, or who produced certain effects in nature to give a message to the suppliant. Such a superstitious attitude, which turns astronomy into astrology, can hardly be expected to develop the historical consciousness that leads to historiography.[4]

But, dismissive as he is, Grayson cannot explain why Mesopotamian scribes found it appropriate to incorporate omen protases and apodoses into a variety of chronographic and didactic texts (one has to compare this with the fact that the Mari "prophetic" texts and the Neo-Assyrian

---

[1] "Mesopotamian Historiography", *Proceedings of the American Philosophical Society* 107 (1963), pp. 461-72.

[2] See already Grayson's attempt to reduce to a minimum the influence of omina on the Babylonian chronicles in "Divination and the Babylonian Chronicles" in *DM*, pp. 69-76; his subsequent remarks in *Assyrian and Babylonian Chronicles* (Locust Valley, NY, 1975), pp. 37 and pp. 43-9; and his introductory dismissal of Finkelstein's position in *Orientalia* N.S. 49 (1980), pp. 143-48.

[3] *In Search of History*. Historiography in the Ancient World and the Origins of Biblical History (New Haven and London, 1983).

[4] *In Search of History*, pp. 77-8.

Ishtar "prophecies", that is, divination texts which seem to speak of the future, do not do so: why specifically chronographic and didactic texts?); and Van Seter's objection simply presupposes the "scientific" (historiographical) character of Mesopotamian historical thought, without taking the trouble to prove it. It may be regrettable, or sad, or even quite exciting that Mesopotamian scribes sometimes described the past in the language of omina; but it is not unthinkable, for they *did* do it.[1]

A similar problem arose in the Assyriological discussion of the relationship between ancient Mesopotamian astrology and astronomy. Already Berthelot had held that the preoccupation of Babylonian astrologers with the periodicities of the heavens "allows us to consider them as not only the first promotors of the sciences, but as the heralds of science".[2] O. Neugebauer, one of the most prominent historians of ancient mathematics and mathematical astronomy, has contested the relationship between ancient mathematical astronomy and astrology throughout his career.[3] Nevertheless, this view was already jeopardised by Oppenheim's demonstration that the same Mesopotamian centres— and some of the same personnel—which produced the most extraordinary feats of early mathematical astronomy were also responsible for astrological matters.[4] That the astrologers of the Neo-Assyrian great

---

[1] See most recently M. de Jong Ellis' ("Observations on Mesopotamian Oracles and Prophetic Texts", *JCS* 41/2 (1989) 159-60) recognition of the common horizons of the omen literature, the Akkadian "prophecy" texts, and the past-relating literature. I do not say "historiographic" literature, as I am convinced that this term is overused, and in such a manner as to prejudice the study of the phenomena and the texts in question.

[2] *La Pensée de l'Asie*, p. 76; and, before him, note Boissier, *Mantique Babylonienne*, p. 63: "mantic practice requires special gifts of observation, which made the haruspices, the augurers and the diviners the forerunners of experimental scientists".

[3] Cf. e.g. in "History of Ancient Astronomy", in (ed. *idem*) *Astronomy and History. Selected Essays*, (New York, et al., 1983), pp. 38-9; and *passim* in virtually everything else he has ever published. Note, however, his spirited defence of a "wretched collection of omens, debased astrology and miscellaneous nonsense" (the phrase was used by E.A. Sarton in dismissal of a study on omina) in *Isis* 42 (1951), repr. in "The Study of Wretched Subjects" in *Astronomy and History*, p.1.

[4] Cf. "Divination and Celestial Observation in the Last Assyrian Empire", *Centaurus* 14 (1969), pp. 97-135.

kings were also astronomers has been a matter of record since the publication of S. Parpola's collections of royal correspondence.[1] Thus there was no tidy distinction in ancient Mesopotamia between "magicians" and "proto-scientists" or "proto-historians". Nor, given our review of the experiences of the social anthropologists, should we have expected this to be the case.

In a way, it is quite extraordinary that the history of the Assyriological investigation of ancient Mesopotamian magic and divination manages in this fashion to recapitulate the social anthropological discussion which had preceded it. The distinction between "magic" and "science", already so problematical for Tylor, Frazer and Mauss-Hubert, and its attendant distinction between "magic" and "empiricism", posed so eloquently by Evans-Pritchard in connexion with the Azande, returned to haunt the work of the Assyriologists even after these false antitheses had largely ceased to trouble social anthropologists. Conversely, as we have seen, the social anthropological study of magic and divination has failed to observe the extent to which magic and divination were central theurgies, that is, religious phenomena, in the ancient "high cultures". This has helped to preserve the fiction of the antithesis between magic and religion .

The latter situation is not entirely the fault of the anthropologists. The Assyriologists have understood the phenomenon of divination as a species of "science", among other things, mainly in deference to the considerable learning of the diviners. Thus, for example, in Oppenheim's previously-mentioned article, he refers to them simply as "experts" and their area of specialisation as a "discipline".[2] At the same time, however, as we have seen, in his *Ancient Mesopotamia* he

---

[1] Cf. *Letters from Assyrian Scholars to the Kings Esarhaddon and Assurbanipal*, Part II, Vol. 2 (Neukirchen-Vluyn, 1983) (= *AOAT* 5/2), p. XXI: "Much of the efforts of the contemporary astrologers appears to have been directed towards predicting astronomical phenomena...in advance, evidently with an eye to capitalize on the king's desire to attach to his service the best prognosticators available. Many of these predictions can be shown to have been based on really primitive methods directly derived from the 'Scriptures'. . . but many turn out to involve more sophisticated methods not to be found in the 'Scriptures'. . . The astronomical knowledge making such predictions possible can only have been acquired through systematic/intensive study and recording of astronomical phenomena".

[2] "Divination and Celestial Observation", esp. pp. 100-1.

discusses this personnel in the context of Mesopotamian religion, just as Nougayrol found it possible to ask himself "whether. . .divination did not constitute the very centre of Babylonian religion".[1] In other words, both disciplines could well have profited one from the other; and it is a great pity that, up to the present, they have not done so. If the Assyriologists themselves cannot decide what sort of personnel they are dealing with, how could scholars from extraneous disciplines dare to comment?

We are now in the middle of the fourth phase of the Assyriological study of Mesopotamian divination. This phase, which naturally overlaps to some extent with the previous phases, has mainly consisted in the production of critical editions of the various omen series, but also in the publication of a number of perceptive analytical studies of the individual phenomena of divination. Here we may mention in particular such names as A. Goetze,[2] A.L. Oppenheim,[3] G. Pettinato,[4] E. Leichty,[5] E.F. Weidner,[6] R. Caplice,[7] E. Reiner and D. Pingree

---

[1] *DM*, p. 16.

[2] A. Goetze, *Old Babylonian Omen Texts* (New Haven, 1957) (= *YOS* 10).

[3] "The Interpretation of Dreams in the Ancient Near East. With a Translation of an Assyrian Dream Book", in *Transactions of the American Philosophical Society*, N.S. 46/3 (1956), pp. 179-353; cf. also *idem*, "New Fragments of the Assyrian Dream-Book", in *Iraq* 31 (1969), pp. 153-65.

[4] *Die Ölwahrsagung bei den Babyloniern*, Vols. I-II (Rome, 1966).

[5] *The Omen Series Summa Izbu* (Locust Valley, N.Y., 1970) (= *TCS* 4); cf. also S. Moren, "New Light on the Animal Omens", in *AfO* 27 (1980), pp. 53-70.

[6] Weidner's edition of the great astrological series *Enuma Anu Enlil* is now venerable, but still the only one available: *AfO* 14 (1944), pp. 172-95; pp. 308-18; 17 (1955), pp. 71-89; 22 (1968-1969), pp. 65-75. However, tablets 15-22 of the series have now been exhaustively treated by F. Rochberg-Halton, *Aspects of Babylonian Celestial Divination: The Lunar Eclipse Tablets of Enuma Anu Enlil AfO*, Beiheft 22, 1988.

[7] The rituals known as *namburbis* by Assyriologists are apotropaic rituals which counter the evil portents of the omina contained in *šumma ālu* (see below), as well as some *šumma izbu* or izbu-like omens. They have been published by R. Caplice in "Namburbi Texts in the British Museum", Or N.S. 34 (1965), pp. 105-31; 36 (1967), pp. 1-38; pp. 273-98; 39 (1970), pp. 111-51; 40 (1971), pp. 133-83; 42 (1973), pp. 508-17; see also Caplice's brief work, *The Akkadian Namburbi Texts: An Introduction* (Los Angeles, 1974) (= *Sources and Monographs. Sources from the*

(together),[1] U. Jeyes,[2] F.R. Kraus,[3] I. Starr,[4] among many other fine scholars.[5]

The Problem of Literacy

We have seen that Mesopotamian divination was very much a literate phenomenon. It is difficult to say, but it may well be this very fact that has kept social anthropologists from concerning themselves with it (i.e., ancient Near Eastern societies did not seem sufficiently "primitive"), besides, of course, the daunting task of approaching societies through a welter of translations, histories, and archaeological reports—all pretty much foreign soil for the anthropologist. However the truth of the matter, the sociologists J. Goody and I. Watt published a common

Ancient Near East, Vol. 1, fasc. 1).

[1] *Babylonian Planetary Omens, Part One: The Venus Tablet of Ammisaduqa* (Malibu, CA, 1975) (= *BPO* 1); *Part Two: Enuma Anu Enlil. Tablets 50-51* (Malibu, 1981) (= *BPO* 2).

[2] E.g. "The 'Palace Gate' of the Liver. A Study of Terminology and Methods in Babylonian Extispicy", *JCS* 30/4 (1978), pp. 209-33; *idem,* "The Act of Extispicy in Ancient Mesopotamia", in B. Alster (ed.), *Assyriological Miscellanies* 1 (1980), pp. 13-32; *idem, Old Babylonian Extispicy. Omen Texts in the British Museum* (Istanbul, 1989).

[3] "Mittelbabylonische Opferschauprotokolle", *JCS* 37 (1985), pp. 127-203.

[4] *The Rituals of the Diviner* (Malibu, 1983) (= *Bibliotheca Mesopotamica* 12 [1983]).

[5] It is to be noted, and regretted (a thing Assyriologists do with ritualistic resignation) that the great Babylonian compendium of extispicy omina for the diviner, *Barûtu*, has never been edited, for which reason I have referred merely to the latest important studies of the phenomenon in the previous notes. The series will probably originally have included as many as 100 tablets (see U. Jeyes, *Old Babylonian Extispicy*, p. 11). Similarly, in spite of a number of excellent preliminary studies, we still have no adequate replacement for F. Nötscher's now very outdated version of the random-sign "serial but non-canonical" collection of omina known as *šumma ālu* (cf. *Or* N.S. 31 (1928), pp. 1-78; pp. 39-42 (1929), pp. 1-247; 51-54 (1930), pp. 1-243). I regret that the preliminary study of *šumma ālu* by S. Moren has not been available to me.

article in a book they edited in 1968,[1] in which they stressed that literacy enables the criticism of existing social traditions, and hence is a powerful force for social development. Goody extended the scope of this claim in a later work;[2] it has generally been well received among social anthropologists.

Here we see an area in which social anthropology had much to learn from Assyriology, and did not learn it. On the other hand, both an Egyptologist and an Assyriologist have taken the trouble to point to the deficiencies in Goody's thesis by showing the extent to which, everywhere in the ancient Near East, literacy was very much a socially conservative force, or at best a neutral one with respect to existing forces for change.[3] In connexion with the ancient Near East, Oppenheim long ago pointed out that, "The desire to maintain a written tradition represents in itself an important culture trait of Mesopotamian tradition."[4]

What this means in the context of the omen tradition is simple to explain. Scribes, including future diviners, were instructed by means of being taught to copy texts, first of one genre, and then of another. Omens were one of the many genre preserved in the scribal tradition. Omens themselves are straightforwardly casuistic in form. They consist of two parts, a protasis, or "if-clause" (e.g. "if (Akk. *šumma*, usually represented by Sum. BE or DIŠ, more rarely TUKUM.BI) the fissure of the gallbladder (of the sacrificial animal) is split in three parts") and an apodosis, or "then-clause" (e.g., "the god will forgive the sin of the man (*sc.*, the client)"). Omens first began to be collected, as far as we can tell, in the Old Babylonian period (ca. 1850-1600), when they

---

[1] "The Consequences of Literacy", in *Literacy in Traditional Societies* (Cambridge, 1968), pp. 27-68.

[2] *The Domestication of the Savage Mind* (Cambridge, 1977).

[3] Cf. J. Baines, "Literacy and Ancient Egyptian Society", *Man* 18 (1983), pp. 572-99; F. Rochberg-Halton, "Canonicity in Cuneiform Texts", *JCS* 36 (1984), pp. 127-44; in all fairness, though, it should be added that the thesis of Goody and Watt did not long survive uncontradicted by their fellow social anthropologists; see e.g. R. Finnegan, "Literacy versus Non-literacy: The Great Divide?", in: R. Horton and R. Finnegan (eds.), *Modes of Thought. Essays on Thinking in Western and Non-Western Societies* (London, 1973), pp. 112-44.

[4] *AM*, p. 13.

existed in short collections. The evidence suggests that the somewhat pedantic scholars of the succeeding Cassite period (ca. 1600-1200) combined and systematised these collections into extensive series.[1] We do not know the extent of literacy in the Old Babylonian and Cassite

---

[1] On scribal phenomena in general, see C.J. Gadd, *Teachers and Students in the Oldest Schools* (London, 1956); Oppenheim, *AM*, pp. 235-49. On scribal schooling in Neo-Sumerian times, see S.N. Kramer, *The Sumerians. Their History, Culture and Character* (Chicago and London, 1963), pp. 229-48; on Sumerian collections of Wisdom literature, see E.I. Gordon, "A New Look at the Wisdom of Sumer and Akkad", in *BO* 17 (1960), pp. 122-52; further, H.L.J. Vanstiphout, "How Did They Learn Sumerian?", *JCS* 31 (1979), pp. 118-26; for a detailed study of scribal teaching in the Old Akkadian period, see Aa. Westenholz, "Old Akkadian School Texts. Some Goals of Sargonic Scribal Education", in *AfO* 25 (1974-1977) pp. 95-110, esp. pp. 106-10; for procedures in the Old Babylonian schools, M.Çig and H.Kizilyay, *Zwei altbabylonische Schulbücher aus Nippur* (Ankara, 1959); further, R.S. Falkowitz, "Round Old Babylonian School Tablets", in *AfO* 29 (1983/84), pp. 18-45; for the library of an Old Babylonian diviner, see D. Charpin, "Les Archives du Devin Asqudum dans la Résidence du 'Chantier A'", *M.A.R.I.* 4 (1985), pp. 453-62; on the unsystematic nature of the Marian archives, see J.M. Sasson, "Some Comments on Archive Keeping at Mari", in *Iraq* 34 (1972), pp. 55-67; for scribal phenomena in Egypt see A. Schlott, *Schrift und Schreiber im Alten Ägypten* (Munich, 1989); on the dissemination of Mesopotamian scribal learning in the Hittite world, see G. Beckman, "Mesopotamians and Mesopotamian Learning at Hattusa", *JCS* 35 (1983), pp. 97-114. On scribal phenomena in Ugarit, see A.F. Rainey, "The Scribe at Ugarit: His Position and Influence", in *Proceedings of the Israel Academy of Science and the Humanities*, 1968, pp. 1-22. On Cassite collection and editing, see Nougayrol, *La Divination*, p.28; further, Rochberg-Halton, "Canonicity...", p. 127 and n. 2; further, Liverani, *AO*, pp. 620-23. Just how scribal schools functioned in the first millennium we do not really know, but see T.N.D. Mettinger, *Solomonic State Officials* (Lund, 1971), pp. 140-57; see also J.P.J. Oliver, "Schools and Wisdom Literature", *JNWSL* 4 (1975), pp. 49-61; A. Lemaire, *Les écoles et la formation de la bible dans l'ancien Israël* (Göttingen, 1981); (critically reviewed by S. Herrmann in *OLZ* 80 (1985), pp. 255-58; attacked by F.W. Golka, "Die israelitische Weisheitsschule oder 'Des Kaisers neue Kleider'", *VT* 33 (1983), pp. 257-71, with a response by Lemaire in "Sagesse et Écoles", *VT* 34 (1984), pp. 270-81). For literature on the perpetuation of Akkadian cuneiform in the Seleucid period, see S.M. Burstein, *The Babyloniaca of Berossus* (Malibu, CA, 1978) (= *Sources and Monographs. Sources from the Ancient Near East*, Vol. 1, Fasc. 5), p. 5, n. 4; and for a brief characterisation see G.J.P. McEwan, *Priest and Temple in Hellenistic Babylonia* (Wiesbaden, 1981) (= *Freiburger Altorientalischen Studien*, Vol.4), pp. 183-87.

periods; in 1983, however, S. Parpola provided evidence that Assurbani-pal's famous library was composed of (more or less) voluntary contributions from private donors, which, among other things, explains why the collection contains so many duplicates of incomplete series of tablets: people were donating their left-overs.[1] Recent publications have shown that the city of Assur contained by the time of its fall in 614 at least 27 private archives.[2]

The evidence from first-millennium Assyria suggests that literacy had become relatively widespread under the Sargonids. This gives us reason for pause. We have seen previously that in societies which practice divination, the phenomenon is regarded as a valuable form of knowledge. Since the Mesopotamian tradition was massively literary, a rise in literacy would have been synonymous with the tradition's becoming more accessible to ordinary folk. This cannot but have resulted in a certain devaluation of its significance.

The Phenomenology of Mesopotamian Divination

Assyriologists have traditionally distinguished between *omina oblativa* and *omina impetrativa*, that is, between those which simply present themselves to the attention of the observer (like a lunar eclipse), and those which the observer himself provokes (like an omen sacrifice, or extispicy).[3] Both, however, depend on the previous knowledge and intention of the diviner (note that most moderns would not recognise a lunar eclipse if they saw one), so the distinction is less than useful.

---

[1] "Assyrian Library Records", *JNES* 42 (1983), pp. 1-29.

[2] O. Pedersén, *Archives and Libraries in the City of Assur. A Survey of the Material from the German Excavations*, (Uppsala, 1986), (= *Studia Semitica Upsaliensis* 6 & 8), Vol.1, pp. 140-45. The collection of literary works in Assur was possibly initiated already in the reign of Tiglath-pileser I (ca. 1114-1076); cf. E.F. Weidner, "Die Bibliothek Tiglatpilesers I." in *AfO* 16 (1952/53), pp. 197-215, esp. pp. 199-202. See, however, Pedersén, *Archives*, Vol.1, pp. 31-2, who disputes the attribution to Tiglath Pileser I. Unavailable to me was K.R. Veenhof (ed.), *Cuneiform Archives and Libraries. Compte Rendu de la XXXe Rencontre Assyriologique Internationale à Leyde (1-3 Juillet 1983)* (Leiden, 1986).

[3] Cf. Jastrow, *Aspects of Religious Belief*, pp. 144-47; Boissier, *Mantique Babylonienne et Mantique Hittite*, p. 3; with qualifications, C.J. Gadd in *DM*, pp. 22-23.

Socially, though, there is certainly a distinction: sheep for the omen sacrifice are expensive, whereas shooting-stars and the like come free. Also, some ominous phenomena are clearly so only by virtue of the conventions of the discipline (e.g., features of the exta of the sheep, which the common man would not be likely to know), and therefore require an extensive education for their interpretation, whereas others (like the birth of monstrous animal or human offspring) are more immediately "portentous". We shall see that there is good reason to believe that Mesopotamian divination existed at numerous levels, from the royal diviners down to private individuals.[1] This being the case, one must recognise that ancient Near Eastern society was permeated by a continuum of ideas and attitudes surrounding divination.

Methods, Geographical and Chronological Distribution
Astrology
Though the practice of linking stellar phenomena with prognostics is attested as early as the Old Babylonian period,[2] the textual witness is

---

[1] In *DM*, p. 37, Oppenheim allowed for a current of "folklore" divination running alongside of his "scholarly" variety. It might be more accurate to say that the basic premises of magical thought and behaviour are accepted by both "high" and "low" strata in any society which embraces magic. The forms of magic actually practised in a given society will then vary as to presumed effectiveness, status, sex, (notional) access to knowledge provided by the method in question, and so forth. At least, this is surely the case among the Azande and comparable African societies, as we have seen; it appears to have been the case throughout the ancient Near East; and, as R. Kieckhefer has shown (*European Witch Trials: Their Foundation in Popular and Learned Culture, 1300-1500* (London, 1976); *Magic in the Middle Ages* (Cambridge, 1990 [1989])), it was also the case in the medieval European tradition.

[2] It is possible that already the Sumerians knew some form of prognostication based on astrology; note that already the Gudea Cylinder (A IV:7-VI:14 = TCL VIII pl. 4-5, ET in Oppenheim, *Dreams*, pp. 245-46) speaks of "The first woman. . . a stylus she held in (her) hand, a tablet of (?) heavenly stars she put on (her) knees, consulting it. . . ."(p. 245). B. Alster, *Studies in Sumerian Proverbs* (Copenhagen, 1975), pp. 102-3 and p. 130, n. 6-7, sees in this a reference to "astral archetypes", whatever that may mean.

limited to the "Venus Tablet of Ammisaduqa",[1] plus text finds from such diverse places as Ugarit, Boghazkeui, Qatna, Mari, and Elam.[2] Oppenheim notes that "the fact that astrological texts were translated into Elamite and Hittite emphasizes the readiness with which this type of divination was accepted outside of Babylonia proper."[3] This should not surprise us; D.L. O'Keefe has shown the extent to which "magical symbolism travels easily and accumulates a history" and we shall see that this is very much the case with virtually all forms of Mesopotamian divination. Only sparsely attested in the second millennium, astrology eventually supplanted extispicy as the pre-eminent form of Mesopotamian divination,[4] and was represented in Assurbanipal's great library by the so-called "canonical"[5] omen series *Enuma Anu Enlil* (originally compiled c.1400-900).[6] In addition to astrological omens, the series also concerns itself with meteorological and seismic phenomena; it will

[1] B.L. van der Waerden, "Babylonian Astronomy I", *Jaarboek, Ex Oriente Lux* 10 (1948), p. 414; see the edition of E. Reiner and D. Pingree (above); and see C.B.F. Walker, "Notes on the Venus Tablet of Ammisaduqa", *JCS* 36 (1984), pp. 64-66, and, above all, W.G. Lambert's thoughtful criticisms in *JAOS* 107 (1987), pp. 93-96.

[2] See Rochberg-Halton, *Aspects*, pp. 5-6, for the continuity of the astrological tradition behind *Enuma anu enlil* from the Old Babylonian period until the Seleucid period. For astrological omens at Ugarit, see M. Dietrich and O. Loretz,"Sonnenfinsternis in Ugarit. PRU 2,162 (=RS 12.61), Das älteste Dokument über eine Totaleklipse", in *Ugarit Forschung* 6 (1974), pp. 464-65; further, M. Dietrich et al. *Mantik in Ugarit. Keilalphabetische Texte der Opferschau— Omensammlungen—Nekromantie* (Munster, 1990) (= *Abhandlungen zur Literatur Alt-Syrien-Palästinas*, Bd. 3), pp. 165-195; for the other sites mentioned, see Oppenheim, *AM*, p. 224 and p. 374 n. 6.

[3] *AM*, p. 224.

[4] See already Oppenheim's study, "Divination and Celestial Observation"; which has been amply confirmed by S. Parpola's *Letters from Assyrian Scholars* (see above).

[5] For the distinction between the broad Near Eastern copying tradition and the canonisation of Biblical works, see F. Rochberg-Halton, "Canonicity in Cuneiform Texts", pp. 127-44.

[6] Cf. B.L.van der Waerden, "Babylonian Astronomy II. The Thirty-Six Stars", *JNES* 8 (1949), p. 18; and see the edition of E. Weidner, above, and the collaboration of E. Reiner and D. Pingree mentioned previously.

originally have consisted of more than 70 tablets coming from Babylon, Borsippa, Uruk, Kish, and Nippur.[1] Note that "astrology" is not to be confused with "genethliology" (horoscopic astrology), which was a very late and relatively rare development within the Babylonian tradition.[2] If ever a case could be made for cultural diffusion, the materials of Mesopotamian astrology provide a particularly impressive example, in part because the omen series was linked to some extent with specifically Mesopotamian forms of astronomical computation, and in part because the very types of observation which were considered significant were so characteristically Mesopotamian.[3] There is considerable evidence of the spread of knowledge of the contents of Enuma Anu Enlil to both India and Egypt in the Achaemenid period, and of Achaemenid and Seleucid-period astronomical and astrological lore to both Egypt and Greece in the Hellenistic period.[4]

---

[1] Cf. Oppenheim, *AM*, p. 225 and p. 374 n. 69. It should be noted that astrological omens were completely lacking from the collection of Tiglath-Pileser I at Assur (cf. Weidner, *AfO* 16 (1952/53), p. 204). Thus the vast collection of Assurbanipal and the extensive correspondence between astrologers and the royal courts of Esarhaddon and Assurbanipal, so effectively demonstrated by Oppenheim and Parpola, represent a major innovation of the first millennium.

[2] Cf. O. Neugebauer, "History of Ancient Astronomy", in (ed. *idem*) *Astronomy and History*, pp. 57-59; on the mysterious origins of the Zodiac, see B.L. van der Waerden, "History of the Zodiac", *AfO* 16 (1952/53), pp. 216-30.

[3] See D. Pingree, "Mesopotamian Astronomy and Astral Omens in Other Civilizations", in H.-J. Nissen and J. Renger, eds, *Mesopotamien und seine Nachbarn* (= *XXV. Rencontre Assyriologique Internationale Berlin, 3. bis 7. Juli 1978*) (Berlin, 1978), pp. 613-31, esp. pp. 617-23. Pingree holds that "The serious misunderstandings of many of the optical and astronomical phenomena mentioned in Enuma Anu Enlil that are displayed by the compilers of the tablets preserved in Assurbanipal's library indicate that there was a break in the tradition" (p. 613). This is not necessarily so; as I shall argue below (in connexion with birth omens), and as I have already suggested previously, the tradents of these materials were not particularly interested in empirical correctness.

[4] I find one feature to which Pingree points as evidence of the diffusion of Mesopotamian astronomical and astrological lore into the Indian cultural ambit especially interesting. This is his argument that the 360-day-year, based on 12 months of 30 days, which is preserved in the treatise MUL.APIN, also influenced the calendrical reckoning in the liturgical calendar in the Rigveda (p. 615). I have previously argued in a number of articles that a 360-day calendar, based on 12

Oil Omens

Also attested for the OB period is prognostication based on the pouring

months of 30 days, is detectable both in the Old Testament and in such extra-Bib-
lical works as Ethiopic Enoch and the Book of Jubilees (see F.H. Cryer, "The
Interrelationships of Gen 5,32; 11,10-11 and the Chronology of the Flood", *Bib* 66
(1985), pp. 241-61, esp. pp. 256-60; "The 360-Day Calendar Year and Early Judaic
Sectarianism", *SJOT* 1 (1987), pp. 116-22; "To the One of Fictive Music: OT
Chronology and History", *SJOT* 2 (1987), pp. 21-27). J.M. Sasson has recently
shown that the same system was possibly in use in ancient Mari (in "Zimri-Lim
Takes the Grand Tour" in *BA*, Dec. 1984, p. 249). A year later (in "'Year:
Zimri-Lim Offered a Great Throne to Shamash of Mahanum'. An Overview of One
Year in Mari. Part I: The Presence of the King", in *M.A.R.I.* 4 [1985] p. 440 n. 10).
Sasson noted that "it may well be that Mari did not try to balance lengths of days
within each month in order to obtain an aggregate of twelve 29-day months, the
normal lunar year. If so, we may then have to regard the Mari year as 12 X 30 =
360 days and have to endure the havoc that this condition will create to our
recreation of a number of festivals and celebrations!" In fact, a Marian *ikribu*
(divining prayer) makes the request for a safe oracle covering the time period of
6 šu-ši u4-ma-tim/ 6 šu-ši (u4)-mu-ši-a-tim, "six sixties of days (and) six sixties of
nights", which shows that the Marian 360-day calendar was known to the local
diviners as well (cf. IM 80213 obv. 8-9; published in G. van Driel, et al. (eds.),
*Zikir Šumim. Assyriological Studies Presented to F.R.Kraus on the Occasion of his
Seventieth Birthday* (Leiden, 1982), p. 274). Moreover, this usage persisted until
quite late; the Neo-Assyrian "diviner's manual" also explicitly informs us that
"twelve are the months of the year, 360 are its days" (cf. A.L. Oppenheim, "A
Babylonian Diviner's Manual", *JNES* 33 (1974) p. 105, line 57); furthermore, a
letter published by Parpola (*Letters from Assyrian Scholars*, I, Nr. 100, pp. 68-69)
shows that Sargonid star-gazers reckoned with a "normal" month of 30 days, as is
also supported by the "astronomical diaries" ((cf. A.J. Sachs-H. Hunger,
*Astronomical Diaries and Related Texts from Babylonia. Vol.I. Diaries from 652
B.C. to 262 B.C.* (Vienna, 1988), p. 38). Moreover, a 360-day-year calendar was in
use in ancient China from the 13th century at the latest; it was an adjunct to the
liturgical scheme employed in tortoiseshell divination, which had been practised in
China ever since the Shang dynasty. Interestingly, however, the Chinese liturgical
calendar was based on 36 weeks of 10 days (cf.Tung Tso-Pin, *Fifty Years of Studies
in Oracle Inscriptions* (Tokyo, 1964), esp. pp. 98-99); Prof. Tung Tso-Pin had
originally conjectured that this scheme was accomodated to a luni-solar intercolated
calendar (in "Ten Examples of Early Tortoise-shell Inscriptions", *Harvard Journal
of Asiatic Studies* 11 [1948], pp. 119-29). It appears that 360-day-year calendars,
liturgical, practical, or otherwise, were universal in the ancient Orient.

of water upon oil or oil upon water in a divining-bowl.[1] The resultant reaction was then classified according to colouration, motion, division or uniting of the oil, its form in relation to the beaker, or to the water. The diviner performed this act with the bowl between his thighs, crouching, facing east, at sunrise. Orientation towards the north and east were regarded as favourable, south and west as unfavourable. The numbers 1-2 (of bubbles formed by the oil) were propitious, while 3-7 were unfavourable. Texts have come down to us from northern and southern Babylon, Boghazkeui, and Assur.[2]

The question as to whether oil divination persisted into the first millennium is not settled; the great Shamash Hymn published by W.G. Lambert[3] refers to the "seer's bowl with the cedar-wood appurtenance". The hymn in question existed in five copies in Assurbanipal's library, so the existence or non-existence of the practice depends in part on whether one regards the reference as a first-millennium archaism. The same applies to the reference to the diviner as an *apkal šamni*, "knower of oil", in Assurbanipal's "In Praise of Shamash";[4] the phrase recurs among the "Ritualtafeln" of the diviner published by Zimmern, where we are also told that the diviner's capabilities include the ability "to look at water on oil".[5] Also, three rescensions of Esarhaddon's so-called

---

[1] A single reference from the Neo-Sumerian period seems to have escaped Pettinato's attention: (E.I. Gordon, *Sumerian Proverbs* (Philadelphia, 1959), Nr. 2.4:) "I looked into the water: (it was) my Fate which was walking there!" Gordon took this to be a possible reference to the practice of hydromancy, which is entirely possible.

[2] Texts were originally published by J. Hunger, *Becherwahrsagung bei den Babyloniern* (Leipzig, 1903) (=*LSS* I,1); modern edition by G. Pettinato, *Die Ölwahrsagung bei den Babyloniern*, I-II; and see Pettinato's introductory remarks in "Zur Überlieferungsgeschichte der aB Ölomentexte", in *DM*, pp. 95-109.

[3] In *Babylonian Wisdom Literature* (Oxford, 1975 [1967]), p. 128, line 53 (ET p. 129).

[4] Cited by Pettinato in *Die Ölwahrsagung*, Vol. 1, p. 20.

[5] H. Zimmern, *Beiträge zur Kenntnis der babylonischen Religion* (Leipzig, 1896), Nr. 24 (p. 116), line 7: šamne ina me na-ta-lu; for *apkal šamni*, read by Zimmern *abkal šamni*, see Nr. 24, line 23 (p. 118). Cf. Pettinato, Vol. 1, p. 20 for other examples. W.G. Lambert made a number of joins to Zimmern's Nr. 24, thus arriving at a fairly complete text, of Neo-Assyrian provenance, which traces the knowledge of oil divination back to the gift of knowledge by Shamash and Adad to

"Babylon Inscription" record that the king resorted to both oil divination and extispicy to assure himself of the correctness of rebuilding Babylon, which his father, Sennacherib, had destroyed.[1]

In short, the diviner continued to be known as a "knower of oil", but the practice of oil-divination seems largely to have dropped out of the official literary tradition. However, as Pettinato has observed, it reappears in Egypt in Demotic texts of the 2nd or 3rd centuries AD which display an astonishing parallelism to the baru-ritual and allow us to suppose that oil divination was imported into Egypt from Babylon".[2] To explain this, as well as the subsequent appearance of similar forms of divination in the ancient Near East, we must either hypothecate a 2,000 year-long process of tradition at the cult level which has somehow fully escaped the countless excavations, or we must assume that this type of divination had become "democratised", that is, popularised, and so dropped out of the "official" tradition. An indication that this was the case is provided by the reference to oil divination in Esarhaddon's "Babylon Inscription". If this type of divination had ceased to be practised, or if it was regarded as of no account, it could hardly have served the obvious purpose of demonstrating that Esarhaddon acted in accord with the divine will, that is, the ideological function of legitimation. Moreover, it occurs in the text in question alongside extispicy, another form of divination which, as I have already mentioned, had mainly lost its official status by the Neo-Assyrian period, and yet which is obviously also assumed to be capable of providing divine legitimation. It is therefore possible that both types of prognostication had dropped out of the *official* tradition, while remaining high in *popular* esteem. If this was the case, it will have accompanied, and perhaps been caused by, the increase in literacy of which I have already spoken.

Enmeduranki, the seventh antediluvian king of ancient Sippar, who then passed on the knowledge to "the men of Nippur, Sippar and Babylon" (cf. "Enmeduranki and Related Matters", *JCS* 21 (1967), pp. 126-38; here p. 132 (text and ET).

[1] Cf. M. Cogan, "Omens and Ideology in the Babylon Inscription of Esarhaddon", in: H. Tadmor and M. Weinfeld (eds.), *History, Historiography and Interpretation* (Jerusalem and Leiden, 1984 [1983]), pp. 79-80.

[2] Pettinato, *Ölwahrsagung*, Vol. 1, p. 24.

Incense Omens

The practice of divination by interpreting the behaviour of smoke arising from an incense-brazier is attested for the OB period alone.[1] The rite was performed, as in the case of oil-divination, with the censer in the lap of the diviner, facing east.[2] I know of no 1st-millennium attestations in Mesopotamia or Syro-Palestine, but the phenomenon was common in the Greco-Roman world,[3] although we obviously cannot speak of "cultural diffusion" in this instance.

Birth Omens

The technique of divination based on the interpretation of monstrous births, whether human or animal, seems to have enjoyed great favour in the OB period and later. Two separate series of omens were collected; one of these, called *šumma sinništu aratma*, after its incipit, deals with human mutations; the other, *šumma izbu*, deals with animal anomalies.[4] Though "canonically" collected into extensive series, the izbu-type omina were nevertheless not as concretely delimited as some others, such as, for example, extispical omina. Thus there is a portion of

---

[1] Only four texts are known at all, which makes it surprising that they continue to recur in histories of divination as a "genre"; the publication of G. Pettinato, "Libanomanzia presso i Babilonesi", *RSO* 41 (1966), pp. 303-27, containing two of the texts, while not exact, nevertheless takes pains to relate the phenomenon to the general divinatory practice. Pettinato's texts were collated and re-published by R.D. Biggs, "A propos des textes de libanomancie", *RA* 63 (1969), pp. 73-74; additional notes plus collation of a third text are provided by E. Leichty in "Literary Notes", in M. de Jong Ellis (ed.), *Ancient Near Eastern Studies in Memory of J.J. Finkelstein* (Hamden [Connecticut], 1977), pp. 143-44; the fourth has been published by I.L. Finkel, "A New Piece of Libanomancy", *AfO* 29 (1983), pp. 50-57.

[2] Cf. Pettinato, "Libanomanzia", p. 307, who shows that the spatial terminology used is identical to that employed in oil divination.

[3] References in Pettinato, "Libanomanzia", p. 308.

[4] See E. Leichty, *Šumma Izbu*; and his introductory remarks to the genre in *DM*, pp. 131-41; see also S.M. Moren, "Šumma Izbu XIX: New Light on the Animal Omens", *AfO* 27 (1980) 53-70; "anomaly" is Leichty's preferred rendering of *izbu*. For *šumma izbu* omens at Ras Shamra-Ugarit, see M. Dietrich, O. Loretz and J. Sanmartin, "Der keilalphabetische šumma izbu-text RS 24.247+265+268+328", in *UF* 7 (1979), pp. 134-40; further, M. Dietrich et al., *Mantik in Ugarit*, pp. 87-165.

izbu-like omina in the great "catch-all" category of *šumma ālu* omens.[1]
Leichty points out that

> Tablets of šumma izbu come from the Old Babylonian period, from
> Boghazkoi in Akkadian, Hittite and Hurrian, from Ugarit in Akkadian
> and Ugaritic, and from Kuyunjik, Assur, Nimrud, Sultantepe, Susa,
> Babylon, Borsippa, and Uruk.[2]

The chronological dispersion of the texts ranges from the Old Babylonian period until well down into the first millennium.[3]

While no rituals are known for warding off the evils portended by
oil or incense omina, some namburbis did exist for countering the
effects of unfortunate izbu portents.[4] We also possess some "reports"
written by diviners of the Sargonid court on various izbus they had been
ordered to investigate.[5] Since apotropaic rituals were the province of the
Mesopotamian exorcist, while omens were the specialty of the diviner,
it is clear that there was an official and well established collaboration
between these two types of specialist, at least in the Neo-Assyrian
world, and perhaps elsewhere and in other times as well (although no
second-millennium namburbis are known). Whether izbu-type omens
were also recognised by the peasantry and dealt with on a more
primitive level is an imponderable, although, given the popularity of this
sort of omen in rural societies as disparate as Shakespeare's England
and modern-day Sicily, it seems very likely.

As Leichty points out, the apodoses of izbu-omina fall naturally

---

[1] Cf. S.M. Moren, "Summa Izbu XIX", p. 53.

[2] *DM*, p. 131.

[3] Some interesting evidence of the very late persistence of izbu-type omen
observation is provided by the so-called "astronomical diaries" recently published
by H. Hunger in completion of the work of the late A.J. Sachs (*Astronomical
Diaries and Related Texts*). Among the numerous observations of heavenly bodies,
the weather, meteors, market-prices, and the level of the Euphrates, we also find
such notices as the remark that "a ewe gave birth and (the young) had no jaw" (No.-
418, lines 9' and 10') and "a she-goat gave birth, and (the kid) had a. . .and the ears
of a fish, and on its head were. . .and a lock like that of a slave" (No.-324, lines
6-7).

[4] Cf. *Šumma Izbu*, p. 12; and Caplice, "Namburbi Texts", *Or* N.S. 34 (1965),
pp. 125-31.

[5] Examples are provided by Leichty in *Šumma Izbu*, pp. 8-11.

into two classes, public and private. The public variety have to do with the well-being of the king, the nation, or the army (e.g., "the prince's/-king's land will revolt against him"); they are stereotyped and also occur in omens from other genres. Private apodoses, as one might expect, strike closer to home (e.g., "that child will not prosper").

Excursus: "Empirical" Omens?

A question which arises in connexion with the izbu-type omens is worth considering. We have seen that Assyriologists have had difficulties in determining the status of the diviner and his various practices. Briefly, they have been aware that the phenomenon itself was often subordinated to the dominant theologies of ancient Mesopotamia; for example, extispicies were usually undertaken as direct questions addressed to the deities Šamaš and Adad. This seemed to suggest that the diviner was a sort of priest.[1] On the other hand, there has long been a perception of the diviner as a scholar, one whose observations of natural phenomena had something of the pre-scientific about them, even though, as we have seen, researchers like O. Neugebauer, A.K. Grayson and J. Van Seters have strenuously opposed the notion of any possible co-existence of "magic" and "science". In the understanding of the various omen-series the "proto-scientific" perception, with its attendant emphasis on the "empirical" nature of omens, has played a much more important rôle than scholars are aware.

For example, in his study of the izbu omina, Leichty has devoted several pages to a study as to whether most of the reported anomalies can, in the way of things, actually occur.[2] With some qualifications, he answers in the affirmative. Ms. Moren is even more certain of the empirical basis of the series, as she invariably translates the preterites of the protases of Tablet XIX in the English past tense (e.g., (omen 1) "If a cow gave birth and the offspring had two heads"). She also

---

[1] The diviner is in fact listed among the members of the priesthood in the excellent survey of these personnel in the OB period by J. Renger: "Untersuchungen zum Priestertum in der altbabylonischen Zeit", 1.Teil, *ZA* 58 (1967), pp. 110-88; 2.Teil *ZA* 59 (1969), pp. 104-246; here 59 (1969), pp. 203-17.

[2] *Šumma Izbu*, pp. 16-20.

defends this decision with the remark that,

> the use of the preterite may be characteristic of the nature of omen formulation. The omen was not originally perceived as hypothetical. It occurred; it was observed. It therefore represented an occurrence as surely past or completed as any other action expressed by a preterite verb.[1]

And yet both Leichty and Moren have, of course, noted that some patently impossible protases sometimes figure in Šumma Izbu. Leichty explains this fact in two ways: some of the omens, like Izbu III 1 ("If a woman gives birth and the child has the ear of a lion") have to be understood "metaphorically".[2] Other cases, however, "can easily be explained as late additions"; and Leichty goes on to say that "It seems obvious that the series was originally based on observed omens and then expanded later".[3] Thus two principles, "metaphor" and "historical text development" are drawn into service to "save the appearances" for empiricism. In reality, though, in spite of the previously-mentioned wealth of Izbu tablets from most of the ancient Near East, there is no demonstrable sequence whereby we can illustrate the addition of "impossible" omens to a previously-existing sequence of "possible" ones. Thus the purported "textual history" is purely *ad hoc*, introduced only for the purpose of "making sense" of apparent nonsense. Moreover, the idea itself is peculiar: what is claimed is that there was an original stage of sober, observationally-minded empiricists, whose carefully-garnered records of animal and human births somehow got into the hands of the sort of lunatic (seen from an "empirical" point of view) who could write the following prognostic: (XVII 76´) "If an anomaly's womb is full of faces. . .one head of a monkey, one head of a lion, one head of a human, one head of a pig—the land will go mad. . . ." In actuality, this is not to postulate historical evolution, but rather *devolution*, that is, the surrender of empiricism to other concerns—and I doubt that Leichty really wants to maintain this.

Another case in point is drawn from the astrological omens preserved in the "canonical" omen series, *Enūma Anu Enlil*. F. Roch-

---

[1] Moren, "Šumma Izbu XIX", p. 55.

[2] *Šumma Izbu*, p. 19.

[3] *Šumma Izbu*, p. 20.

berg-Halton has in her study of this series called attention to the fact that there is an anomaly in connexion with the lunar eclipse omens. In the nature of things, lunar eclipses can only occur on only one of four possible days grouped around the middle of the lunar month. Mesopotamian observers were well aware of this; they were even able accurately to *predict* lunar eclipses by some time in the Achaemenid period. The question is, then, why the series in question also contains, both in its early and in its late versions, omens based on eclipses (notionally) taking place on "impossible" days.[1]

My point is that the concern to regard omen texts as "protoscience" imports yet again the false distinction between magic and science/empiricism into the study of the texts (in Moren's case, even into her philological understanding of them![2]) and the phenomenon they represent. To exemplify the dangers of this, note that a similar confusion has plagued the social anthropological perception of, for example, cannibalism, for quite some time. Inclined to disbelieve in "witches", anthropologists paid only scant attention to native claims that witches devour the flesh of their victims. However, with visions of missionaries boiling in the tribal pot in the backs of their minds, they were more than willing to credit the claim of tribe B that members of tribe A are cannibals. Contemporary research indicates that actual cannibalism, ritual or otherwise, is a rare phenomenon indeed.[3] Accordingly, what is really of interest is not whether event A or B can take place, but what is signified by the various *claims* that it has. With this point and our previous discussion of Evans-Pritchard and the Azande in mind, it might seem to be a better idea to attempt an analysis of the symbolisations involved in the omen protases and apodoses, and in the juxtapositions of protases and apodoses. Moreover, the symbolisations present in

---

[1] Rochberg-Halton, *Aspects*, pp. 25; 38-40.

[2] The key which activates the Akk. preterite in omens is the introductory *šumma*, as in law codes; the latter do not necessarily reflect events which have ever taken place (many prohibitions seek to prevent certain kinds of behaviour, not merely to punish them), so there is no grammatic-syntactical apriori case for Moren's assumption. See R. Westbrook, "Biblical and Cuneiform Law Codes", *RB* 92 (1985) pp. 247-64, here esp. p. 253 and n. 27.

[3] See similarly, with rich irony, I.M. Lewis, "The Cannibal's Cauldron", in *Religion in Context*, pp. 63-78, esp. pp. 69-70.

omens are not isolated phenomena, as is proved by, among other things, the collaboration between the diviner and the exorcist in the case of the izbu omens; symbolisations arise out of the context of the society as a whole, and may, as D.L. O'Keefe has argued, ultimately derive from native systems of classification. Thus omen texts must further be approached through the vantage of the assumptions pertaining to them, which in the context of Assyro-Babylonian societies means the theologies in which they play an explicit rôle. Also, there is the question of the constitutive rules governing the sort of phenomena that, in this case, can count as "anomalies".[1] Finally, it would be useful if we could examine a series of actual "case histories", from the discovery of an anomaly to its being reported to a diviner for interpretation and possible ritual action by the exorcist, which might tell us something about the social significance (use) of the phenomenon.

A point of comparison presents itself. I mentioned in the introduction to this work that it would be a mistake to imagine that any ancient society possessed a conception of "empiricism", and that this is one of the primary factors separating ancient mentalities from our own. As I there showed, even in cases where precise observation of stellar events was essential to their understanding, Babylonian scholars had no hesitation to fill non-observed data into their schemata.[2] However, since

---

[1] In this connexion, Leichty's observation (*Šumma Izbu*, p. 19) that some of the most common human birth defects, like harelip and cleft palate, do *not* figure in the series may prove important. This is surely problematical for the assumption of the "empirical" basis of these omens. I am, of course, not denying that Mesopotamian diviners knew the outcomes of normal births, any more than I am claiming that they did not know, in the case of the omen sacrifice, what the insides of a sheep look like (on their anatomical knowledge, see J.-H. Scharf, "Anfänge von systematischer Anatomie und Teratologie im alten Babylon", *Sitzungsbericht der Sächsischen Akademie der Wissenschaften. Mathematisch-naturwissenschaftliche Klasse* 120 (1988, Berlin). I am merely claiming that their purposes were other than empirical-classificatory, and that the study of what they were up to is not well served by comparing it with what they did not intend.

[2] This remained true even in very late periods in Mesopotamian history; in a fine study ("A Classification of the Babylonian Astronomical Tablets of the Seleucid Period", *JCS* 2 (1948), pp. 271-90), A. Sachs observed that "A somewhat startling result is that all classes of Seleucid astronomical texts contain at least some predictions" (p. 271; by "predictions", Sachs means figures that were extrapolated from existing observations rather than observed). Similar observations by O. Neuge-

we can compute what they must have been able to see, and what not, we can catch them at it, and correct their figures: but we are prepared to do so precisely because we are "empiricists", and they were not; they would have been quite content (and, historically, *were* quite content) to transmit non-observed data to posterity. Now with respect to precise phenomena like heliacal rising times and the like, the numbers either fit or they do not, so we can always detect bad data. But, faced with the multitude of things that can go wrong in the transmission of genetic information, there is no way to determine which izbu omens are based on observed phenomena (except for the obvious absurdities), and which are not. Accordingly, the correspondence of any omen to the "real" world is to be demonstrated and not assumed.

Excursus: The So-Called "Historical" Omens

This insight must have consequences for the philological understanding of individual omina, although Assyriologists appear, as a group, not to have realised this as yet. Moreover, it has important implications for a discussion which the Assyriologists have conducted for quite some time, namely the question of the historicity of the so-called "historical omens".

Assyriologists have been aware of the category of so-called "historical omens" for quite some time. They are simply omens whose apodoses refer to various Mesopotamian kings of the dim past, such as Sargon the Great (ca. 2334-2279), Naram-Sin (ca. 2254-2218), and Amar-Suen (ca. 2046-2038), as well as such quasi-mythical figures as Gilgamesh. Example: "If the gall-bladder (in an extispicy) is formed like

bauer are presented in "Some Atypical Cuneiform Texts.I", *JCS* 21 (1967), pp. 183-218. If Johannes Kepler and Tycho Brahe had "fudged" their observational data in trying to derive the structure of the solar system, the "Copernican Revolution" — the breakthrough of modern empiricism — could not have taken place; cf. T.S. Kuhn, *The Copernican Revolution. Planetary Astronomy in the Development of Western Thought* (New York, 1959 [1957]), pp. 185-260. The distinction is relatively simple: Babylonian and Assyrian observations were pragmatic, that is, only as precise as they had to be in order to achieve one or another fairly concrete and delimited goal (e.g., an intercalation sequence for harmonising the lunar and solar calendars). An empiricist may have a particular goal in mind, but he will exclude no data in his pursuit of it.

a lizard (it is) an omen of Sargon". Texts and/or varying degrees of commentary have been published by M. Jastrow,[1] J. Nougayrol,[2] A.L. Oppenheim,[3] A. Goetze,[4] J.J. Finkelstein,[5] E. Reiner,[6] I. Starr,[7] and J. Cooper,[8] among others. Scholars have been willing to invest these statements with varying amounts of plausibility,[9] but the more recent scholars in the above list have grown cautious. As outlined by Jastrow, the ominous "signs" recorded in connexion with a given historical figure are those which were observed on the occasion of a sacrifice immediately preceding some important event in the life of that figure, which explains why the "signs" were recorded. Goetze finds this likely in view of the practice of modelling certain especially significant configurations of the liver for teaching purposes.[10] E. Reiner, however, points out that

---

[1] *Die Religion Assyriens und Babyloniens*, pp. 213-44; *Religious Belief in Babylonia and Assyria*, pp. 175-180.

[2] "Note sur la place des présages historiques dans l'extispicine babylonienne", in *Ecole Pratique des Hautes Etudes , Section des Sciences Religieuses, Annuaire* (1944-45), pp. 5-41. And see the historicising interpretation of A. Spycket, "Illustration d'un text hépatoscopique concernant Sargon d'Agade (?)", *RA* 40 (1945-46), pp. 151-56.

[3] In his previously-mentioned article, "Zur keilschriftlichen Omenliteratur", pp. 199-228.

[4] "Historical Allusions in Old Babylonian Omen Texts", *JCS* 1 (1947), pp. 253-66.

[5] *Proceedings of the American Philosophical Society* 107 (1963), pp. 461-72.

[6] "New Light on Some Historical Omens", in: *Anatolian Studies Presented to Hans Gustav Güterbock on the Occasion of his 65th Birthday* (Istanbul, 1974), pp. 257-61.

[7] "Notes on Some Published and Unpublished Historical Omens", *JCS* 29 (1977) pp. 157-66; *idem*, "Historical Omens Concerning Ashurbanipal's War Against Elam", *AfO* 32 (1985), pp. 60-67 (containing an interesting "modern" omen referring to Assurbanipal).

[8] "Apodictic Death and the Historicity of 'Historical' Omens", in: B. Alster (ed.), *Death in Mesopotamia. XXVIe Rencontre assyriologique internationale* (= *Mesopotamia* 8) (Copenhagen, 1980), pp. 99-105.

[9] E.g. Jastrow *(Religious Belief*, p. 175) and also Ungnad *(Die Deutung der Zukunft*, p. 5) were quite convinced of their historical reliability.

[10] "Historical Allusions. . .", p. 265.

much of the "information" preserved in such apodoses is purely anecdotal, and, as such, of little "historical" interest.[1] J. Cooper has very sensibly asked the question that, if a given configuration actually occurred in a sacrifice prior to, say, the death of ruler X by a "cylinder seal", how does it happen that the "cylinder seal" (or Amar-Suen's "bite of a shoe") death is also attested for ruler Y? He further points out that the entire tendency of omen apodoses was to interpret them "in a general way, as simply favorable or unfavorable".[2] This observation has been further developed by I. Starr, who, having already published an omen which records the death of Amar-Suen from both "the goring of an ox" and "the bite of a shoe",[3] logically concludes that

> for purposes of prediction, the historical worth of the so-called historical omens or lack thereof is quite irrelevant. Within the corpus of apodoses as a whole the historical omens served as any other, i.e., they were either favorable or unfavorable. The wording of these apodoses was relevant only in as much as it defined the nature of the omen: favorable or unfavorable, as the case may be.[4]

Since it does not seem likely that two separate Mesopotamian kings were attacked by cylinder seals, nor that poor Amar-Suen died two different ways, one is forced to agree with Cooper and Starr. The interest of this in our connexion, however, is that we have already seen in the case of the izbu-omens that the protases of omens need not be based on experience; now we have to conclude that the apodoses may be equally non-empirical. Once again, considering our review of the social anthropological material on divination, this can hardly be surprising: but it may help to point Assyriologists on the way to a more fruitful interpretation of the omen tradition. If, as I have previously argued, divination is a species of performative utterance, then it is implicitly non-empirical (i.e., a command or a promise can neither be true nor false).

---

[1] "New Light on some Historical Omens", *passim*.

[2] "Apodictic Death and the Historicity of 'Historical' Omens", *passim*.

[3] "Notes on Some Published and Unpublished Historical Omens", p. 161, lines 1-3.

[4] "Historical Omens Concerning Ashurbanipal's War Against Elam", p. 63.

The Interpretation of Dreams

Dreams were regarded as significant already in Neo-Sumerian times. In one of the texts of the Dumuzi cycle(s), Dumuzi (Babylonian Tammuz) has a troubling dream; on awakening, he cries out,

> Bring, bring, bring my sister! Bring my Geštinanna, bring my sister! Bring my tablet-knowing scribe, bring my sister! Bring my song-knowing singer, bring my sister! Bring my skilful girl, who knows the meaning of words, bring my sister! Bring my wise woman, who knows the portent of dreams, bring my sister![1]

The reference to Dumuzi's sister as a "tablet-knowing scribe" in connexion with the interpretation of dreams suggests that already in Neo-Sumerian times, dream interpretation was a learned skill, the province of literate specialists. Interestingly, in the famous epic of Gilgamesh, the Sumerian version of the text records that Gilgamesh's mother interpreted her son's dream-warning of the advent of Enkidu, suggesting that dream interpretation may, in Sumerian times, have been a female office.[2] By way of contrast, when Gilgamesh and Enkidu later on take turns interpreting each other's dreams, they almost invariably get it wrong, with catastrophic consequences.[3] But, whether the dream-interpreter was exclusively female or not in Neo-Sumerian times,

---

[1] Cited in B. Alster, *Dumuzi's Dream. Aspects of Oral Poetry in a Sumerian Myth* (Copenhagen, 1972) (= *Mesopotamia* 1), Sumerian text p. 54, lines 19-24, ET p. 55.

[2] On Dumuzi's sister, see Falkenstein in *DM*, pp. 63-64; on the female dream-interpreter, see Oppenheim, *Dreams*, p. 221: Sum. *sal.ensi*; Akk. *ša'iltu*.

[3] It is hard to point to a useful translation of the text in any language because the Epic of Gilgamesh was never "canonical" (cf. Oppenheim, *AM*, p. 256), and therefore varied hugely from society to society and language to language. In A. Heidel's (*The Gilgamesh Epic and Old Testament Parallels* [Chicago and London, 6th edn 1967 (1946)]) eclectic and now very outmoded edition the dream sequences of Gilgamesh and Enkidu are located on V iii 32-43 (p. 46: wrongly interpreted by Enkidu as favourable), V iii 47-iv 1-22 (where the dream must, in spite of Heidel's translation, have been had by Gilgamesh and wrongly interpreted by Enkidu: one did not interpret one's own dream). The Standard Babylonian version has recently been published by S. Dalley in a popular and accessible form (*Myths from Mesopotamia. Creation, The Flood, Gilgamesh and Others* (Oxford and New York, 1991), pp. 39-135); the dream sequences are recorded on Tablet IV, i-iii (pp. 67-70).

the practice is well attested in Mesopotamia as an "academic" discipline from the OB period until the latest times. The technical name for the dream interpreter/ess was *ša'il(t)u*.

Divination by the interpretation of dreams is represented in the Old Babylonian period by a Babylonian fragment dating to this era, and by another from Elamite Susa which is presumably contemporaneous.[1] There are also a number of fascinating dream reports from Mari which have recently been studied in some depth by Sasson.[2] Dream omens were copied systematically and with surprisingly little elaboration over the centuries until they were finally collected in the form known to us by the scribes of Assurbanipal in the Neo-Assyrian period.[3] Oppenheim distinguishes between the "message" dream, containing unambiguous contents, and the "symbolic" dream, which requires interpretation by comparison with the omen collections.[4] At a late date (presumably the 8th century BCE), the collection of dream omina was prefaced by a series of incipits of incantations for warding off the consequences of untoward dreams, and followed by the incantations themselves, making it a sort of "how-to" book.[5] Oppenheim feels that dream omina did not enjoy high standing in Mesopotamia proper, and were only collected by Assurbanipal's scribes for the sake of scholarly completeness.[6] This

---

[1] Cf. Oppenheim, *Dreams*, pp. 243; 259-60.

[2] Oppenheim's study appeared too early in the course of the publication of the Marian materials for him to do more than merely refer to them; see J.M. Sasson, "Mari Dreams", in *JAOS* 103 (1983), pp. 283-93.

[3] *Dreams*, p. 242; the Assyrian Dream-Book actually appears in various Sargonid lists as ÉS.QAR. Za-qi-qu, after the "god of dreams" who serves as "messenger", ^{d}Zaqiqu.

[4] *Dreams*, pp. 205-12; this distinction was already made by Artemidorus in the 2nd century AD; cf. G. Luck, *Arcana Mundi. Magic and the Occult in the Greek and Roman Worlds* (London, 1987 [1985]), p. 291. Artemidorus' terms are "theorematic" and "allegorical" dreams, respectively. Further on dream interpretation in the classical world, see R.C. White, "Techniques in Early Dream Interpretation", in G. MacRae (ed.), *SBLSP*, (Missoula (Montana), 1976) pp. 323-36, and, with extensive references, G. Luck, *Magie und andere Geheimlehren in der Antike* (Stuttgart, 1990), pp. 292-302.

[5] *Dreams*, pp. 294-96.

[6] *Dreams*, p. 296.

conclusion is surely questionable, since dreams and their interpretation, if not actually well represented in the omens which have come down to us, figure prominently in literary contexts throughout the history of Mesopotamia: in the dream of Gudea of Lagash (ca.2143-2124),[1] those of Gilgamesh and Enkidu, and as we have seen, of Dumuzi, the troubled dreams of the sufferer in the famous Cassite work "I Will Praise the Lord of Wisdom" (Ludlul bel Nemeqi),[2] as well as his (dreamed) experience of restoration,[3] and countless appearances in official inscriptions. Moreover, as is well known, the phenomenon of dream interpretation, even preserving the distinction between the two sorts of dreams, spread throughout the ancient Near East in the first millennium and ultimately reached the classical world.[4] There is therefore reason to suspect that, as in the case of oil divination, the phenomenon had become "popular"; it was no longer cultivated by the élite of diviners and exorcists because it had been assimilated by the populace in general. Artemidorus relates that every marketplace in Greece had its dream diviners, which suggests, at least indirectly, that this may have been the general trend.[5]

A single feature of the category of "symbolic" dreams to which we shall return is that only the *objective features* of a dream were regarded as significant; the dreamer's subjective state was totally without significance. Oppenheim goes so far as to say that

> the physiological status. . .remains without importance. Whether he
> be asleep, in an enthusiastic frenzy or waking, these "signs" convey
> their meaning to the person who is intelligent enought to notice them
> (as being meaningful) and trained to understand them.[6]

---

[1] Gudea Cyl. A IV:7-VI:14 = TCL VIII pl.4-5, ET in Oppenheim, *Dreams*, p. 245 (a "message" dream legitimating Gudea's construction of a temple).

[2] As it is called in the collophons of the poem; Lambert, though, calls it "The Poem of the Righteous Sufferer", although "righteousness" as such is not a Babylonian concept; cf. W.G. Lambert, *Babylonian Wisdom Literature*, pp. 33-61 for text and ET; for the Cassite date, see p. 26. The sufferer's troubled dreams are on pp. 32-33, lines 52-54; pp. 38-39, line 7; pp. 42-43, line 82.

[3] *Babylonian Wisdom Literature*, pp. 48-51, lines 9-44.

[4] Cf. e.g. G. Luck, *Arcana Mundi*, pp. 230-31.

[5] Luck, *Arcana Mundi*, p. 291.

[6] Oppenheim, *Dreams*, p. 238.

Speech Omens

Roughly everything that is known about the ancient Near Eastern genre of speech omens is contained in a single slim article by A.L. Oppenheim, which should not allow us to think that the genre was unimportant or little used. Called in Sumerian *inim.gar* = Akkadian *egirrû*,[1] the speech omen is a chance-heard remark or sound which is perceived as portentous by its hearer. Thus the mental set of the hearer is all-important: if he is not predisposed to hear an egirrû, then he will not. Seen from the other side of the coin, the speech omen is a serious matter, since unwittingly to convey an unfortunate egirrû to someone else is virtually the same as to curse him. Thus Oppenheim cites numerous maledictions among the curses inscribed on kudurrus (boundary-stones) of the sort: "May god X, the great god, make his egirrû evil"![2] If the speech omen were only a portent, it would hardly be able to serve as a curse on kudurrus, so it appears (although Oppenheim does not suggest it) that there was no conceptual boundary between a bad omen and the evil portended by it. Oppenheim feels that the speech omen was not particularly important because it plays no appreciable rôle in the *literary* tradition of the diviner and exorcist. This was in reality an odd position from an historical point of view, as Oppenheim was elsewhere at pains to emphasise the limits of our source materials. In this connexion, we should once again note *where* this omen is mentioned: in an "historical" inscription of Assurbanipal, recording divine encouragement for his successful struggle against the Elamites, in a public inscription of Esarhaddon, on Gudea's famous building inscription (Cyl. A XX:3), plus in assorted letters, hymns, and the famous "vade mecum" of the Mesopotamian exorcist.[3]

---

[1] A.L. Oppenheim, "Sumerian: inim.gar, Akkadian: egirrû, Greek: kledon", *AfO* 17 (1954-56), pp. 49-55; W.H.P. Römer reads Sumerian *inim.gar* as *igarra*, which would make sense of the Akkadian loan; however, he does so with some hesitation; cf. M. Dietrich, et al. (eds.), *Deutungen der Zukunft in Briefen, Orakeln und Omina* (Gütersloh, 1986) (= *Texte aus der Umwelt des Alten Testaments* II.1), p. 22, (b).

[2] "Sumerian: inim.gar", p. 51.

[3] References in "Sumerian: inim.gar", pp. 49-51; for the "vade mecum", see H. Zimmern, "Ein Leitfaden der Beschwörungskunst", *ZA* 30 (1915-16), pp. 205-29; the egirru-omen is mentioned (though not understood by Zimmmern) rev. line 2 (pp.

Now we do not really know whether the people uttered favourable *inim.gar* when Gudea proposed to build his temple; but it is obvious that his scribes thought someone would be impressed if it were thought that they had; a consideration which applies to the notices of Esarhaddon and Assurbanipal as well. For over a thousand years, then, the speech omen was held in sufficient respect that it could be mentioned in legitimating contexts as a clear sign of the divine approval. Obviously, we have to do with a type of omen which traditionally excited popular awe. To illustrate the import of this, one has only to consider its opposite in our times, as, for example, the dismay of the popular press when it was recently revealed that President Reagan's wife had been consulting an astrologer; the fact was certainly *not* the kind of thing the White House wanted bruited about. Of course, had Mrs. Reagan consulted one of the "think tanks" which are sanctioned by the technocratic imagination of the times, one suspects there would have been little to-do.

Finally, the omen series *šumma ālu* (see below) records a few features enabling one to determine if the sense of a speech omen is positive, negative, or especially reliable (three repetitions of the omen); it further characterise them as they are heard in front of or behind the hearer, and whether they appear to be near or far. All of these sound like attempts to systematise the speech omen along the lines of the north-south-east-west orientations of the oil or incense omens.

Šumma Ālu

I have generally attempted to avoid the jargons of sociologism and Assyriologism in this work. In connexion with the omen series known as *šumma ālu*, after its incipit (*šumma ālu ina mele šakin*: if a city is situated on a hill), no single term happens to be adequate because the series is both capacious and amorphous. Originally published by F.

210-11, text and trans.). According to A. Finet ("Un cas de clédonomancie à Mari", in: G. van Driel et al. (eds.), *Zikir Šumim* (Leiden, 1982), pp. 48-56, the speech omen also figured in ancient Mari, where, additionally, procedures existed for impetrating it.

Nötscher, we have been promised a new edition for some time,[1] but we shall have to soldier on without it for a while yet. The *šumma ālu* omina consist largely of "surprise encounters", like two, three, or more snakes entwined on the path ahead of one; a dog, wolf, fox, or other animal entering a city; a cry (said to be from an etimmu or "evil ghost") being heard in one's house in the night; but also, as we have seen, of omens reminiscent of izbu omina,[2] prognostics based on various ways of love-making[3] and much more besides. The series is vast—over 120 tablets at last count—and disorderly, and almost all of them derive from the first millennium.[4] As mentioned previously, the series of namburbi-conjurations[5] are specifically designed to counter the portents found in *šumma ālu*; in fact, the individual namburbis usually quote the incipit of the relevant *šumma ālu*-omen to which they correspond (i.e., to which they offer an antidote), a feature which sometimes aids the reconstruction of texts of both series.

The overwhelming majority of the ālu-omens are so-called "private" omens, although some do refer to events transpiring in the presence of the king, or which otherwise pertain to him. This preponderance led already Nötscher to acknowledge that the series represented divination at the popular level: these were the "small magics of the

---

[1] Ms. S.M. Moren noted back in 1977 that she, A. Guinan and E. Leichty were engaged in this "lengthy and complicated undertaking" ("A Lost 'Omen' Tablet", *JCS* 29 (1977), p.65 n. 1.

[2] So much so that Moren, "Summa Izbu XIX", p. 53, points out that they can frequently only be properly disentangled on the basis of the logogram used for "šumma".

[3] Tablet 104 of Šumma Alu (= CT 39 44-46), which Nötscher could not bring himself to translate; cf. R.D. Biggs, *ša.zi.ga: Ancient Mesopotamian Potency Incantations* (Locust Valley, 1967) (= *TCS* Vol. 2), p. 1, n. 6.

[4] The exception is D.B. Weisberg's text, "An Old Babylonian Forerunner to Summa Alu", *HUCA* 40-41 (1969-70), pp. 87-105, which proves that augury (prognostics based on the flight of birds) was also practised in Mesopotamia, and was not, as often supposed, a specifically Western phenomenon. At the other end of the Mesopotamian time scale—the Seleucid period—we find reference to šumma alu-like phenomena in the "astronomical diaries" published by Sachs and Hunger (*Astronomical Diaries and Related Texts*); cf. e.g. No. -567, obv. line 7: "That month, a fox entered the city".

[5] See R. Caplice, "Namburbi texts in the British Museum".

everyday" of which Jakob Grimm and, later, Mauss and Hubert spoke. Thus it is intelligible that some *šumma ālu* omens spread in the periods subsequent to the Neo-Assyrian as far afield as to India.[1] The question as to how they entered the stream of literary tradition alongside of the great "academic" omen series like the astrological and extispical omina demands some sort of answer.

When we consider that the vast majority of the ālu texts are Neo-Assyrian, and, further, that already Oppenheim had pointed to a prodigious decline in the number of "specialists" in Assyria who styled themselves "diviner", with respect to the title of "exorcist",[2] an answer seems to suggest itself. The "popular" omens of the *šumma ālu* type must have been written down by the non-diviners, that is, either the "scribes"[3] or the "exorcists"[4], as a facet of their appropriation of the matter of divination. This is further supported by the intimate connexion, pointed to above, between *šumma ālu* and the apotropaic *namburbi* rituals, as the exorcists were the pre-eminent practitioners of defensive magic. It is also supported by the proliferation of exorcistic literature and the evolution of exorcistic rituals during the Neo-Assyrian period.[5]

---

[1] Cf. D. Pingree, "Mesopotamian Astronomy and Astral Omens", in Nissen and Renger (eds.), *Mesopotamien und seine Nachbarn*, pp. 617-18. P. Artzi and Mrs. Warda Lask, "'The King and the Evil Portending, Ominous Sign in His House' (EA 358)" (in the same work, pp. 317-20), offer a reconstruction of Knutzon's EA 358 which strikingly recalls both *šumma ālu* and the *namburbi* series; which, if correct, would be a very early attestation of these materials.

[2] "Divination and Celestial Observation", esp. p. 100; strikingly supported by the texts published in Parpola's *Letters from Assyrian Scholars*, Pt.1: of 317 letters sent by various "specialists" (or "scholars") to Esarhaddon and Assurbanipal, only 6 are from diviners (i.e., from practitioners who style themselves *bāru*), pp. 1-273.

[3] That is, those experts on astrology who styled themselves "scribes of *enuma anu enlil*" (i.e., the astrological omen series).

[4] Either Akk. *ašipu* or the Sum. loanword *mašmašu*. We shall consider the question of personnel in more detail presently.

[5] Although dating back in part to the Old Babylonian and Cassite periods, the exorcistic series of incantations known as *Maqlu* (defending against witches and sorcerers) and *Šurpu* (defending against manifold breaches of tabu) are mainly even known to us thanks to copies preserved in Nineve, Assur, and elsewhere in the former Neo-Assyrian empire (G. Maier, *Die assyrische Beschwörungs sammlung Maqlu* (Berlin, 1937), whose version is based on the "von den Gelehrten

Here we might pause to consider the social anthropological studies in Africa and elsewhere from the 1950s and later which have tended to show that massive changes in the character of magic in a given society are indicative of fundamental social change: they are in many respects a reaction against acculturation.

In this connexion, it is not difficult to argue for an understanding of first-millennium Assyria as a society under severe pressure from a variety of sources. To begin with, the end of the second millennium and the beginning of the first millennium in Assyria witnessed a pronounced demographic decline, the causes of which are still not entirely evident.[1] Moreover, the incessant Assyrian wars against three different fronts, which lasted from the turn of the millennium until the downfall of the Neo-Assyrian empire,[2] with the accompanying resettlement of foreign-

---

Assurbanaplis redigierte Text" (p. 1); E. Reiner, *Šurpu. A Collection of Sumerian and Akkadian Incantations* (Graz, 1958), esp. pp. 1-2). The "patients" who were treated by the exorcist were largely private persons. The popularity of the series — which were performed together, first Maqlu, then Šurpu—is indicated by the previously-mentioned Wisdom text, *Ludlul bel nemeqi*, of which pieces of seven different copies were found in Assurbanipal's library at Kuyundjik, which indicates, according to Parpola's theory, that at least seven complete editions were in circulation in private collections. In Ludlul, there are numerous features which recollect the phrasing of both Maqlu and Šurpu (cf. W.G. Lambert, *Babylonian Wisdom Literature*, pp. 26-27).

As far as the development of exorcistic series is concerned, the most notable Neo-Assyrian innovation was the ritual lustration series known as *bit rimki*, the purpose of which was to cleanse the king from all manner of defilements, whether deriving from ritual abuse, witchcraft, lunar eclipses, or whatever. Cf. J. Læssø, *Studies on the Assyrian Ritual and Series bit rimki* (Copenhagen, 1955), pp. 89-93. Note also that the Sargonid kings took pains to keep themselves informed as to both omens and the appropriate magical defences (e.g., ABL 355, letter to Esarhaddon from Balasi, ET in A.L. Oppenheim, *Letters from Mesopotamia* (Chicago and London, 1967), p. 162, nr 105; ABL 370, in the same, pp. 165-66, nr 108; ABL 353, in the same, p. 166, nr 109. See also Mar-Ištar's letter to Assurbanipal, ABL 338, in the same, pp. 162-65, nr 106). Particularly Assurbanipal's knowledge of both omens and incantantions was extensive, as is well known today; cf. Liverani, *AO*, p. 808; Labat, in *Die altorientalischen Reiche*, Bd. III, pp. 91-92.

[1] Cf. Liverani, *AO*, pp. 765-66.

[2] I.e., against the mountain peoples, who were normally only held in check by the buffer state of Urartu; against the peoples of the West and the Mediterranean

ers on Assyrian soil,[1] meant automatic confrontations between social horizons, values, and expectations, which could only have led to some degree of disorientation among the populace.[2] Thus it is not surprising to discover that, like other Near Eastern countries, at least towards the end of the 8th and the beginning of the 7th century, Assyria exhibited repristinatory tendencies which took the form of a harking back to the distant past.[3] As a concomitant to this, official pronouncements of the apparatus of state went from more or less "realistic" descriptions of Assyria's numerous warlike engagements with foreign powers to self-serving "ideological" formulations in which Assyria's enemies were portrayed as "oath-breakers".[4] This attests to the emergence of a need for self-justification, and implies that the simple business of being Assyrian was no longer quite as simple as before. Also, in the Assyria of Esarhaddon and Assurbanipal we find indications of a burgeoning individualism in the literary tradition and in the graphic arts,[5] which

---

coast; and against the Babylonians and Elamites. See Oppenheim, *AM*, pp. 166-67.

[1] A phenomenon which contributed to the "Aramaisation" of Assyria, one prominent social feature of which was the increasing use of Aramaic as the vernacular; see Liverani, *AO*, pp. 731-32. However, this phenomenon deserves to be much more intensively studied than has been the case up to the present.

[2] Cf. R. Labat's contribtion in E. Cassin et al. (eds.), *Die Altorientalischen Reiche,* Bd. III. *Die erste Hälfte des 1.Jahrtausends* (Frankfurt am Main, 1984 [1967]), p. 82.

[3] Most clearly symbolised by the regnal name of Sennacherib's predecessor, Sargon (II), and most clearly realised in Assurbanipal's commissioning of agents to collect works for his library from all over his far-flung empire. This general repristinatory tendency was observed by H. Friis in connexion with developments in Egypt and Nabonidus' Babylon and seen in relation to the Israelite development of "historical" interests in "Eksilet og den israelitiske historieopfattelse", *DTT* 38 (1975), pp. 1-16; Ms. Friis' article has subsequently appeared in German in "Das Exil und die Geschichte", in *DBAT* 18 (1984), pp. 63-84.

[4] Cf. Liverani, *AO*, p. 844; more extensively, H. Tadmor, "History and Ideology in the Assyrian Royal Inscriptions", in F.M. Fales (ed.), *Assyrian Royal Inscriptions: New Horizons in Literary, Ideological, and Historical Analysis* (Rome, 1981), pp. 13-35.

[5] Cf. R. Liwak, "Literary Individuality in the Hebrew Bible", in B. Uffenheimer and H.G. Reventlow (eds.), *Creative Biblical Exegesis. Christian and Jewish Hermeneutics through the Centuries* (Sheffield, 1988) (= *JSOTSup* 59), p. 92.

might be taken to suggest that consciousness of self qua Assyrian was being challenged and perhaps fragmented.[1] In addition to this, we must consider the effects of the apparent increase in literacy of which I have spoken before, which in the Neo-Assyrian empire manifested itself in the establishment of private libraries. This in itself meant that materials which were once the province of a small group of specialists became more amenable to appropriation by others.[2] Finally, economically considered, it is possible that the concentration of provincial administration in the new provincial capitals that were established by Tiglath

[1] In saying this, I do not mean to imply that Assyrians were previously less fully realised individuals than came to be the case, i.e., that they were emerging from a consciousness of self as rooted in the social whole, and that they were developing a sense of person in contradistinction to society. Wheeler Robinson's never very well-defined notion of "corporate personality" has been killed about as effectively as a theory can be by J. Rogerson (in "The Hebrew Conception of Corporate Personality: A Re-examination", in (B.Lang [ed.]), *Anthropological Approaches to the Old Testament* (Philadelphia and London, 1985), pp. 43-59 (a revision of his original article in *JTS* 21 [1970], pp. 1-16). One has only to read Assyrian court cases to find brothers cheerfully suing brothers for a larger share of their inheritance, or trying to do adopted sons out of their share, to note that such supraordinate concepts as "family", "lineage", "clan" or "tribe" did not diminish an Assyrian's awareness of self. What I do mean, though, is that the manifold stresses and strains on Assyrian society were forcing its members to confront the nature of their self-identification.

[2] Under the rubric "Geheimwissen" in the *RLA* one notes that certain late texts—including omens—were frequently stamped with the predicate *pirištu ša ilani rabûti*, "secret of the great gods", or the like. However, texts bearing such predicates do not fall into any well-defined categories, and some of the materials in question were immediately accessible to anyone who could read. It is accordingly unlikely that there ever existed a specific category of "arcana" which Assyro-Babylonian scribes tried to protect. One wonders, then, whether this sort of predicate is not to be socially explained, that is, as an expression of the attempts of the tiny literate stratum with a vested interest in keeping knowledge of the stream of literary tradition from the hands of a broader substratum who could read, but who lacked a formal introduction to the tradition. This distinction may have been parallel, if not identical with, that between scribes versed in cuneiform and those familiar with Aramaic. On the learned character of texts bearing such subscriptions, see most recently A. Livingstone, *Mystical and Mythological Explanatory Works of Assyrian and Babylonian Scholars* (Oxford, 1986).

Pileser III (744-727) resulted in the impoverishment of the older towns and their outlying villages.[1] None of these indications is sufficient by itself to point to the sort of social tensions which might have led, in first-millennium Assyria, to a rise in the employment of the "defensive magics" of the exorcist. But, taken together, they might well provide explanatory background for this phenomenon. If so, then the proliferation of "scribes" and "exorcists" in the royal administrations of Esarhaddon and Assurbanipal was not an isolated phenomenon; it must have reflected quite general tendencies in Assyrian magical practice, also at the non-literary level which eludes our ability to determine.

Physiognomic and Diagnostic Omens

Physiognomic and diagnostic omens are a grand catch-all corpus of materials which bases its predictions either on observed physical characteristics of a subject, or on peculiarities of his behaviour.[2] The principles of observation employed in these omens are clearly analogous to those employed in divination for the purpose of ascertaining the cause or nature of a disease, with which they in fact share some features of vocabulary. To us they are reminiscent of such "modern" phenomena as phrenology or palmistry. The genre was well dispersed in both space and time; texts come to us from Hittite Hattusa which were based on Old Babylonian originals, but mainly from late Assyrian copies the textual tradition of which, however, also goes back to Old Babylonian

---

[1] As is hesitantly argued by J.N. Postgate in "The Economic Structure of the Assyrian Empire", in M.T. Larsen (ed.), *Power and Propaganda. A Symposium on Ancient Empires* (Copenhagen, 1979), pp. 216-17.

[2] Cf. Oppenheim, *AM*, p. 223; Nougayrol, *La Divination*, pp. 55-56. Texts have been edited by, among others, F.R. Kraus, "Ein Sittenkanon in Omenform" in *ZA* 43 (1936), pp. 77-113; *idem*, "Babylonische Omina mit Ausdeutung der Begleiterscheinungen des Sprechens", in *AfO* 11 (1936-37), pp. 219-30; *idem*, *Texte zur babylonischen Physiognomatik* in *AfO* Beiheft 3, (Berlin, 1939); *idem*, "Weitere Texte zur babylonischen Physiognomatik", in *Or* N.S. 16 (1947), pp. 172-206; F. Köcher and A.L. Oppenheim, "The Old Babylonian Omen Text VAT 7525" in *AfO* 18 (1957-1958), pp. 62-80; S.M. Moren, "A 'lost' omen tablet" in *JCS* 29 (1977), pp. 65-72.

times.[1] A large number of omens of the physiognomic-diagnostic type are to be found in *šumma ālu* (see above); in fact, the rules separating one category from another are by no means clear. A single feature deserves special comment, namely Labat's observation that "the interpretative principle which governs a prognostic prediction differs wholly from that pertaining to an ordinary prediction. An observation which would ordinarily be favourable proves to be unfavourable for a sick person, and *vice versa*".[2]

Extispicy: The Omen Sacrifice

The omen sacrifice may be traced back to Sumerian times, although, as with most other divinatory practices, no Sumerian extispical omina are preserved.[3] Already in Old Babylonian times, however, extispicy was regularly practised, as a considerable number of published texts and

---

[1] For medical omens, see J.V. Kinnier-Wilson, "The Nimrud Catalogue of Medical and Physiognomical Omina" in *Iraq* 24 (1962), pp. 52-63; *idem*, "Two Medical Texts from Nimrud", *Iraq* 19 (1957), pp. 40-49; see esp. R. Labat's reconstruction of the series *enuma ana bit marsi ašipu illiku* ("when the exorcist goes to the patient's house"), "Un traité médical Akkadien" in *RA* 40 (1945-46), pp. 27-49. On the similarity of observation used in diagnostic and physiognomic omens, see the same, p. 37, where Labat also distinguishes the three main types of physiognomic omens: *šumma alamdimmu*, concerned with peculiarities of the body; *šumma liptu*, dealing with spots or marks on the skin; and *šumma kataduggu*, which covers habitual behaviours of speech, deportment, and thought (the last category is amply represented by Kraus' "Sittenkanon"). As much of the forty-tablet series as it has been possible to reconstruct has been published by Labat, *Traité akkadien de diagnostics et prognostics médicaux*, Vols. 1- 2 (Paris and Leiden, 1951). For a very general introduction to Mesopotamian magical medicine, see *idem*, "Médecins, devins et prêtres-guerisseurs en Mésopotamie ancienne" in *Archeologia* 8-13 (1966), pp. 11-15. See also F. Köcher, *Die babylonisch-assyrische Medizin in Texten und Untersuchungen*, Vols.1-3 (Berlin, 1963-64), which is, however, purely for the specialist.

[2] Labat, "Un traité médical Akkadien", p. 37.

[3] Falkenstein in *DM*, pp. 45-50; further references and mentions in Sumerian inscriptions and the like in W.H.P. Römer's treatment in M. Dietrich et al. (eds.), *Deutungen der Zukunft*, pp. 17-55; and see esp. Römer's version of the only known Sumerian omen collection (based on the behaviour of the king) in *ibid.*, pp. 53-55.

studies show.[1] As we have seen, the extispical omens were probably collected and edited into sizable corpora during the Cassite period, although direct evidence for Cassite extispicy is rare.[2] Texts of the omen sacrifice were preserved in Assyria which derive from the time of Tiglath-Pileser I (ca. 1114-1076),[3] and, as mentioned previously, the vast majority of materials on extispicy have been preserved in Assurbanipal's famous library at Kuyundjik, and hence attest to Neo-Assyrian practice.[4] Outside of Babylonia and Assyria, the practice of extispicy is attested through-out the ancient Near East, from Elam to the Hittite kingdom, Ugarit, Megiddo and Hazor.[5] Interestingly, there is no evidence that the practice ever gained a foothold in Egypt;[6] perhaps the understanding of the body fostered by the mortuary cult

---

[1] Cf. e.g. A. Goetze, *Old Babylonian Omen Texts*; J. Nougayrol, "Textes hépatoscopiques d'époque ancienne conservés au musée du Louvre"; Jeyes, *Old Babylonian Extispicy*.

[2] See the few fragments published by E.F. Weidner in *AfO* 16 (1952/52), pp. 74-75; both OB and Cassite extispicy reports were published by Goetze in *JCS* 11 (1957), pp. 89-105; see further F.R. Kraus, "Mittelbabylonische Opferschau-protokolle", *JCS* 37 (1985), pp. 127-203.

[3] As we see in Weidner's catalogue of Tiglath-Pileser's library; *AfO* 16 (1952/53), p. 210, nr. 77; and see H. Tschinkowitz, "Ein Opferschautext aus dem Eponymenjahr Tiglatpilesers I.", in *AfO* 22 (1968/69), pp. 59-62.

[4] Cf. e.g. J.A. Knudtzon, *Assyrische Gebete an den Sonnengott* (Leipzig, 1893), texts Nrs. 1-154, pp. 72-276 (texts and trans.); G. Klauber, *Politisch-Religiöse Texte aus der Sargonidenzeit* (Leipzig, 1913); discussed at length by M. Jastrow in *Die Religion Babyloniens und Assyriens*, pp. 174-415. See also J. Denner, "Der assyrische Eingeweideschautext II R.43", pp. 180-220; Parpola, *Letters from Assyrian Scholars* I, Nrs. 2, 113, 116, 246, 340.

[5] Cf. Oppenheim *AM*, p. 213; for extispicy at Ugarit see P. Xella, "L'influence Babylonienne à Ougarit, d'après les Textes Alphabétiques Rituels et Divinatoires", in Nissen and Renger (eds.), *Mesopotamien und seine Nachbarn*, p. 328; p. 337, n. 52; further, M. Dietrich et al., *Mantik in Ugarit*, pp. 1-85; 241-279; in the region later known as Israel, see B. Landsberger and H. Tadmor, "Fragments of Clay Liver Models from Hazor", *IEJ* 14 (1964), pp. 201-18. For the Hittite evidence, see A. Kammenhuber, *Orakelpraxis, Träume und Vorzeichenschau bei den Hethitern* (Heidelberg, 1976), p. 70, Nrs. 15-16; pp. 73-74; pp. 110-111; pp. 134-136.

[6] In spite of Herodotus' claim that "divination by the inspection of sacrificial victims also came from Egypt" (*Histories*, Bk. II, 59-60).

there simply ruled out the possibility of understanding the exta of an animal as a medium of communication.

So far I have referred mainly to extispical omens which have come down to us either in isolated reports of actually-undertaken extispicies or in the compendia of the Neo-Assyrian period. In reality, the materials pertaining to the omen sacrifice are of five types, in addition to the individual omens which eventually made their way into the late (largely Assyrian) compendia: 1) reports 2) queries 3) prayers 4) tamitus 5) plastics. 1) The reports. The "reports" (or "protocolls" —F.R. Kraus) are just what the term implies, accounts of actual extispicies which were undertaken for some purpose. Such records, usually composed more or less as letters, have been preserved stretching from the Old Babylonian era to the time of Sargonid Assyria, plus a few inscriptions of Nabonidus which may reflect actual reports or else are literary imitations of such.[1]

1) The Report

The *report* begins with an introductory statement such as "one lamb (for the) diviner's ritual, (a sacrifice for) the god DN"; then follows a mention of the subject on whose behalf the ritual is undertaken, e.g., "for the well-being of NN"; then the anatomical details observed in the course of the ritual (e.g., "the 'path' was present"); finally, the diviner closes by noting whether the omen was favourable, unfavourable, or sufficiently unclear as to merit a further extispicy (sometimes called either a "cross-examination" or a "check-up" by Assyriologists).[2] In Neo-Assyrian reports, the various observed states of the exta are often connected with (more or less appropriate) apodoses from the "canonical"

---

[1] In addition to the materials mentioned above, see Klauber, *Politisch-religiöse Texte*, pp. xxv-xxxv. On the genuineness of the Nabonidus inscriptions, see Gadd, *DM*, pp. 32-34, who takes them to be genuine, while admiring their literary qualities; Starr (*The Rituals of the Diviner*, text and translation pp. 127-28, commentary, p. 126) regards them as literary imitations because of their wealth of positive protases; Kraus ("Mittelbabylonische Opferschauprotokolle", p. 128) however, claims that "the selection and sequence of these protases seem to this writer. . . to have been impossible without some relationship to practical extispicy". Which does not actually rule Starr's view out of court.

[2] For details, see Goetze, "Reports", pp. 94-95; Starr, *The Rituals of the Diviner*, pp. 107-21.

compendia.[1]

2) The Query

The query is solely an Assyrian genre, although it bears notable similarities with a report written in Mari in the Old Babylonian period; it is a formal request addressed to a god (usually Šamaš) for an oracle; it is followed by the question itself, which is carefully worded (e.g., "the army, which is to be sent out against NN, will NN not capture it, nor defeat it, nor cause it to be defeated. . . as they have left the gate of the city of X, will they return safely through the gate of the city of X"?). Often the period of time for which the extispicy is expected to be valid (Akk. *adannu*) is stipulated ("for the next three months/two years, etc."). Queries are also often equipped with so-called *ezib*-lines, that is, instructions for the god in question to disregard some features which might otherwise invalidate the oracle (e.g., "*ezib* whether today is a favourable or unfavourable day"). The question is then stated once more, after which the diviner's observations follow, although his observations are couched in the language of the omen compendia (e.g., "BE = šumma, if there is a 'path'. . .").[2]

3) The Prayer (*ikribu*)

The prayers of the omen sacrifice are literary products of some beauty, which, however, were intended to preface actual consultations. As the preparations for the omen sacrifice apparently were quite extensive, it seems that it was only possible to perform the ritual twice a day; or else that the Assyro-Babylonian worldview found only two times appropriate for the sacrifice: at dawn and at night (not at dusk: the constellations of the Pleiades and Orion are both addressed, and so must be fully visible). Old Babylonian prayers for the morning rite have been published by, among others, Goetze[3] and Starr.[4] The shorter of the two texts totals

---

[1] Cf. J. Aro, *DM*, p. 110.

[2] See J. Aro, who suggested the designation "query" in *DM*, pp. 109-10; more specifically on the *ezib*-lines, see Knudtzon, *Assyrische Gebete*, pp. 24-43. On the query in Mari, see Starr, *The Rituals of the Diviner*, p. 109.

[3] "An Old Babylonian Prayer of the Divination Priest", *JCS* 22 (1968), pp. 25-29.

66 lines; the longer reaches a grand total of 142 lines. Both are addressed to "Šamaš, lord of judgement; Adad, lord of the extispicy--ritual (*ikribu*) and divination". Both describe the setting of the ritual at considerable length, and require to be studied in depth in terms of their relations to Assyro-Babylonian symbols, concepts, and religious behaviour as a whole. This has not been done as yet, although Starr has made a beginning. Prayers for the evening rite have been published by Dossin,[1] and von Soden,[2] with revision and commentary by Oppenheim.[3] In them, we are expressly told that, Šamaš and Adad having retired, the diviner makes his supplication for a favourable omen to the "great gods of the night". Oppenheim feels that the night ritual was merely preparation for the next morning's extispicy,[4] but this seems unlikely, as the diviner directly requests that the "shining Fire-star, heroic Irra, Bow-star. . .stand by and put a propitious sign on the lamb".[5] If a day-ritual were implied, would one not simply address Šamaš and Adad themselves? In any event, as Oppenheim notes, the "prayer to the gods of the night" dropped out of the tradition between the Old Babylonian and the Neo-Assyrian periods, so it seems that the

---

[4] In *The Rituals of the Diviner*, pp. 30-44 (text and translation), pp. 44-106 (commentary). Starr defines *ikribu* as "extispicy-ritual-cum-prayer" (p. 45), rather than as the accompanying prayer; but the word remains part of a text, as do all the instructions and descriptions of ritual activity.

[1] "Prières aux 'Dieux de la Nuit' (AO 6769)", *RA* 32 (1935), pp. 179-87.

[2] In *ZA* 43 (1936), pp. 305-08; German trans. in A. Falkenstein and W. von Soden (eds.), *Sumerische und akkadische Hymnen und Gebete* (Zurich and Stuttgart, 1953), p. 274. Von Soden's text was originally published by W. Schileico in *Izvestiia Akademii Istorii Materialnoj Kultury* 3 (1921), pp. 144-52.

[3] "A New Prayer to the Gods of the Night", *Studia Biblica et Orientalia* 3 (1959), pp. 282-301. Oppenheim shows that the beautiful description of the night scene enjoyed by the celebrant became a topos susceptible to reinterpretation and re-employment in Mesopotamian magic, as it after the Old Babylonian period re-emerged as an introduction to a Neo-Babylonian *namburbi* conjuration. Two further Old Babylonian *ikribus* have been published, though without commentary, by L. de Meyer, "Deux prières ikribu du temps d'Ami-saduqa", in: G. van Driel, et al. (eds.), *Zikir Šumim* (Leiden, 1982), pp. 271-79.

[4] "A New Prayer. . . ", p. 298.

[5] "A New Prayer", p. 296.

rite at daybreak won the field in the end.[1]

4) The *tamitu*

The *tamitu* is essentially simply a "query" addressed to Šamaš and Adad, rather than to Šamaš alone; moreover, it is found solely in the ambit of the Babylonian language.[2] Texts of *tamitus* date from the Old Babylonian period down to some time prior to the Neo-Assyrian era; they come from Nineve, Assur, Babylon, and Nimrud. The names of the enquirers are almost always blank, suggesting that only the answers, like juridical precedents, were of interest. The questions posed were of two types: so-called "safety *tamitus*", which ask whether all will be well with the enquirer for the year to come; and questions about specific projects of the enquirer. Only positive replies to the various enquiries have been preserved.[3]

5) Plastics

"Plastics" is my own term for the curiously-shaped communications usually called "liver (sometimes lung) models" (French "maquettes") by Assyriologists. As indicated above, scholars have regarded them as preserving particularly interesting features of a given case,[4] or else as

---

[1] "A New Prayer", p. 296. Interestingly, in her recent Presidential Address to the American Oriental Society (repr. in *JAOS* 105 [1985], pp. 589-95) E. Reiner sides with Oppenheim on the grounds that a recently-published Old Babylonian *ikribu* addresses the "star" Venus as Ninsianna, a male god. Venus was thought to be male when it appeared as the morning-star, and female in its nocturnal rôle (p. 591). This is indisputable; and yet Oppenheim's text also addresses the Pleiades, which are certainly not visible by the time of the first visibility of Venus in the early morning.

[2] As Rochberg-Halton (*Aspects*, p. 18) has noted, the lunar eclipse omens of the *enuma anu enlil* astrological series are also characterised as *tamiātu*, though for no reason that is apparent to us.

[3] All that is known of the *tamitus* comes from W.G. Lambert (*DM*, pp. 119-23), who promised us an extensive publication twenty-seven years ago. We are still waiting. Failing Lambert's edition, the only more or less complete *tamitu* is that published by E.F. Weidner, "Keilschrifttexte nach Kopien von T.G.Pinches", *AfO* 11 (1936-37), pp. 358-69.

[4] E.g. Goetze, "Historical Allusions", p. 265.

anatomical teaching models for would-be diviners.[1] In support of the former theory is the fact that some such models are inscribed with (whole or partial) omen protases, beginning with *šumma*. In support of the latter is the fact that many models lack precisely such protases, and identify instead various anatomical features. Over thirty years ago, A. Goetze observed that, "veterinarians cannot agree whether a modelled object is meant to represent a sheep's lung or a sheep's liver".[2] This being the case, it is worth considering that the societies which have produced such models, ranging from ancient Syro-Palestine to Anatolia and throughout Mesopotamia, and dating from as far back as the Old Babylonian and as late as the Neo-Babylonian periods, actually possessed a fairly good representative art which, in the late periods, even bordered on the realistic. Why, then, would their diviners convey what was obviously to them valuable information in plastic forms which our modern "empirical" scholars (e.g., Goetze's veterinarians) cannot identify at all? The answer, it seems, is that the "liver models" are in reality something else, namely composite-media communications about actual consultations; they are a type of "report" *sui generis*, with their own appropriate hermeneutical keys, as has recently been argued by J.-W.Meyer.[3]

The Procedure of Extispicy

After employing some form of divinatory prayer, the diviner apparently whispered the words of the question to be answered into the ears of the sacrificial victim (almost always a sheep, though some few bird-extispicies are known). After being killed, the victim lay on its back, and the diviner stood at its hind end. M.I. Hussey has reconstructed the subsequent procedure:

[1] E.g. Nougayrol, "Le foie 'd'orientation'", pp. 31-50.

[2] "Reports on Acts of Extispicy from Old Babylonian and Kassite Times", *JCS* 11 (1957), pp. 89-105; here p. 97.

[3] *Untersuchungen zu den Tonlebermodellen aus dem Alten Orient* (Neukirchen-Vluyn, 1987) (= *AOAT* 39). While Meyer's choice of literature is idiosyncratic (he seems, remarkably for a German scholar, to read better French than English), his semiological approach to the models in question is exciting and must provoke future discussion.

the skin was then cut along the mid-ventral line; that the cartilages
which connect the ribs to the sternum were cut; that the skin and ribs
were folded backward so that the internal viscera could be seen. . .;
that the first inspection was made in the lamb's body. . ..[1]

Thus the positions "right" and "left", which play an important rôle in
omen collections, refer to the organs as seen by the diviner.[2] The
general direction of investigation was from fore-end to rear, from the
ventral surface towards the dorsal one, circling in counter-clockwise
fashion, the liver receiving special attention. The organs were clearly
subjected to a second examination after removal from the body of the
animal, since features are mentioned which could only be observed after
this procedure.

It would be a serious mistake to imagine that only the liver of the
sacrificed animal was examined (i.e., there was never a discipline of
"haruspicy" in ancient Mesopotamia); in fact, all the exta were
examined according to a sequence which was established already in the
Old Babylonian period, and which remained standard practice as long
as we have textual evidence.[3] There were, however, significant
departures from this pattern.[4] It is to be noted that the answers which
the diviner obtained could be positive, negative, or uncertain. In the
last-mentioned case the standard practice was simply to wait a bit and
then try another extispicy, and yet another, and so on, until a favourable
answer was obtained.[5] We have seen previously that similar practices

[1] "Anatomical Nomenclature in an Akkadian Omen Text", *JCS* 2 (1948), pp.
21-32.

[2] This was observed already by J. Denner, "Der assyrische Eingeweideschautext
II R.43", p. 183.

[3] Cf. e.g. Nougayrol, "Rapports paléo-babyloniennes d'haruspices", p. 233; Starr,
The Rituals of the Diviner, pp. 68-69. For another recent account of the phenomenology of the omen sacrifice, see U. Jeyes, "The Act of Extispicy in Ancient
Mesopotamia: An Outline", B. Alster (ed.), *Assyriological Miscellanies* 1 (1980), pp.
13-32.

[4] As pointed out by F.R. Kraus, "Mittelbabylonische Opferschauprotokolle", p.
164.

[5] Cf. already C.J. Gadd in *DM*, pp. 27-28. Also common, at least in Old
Babylonian times, was the immediate "cross-examination" of an extispicy by a
second one, to ensure that the first was no isolated fluke, but a legitimate

among the Azande in connexion with the *benge* poison-oracle led Evans-Pritchard to conclude that the Azande must have a different understanding of time from ours. But, as I pointed out at that time, the reason for this behaviour is simply that divination is a species of "performative utterance", one which is coupled with a symbolic model which enables the questioner to realise his plans, fears, hopes and projects on an ideal plane. Hence it is in principle unrelated to concepts of time. Of course, this does not rule out the possibility that a given society may have developed one or more ideologies to explain the apparent lack of logic inherent in such behaviour, a development which is only to be expected in traditional societies which have had, like all contemporary "primitive" societies, at least some contact with the developed world.

The terminology employed by the diviner to designate the various parts of the exta is of bewildering complexity, and for a number of reasons. For one thing, and possibly the most important reason, the ancient diviners were not concerned with descriptive anatomy. This means that, to them, the insides of an animal had no functional significance; they were instead regarded as instruments of communication, which explains why numerous features, such as depressions left on the liver by the pressure of other organs, were assigned ominous meaning, although a modern anatomist would find little in such features to interest him. Then again, as is the case with other forms of Mesopotamian divination, the diviners were not solely concerned with the empirically *possible*; there are accordingly references to animals with odd numbers of "convolutions" of the intestine, which, since this would entail that the animal in question had managed to grow to maturity with an intestine which failed to exit its body, a phenomenon which, in the nature of things cannot occur.[1] There are also references to animals

---

communication. See already Nougayrol, "Rapports paléo-babyloniennes d'haruspices", p. 222, lines 12-14 and n. 31.

[1] As only the (to my knowledge) second Assyriologist to do so (the other was R.D. Biggs), R.K.G. Temple actually took the trouble to compare the texts with slaughterhouse animals instead of the usual highly idealised specimens in anatomical textbooks ("An Anatomical Verification of the Reading of a Term in Extispicy", *JCS* 34 [1982], pp. 19-27). On doing so, he found that the feature called in the texts *tiranu*, usually rendered "large colon", was actually the "spiral colon" of the sheep.

lacking a *libbu* (heart), which, all things considered, makes it unlikely (to say the least) that the animal could have reached the age and condition suitable for sacrifice.[1] Nevertheless, even in spite of these limitations, Assyriologists have done yeoman's service in elucidating many of the features which were significant to the diviner.[2]

The Interpretation of the Omen Sacrifice

Assyriologists have for many years contented themselves with only very occasional and sporadic attempts to determine how the diviner interpreted the exta of the sacrificial animal.[3] Since the diviner investigated

---

Temple was unable to solve the symmetry problem, however, and so suggested that a degenerative condition of the colon may leave a section of it almost invisible; thus a lamb might look as if it had only 11 or 13 "convolutions". While Temple may very well be right, my point is that, as we have seen, other omens sometimes have features which have nothing to do with what can occur (moreover, as parts of performatives, even if they can occur, this is unimportant). And, since the diviner obviously knew what the insides of a sheep looked like, perhaps he was also able to see the almost-invisible degenerate "convolution". He may therefore have meant something quite different by postulating an anatomically impossible case.

[1] Cf. e.g. YOS 10 42:16: *šumma libbu la ibašši miqitti rubim*: "if there is no heart, downfall of the prince"; and compare Cicero, *De Divinatione* 1,118-19, cf. 2,35-36, for a supposedly "authentic" Roman case in which the sacrificial animal is said to have lacked a heart.

[2] In addition to the many studies of J. Nougayrol, mentioned previously, and that of M.I. Hussey, see such recent investigations as: L. Rost, "Der Leberlappen", *ZAW* 79 (1967), pp. 35-41; R.D. Biggs, "Qutnu, masrahu and related terms in Babylonian extispicy", *RA* 63 (1969), pp. 159-67; *idem*, "A Babylonian Extispicy Text Concerning Holes", *JNES* 33 (1974), pp. 351-58; I. Starr, "Notes on Some Technical Terms in Extispicy", *JCS* 27 (1975), pp. 241-49; *idem*, "An Additional Note on a Technical Term in Extispicy", *JCS* 30 (1978), pp. 170-172; *idem*, "Omen Texts Concerning Holes in the Liver", *AfO* 26 (1978/79), pp. 45-55; U. Jeyes, "The 'Palace Gate' of the Liver. A Study of Terminology and Methods in Babylonian Extispicy", *JCS* 30 (1978), pp. 209-33; R.G. Temple, "An Anatomical Verification"; I. Starr, "Omen Texts Concerning Lesser Known Parts of the Lungs", *JNES* 42 (1983), pp. 109-21; *idem, The Rituals of the Diviner, passim*; Jeyes, *Old Babylonian Extispicy*, esp. pp. 51-92.

[3] Cf. e.g. M. Jastrow, *Religious Belief*, pp. 143-206; A. Ungnad, *Die Deutung der Zukunft, pp. 9-14; G. Klauber, Politisch-religiöse Texte aus der Sargonidenzeit* (Leipzig, 1913), pp.XXXV-LVI; J. Denner, "Das assyrische Eingeweideschautext II R.43", pp. 180-220.

numerous organs and details of the individual organs, and, further, since the omen compendia list at least one apodosis for each "sign" present in the exta, it has always been obvious that the final prognosis represented some sort of "sum" of the various "prognoses", but just how it was arrived at has long been mysterious. However, it was noted fairly early that the positions left and right with respect to the diviner play an important part in the diviner's "arithmetic"; this led to the assumption that such references implied the use of a *pars familiaris—pars hostilis* system, as practised by diviners in classical times.[1] But just how the manifold protases and apodoses fit into such a system has only recently come to some extent into focus, thanks to the efforts of I. Starr.[2]

Starr has devoted great attention to the text HSM 7494, originally treated by M.I. Hussey.[3] The text is a lengthy *ikribu* (divination prayer) which asks the gods Šamaš and Adad to place favourable ominous signs on the right sides of the organs of the sheep, and unfavourable ones on the left. Clearly, the left side represents the enemy, opponent, or whatever, while the right side symbolises the diviner's client. Starr has then shown that "favourable" label simply designates the presence of a feature of the exta that was to be expected; absence, degeneration, engorgement, or similar unusual characteristics of the same anatomical details accordingly signify departures from the "norm", and are *per definitionem* unfavourable. Therefore every favourable characteristic on the right side represents a "plus" for the subject of the enquiry and a "minus" for the opponent, and *vice versa*. If the diviner did not know the plus or minus value of a given "sign", his next step was to consult the compendia of omens. Then all he had to do was to summarise the number of plusses, subtract the number of minusses, and produce an aggregate sum. If the plusses and minusses more or less cancelled each other out, the result was uncertain (*pitrustum*), so that a "cross-examina-

---

[1] Cf. already Ungnad, *Die Deutung der Zukunft*, p. 11.

[2] "In Search of Principles of Prognostication in Extispicy", *HUCA* 45 (1974), pp. 17-23; *The 'Baru' Rituals*, Yale University Ph.D. (New Haven, 1974); *The Rituals of the Diviner*.

[3] "Anatomical Nomenclature", pp. 21-32.

tion" (*piqittum*) (or "check-up") was indicated.[1] Accordingly, what remains for Assyriolgists to do at present is to publish the full corpus of the apodoses of extispicy, with a view to discovering whether they were regarded as "positive" or "negative". In addition to Starr's efforts, U. Jeyes has made a start on this, if only a start.[2]

Starr's insight that the "normal" state of the exta is the diviner's point of departure, and that deviations from the norm are inherently negative, has some interesting implications. I cited R. Labat above to the effect that, in connexion with medical and diagnostic divination, any observation which normally bears a positive significance suddenly receives a negative apodosis when the enquirer is a sick person, and vice versa. J. Nougayrol likewise noted over thirty years ago in a study of omen sacrifices undertaken on behalf of the sick that, in the Old Babylonian period, when an omen protasis is followed by two apodoses, they are normally semantically parallel. However, he added that at some point between the Old Babylonian and Cassite periods this practice changed, so that we suddenly find, first, a positive apodosis, followed by the rubric "if for a sick person", and then a negative one.[3]

If the analogy of the condition of the exta of the sacrificial sheep holds, the enquirer in an extispicy was presumed to be in a cultically pure state. This is immediately obvious once one acknowledges that the "ideal" enquirer was the king, as so many apodoses show. When we consider the immense cultic effort that was ordinarily invested in ensuring the king's unobjectionable cultic status in ancient Mesopotamia, then it is clear that he was apriori "pure". Also, the rite of extispicy itself was accompanied by extensive rites of self-purification which no doubt extended to the enquirer, whether he was personally present or only represented by the "fringe" of his garment, or the trace of his fingernail on a clay tablet. The obvious analogy to this is the fact that the normal state of the exta is considered to be a positive sign. Conversely, however, it was universally held in the ancient Near East

---

[1] Cf. Starr, "Notes on Some Technical Terms", pp. 243-46; Goetze, "Reports on Acts of Extispicy", p. 95 and n. 40.

[2] "Death and Divination in the Old Babylonian Period", in B. Alster (ed.) *Death in Mesopotamia*, pp. 107-21, esp. pp. 116-21; *idem, Old Babylonian Extispicy*, pp. 38-96.

[3] "Présages Médicaux de L'haruspicine Babylonienne", pp. 8-12, esp. p. 12.

that illness was the result, not necessarily of sin (an anachronistic concept which can only with difficulty be harmonised with ancient Near Eastern patterns of belief and praxis), but at least of disharmony with the divine. Thus, for example, we read in Šurpu the prodigious list of trepasses which the sufferer may inadvertently have committed, and for which the cleansing ritual was the appropriate remedy. Therefore a sufferer was by definition in the opposite cultic state from the "normal" enquirer, so it is not only intelligible, but also logical, that the "normal" apodoses have the reverse significance for him. According to Nougayrol, this conclusion seems to have been drawn in the Cassite period.[1]

In the terms of structuralist anthropology, this simple reversal of the "sign-value" of the status of the enquirer as a result of illness reflects a phase in the assimilation of nature (in this case the spectrum of human physical states ranging from health to grave illness) to culture (i.e., categorisation, via the agency of divination: a social product).

Unusual Genres

Though there were a fair number of phenomena pertaining to the tradition of Mesopotamian divination which cannot be said to have been central to the tradition,[2] we shall confine ourselves here to speak of only two of them, namely necromancy, divining by contact with the dead, and a "genre" which has only recently been fully identified as such (it had no independent rubric in ancient times), the prophecy. The former is included here in spite of its clearly marginal status in the ancient Near East simply because of the interest that invariably accrues to it here in the West; the latter is included because of its obvious relevance to discussions of "historical" and "chronographic" thought in the region in remote times.

---

[1] "Présages Médicaux de L'haruspicine Babylonienne", p. 12.

[2] Cf. e.g. such phenomena as lot-casting, (E. Reiner, "Fortune-Telling in Mespotamia", *JNES* 19 [1960], pp. 23-35), or predictions apropos human and natural phenomena based on the month of their occurrence (cf. R. Labat, *Un Calendrier Babylonien des Travaux, des Signes, et des Mois (Séries iqqur ipuš)* (Paris, 1965).

Necromancy

Virtually all that is known of divining by the dead has been assembled in a single, thorough article by I.L. Finkel in *Archiv für Orientforschung*,[1] plus a recent monograph by J. Tropper.[2] As Finkel points out, the necromancer/ess was known as *mušelu / mušelitu* [3] *etemmi*, or *ša etemmi*, where the terms used for the dead were either *utukku* or *etemmu* (both meaning "ghost"), although *ilu*, "god, spirit" was sometimes used as well.[4] Otherwise, outside of a few mentions in letters from as far back as the Old Akkadian period, the only really tangible evidence for the practice consists of one Late- and one Neo-Babylonian text. Both texts are clearly products of late reflection and development of the tradition; one of them reflects the terminology and concepts of both *šumma alu* and the *namburbi* series, indicating that the *namburbis* were not only capable of combating unfortunate omens, but perhaps also of deriving information from elsewhere themselves.[5] One of the two texts requires the summoning of the *etemmu* into a handy skull provided for the purpose. The summoner is instructed, after completing the ritual, to "speak (to the skull), and it will answer". About the only other relevant information bearing on this practice is to be found in the Old Testament and the Talmud.[6]

For his part, Tropper attempts to examine the phenomenon of necromancy in the light of the ancient Near Eastern cults of ancestor worship, a praiseworthy attempt to change the frame of reference of necromancy studies from the phenomenology of obscure "magical" practices to the wider field of a neglected aspect of ancient Near Eastern religious life. Unfortunately, there is little he can do to overcome the

---

[1] "Necromancy in Ancient Mesopotamia", *AfO* 29 (1983), pp. 1-17.

[2] *Nekromantie. Totenbefragung im Alten Orient und im Alten Testament* (Neukirchen-Vluyn, 1989) (= *AOAT* 223).

[3] the *š*-stem (causative) participle of Akk. *elû*, "to ascend", hence "he/she who brings up (the dead)".

[4] "Necromancy in Ancient Mesopotamia", p. 1.

[5] "Necromancy in Ancient Mesopotamia", p. 7.

[6] "Necromancy in Ancient Mesopotamia", pp. 13-15. See also K. van der Toorn, "Echoes of Judaean Necromancy in Isaiah 28,7-22", *ZAW* 100 (1988), pp. 199-217, which, however, is rather apologetic in its orientation.

dearth of sources already indicated by Finkel. Thus, for example, the few references to the *mušelu/mušelitu* Tropper is able to unearth in the Sumero-Akkadian lexical series[1] awaken no confidence in the notion that necromancy was a widespread practice. Surely no Assyriologist would be prepared to accept lexical evidence without correlative evidence in the vast mass of Akkadian correspondence, legal documents, and archival materials available to us—and it is precisely such evidence that we lack.

Tropper himself is aware that one of his lexical attestations (MSL 12,104:18) lists the *mušelitu* woman immediately after the "sorceress" (kaššaptu);[2] but if he had read any of the fairly extensive social anthropological literature on magic that has appeared since Evans-Pritchard, he would have known that the latter designation is most unlikely to have been a "calling". It was, rather, more probably a socially stigmatic accusatory term which figured in witchcraft accusations and in the countermagic of the exorcist.

Nor can Tropper's examination of the Ugaritic evidence[3] change the impression of the rarity of the phenomenon, as it develops that, alongside of texts showing the existence of the ancestor cult at Ugarit (a phenomenon we have long been aware of), only a single difficult and fragmentary text (KTU 1.124) might, with some good will, be taken to represent a series of oracular questions addressed to the dead.[4] Finally, it is also the case that Tropper has not cast his net wide enough by expanding his focus from the phenomenology of magic to religious practice. Comparison of the ancient Near Eastern ancestor cults with similar practices in existing traditional societies might have served as a

---

[1] *Nekromantie*, pp. 58-60.

[2] *Nekromantie*, p. 60.

[3] *Nekromantie*, pp. 123-60.

[4] *Nekromantie*, pp. 151-56. In this connexion it might be mentioned that the narrative scheme of KTU 1.124 in which questions as to the healing of a young prince are addressed to a mythical ancestor, who replies with ritual instructions, can hardly be considered a necromantic act in *senso strictu*. The pattern is simply that of obtaining legitimating authority for a conjuration, a standard feature of the Marduk-Ea and other central Mesopotamian incantations. This possibility has been overlooked by Dietrich et al. in *Mantik in Ugarit*, pp. 205-40, where KTU 1.124 is compared with the *tamitu* texts.

useful safeguard against the tendency to assume that, where veneration
of the ancestors may be safely assumed, it may be likewise assumed that
one invariably attempts to derive information from them. Tropper's
investigation remains, however, useful, in particular as regards the Old
Testament, as we shall see later.

Akkadian "Prophecies"

To begin with, in dealing with the texts of this genre there is a
terminological problem which is practically insoluble.[1] The texts all
contain, or seem in their fragmentary condition to contain, statements
about the course of future history, some of which have been placed in
the mouth of a ruler from the distant past or a god. On the other hand,
the "future" they envision seems cyclical and may or may not end in a
final time of blessedness; thus the analogy to the late Biblical and
extra-Biblical apocalypses suggests itself, and some scholars prefer this

---

[1] As is well known, there is a considerable epistolary literature from ancient
Mari and from the Neo-Assyrian courts in which the desires, warnings and
assurances of the gods are communicated to the respective sovereigns.
Unfortunately, it will not be possible to examine these materials, which clearly also
have a claim to the title of "prophetic communications", in these pages. This is so
more for reasons of space and because of my primary concern to deal with the
so-called "technical" means of divination than because of any apriori theoretical
distinction between these and other types of revelation. All of them are varieties of
divination, which means that they are, Marian, Assyrian and Israelite alike,
manifestations of the wider province of magic. Cf. my "Der Prophet und der Magier.
Bemerkungen anhand einer überholten Diskussion" in: R. Liwak and S. Wagner
(eds.), *Prophetie und geschichtliche Wirklichkeit im alten Israel. Festschrift für
Siegfried Herrmann zum 65. Geburtstag* (Stuttgart, 1991), pp. 79-88. In this
connexion it is regrettable that most OT scholars, and even some Assyriologists,
have traditionally attempted to distinguish between Israelite and other ancient Near
Eastern "prophetic" phenomena. The literature alone on these materials is too
extensive to mention here; the reader is accordingly referred to M. Weippert,
"Assyrische Prophetien der Zeit Asarhaddons und Assurbanipals", in F.M. Fales
(ed.), *Assyrian Royal Inscriptions: New Horizons in Literary, Ideological and
Historical Analysis* (Rome, 1981) (= *Oriens Antiqui Collectio* 17), pp. 71-104, for
the Neo-Assyrian prophetic texts, and, for the Marian and other Old Babylonian
materials, to the investigation by M. de Jong Ellis in "Observations on Mesopotamian Oracles and Prophetic Texts: Literary and Historiographic Considerations", *JCS*
41 (1989), pp. 134-46.

designation. We have known about these texts for quite some time,[1] but it was only in recent times, with the publication of new texts, that the discussion has gathered momentum. The breakthrough came when a number of texts, called for convenience A,B,C, and D were published by A.K. Grayson and W.G. Lambert.[2] In addition to a fine edition of the texts in question, the authors also made extensive references to related literature, and explicitly drew parallels with the Book of Daniel. Here, too, Grayson made the unfortunate statement that the fact that

> the Babylonians did regard history as cyclical is well attested by historical omens. . .The same natural phenomenon is always (in theory) accompanied by the same historical event.[3]

I have referred previously to Grayson's assumption of an antithesis between "historical" thought and omens. This particular statement shows a lack of reflection about the nature of history[4] as well as a lack of insight into the phenomenology of omens, and Grayson's collaborator, Lambert, was not slow to renounce the idea.[5] Grayson and Lambert's effort was soon followed by an article by W.W. Hallo,[6] who compared the intervals of time mentioned in the "cycles" described in the texts with the chronology of Mesopotamian history, found a fair degree of co-incidence, and so concluded that the cycles are *vaticinia ex eventu*. This insight enabled Hallo to identify many of the events mentioned in

---

[1] Cf. H.G. Güterbock, "Die historische Tradition bei Babyloniern und Hethitern", *ZA* 42 (1934), pp. 79-86 (the Marduk prophecy, called by Güterbock "naru-Literatur").

[2] "Akkadian Prophecies", *JCS* 18 (1964), pp. 7-23.

[3] "Akkadian Prophecies", p. 10.

[4] How can one organise *any* experience without some standard of comparison? Without some sort of pattern shaping one's expectations, every experience would be foreign and unintelligible. But, of course, this does not mean that one identifies the pattern with the perceived reality. See K.R. Popper, *The Poverty of Historicism*, (London, 1972 [1957]), pp. 9-11; pp. 146-47.

[5] Cf. W.G. Lambert, "History and the Gods: A Review Article", *Or* N.S. 39 (1970) 175 n. 7: "The reviewer would like to take this occasion to say that he does not and has never accepted the idea that the Babylonians conceived history cyclically".

[6] "Akkadian Apocalypses", in *IEJ* 16 (1966), pp. 231-42.

Grayson-Lambert's Text A with a fair degree of probability.

In 1967, R.D. Biggs entered the fray with the claim that "the 'prophecies' must. . .be considered simply a peculiar part of the vast Mesopotamian omen tradition".[1] Earlier scholars had been aware that the language in some of the prophecies/apocalypses reflects that which is employed in omen *apodoses*; in publishing a new text fragment of Text B and a version of LBAT 1543, Biggs was able to show that some omen *protases* are also present as well. Moreover, Biggs identified the language of the omens in question as characteristic of astrological omina; thus he questioned the relevance of the texts to Mesopotamian history, and held that "The purpose of this literary genre may be guessed at, but the fact remains that we do not know".[2] Undeterred by Biggs' claims, the very learned Assyriologist, R. Borger published a finely-detailed study and textual edition of both the Marduk and the Sulgi "prophecies".[3] Borger anchors the "Marduk" text, which speaks of Marduk's return to Babylon from Elam, in the reign of Nebuchadnezzar I (1127-1105), as this king is known to have retrieved the stolen statue of Marduk from its captivity in Elam.[4] Borger also cautiously embraces Hallo's date for Grayson-Lambert's Text A to the end of the 11th century, accepts the notion that we have to do with *vaticinia ex eventu*, but points out that it is nevertheless difficult to term the texts in question apocalypses because of "the lack of any kind of eschatology in the Akkadian texts"[5]

An excellent introduction to the whole question, including a translation of the so-called "Dynastic Prophecy", was published by Grayson in 1975.[6] Having taken Biggs' point about astrological material in Text B and LBAT 1543 seriously, Grayson "saves" the remaining

---

[1] "More Babylonian 'Prophecies'", *Iraq* 29 (1967), pp. 117-32; here p. 117.

[2] "More Babylonian 'Prophecies'", p. 117.

[3] "Gott Marduk and Gott-König Šulgi als Propheten", *BO* 28 (1971), pp. 3-24.

[4] "Gott Marduk und Gott-König Šulgi", p. 21.

[5] "Gott Marduk und Gott-König Šulgi", p. 24.

[6] *Babylonian Historical-Literary Texts* (Toronto and Buffalo, 1975), pp. 13-40.

"prophecies"[1] for the historical interpretation by the simple expedient of excluding Text B and LBAT 1543 from the corpus of the "prophecies".[2] His view finds tacit, if not explicit support in W.G. Lambert's subsequently-published historicising interpretation of the Marduk and Uruk prophecies.[3]

In recent times, R.D. Biggs has returned to the question and demonstrated that also as far as Grayson-Lambert's Text A is concerned, "the phraseology of the predictions. . .is largely that of astrological omens".[4] He further points to coincidences of terminology and geographical designations between astrological omina and all of the remaining prophecies.[5]

In sum, up to the present the main disputants as to the nature of the "prophecy" texts seem to be arguing at cross-purposes. Oddly, what they have in common is the view that, if the texts are based on omens, the events referred to cannot have taken place, or rather, that no actual events are referred to. No one seems to have grasped the point that correspondence with empirical facts *may* be presupposed in omens, although "correspondence with the facts" is not their primary purpose and certainly cannot be assumed *apriori*.

The most recent contribution to the discussion has been a lengthy article by M. de Jong Ellis.[6] Ms.de Jong Ellis sees the difficulties scholars have had in getting a grip on the "prophecy" texts as at least in part the result of the failure of our attempts to classify the works in

---

[1] I.e., the "Dynastic Prophecy", Text A, the Uruk Prophecy, the Marduk Prophecy, and the Sulgi Prophecy; see Grayson, *Babylonian Historical-literary Texts*, pp. 14-15, n. 4-8.

[2] Grayson, *Babylonian Historical-literary Texts*, p. 15 and n. 11-15.

[3] *The Background of Jewish Apocalyptic. The Ethel M.Wood Lecture delivered before the University of London on 22 February 1977* (London, 1978), pp. 1-20; here pp. 9-13.

[4] "The Babylonian Prophecies and the Astrological Traditions of Mesopotamia", *JCS* 37 (1985), pp. 86-90; here p. 87.

[5] "The Babylonian Prophecies and the Astrological Traditions of Mesopotamia", pp. 88-90.

[6] "Observations on Mesopotamian Oracles and Prophetic Texts: Literary and Historiographic Considerations", *JCS* 41 (1989), pp. 127-86, on the "prophecies" (which Ms. de Jong Ellis redefines as "literary predictive texts") see pp. 146-86.

question. As she puts it,

> My basic argument with the current classificatory pattern is that it elevates a category established for the convenience of modern scholars into a 'more abstract classification'. This is done without consideration of all appositie material, including the possible relevance of the serial classification the ancient scribes made for their convenience. . . Modern work. . . has not dealt with either the 'genres' or the texts assigned to them through the kind of analysis practiced by the modern literary critic, which takes into account the mutual interdependence of textual witnesses and the society that produced them.[1]

Naturally, this sort of critical remark is easier to present than is, say, the introduction of a new taxonomy or an exhaustive analysis of the background underlying the taxonomic choices of the ancient scribes. Nevertheless, Ms. de Jong Ellis has made a bold attempt to point to at least some of the political, historical and social features which these texts may be claimed to have in common. In particular, I should like to emphasise her acknowledgement of the common ground shared by these texts, the omen literature, and other past-relating literature[2]—a conclusion that would greatly have pleased the late J.J. Finkelstein, whose original insight pointed in this direction.

Divination as an Intellectual Activity: Omens and the Literary Tradition

A difficulty with the modern study of the omen literature and its underlying phenomenology is that the course of this study has necessarily followed strictly form-critical lines, that is, scholars have mainly been content to pay great attention to the individual genres of the literary tradition. They have not, however, devoted equal time to the relationship between the omen literature and the other literatures which composed what A.L. Oppenheim termed the Mesopotamian "stream of tradition". This is entirely understandable, as the Mesopotamian genres are gnomic in style; hence, the attempt to bridge the gap between the genres inevitably entails a degree of speculation which most scholars would not

---

[1] "Observations on Mesopotamian Oracles", p. 155.

[2] Cf. "Observations on Mesopotamian Oracles", esp. p. 159.

want to risk. But a problem does not happen to go away simply because one prefers to avoid it, and it is in any case only by synthesis that we can derive a model, that is, a theory, which may be corrected, amended, or discarded, and so provide a basis to prompt future research.

One stumbling-block that must be overcome is the assumption that omens attempt in some fashion to "predict the future". As I suggested in the third chapter of this work, like many other magical acts, what they actually do is either to provide models for action, or else, being performatives, they are themselves the action in question. Now performatives, as I have maintained, consist of two elements, the performative proper, whether spoken or enacted (e.g., "I hereby promise, swear, bequeath," etc.), and the "complement" (i.e., what is promised, sworn, bequeathed, etc.). When a Mesopotamian king asked his diviner whether the gods approved of his project to invade a neighbouring territory, the diviner's "question" carefully mapped out the project, naming the towns and villages to be occupied along the route and even specifying the route of return. This, I submit, is the literary mimesis[1] of (projected) reality; the diviner makes a verbal model of the planned course of action. This model, then, is the "complement" of the performative, that is, of the act of divination itself, whether this might take the form of an omen sacrifice, an oil omen, or whatever. The diviner's "yes" may be interpreted as a promise: a promise which the gods themselves have pronounced. Like the "I do" in the wedding ceremony, it is the act itself.

Acknowledgement of the fact that divination does not actually "predict the future" allows us to compare the literature of divination with other ancient literary forms whose purpose it is to model action, and so to enable man to face the challenges of his existence.[2] Seen in this light, the omen texts may be understood without further ado to be the immediate complement to the literature of defensive magic, that is, to the incantations whose function it is to protect against pollution, to

---

[1] For the concept, see E. Auerbach, *Mimesis* (Berne), 1946; ET (Princeton, 1957 [1953]); see, above all, "Odysseus' Scar", pp. 1-20.

[2] Of course, not only "action" is modelled; the questioner may ask as to whether X has stolen his money, or whatever. This, too, is a variety of model-building, only of ideation, rather than of action: the questioner desires certainty as to his suspicions, and the performative warrants (or does not) that certainty.

repel demons, witches, sorcerers, or the like. The fact that the king's fear of military defeat, which prompts him to seek the counsel of the diviner, is intelligible to us in rational-"empirical" terms, while the believer's fear of demons or witches is not, is neither here nor there. The distinction, as I have by now argued many times, was unknown in the societies in question. The Marian diviner Asqudum (see below) found it as sensible to enquire as to the prospects for the grain harvest as he did to investigate the (ominous) import of a lunar eclipse. His counterpart, the conjurer (see below), found it likewise sensible to perform an incantation warding off the evil consequences of a lunar eclipse, even after lunar motion had been sufficiently well described mathematically to enable him to say with certainty when the phenomenon would take place.

It is a commonplace that historiography is not about the past, but about the present, that is, that the questions which can be directed towards the past are unique to the period of social development which gives rise to them. I have already argued in the introduction to this work that the ancient world had no historical writing, that is, no self-critical, empirically orientated way of posing questions of the past so as to produce falsifiable models. Another way of putting it would be to say that in our world historiography is a specialised province of the theory of knowledge (epistemology), which it certainly was not in the ancient world. The ancient world did, however, produce a considerable literature about the past which manifested itself in king lists, chronicles, annals, royal inscriptions and in the foundation deposits of temples and other structures.[1]

The purpose of this literature was clearly not to tell "how it was", but to glorify the deeds (whether military or "cultural", i.e., construction enterprises) of the king or, occasionally, of members of his line, where filial piety was involved, which is the same thing (even in Assyria, where the prevailing ideology promulgated a largely fictive dynastic continuity).[2] Thus these writings obviously served the purpose of

---

[1] See the fundamental study by A.K. Grayson, "Histories and Historians of the Ancient Near East: Assyria and Babylonia", *Or* 49 (1980), pp. 140-94.

[2] Cf. e.g. H. Tadmor, "History and Ideology in the Assyrian Royal Inscriptions", in Fales (ed.), *Assyrian Royal Inscriptions*, pp. 13-35; P. Garelli, "La conception de la royauté en Assyrie", in the same, pp. 1-11. Already the great S. Mowinckel had

legitimating the present order and hence were pragmatically designed to enable the king to exercise his authority: an entirely present-orientated concern. They are in this sense fully comparable with the various extispicies which were undertaken to shore up the authority of a royal appointment or accession to the throne. For this reason it is perhaps not so inexplicable as A.K. Grayson thinks that some few seemingly "historical" documents incorporate phrases from omen protases and apodoses. Conversely, we note that documents which seem to speak of future developments in terms of vaguely characterised royal "reigns", such as the prophecy/apocalyptic texts (see above), also do not hesitate to employ the language of omina. Once again it seems that distinctions which are completely obvious to us were not necessarily ever drawn, or at least not fully drawn, in ancient Babylonia and Assyria.

Finally, there is that amorphous mass of texts of all types, proverbs, fables, instructions, didactic tales, and so forth which go by the name of "Wisdom" in Assyriological and Old Testament parlance.[1] The difficulties of arriving at a formal definition of the phenomenon are notoriously legion, so that we are perhaps best advised simply to acknowledge that the category is a catch-all, and that its boundaries are very poorly defined. This is especially the case as far as past-relating ("historical") texts is concerned, as no obvious formal distinctions present themselves between stories told about the past for one purpose or another and similar stories which are told about the past in order to

---

acknowledged the self-serving character of ancient Near Eastern "historical" inscriptions; cf. "Die vorderasiatischen Königs- und Fürsteninschriften: eine stilistische Studie", in: *Eucharisterion. Festschrift Herrmann Gunkel dargebracht,* Vol.1 (Göttingen, 1923) (= *FRLANT* 19), pp. 278-322. Naturally, I am not claiming that all ancient Babylonian-Assyrian past-referring texts served the king alone. Obviously, they served many other aims as well, such as persuading subject peoples of the rightness of their subjugation. Some, like the Babylonian "chronicles", may even be held to evidence a "scholarly" concern to gather together as much inscriptional material as possible—though, once again, I would contest the notion that this effort has anything to do with what might be termed "historiographical" interests.

[1] Like most of our terminology, "Wisdom" represents the superimposition of an artificial category of uncertain contents onto a wide field of phenomena for which the ancient Mesopotamians themselves had no term. As Lambert points out, Akk. *nemequ(m)*, "wisdom", and its parallels have to do with "skill in cult and magic lore" (*Babylonian Wisdom Literature*, p. 1).

"improve" their hearer.[1]

For our purposes it is sufficient to note the fact that some of the contents of this "grab-bag" tend to describe what might be termed normative outcomes of habitual behaviour. Thus, for example, a Sumerian proverb informs us that "When drinking beer, all the harvest is drowned".[2] Similarly, the Old Testament notes that "He who guards his mouth preserves his life; he who opens wide his lips comes to ruin" (Prov 13.3). It has long been noted that this tendency of some Wisdom materials to assume that characteristic or habitual actions have characteristic results presupposes a belief in an orderly cosmos. The wise man, it is maintained, will profit from Wisdom instruction and so be in a position to pilot his way through life's vicissitudes. Some scholars have gone so far as to compare this hypothetically benign world order with the Egyptian concept of *ma'at* and the Sumerian concept of the *me's*, both of which seem to express some such notion of world order.[3]

I feel, however, that it is difficult to maintain the existence of such abstractions in connexion with societies which never expressed themselves in terms of universalising concepts. It would perhaps be more appropriate simply to note that ancient Mesopotamian proverbs often relate general moral acts to general outcomes; the same, it should be noted, is the case of certain classes of omens. In 1936, F.R. Kraus published under the title "Ein Sittenkanon in Omenform" a series of Old Babylonian omens which link certain physical features of individuals to specific prognostics (physiognomical omens). However, some of the omens in Kraus' publication also link certain types of general behaviour to equally *general* prognostics, as for example: "if he repays good

---

[1] Cf. e.g. J.L. Crenshaw's strictures in "Method in Determining Wisdom Influence upon 'Historical' Literature", *JBL* 88 (1969), pp. 129-42.

[2] Sum. *KAS kurun₂ nag-nag/guru₇ sè-LAGAB-LAGAB*; Cf. B. Alster, *The Instructions of Suruppak. A Sumerian Proverb Collection* (Copenhagen, 1974), p. 14 IIa 225; ET p. 18.

[3] For the Egyptian concept, see A.K. Grayson and D.B. Redford, *Papyrus and Tablet* (Englewood Cliffs NJ, 1973), pp. 6-7; further, A. Volten, "Der Begriff der Maat in den ägyptischen Weisheitstexten" in: *Les Sagesses du Proche-Orient Ancien* (Paris, 1963), pp. 73-99; for the *me's* see S.N. Kramer, *The Sumerians*, pp. 115-16.

deeds, the whole of him will prosper".[1] Kraus himself later published more such material; the list was further expanded by another tablet published by F. Köcher and A.L. Oppenheim.[2] All of these collections date from the Old Babylonian period, and some of them reveal contacts with the massive collection of omens known as *šumma alu*,[3] which suggests that the kind of conceptual overlap in question was not a temporally isolated phenomenon, but one which persisted in Mesopotamian tradition.

Conversely, it may be pointed out that some proverbs from the earliest collections tend to relate entirely specific actions to equally specific prognostics, a feature otherwise common to the omen collections, with the formal difference that the proverbs are characteristically admonitory, rather than casuistic, thus: "Do not curse a ewe, you will give birth to a daughter",[4] or: "Do not throw a lump (of earth) into a sieve, you will give birth to an heir".[5] Of course, these are to be compared with the many omens of a number of different classes which bear on the question of the sex of future offspring. These two examples by no means exhaust the witness available. In short, a degree of overlap between the aims and styles of omens and proverbs is detectable in ancient Mesopotamia from the earliest times.

A fascinating mixture of ominous style and content with an essentially didactic text is offered by the famous "Advice to a Prince", originally published by F.M.T. Böhl as *Der Babylonische Fürstenspiegel*, and subsequently published in magisterial form by Lambert.[6] Briefly, this short document (written on a single tablet) imitates the style

---

[1] *šumma gi-mil-li u-ta-ar ka-lu-šu i-ta-ab-šu*; *ZA* 43 (1936) 96-97 (text and German trans.).

[2] "The Old Babylonian Omen Text VAT 7525", *AfO* 18 (1957-58) 62-80.

[3] "The Old Babylonian Omen Text VAT 7525", p. 67.

[4] Cited in Alster, *Šurrupak*, p. 49, line 249. I have slightly corrected Alster's English.

[5] *Šurrupak*, p. 49. Of course, the logic of this twin pair of admonitions is baffling; it was not unusual in the ancient Near East to want to avoid the birth of daughters, but what on earth was the objection to sons (i.e., "heirs")?

[6] For the "Fürstenspiegel", see Böhl, *MAOG* 11 (1937); for the "Advice", see W.G. Lambert, *Babylonian Wisdom Literature*, pp. 110-15.

and contents of omens, with the exception that the introductory "šumma" (if) is lacking. The point is that if the monarch fails to adhere to some common and, or so the text presupposes, universally respected moral precepts (e.g., "If he does not heed the justice of his land, Ea, king of destinies, will alter his destiny and will not cease from hostilely pursuing him"[1]), or abridges the *kidinnutu*-status (i.e., city-state rights)[2] of the citizens of Nippur, Sippar, or Babylon, then divine retribution is sure to follow. The references to the rights of the citizens of the three main Babylonian cities has prompted some scholars (e.g., Böhl) to set the date of the document quite late, that is, to the time of the Assyrian domination of Babylonia. Lambert, however, points out that the king in question is considered to be a native,[3] which rules out an Assyrian interloper, and so points to the period between 1000 and 700 BC. Liverani, by contrast, takes the protests of the cities to represent the resentment of the citizens of late second-millennium or early first-millennium Babylonian cities towards the ever-increasing powers of an increasingly centralised—and hence tyrannical—monarchy.[4]. Whatever the truth of the matter, it should be clear that in the "Advice to a Prince" we have a text in which the didactic and ominous traditions flow together in the interests of political ideology. Moreover, this ideology borders on forming a concept of natural law, above the demands of which no man, not even the king, is elevated. Once again, however, as I have already stressed, this conclusion is not stated in terms of universalising statements, but concretely, through the grainy particularity of a collection of omens (or rather, an imitation of one).

In this connexion, it might be added that the notion that a king has perforce to observe the dictates of the omens is the main thrust of a didactic text deriving from as far back as the Old Babylonian period. This is the so-called "Cuthaean Legend of Naram-Sin", a "pseudo-auto-biographical" composition which relates how the fabled Akkadian monarch (he reigned around 2254-2218) attempted, against the advice

[1] *Babylonian Wisdom Literature*, p. 113, lines 19-22.

[2] Cf. Oppenheim, *AM*, pp. 120-24. The *kidinnutu* status involved freedom from certain taxes and obligations, like corvée-service, with respect to the crown.

[3] *Babylonian Wisdom Literature*, p. 111.

[4] *AO*, pp. 772-73.

of his diviners, and with predictably unfortunate consequences, to resist the invasion of his kingdom by a strange people with "raven-like" faces.[1] After some chastening experiences, however, he resigns himself to abide by the divine will, and is assured that in the course of time his mysterious enemy will be destroyed.

To summarise briefly: the omen literature is complementary to the ancient Mesopotamian defensive-magical literature, and shares a kinship of ideological intention with much of the "historical" literature of its day. Further more, both the Wisdom and ominous traditions had certain features and interests in common from as far back as we can determine. Moreover, there is evidence at an early date of the interpenetration or confluence of both traditions. Finally, in the first millennium, this tradition of magical or "mantic" Wisdom was so firmly established as to serve the interests of political ideology and to play a rôle in the composition of past-referring (or "historical", if you will) texts, and in the production of the strange genre of future-referring texts known as "prophecies" or "apocalypses". Of evidence for this tradition in Syro-Palestine we shall hear more in the second part of this work.

The Actors

The Diviner (*bārû*)

The pre-eminent Mesopotamian diviner was the bārû, usually translated "seer"; his Sumerian title, which is regularly attested in Akkadian texts, was *máš.šu.gíd.gíd* (in Mari: *máš.šu.su$_{13}$su$_{13}$*), literally "he who stretches out his hand to the goat" (i.e., to sacrifice it), although to the best of my knowledge goats are never attested as the objects of the omen sacrifice.).[2] The "stretching out of the hand" is reflected in the common Akkadian designation for the omen sacrifice as *lipit qati*, literally, "the

---

[1] The best text available is that of O.R. Gurney in *Anatolian Studies* 5 (1955), pp. 93-113. Further references as well as references to related texts in: A.K. Grayson, *Babylonian Historical-Literary Texts*, p. 8, n. 10-11.

[2] Birds sometimes are, though; see J. Renger, *ZA* 59 (1969) 208, n 944. For other Sumerian designations of the diviner, see Falkenstein, *DM*, pp. 45-52.

touch of the hand".[1] The bārû was also commonly designated LU.ḤAL.[2] As we have seen, in the second millennium the bārû's major fields of competence were extispicy, that is, the omen sacrifice, and oil divination.

In spite of repeated laments by Assyriologists about the absence of an adequate descriptive investigation of the activities of the bārû, none has as yet appeared, and we have for a long time had to make do with what little can be gleaned from the references in the *CAD*,[3] von Soden's *AHw*,[4] the previously-mentioned article by J. Renger,[5] an article by A. Finet in *La Divination en Mésopotamie Ancienne et dans les Régions Voisines*,[6] on the diviner in ancient Mari, and an article which has recently appeared in the French periodical *M.A.R.I.*[7] This unsatisfactory state of affairs has now been improved somewhat by the magisterial publication of Marian texts by J.-M. Durand, D. Charpin et al.[8] The discussion has unfortunately also been somewhat obscured by U. Jeyes' recent contribution on the status and activities of the bārû.[9]

As I have indicated earlier, the discussion has not been aided by the fundamental ambiguity which runs throughout the Assyriological

---

[1] On *lipit qati* see already Goetze, "Reports on Acts of Extispicy", p.94; and the *CAD*, sub *liptu*. The most common alternative designation was *nepešti bari(m)*, "ritual of the baru".

[2] Cf. Oppenheim, *AM*, p. 212; Falkenstein, *DM*, p. 47.

[3] Vol. 2-B, pp. 121-25.

[4] Bd. I, pp. 109-10.

[5] In *ZA* 59 (1969), pp. 104-246; on the *bārû* pp. 207-17.

[6] (= *DM*): "La place du devin dans la société de Mari", pp. 87-94.

[7] D. Charpin, "Les Archives du Devin Asqudum dans la Résidence du 'Chantier A'", *M.A.R.I.* 4 (1985), pp. 453-62.

[8] *AEM* I/1-2 (Paris, 1988) (= *ARM* XXVI).

[9] In *Old Babylonian Extispicy*, pp. 15-37. Ms. Jeyes' procedure here consists of taking a number of extremely cryptic references in omen protases (as, e.g., "the one who walks in front of the army", pp. 21-22) as if they inevitably refer to the diviner himself. She thus arrives at a picture of the social importance of the diviner to which, I think, few would subscribe. This does not, however, detract from the value of Ms. Jeyes' other observations as to the meanings of the various terms for the exta of the sacrificial animal (pp. 51-96).

approach to the study of the diviner as to the diviner's "secular" (i.e., quasi- or proto-scientific) or "cultic" (i.e., quasi-priestly) status. As I have argued throughout this study, such ambiguity represents the importation of anachronistic concerns about the distinction between "science" (itself by no means an unambiguous concept in Western society: consider, for example, the long-standing—and fairly meaning-less—discussions as to whether such disciplines as sociology or psychology may be termed "scientific"; or the difference between English "science" and German "Wissenschaft".) and "religion" (the ambiguity of which needs no further comment) into the study of the ancient Near East. It is of a piece with now-discredited socio-anthropo-logical attempts to distinguish between "pre-logical" or "proto-scientific" and "magical" or "magico-religious" thought.

In reality, there is no great mystery about the status of the bārû/diviner. From the earliest published Akkadian extispicy reports to the latest ones, we find him undertaking extispicies to enquire of such deities as Marduk, Enlil, Annunitum, Nana, Ishtar, Šamaš and Adad[1] (in tandem), or merely Šamaš (alone).[2] Furthermore, although it is true that the diviner's art was the object of some reflection in late periods, so that a number of more or less "esoteric" commentaries on the practice appeared, note that even these frankly speculative works are often "theologies" of divination; they trace the origin of the diviner's art back to an original gift from the gods.[3] The diviner's reports characterise his

---

[1] All of the preceding deities, and more, figure in reports of the Old Babylonian and Cassite periods.

[2] E.g., in the Neo-Assyrian reports and queries. Although we shall deal more extensively with the subject presently, it is worth remarking here that also both ancient Mesopotamian conjuration and one of its primary antitheses, namely black magic, were explicitly theistic as well. See, most recently, the brief but excellent study of M.-L. Thomsen, *Zauberdiagnose und Schwarze Magie in Mesopotamien* (Copenhagen, 1987) (= *Carsten Niebuhr Institute of Ancient Near Eastern Studies* 2). Unavailable to me was T. Abusch, *Babylonian Witchcraft Literature. Case Studies* (Atlanta, 1987).

[3] Lambert, "Enmeduranki and Related Matters", p. 132 (text and trans.); and cf. Berossos' account of the Flood (probably Seleucid period), where "Cronus" (= Akk. Ea) instructs Xisouthros to bury the sacred books to preserve them from the Flood (S.M. Burstein, *The Babyloniaca of Berossus* (Malibu; CA, 1978), p. 20: 2/1. Gadd, *DM*, p. 25, n. 3 points out that these must have included the works on divination,

activity with such terms as Sumerian SIZKUR, "sacrifice"[1] or Akkadian *niqû*, with the same meaning.[2] The sacrificial activities were introduced by prayers, some of which even manage to aspire to beauty. Since the extispicy was considered a form of sacrifice, it was explicitly assumed to be capable of mollifying an offended deity.[3] Also, as we have seen previously, the late periods saw the application of various tags signifying "esoterica" to a wide range of literary products; however, in particular works on extispicy and divination in general seem to have enjoyed the designations *nisirti/pirišti ilāni rabûti*, "secrets of the great gods".[4] Furthermore, divination was conceived throughout its history as a function of the "judicial" activities of the gods, who met in assembly (Akk. *puḫur ili*) under the presidence of Šamaš, the pre-eminent guarantor of justice.[5]

---

although "these were already in keeping of the *maru ummane* (lit. "wisemen"), who had been taken into the ark" in the Gilgamesh Epic.

[1] E.g., Goetze, "Reports on Acts of Extispicy", p. 94, text (1).

[2] Cf. e.g. J. Renger, "Priestertum" (I), pp. 208-9 and n. 954.

[3] E.g. *ana nipešam ana ilim zenim lišepišusu*, "let him perform the ritual for the angry god" (Goetze, "Reports on Acts of Extispicy", pp. 94-5 (text Nr. 16); cf. the same, p. 95, Nr. 15: *tertum immer ezzim šalmat*, "omen consultation, sheep, (for the) angry (one/god): favourable" (my trans.; for *tertum* as "omen consultation" or "extispicy", see *AHw*, III, p. 1350).

[4] Cf. Starr, *The Baru Rituals*, p. 76 and n. 116; further, note the fact that in so-called "primitive societies", it is by no means unusual for divination to be kept secret or at least highly privileged; see J. Middleton, "Secrecy Among the Lugbara", in K.W. Bolle (ed.), *Secrecy in Religions* (Leiden, New York, et.al., 1987), pp. 25-43.

[5] See the Old Babylonian divining-prayers (ikribus) published by Goetze ("An Old-Babylonian Prayer of the Divining-Priest", pp. 25-29) and Starr (*The Rituals of the Diviner*, pp. 30-44), and compare those of Knutzon, *Assyrische Gebete*, esp. Nrs. 42,5; 43,7; 44,6; 46,5, etc. (Akk. *purussu*, "[legal] decision"); further on the juridical character of the *bārû* ritual, see Starr, *The Rituals of the Diviner*, pp. 56-59; and note that the juridical metaphor was probably the single most dominant metaphor of the entire "common theology of the ancient Near East" (the phrase is M. Smith's, *JBL* 71 [1971], pp. 134-47): A. Gamper, *Gott als Richter in Mesopotamien und im Alten Testament. Zum Verständnis einer Gebetsbitte* (Innsbruck, 1966). The notion that the "assembly of the gods" determines outcomes in the human world goes back to the realm of Sumerian thought; cf. T. Jacobsen, *The Treasures of Darkness. A*

In short, the *bārû* was held (and no doubt also held himself) to be a cultic functionary whose primary activity was to mediate between the gods and man.[1] This is the "manifest content", to decline momentarily to "sociologese", of the innumerable references to the diviner's activities that we find in ancient Near Eastern documents. What seems to have misled Assyriologists into believing him to have been a "proto-scientist" or "specialist" has been, for one thing, the evolutionistic notion that Mesopotamian divination was originally non-theistic and that it was only secondarily "theologised".[2] The reason for this position, as we have

History of Mesopotamian Religion (London, 1978 [1976]), pp. 86-91; of the rôle of this conception in Syro-Palestine we have heard perhaps a bit too much in recent times, but see F.M. Cross, *Canaanite Myth and Hebrew Epic* (London and Cambridge [MA], 1973), pp. 177-86; P.D. Miller, Jr., *The Divine Warrior in Early Israel* (Cambridge; [MA], 1973), *passim*.

[1] This conclusion differs strongly from that arrived at by J.-M. Durand, *AEM* I/1, pp. 61-62. Durand emphasises that the diviner is never connected with a particular god or sanctuary, that we never see him carrying out specifically cultic actions, and that we never see him manifesting religious fervour of any sort: "One gets an ultimate impression of the baru as the cold announcer of the divine verdict" (p. 62). As far as the first point is concerned, the Marian diviners had to go to the places concerning whose well-being they were expected to enquire, so connexion with a sanctuary would hardly be expectable. The god in whose name the enquiry was undertaken will probably have been determined by the diviner's client, who no doubt had his own preferences (particularly if the client was the king, and he had been informed that DN x was unsatisfied with him for one reason or another). Anyone attracted to Durand's second point should take the trouble to read A. Goetze's *ikribu* in "An Old-Babylonian Prayer of the Divining-Priest", pp. 25-29, in which the diviner personally (the *š*-causative, indicating that he might have had someone else do the ritual labour, is *never* employed) purifies himself (obv. l.1-8), censes the locale (obv. l.14-15), describes the ceremonial meal which he has prepared for the gods (obv. l.19-rev .l.52), and invokes all the great gods to attend (rev. l.55-65). I confess that I am unable to judge the religious fervour of people who have been dead for 4,000 years, and whose only surviving correspondence has to do with the practical aspects of their craft (not to mention Evans-Pritchard's point, alluded to in the second chapter of this work, that it is idle to attempt to classify the religious character of specific types of behaviour on the basis of the emotions associated with them: a ritual act retains its liturgical character whether the officiating priest is "enthusiastic" or bored silly by it.).

[2] Cf. e.g. H.W.F. Saggs, *The Encounter with the Divine in Mesopotamia and Israel* (London, 1978), pp. 131-37. Saggs is over-interpreting Oppenheim on this

seen, has been the Assyriologists' very praiseworthy acknowledgement of the fact that the diviner belonged to an extremely learned class of individual. But if they had instead studied the comparative materials provided by modern linguistics and social anthropology, they would have known that the linguistic skills of the diviner are in many ways unremarkable, as bi- or multi-lingualism occurs in a great many societies round about, including the so-called "primitive" ones.[1] Moreover, as far as the diviner's compendious knowledge is concerned, social anthropology has amply demonstrated that extraordinary feats of classification and manipulation of symbols in highly complex interlocking systems are also very common, even in societies which are much more "primitive" than were those in ancient Mesopotamia.[2]

point; as we have seen, Oppenheim's study of divination in *Ancient Mesopotamia* is part and parcel of his study of Mesopotamian religion; similarly, he has overseen Oppenheim's remark (*DM*, p. 39) that, while the addresses to Šamaš and Adad may represent a secondary "mythologization" of the phenomenon, he characterises the original phenomenon as "a much deeper and earlier *religious* relationship (emphasis mine) between what one could well call the 'dispenser of signs' and those for whom they were meant. . . ." Oppenheim's distinction was not between non-religious and religious divination, but between religious and *theistic* divination.

[1] Cf. J. Lyons, *Language and Linguistics* (London, New York, et al., 1985 [1981]), p. 281: "Two well-known examples of officially bilingual countries are Canada and Belgium, each of which has experienced language-problems...An equally well-known example of an officially multilingual country...is Switzerland. Other countries, though not officially bilingual (or multilingual), have two (or more) different languages spoken within their borders. *Most* (emphasis mine) countries of the world fall into this latter category". Of course, the lion's share of Assyriological studies have been carried out by scholars from Germany, France, Britain, and America: virtually monolingual countries all, which makes one wonder just how well scholars in these three linguistic communities have perceived the character of ancient Near Eastern civilisations. With their pronounced social interests, only the Italian orientalists and ancient historians have so far acknowledged the character of ancient bi- and multi-lingualism; cf. E. Campanile, G.R. Cardona and R. Lazzeroni (eds.), *Bilinguismo e biculturalismo nel mondo antico. Atti del colloquio interdisciplin are tenuto a Pisa il 28 e 29 settembre 1987* (Pisa, 1988).

[2] Cf. e.g., from a structuralist point of view Lévi-Strauss' *La Pensée Sauvage* (Paris, 1962); from a "symbolist" perspective, V. Turner, *The Forest of Symbols* (Ithaca, 1970); from a "cognitive-competence" vantage, see C.O. Frake, "Cognitive Maps of Time and Tide Among Medieval Seafarers", *Man* 20 (1985), pp. 254-70;

Against this, it might be objected that the ancient Mesopotamian diviner was highly *literate*; that his perpetuation of the tradition of divination was by means of an ancient and traditional stream of *written* tradition; and that this fact distinguishes ancient Mesopotamian phenomena from all modern equivalents. I would reply by citing R. Finnegan, who remarks that

> In all societies literature is likely to have many different aims in different contexts—to delight, propagandize, moralize, shock, cajole, entrance, eulogize, inform—and we can take no such short cut to their analysis as to suggest that these differences coincide exactly with the differences between literate and non-literate. . .it is difficult to maintain any clear-cut and radical distinction between those cultures which employ the written word and those which do not.[1]

Precisely what is fascinating for the social-anthropological and historical study of the ancient Near East is the fact that in the societies in question we find co-existing side by side phenomena which in our societies are concomitants of capital-intensive economies, secularisation, extensive socio-economic development, and so on. In their own context, however, such phenomena as ancient literacy, numeracy, magic, astronomy, and so on played only a relatively minor part in the development of the respective societies.

However, concluding that the diviner was a cultic functionary answers only one of the many possible questions about his social location. Above all, there remains to be answered the question of his specific position within the cult. It is often held that the diviner operated in virtually total independence of the temple cult, or that he never figures among temple personnel.[2] However, the late (Neo-Assyrian) apology for the diviner published by H. Zimmern and completed by W.G. Lambert[3] claims that the diviner must be

> a benediction priest (*karib*) of the king, a long-haired priest of Šamaš.

A. Gell, "How to Read a Map: Remarks on the Practical Logic of Navigation", *Man* 20 (1985), pp. 271-86.

[1] In Horton and Finnegan (eds.), *Modes of Thought*, pp. 134-35.

[2] E.g., Oppenheim, *AM*, pp. 81-82; Renger, "Priestertum" (2), p. 215.

[3] Zimmern, *BBR*, pp. 117-21 = Nr. 24; Lambert, "Enmeduranki and Related Matters", p. 132.

. . .begotten by a *nisakku*-priest of pure descent: if he is without
blemish in body and limbs he may approach the presence of Šamaš
and Adad where liver inspection and oracle (take place).[1]

This is sometimes regarded as merely a late attempt to pump some
dignity into a discipline that had fallen onto hard times; but, as Starr has
shown, we know of at least one family in ancient Sippar (Cassite
period) whose scions were *šangu*-priests and *bārûs* for a period of over
two centuries.[2] Since the *šangu* (Sum. LU.ŠANGA) was the
highest-ranked of the Mesopotamian priests, at least in the Old
Babylonian period,[3] he had no need to add lesser titles to his name.
This means that if a *šangu*-priest also functioned as a diviner, it is
unlikely that he would ordinarily call attention to the fact in contracts
and the like, where his titulature would normally appear. So it is in fact
possible that there were many diviners who were not just affiliated with
the ancient temples, but actually in charge of them; but, if so, we will
never be able to show that this was the case.[4] There is, then, no *apriori*
reason why the diviner could not be associated with the temple cults in
ancient Mesopotamia, and in fact we find a *bārû* as the recipient of
temple rations as late as the Seleucid period in Babylonia.[5]

But apart from these few references, plus any number of virtually
valueless mentions of him as a witness to Mesopotamian contracts, and
so forth, the diviner mainly appears to us in connexion with the palace
and palace affairs. In the Old Babylonian period there are sporadic

---

[1] Lambert, "Enmeduranki", lines 25-29. It is to be noted that already in Old
Babylonian Mari a certain tendency existed for the diviner-calling to be transmitted
in families; cf. J.-M. Durand, *AEM*, I/1, p. 7.

[2] *The Baru Rituals*, p. 221 n. 119; the text cited is a *kudurru* (boundary-stone)
originally published in L.W. King, *Babylonian Boundary Stones* I-II (London, 1912),
I, pp. 122ff.

[3] Cf. Renger, "Priestertum", (2), pp. 104-21.

[4] This is not merely a gratuitous hypothesis. One of the first rules of
Assyriology is that divergences from the standard patterns of scribal practice are
significant, so the previously-mentioned case of *šangu-bārûs* requires attention.
There was also a priest in ancient Ugarit who claimed to be both *šangu* and *bārû*;
cf. Nougayrol in *DM*, p. 14 and n. 4.

[5] Cf. G.J.P. McEwan, *Priest and Temple in Hellenistic Babylonia* (Wiesbaden,
1981), p. 15.

references to a *wakil/šapir bāri*, usually translated "overseer", which indicates that the diviners formed guild-like associations.[1] Diviners are attested in the Old Babylonian period alone at such sites as Dilbat, Hana, Kiš, Larsa (extensively), Mari (extensively), Nerebtum, Nippur, Sippar (extensively: and intelligibly, as Sippar was the centre of the Šamaš cult), and Šaddapum.[2]

We are best informed about the activities of the diviner at Mari in the Old Babylonian period.[3] The Mari letters inform us, for example, that Zimri-Lim's personal diviner accompanied him on military expeditions, and that all of three diviners accompanied Yasmaḫ-Addu on his campaigns. Military units usually had a diviner with them, whether the king accompanied them or no. The famous Marian diviner, Asqudum, seems to have made a circuit of four towns in the realm in order to undertake extispicies for their well-being. Furthermore, towns which were allied with Mari, which were of a certain significance (*pattum/patum*) and which enjoyed an exposed situation (in military-geographical terms), seem to have had resident diviners. Several of the Marian diviners appear to have held high administrative offices.[4]

---

[1] Falkenstein, *DM*, p. 47; Renger, "Priestertum" (2), p. 214.

[2] Renger, "Priestertum" (2), pp. 204-07.

[3] On Mari's general situation at this time, see Liverani, *AO*, pp. 372-90.

[4] The preceding is from Finet, *DM*, pp. 90-92. J.-M. Durand, *AEM* I/1, p. 32, n. 131 defines the "ville pattum" as unrelated to the districts of the Codex Hammurabi; he renders the word patim instead, and suggests the meaning "ville de frontière", which better agrees with the political and military situation. It should be noted that F.R. Kraus has expressed serious doubts about the alleged high positions of the diviners at Mari; "Mittelbabylonische Opferschauprotokolle", pp. 156-57, n. 70: "Whether the senders of the three 'Mari letters' L, M and N are to be regarded as barus depends on whether bearing this title was optional in Mari. . . if this was the case, one must necessarily conclude that some Marian diviners enjoyed high administrative office. . . However, the diviners' protocols in their letters show their sender just as little as their recipient, the king, to be a diviner". Kraus has a point; some Mesopotamian kings (e.g., Šulgi and Assurbanipal) styled themselves diviners or boasted of their knowledge of the phenomenon, although there is no reason to think that these were other than ideologically "borrowed feathers", as it were. But this very fact suggests that the Marian figures really were diviners: if kings bragged of their divining skills, could lesser mortals have dared do so, if it was not actually the case? The seal employed by Asqudum, as his newly-discovered archive at Mari

As far as Asqudum is concerned, we are fairly well informed, even though the attestations of his name seem to have dwindled somewhat lately owing to Durand's acknowledgement of the fact that there were numerous homonymous Asqudums.[1] In addition to making his mantic "circuit court", he apparently led military expeditions on occasion,[2] and in fact it was once even held that he drowned on one of them while crossing a river.[3]

He was married to a princess, the daughter of Yaḫdun-Lim, and another of the princesses apparently lived in their household.[4] His son, Kabi-Adad, was one of the "servants of Zimri-Lim".[5] Asqudum's royal alliance was probably not the only one made by a diviner in the vicinity in this period.[6] The bît Asqudim (house of Asqudum) covered more than a thousand square metres;[7] provisional analysis of its administrative documents shows that it was "managed accordign to the same administrative principles as was the place of Zimri-Lim, the difference being more one of level than of essence. . .this great house strikes one as a scaled-down palace".[8]

As we have seen, our information ends with the Old Babylonian period. We possess a very few letters to Sargonid kings which show that

---

shows, reads simply (*M.A.R.I.* 4 [1985] 456) zimri-lim / šakin ᵈdagan / asqudum / MAŠ.ŠU.SU₁₃.SU₁₃: "Zimri-Lim, officer of Dagan, Asqudum, diviner".

[1] *AEM* I/1, p. 5. The problem extends to cover many other figures in the Marian correspondence; see the same, p. 4.

[2] *ARM* 5,65.

[3] Cf. Charpin, "Les archives du devin Asqudum", p. 461. J.-M. Durand, however, shows unequivocally that this must have been another Asqudum, as the drowned A. died in the 4th year of Zimri Lim, while texts from the "dead archive" in the house of the diviner A. show that he was still active as late as Zimri Lim 8 (*AEM* I/1, p. 78). Nougayrol lists numerous Old Babylonian omina which speak of the diviner's taking a leading part in military activities in "Textes hépatoscopiques", *RA* 40 (1945-46), p. 87, n. to lines 3f.

[4] "Les archives du devin Asqudum", p. 456.

[5] "Les archives du devin Asqudum", p. 456.

[6] "Les archives du devin Asqudum", p. 457.

[7] "Les archives du devin Asqudum", p. 453.

[8] "Les archives du devin Asqudum", p. 461.

the diviner continued to be associated with the court, and that he was in fact a royal functionary, like the omnipresent "scribe of Anu and Enlil" (astrologer). We also possess some reports and queries which show that the diviner continued to practise his speciality, the omen sacrifice. I have previously linked this apparent decline in the diviner's fortunes with widespread changes in Neo-Assyrian society, changes which led to social discontent and which manifested themselves in a change in the amount and kind of magic that was practised. Defensive magic was very much "in", as was the clockwork-efficient magic of astrology. Perhaps nothing could emphasise this change more trenchantly than the fact that we actually possess a few *namburbi's* (normally apotropaic rituals) from Sargonid times which are intended "to enable the diviner to see and to get a great name" and "to divine for the wise".[1] One can hardly imagine the extispicies of the aristocratic diviners of Mari requiring assistance from other sources!

By the same token, however, I have emphasised that the omen sacrifice continued to be cited in legitimating contexts, in royal inscriptions and the like, which means that it had not lost its prestige in the popular eye, however much it may have suffered in the esteem of magical professionals. Moreover, if this prestige was a fiction, it was at least one which even the exorcists continued to respect. Adad-sumu-usur, an exorcist-cum-astrologer of Aššurbanipal,[2] wrote a sycophantic letter to the king urging his son's case for promotion to the royal court at some time around April of 666. In his letter, the exorcist enthuses that

> Anšar, the king of the gods (himself) called by name the king, my lord, to the kingship of Assyria, (and) the gods Šamaš and Adad, through their reliable extispicy (ina birišunu kini) established the king, my lord, for the kingship of the world. . .[3]

Finally, it is also clear, although the evidence is meager, that Sargonid diviners were still engaged in the production of new omen apodoses

---

[1] Published by Zimmern, *BBR*, pp. 112-15. See also the *namburbi* published by Caplice in *Or* N.S. 40 (1971), p. 174.

[2] Two of his letters to Assurbanipal, dealing with astrological topics, are rendered in Parpola, *Letters from Assyrian Scholars*, I, Nrs. 119 and 120.

[3] Parpola, *Letters from Assyrian Scholars*, I, Nr. 121, Obv. 5-8. For commentary, see Parpola II, pp. 103-07.

until very late in the 7th century, so the practice as such had hardly petrified, as one might otherwise have been tempted to believe.[1]

The Conjurer/Exorcist

The *mašmašu* (the word is an Akkadian loan from Sumerian LU.MAŠ.-MAŠ, the "purifier"),[2] also known as *ašipu*,[3] is possibly a common designation for a number of priests whose essential function was the cure of the sick and the warding off of untoward portents. His functions in the Old Babylonian period are far from clear, whereas his rôle from the Cassite period and later, when the great series of defensive magic (*Šurpu, Maqlu,* etc.) began to be assembled, is much more plain. As we have seen, it was to the conjurer that one addressed onself to dispel the consequences of an unfortunate *izbu* (misbirth) portent, and he was also equipped with *namburbis* for dispelling most of the evils threatened by the omens in *šumma ālu*. It is likely that, in the event that such prestigious forms of divination as extispicy or astrology produced threatening portents, the *mašmašu/ašipu* made use of *namburbis* of extreme generality to combat them.[4]

---

[1] Cf. I. Starr, "Historical Omens Concerning Ashurbanipal's War Against Elam", pp. 60-76, esp. pp. 62- 63. As an imponderable one might mention the fact of the adoption of the omen sacrifice by the Greeks, which no doubt took place in the Neo-Assyrian period and under Assyrian influence. It seems unlikely that foreigners would have borrowed a tradition which had fallen into disrepute in its own country. This may indicate, as I have suggested earlier, that the omen sacrifice retained considerable popular prestige, even if its status within the official tradition had declined.

[2] See already A. Ungnad, "Besprechungskunst und Astrologie in Babylonien", *AfO* 14 (1941-44), p. 252.

[3] From Old Babylonian *(w)asipum*; cf. Renger, "Priestertum", (2), p. 222, and see n. 1071-76 for further lexical parallels.

[4] See R.I. Caplice, *The Akkadian Namburbi Texts*, pp. 8-9, and see Text Nr. 13, pp. 21-23. A late text from Assur, sometimes called the "vade mecum of the exorcist", contains an extraordinary list of conjurations and omen series with which

There is, as I have repeatedly argued, no clear dividing-line between profane and sacred, "empirical" and "magical" in ancient Near Eastern society—or, for that matter, in any society in which uses magic. I mentioned previously that Assyriologists conventionally distinguish between the conjurer/exorcist (*mašmašu/ašipu*) and the "lay practitioner" of medicine (Akk. *asu*). The distinction has no merit; it is based solely on the fact that the latter utilises almost exclusively various (seemingly spurious) *materia medica* and even undertakes elementary operations, while the former may use such things, but in particular is known for his use of conjurations. But all this in reality means is that it was assumed that the *mašmašu* was a "knower of incantations" plus a "knower of the properties of 'medicines'", while the latter was merely a "knower of the properties of 'medicines'". In the absence of causal explanatory hypotheses, the only justification for using one or another "medicine" is some "property" it is asserted by tradition to contain. And, whatever underlies such a tradition, it is certainly not based on empirical testing. Accordingly, the only difference between these two types of specialist lies mainly in the degree of formality of their training; the *mašmašu* is known to have had extensive series of written materials at his disposal, while we have no idea where the *asu* derived his knowledge. In all likelihood, it was folk-traditional. In other words, both practitioners were users of "magic", but at different ends of the social scale applying to magical behaviour.

The conjurer was a practitioner of "medicine" to the extent that he was concerned with the objective symptoms of his patients in order to heal them. These symptoms, however, were regarded as ominous "signs" giving information as to the divine or demonic "cause" of a specific illness, or as to the probable course of the illness. Thus, for example, the exorcist might take the pulse of his patient, but its beating was merely a "sign" of one sort or another, and, naturally, was not seen in relation to the strength of the heart or the state of the circulatory

---

the exorcist was (at least theoretically) supposed to be conversant, all of which are rubricised as *mašmašutu*, "lore of the exorcist"; cf. H. Zimmern, "Ein Leitfaden der Beschwörungskunst", pp. 205-29, text and trans. pp. 206-13. Note that the text insists that the diviner be able to master astrological omens as well as those of *šumma ālu*, *šumma izbu*, *egirrus*, and so forth.

system.[1]

One feature of the exorcist's discipline requires explicit mention. This is the fact that every aspect of the evils which the exorcist combated were held ultimately to derive from the gods themselves. There is no question of any "secondary theologisation" or rationalisation of some more "primitive" conception, as this perception of apotropaic magic is present from the earliest texts to the latest ones. Thus, for example, a violation of one or another purity tabu might lead the gods to withhold their protection from the individual, so that he might become prey to a demon.[2] Alternatively, a black magician might succeed in "polluting" his victim either by means of a spell, a curse, or by bringing him into contact with implicitly unwholsome *materia magica*, so that the gods would desert him.[3] But the entire phenomenology of defensive magic was based on the assumption of the sovereignty of the gods in deciding such aspects of men's fate.

As we have seen, in the first millennium the title "mašmašu" embraced quite a variety of different practitioners, ranging from those proficient in the series "when the exorcist goes to the patient's house" to *šumma ālu*, *šumma izbu* and their appropriate *namburbis*, and ultimately to the great astrological series *Enuma Anu Enlil*. We have virtually no evidence (i.e., there were no "reports" or the like) of the *mašmašu/ašipu* working as a private practitioner, although the features of the omen series in question, and particularly the apotropaic rites over which he presided, show that in addition to the king, his clientele must have consisted largely of private persons.[4] Where we are supplied with

---

[1] Cf. above all R. Labat, *Traité Akkadien de Diagnostics et Prognostics Médicaux*, pp. xxi-xxxiii; also J.V. Kinnier Wilson, "The Nimrud Catalogue of Medical and Physiological Omina", pp. 52-63, esp. pp. 61-62. For a thorough study of the "signs" which the exorcist took to indicate the influence of black magic, see M.-L. Thomsen, *Zauberdiagnose*, pp. 50-57.

[2] Thomson, *Zauberdiagnose*, p. 11.

[3] Thomson, *Zauberdiagnose*, p. 12.

[4] Especially the previously-mentioned *namburbis* presuppose this, as their setting is almost invariably a more or less *ad hoc* assemblage of transportable altars, braziers, and the like. Furthermore, the series of diagnostic omens show that the exorcist did in fact make "housecalls" (e.g., "when the exorcist goes to the patient's house").

evidence, we learn of the *mašmašu's* rôle as an agent of the Sargonid government, as the considerable correspondence published by Parpola demonstrates.

What Did it All Mean?

Meaning, as I showed in the introduction to this work, has been variously construed by social anthropologists at various points in the history of the discipline. We have, for example, seen meaning as historical development, meaning as a-historical "survival", meaning as the function of social structures, meaning as social structure itself, meaning as the organisation of concepts, and meaning as the cognitive competence of social actors, to name but a few varieties. Therefore, in speaking of the "meaning" of divination in the context of the ancient Near East, it is clear that more than one type of meaning must be considered.

        In the first rank, we should consider what meaning was assigned by the actors themselves to the phenomenon. This sort of meaning, termed by social anthropologists "manifest content", is based on so-called "native exegesis", meaning the statements of those who used or were in continuous contact with ancient Near Eastern divination. As we have seen in our study of the diviner, he and his co-religionists considered his function to be purely cultic; which, of course, did not rule out his playing a number of important rôles in what we would consider to be a "secular" capacity (Mesopotamian kings, whether "sacral" or no, were important figures in their respective cults; but they, too, had rather extensive secular competencies). The diviner was an indispensable intermediary between man and the divine realm. The concept of intermediation has played an important part in recent studies of primitive societies; it is necessary in this connexion to distinguish between central-cult and peripheral-cult intermediation. In the former, the intermediary enjoys a well-established status as an agent of the normative institutions of social control; in the latter, his intermediation, as is often in the case in various possession cults, may take the form of social protest on behalf of the powerless and socially disenfranchised.[1] There are no indications that I know of that the Mesopotamian diviner ever represented the socially powerless.

On the level of social psychology, we may conjecture that the diviner allayed anxieties across a broad front of social behaviours. As Oppenheim pointed out over fifty years ago, the apodoses of extispical omina reflect approximately all facets of the social life of ordinary people.[2]

The famous statement, "O Šamaš, rise from the cedar mountain. . . .the diviner brings you cedar; the widow *mašḥatu*-flour; the poor woman oil; and the rich man brings you a lamb"[3] may imply, since the diviner was pre-eminently the intermediary between men and the sungod, that he practised oil divination in less important matters or for less wealthy clients. As I have suggested, this omen may have lacked prestige at the "official" level, while it continued to enjoy great popular respect. We saw in the case of Evans-Pritchard's Azande that the sophisticated circles of the Avongara court were openly contemptuous of much of the magic that flourished among the people in general, and that the court tended to utilise magic rather less than did ordinary people. If this analogy holds, we should recall that every document we possess of ancient Near Eastern divination derives from the upper echelons of society, that is, from the tiny literate minority. This implies that many more types of divination and other magics may have been practised in society at large than we shall ever have evidence for.
Alleviation of the crises of daily life, though, was only one of the facets of the diviner's calling. I have repeatedly pointed in the course of this study to the fact that divination and conjuration supplemented one

---

[1] On the notion of "intermediation", see already G. Lienhardt, *Divinity and Experience*, pp. 80-83; for its role in recent Old Testament scholarship, see R.R. Wilson, *Prophecy and Society in Ancient Israel* (Philadelphia, 1980), pp. 28-33; *idem*, *Sociological Approaches to the Old Testament* (Philadelphia, 1984), pp. 71-72; for literature on protest-possession cults, see the same place, p. 71, n. 13, and esp. I.M. Lewis, *Ecstatic Religion*, passim ; further, the same, *Religion in Context*, pp. 49 and esp. 54.

[2] "Zur keilschriftlichen Omenliteratur", pp. 199-228.

[3] Cited in Oppenheim, "The Interpretation of Dreams", pp. 340-41; ET on p. 301.

another throughout ancient Mesopotamia. Thus, for practically every portent of ill-omen which the omen series could produce there existed either general or specific remedies which the exorcist/conjurer might use. Indeed, it seems that in the socially turbulent first millennium the exorcist simply took on the job of divining himself; in effect, he was "working both sides of the street".

The interdependence of divination and conjuration shows that ancient Mesopotamian societies were, no less than Evans-Pritchard's Azande, "magical societies". Every facet of human existence was comprehended within the theologically and highly ethically polarised continuum of ancient Near Eastern magical praxis. I say "praxis", rather than "thought" quite intentionally; rather too many highly generalising studies have appeared which tend to universalise a few native statements, although there is no evidence that such conclusions were ever drawn by members of the societies in question. It is important that we not present ancient Near Eastern societies as possessing a unity of outlook and perception which was in fact foreign to them. In fact, the few late texts we possess which might be taken to reflect attempts to generalise on the basis of divinatory practices remain relentlessly specific; either they attempt to find common denominators among the (already existing, concrete) omen apodoses,[1] or they attempt to chain more than one type of divination together to ensure more accurate "prediction",[2] or else they combine omens with the relevant apotropaic incantations to nullify them.[3]

Divination, as I argued in my section on magic (ch. 2), and in the recent section on divination as an intellectual activity, is a species of performative, plus a "complement", that is, it is an act which affirms or denies a symbolic representation of (projected) reality. When the diviner invoked Šamaš in the course of a consultation, this act took place; and all the reports, queries, tamitus, plastics, and so forth which have come down to us attest to the unique importance of the act itself. What this immense expenditure of personal and social resources actually resulted in was usually a simple binary answer to the client's question, although

---

[1] E.g. J. Denner "Der assyrische Eingeweideschautext II R.43", *passim*.

[2] Cf. Oppenheim, "A Babylonian Diviner's Manual", *passim*.

[3] E.g., the *namburbis* and the omina of *šumma ālu* and *šumma izbu*.

"maybe, ask again" was also a possibility. The praxis was thus comparable to that employed in Zande and many other African societies. Acknowledgement of this fact leads to the further observation that ancient Near Eastern societies display all the major features of relatively modern, though "primitive" societies, in which the "magico-medical syndrome" has been closely studied by modern social anthropologists. In all such societies we find divination, witch-fears, and incantations linked loosely together and complementing one another. The pattern obviously also holds true of ancient Near Eastern societies: a fact which should caution us not to over-estimate the importance of literacy in the ancient "high cultures". A peculiarity of the ancient Near Eastern variety of the "magico-medical syndrome" is that divination is never used, so far as I am aware, to determine the identity of witches or sorcerers so as to combat them.[1] Purely as speculation we may suppose that this was because, in the last analysis, the practitioner of black magic was devoid of significance; only the gods determined who might or might not be afflicted by black magic, so the magician was merely an incidental link in the chain of the victim's suffering. Divination was, however, extensively used in connexion with illness and other suffering; but it is again characteristic of the societies in question that, in the event, the purpose was solely to put a time-limit (Akk. *adannu*)[2] to the sufferings, to discover whether the sufferer would recover, or to determine the (supernatural) cause of the illness.[3]

I have referred a number of times in the course of this study to various ideological uses of divination. The concept of "ideology" is sometimes misunderstood in Assyriological and Old Testament research,

---

[1] As M.-L. Thomsen has shown (*Zauberdiagnose*, pp. 21-29), the sorcerer/sorceress in ancient Mesopotamia is invariably anonymous in the incantations which have come down to us, and the only personal procedures envisaged to combat them were juridical. See also S.D. Walters, "The Sorceress and Her Apprentice. A Case Study of an Accusation", *JCS* 23 (1970), pp. 27-38.

[2] Cf. e.g. Lambert, *Babylonian Wisdom Literature*, pp. 44-45, line 111: "nor has the diviner (Akk. *bārû*, written LU.ḪAL) put a time limit on my illness"; see also J.J.M. Roberts, "Of Signs, Prophets, and Time Limits: A Note on Psalm 74:9", *CBQ* 39 (1977), pp. 474-81; see also the *CAD*, sub *adannu*.

[3] Cf. e.g. Nougayrol, "Présages médicaux de l'haruspicine babylonienne", pp. 5-14.

so it will be necessary to say a few words on this topic here.[1] "Ideology", as understood here, is simply a projection of self-understanding. The classic example[2] is the insurance agent who characterises himself as an "investment counselor". On the one hand, of course, he is a businessman, and as such has every intention of making as much money from his clients as he can; to this extent his "ideology" is self-serving. On the other hand, it happens to be true (at least in most Western societies) that his clients are well advised to invest some of their capital on insurance, rather than, for example, to use it on consumption. So the ideology may actually be beneficial to those it attempts to impress, even if it is never, strictly speaking, "altruistic". However, ideological self-legitimation may also serve the purposes of social control.

In this connexion we should note that the "message dreams" which we find throughout the ancient Near East, from Gudea of Lagash to Thutmoses IV or Gyges of Lydia all serve as legitmating instances for the monarchies in question, or for projects undertaken by the various monarchs. Similarly, both extispicy and oil divination were used to legitimate both ascensions to the throne and high appointments. The latest attested such use was Nabonidus' attempt to install his daughter as priestess in his newly revived cult of the moon-god Sin at ancient Harran.[3] That this attempt met with resistance from the priesthood in Babylon shows that divination was only one of the many social instances of legitimation in ancient Near Eastern societies, and by no means the most powerful.[4] Of one thing we can be certain: monarchs

---

[1] For example, M. Liverani (e.g., "The Ideology of the Assyrian Empire", in (M.T. Larsen, ed) *Power and Propaganda. A Symposium on Ancient Empires* [Copenhagen, 1979], pp. 279-317) sometimes exhibits a two-dimensional Marxian tendency to imagine that all ideology is a product of fascist oppression.

[2] Originally suggested by Peter Berger in a lecture I attended many years ago. Of course, the concept has many other ramifications. For convenience see K.L. Younger, *Ancient Conquest Accounts. A study in Ancient Near Eastern and Biblical History Writing* (Sheffield, 1990), pp. 47-51.

[3] See Gadd, *DM*, pp.33-34; E. Reiner, "The Uses of Astrology", p. 591.

[4] However, the traditional view that Nabonidus' kingship was in fact endangered by his advocacy of the moon-god Sin—as evidenced by his daughter's appointment—is probably considerably exaggerated; see A. Kuhrt, "Nabonidus and the Babylonian Priesthood", in M. Beard and J. North (eds.), *Pagan Priests. Religion*

used divination to provide legitimacy when alternative legitimising agencies were either unavailable or inadequate, which is why it so frequently appears in our sources in connexion with someone's seizure of power or ascension to the throne in spite of numerous other contenders (e.g., Esarhaddon, Assurbanipal). But in spite of its use as an instrument of social control, there is no sign that divination was ever blatantly manipulated for political ends as was later to be the case in classical times.[1]

In chapter three I stressed the fact that divination is "a set of socially defined and structured procedures for producing (notional) knowledge in a society from what are presumed to be extra-human sources". Since divination is always held to produce real knowledge, and, as I have also mentioned, since access to knowledge is invariably restricted in any society (whether by economic pressures, fiat, tabu, or whatever is unimportant), one should note that access to the sort of knowledge produced by divination in the ancient Near East was also in many ways severely restricted. Thus, for example, to take only the most obvious point of departure, there were virtually no female diviners, so that, in spite of the fact that women apparently could consult the diviner, there was no doubt a good deal they could not talk meaningfully with him *about*. Admittedly, there was, as we have seen, a female dream-interpreter (*ša'iltu*), but I have argued that dream interpreting was among the types of divination which became "popular" in the course of the first millennium, and so was of lesser authority. This, too, is reminiscent of the sexual restrictions applying in Azande divination. Nor do we have any evidence that I know of that there were ever any female astrologers ("scribes of *Enuma Anu Enlil*").

A very important witness to the restriction of knowledge has been provided us by the Mari texts. Here we learn that the various so-called "prophetic" reports were not considered to be self-validating, that is, they were not taken as expressions of the divine will without further ado. Instead, we find repeatedly that they had to be subjected to the secondary control of the king's diviners, who validated or invalidated

and Power in the Ancient World (London, 1990), pp. 117-56.

[1] See, e.g., L.R. Taylor, *Party Politics in the Age of Caesar* (London, 6th edn 1971), pp. 78-90. For an excellent survey of divination in ancient Rome see J. North, "Diviners and Divination at Rome", in *Pagan Priests*, pp. 51-71.

such reports by means of the omen sacrifice.[1] Just how extensive this practice was, we cannot say—and it is important to remember that the (apparently) very exalted rank of the diviner at Mari may not reflect the situation elsewhere. Nevertheless, the analogy provided by the use of the poison oracle among the Azande and other African peoples suggests that an "oracle of last resort" was perhaps to be expected, and that, in the second millennium, at least, this was probably extispicy.

If it was the case that the ancient Near East knew of a hierarchy of ominous knowledge, then access to such knowledge was clearly directly proportional to income and social status: most could afford oil, while not everyone could manage a sheep. Another very important indication of the restrictions placed on ominous knowledge is provided by the recent publication by J.-M. Durand of the Marian "diviners' protocol".[2] The document is the text of the oath which diviners active in the employ of Zimri Lim were obliged to swear. Here we learn that Marian diviners were obliged to reveal any unpleasant portents to the king and, moreover, that they were no less obliged to keep silent about such matters to anyone else (lines 1-10). Furthermore, the diviners were to keep silent about any privileged information which the king might reveal to them or to a colleague in whose extispicy they assisted (lines ll-16). Naturally, they had to swear not to assist by divination anyone seeking to rebel or to murder the king; conversely, if they learned by divination or by participating in a colleague's divination of such threats against the crown, they were obliged to report the matter immediately, either personally or in writing (lines 23-30).

Finally, in the first millennium, we discover that Assyrian diviners, both astrologers and practitioners of extispicy, were formally required by the sovereign to report whatever unfortunate portents happened to turn up in the course of their duties.[3] A Neo-Assyrian letter even shows that diviners who failed to comply with this requirement would not only be reported to the king, but perhaps suspected of

---

[1] See above all W.L. Moran, "New Evidence from Mari on the History of Prophecy", *Biblica* 50 (1969), pp. 15-56. This practice is also attested for the Neo-Assyrian period; cf. Reiner, "The Uses of Astrology", p. 591 and n. 6-7.

[2] *AEM* I/1, pp. 13-15 (text 1 = M.13091).

[3] See ABL 1216, published in Parpola, *Letters from Assyrian Scholars* (II), p. 50.

complicity in subversive activities.[1] Final confirmation of the importance placed on mantic information is provided by the famous "Vassal Treaty of Esarhaddon (with Ramataya of Urakazabanu)", where we read (lines 108-122) that anyone who heard rumours of plots against Esarhaddon or his crown-prince, Assurbanipal, was obliged to report the matter to Assurbanipal;[2] among the figures explicitly mentioned as required to report are the *ragimum*, the *maḫḫum* (both extatics), and the *ša'ilum* (dream- or, in this context, perhaps simply "oracle priest").[3] It is interesting that Esarhaddon makes no such demand of his vassal's extispicy priests or astrologers; did he assume that they would remain loyal to their sovereign in any case,[4] or did he simply assume that his own court diviners would keep him informed on that level of divination? Whatever the answer may have been, these examples provide important objective evidence of the political control of (notional) knowledge in ancient Near Eastern societies, a principle of control which extended from the Old Babylonian to the Neo-Assyrian periods.

---

[1] S. Parpola, "A Letter from Šamaš-šumu-ukin to Esarhaddon", *Iraq* 34 (1972) pp. 21-34 (the text is MB 135586 = 1971-7-5).

[2] Trans. Wiseman; text and trans. conveniently in *ANET*³, pp. 534-41.

[3] Reading according to Borger's "Ergänzungen" in *ZA* 54 (1960), p. 178.

[4] Note that already in the Old Babylonian period, at a time when Mari and Babylon were uneasy allies, the Marian diviner Erib-sin found it possible to complain that his colleagues, the DUMU.MEŠ MAS.ŠU.GÍD.GÍD ša ḫa-mu-ra-pi, "the diviners of Hammurabi", refused to share information by undertaking extispicies together with him (cf. Nougayrol, "Rapports paléo-babyloniens d'haruspices", Text "M", lines 33-40). Given the use of the "diviners' protocol" at Mari at this time (see above), this can hardly be surprising.

CHAPTER 4

SOME QUALIFICATIONS

In the previous section, I presented the main features of Mesopotamian divination. In the course of this examination, I often had occasion to point to the extent to which one or another phenomenon was attested in societies which were quite distant from Mesopotamia proper. It suffices to consider that evidence for the omen sacrifice in its Mesopotamian garb has been found archaeologically or is literarily attested for such diverse locales as ancient Elam, the Hittite and Mitannian (Hurrian) empires, Syro-Palestine (Megiddo, Hazor and Ugarit),[1] Greece, and Etruria (i.e.,among the Etruscans), although the Mesopotamian heritage of the last two is not fully established. Astrology, as we have also seen, was a far-traveler as well, as was divination by the examination of anomalous births (*izbus*). Then there were the more popular varieties of divination, such as dream interpretation, oil omens, "chance encounters" (*šumma ālu*), and the like, all of which seem to have had a far-flung life of their own at levels which our sources only dimly allow us to perceive. However, as I argued in the second chapter of this work, magic is frequently able to borrow foreign materials and practices precisely because they are foreign, that is, essentially unknown. This quality of "blankness" enables the domestic practitioner to accomodate foreign usages to domestic magical practices without perceptible tension. If anything, they merely become an extension of his own arsenal of magical practices. In other words, we must remember the Scottish rugby cap: not everything that is borrowed has the same social significance in

---

[1] Evidence for extispicy in 13th-12th century Megiddo and Hazor: B. Landsberger and H. Tadmor, "Fragments of Clay Liver Models from Hazor", *IEJ* 14 (1964), pp. 201-18. For a fairly full account of Mesopotamian influence at Ugarit, see P. Xella, "L'influence babylonienne à ougarit, d'après les textes alphabétiques rituels et divinatoires", in: H.-J. Nissen and J. Renger, *Mesopotamien und seine Nachbarn*, pp. 321-38.

its new home as it enjoyed in its old one. It will accordingly be necessary briefly to discuss the practice of divination in two ancient societies which were recipients, at least to some extent, of the Mesopotamian magical heritage, namely Egypt and the Hittite empire, merely in order to see what was in these countries the relationship between domestic and imported practices.

Divination in Egypt

First and foremost, one should be aware of the fact that the primary form of divination practised in ancient Egypt was the oracle, as was acknowledged by Egyptologists at an early date.[1] There are literary allusions to oracles prior to the New Kingdom, but, to the best of my knowledge, no oracular enquiries from before this period have survived. Various oracular practices persisted in Egypt until the 7th century AD,[2] so it is evident that, as was the case with Mesopotamian divination, here, too, we have to do with a phenomenon which spanned the millennia.

Egyptian oracular divination was explicitly theistic, as in Mesopotamia. As such, the oracles of the most-revered deities were correspondingly respected. Since access to the temples in Egypt was denied the populace, it was only possible to consult the deity in the

---

[1] Cf. A.M. Blackman, "Oracles in Ancient Egypt", *JEA* 11 (1925), pp. 249-55; 12 (1926) 176-85; O. Kaiser, "Das Orakel als Mittel der Rechtsfindung im alten Ägypten", *ZRG* 10/3 (1958), pp. 193-208; and above all the contribution by J. Černy in R.A. Parker's *A Saite Oracle Papyrus from Thebes in the Brooklyn Museum*, (Providence; RI, 1962), pp. 35-48. See also the summary by J. Leclant in *La Divination*, pp. 1-18. Černy's article remains the standard study on the Egyptian oracles and accordingly forms the basis of the following remarks. A. Barucq's article "Oracle et divination" in *Dictionnaire de la Bible. Supplément* (6 [1960] cols. 761-65) is also very informative. Leclant's article includes extensive references to the sources, as does the article "Orakel" in *Lexikon der Ägyptologie*, IV, pp. 600-9.

[2] Leclant, p. 10; cf. Černy, *A Saite Oracle Papyrus*, p. 47. For oracles of the Hellenistic period see K. Preisendanz, *Papyri Graecae Magicae* (Leipzig and Berlin, Vol. II, 1931); oracle requests: papyri Nrs. xxvi, xxxa, xxxb, xxxc, xxxd, xxxe, xxxf, xxxia-b-c. Fascinating is the attempt of a rationalising Hellenised Egyptian prefect to ban the practice of divination in Egypt in AD 198/199; cf. R.L. Fox, *Pagans and Christians in the Mediterranean World from the Second Century AD to the Conversion of Constantine* (London, 1988), p. 213.

course of processions of his image outside of the temple. The "road of the god" was a characteristic emphasis of temples of the New Kingdom and later, and it is accordingly significant that it was at this time, when the divine image became truly mobile, that we find oracles being delivered *extra muros*. That this took place in connexion with religious festivals is attested by the fact that the dated oracles we possess are without exception dated to festal occasions.[1]

During such excursions, the image was concealed within a curtained shrine which was borne in a boat on the shoulders of the temple servants (the priests). A few cryptic verbs, *hn*, "to lean (?)", *wsd*, "to bow", said of the image, seem to have signified assent to a question, while *n'j m h3.f*, "to go (lean) backwards", or alternative expressions, signified dissent.[2] In short, the procedure was a simple binary oracle, like so many we have seen in this study. All of this seems to presuppose that individuals simply shouted their questions, answerable in yes-or-no form, and received their answers from the attendant priests, who alone were able to observe the motions of the divine image. However, it was also possible to pose such questions in *written* form by submitting to the priests a positive statement and its opposite, one of which would be returned to the questioner.[3]

In late times, it seems that the divine response was pronounced by the (stationary) statue of the god, thanks to the ingenious use of a speaking-tube by the priests, or by a niche hollowed in the cult statue to conceal the priest. This has sometimes led Egyptologists to the Tylor-like conclusion that the priests were corrupt, and to the parallel claim that the Egyptians seem on occasion to have questioned the results

---

[1] For this paragraph, see J. Assmann, *Ägypten. Theologie und Frömmigkeit einer frühen Hochkultur* (Stuttgart, Berlin et al., 1984), p. 43. On access to the temple, see also H. Brunner, *Altägyptische Religion. Grundzüge* (Darmstadt, 1989), pp. 88-91, esp. p. 91.

[2] Çerny, *A Saite Oracle Papyrus*, pp. 43-45. It should, however, be added that far from all Egyptologists are completely convinced by Çerny's reconstruction.

[3] Cerny, *A Saite Oracle Papyrus*, p. 45.

of individual oracles.[1] There is no reason for this suspicion, however reasonable it might seem on occasion. Speaking-tubes and other gew-gaws are simply dramatically effective means of transmitting an oracular decision; they have no bearing on the sincerity of the oracles thus pronounced. In point of fact, we do not know how the priests actually arrived at their judgements, and there is no evidence that they were ever suspected of bad faith. Admittedly, Blackman points to a case in which a man accused of theft rejects a preliminary oracle, and only concedes his guilt when a second oracle confirms the first.[2] But in reality, this is no different from the conclusion of the Azande that a threatening oracle has no bearing on any subsequent oracle, or that even a positive (accusatory) oracle requires verification by yet another oracle. Nor, as we have seen, were Mesopotamian diviners hesitant to renew their questioning in the event of an unfavourable result. Moreover, we should not even be surprised to learn that disappointed enquirers sometimes sought redress from the oracle of another cult; in a polytheistic society nothing could be more logical than to try the oracle of another deity, if one's own cult oracle has been found wanting. The difficulty scholars have had acknowledging this, as I have previously argued, stems from their assumption that divination "predicts the future" in a categorical fashion. As H. Brunner has pointed out, eloquent evidence that the priests produced their oracles in good faith is provided by the fact that a high priest of Amon ensured that an oracle of Amon proclaiming life everlasting for himself and his wife was enclosed in their sarcophagi. This he would surely not have done, had he had reason to be cynical about the production of such oracles.[3]

---

[1] Cf. Barucq, "Oracle et divination", col. 764: ". . . the priests were the bearers of the statue, and one may suspect that on such important occasions as the confirmation of a new monarch or the nomination of a high priest, it will have been just as much the will of the king that the clergy interpreted as that of God". See also Çerny, *A Saite Oracle Papyrus*, pp. 40-41.

[2] Blackmun, "Oracles in Ancient Egypt", pp. 249-55; F. Kammerzell has provided the most recent translation in German in M. Dietrich, K. Hecker, et al. (eds.), *Deutungen der Zukunft in Briefen, Orakeln und Omina* (Gütersloh, 1986) (= *Texte aus der Umwelt des Alten Testaments* II/1), pp. 123-26.

[3] Cf. H. Brunner, *Altägyptische Religion*, p. 120. Curiously, however, Brunner nevertheless speaks of the speaking-tube practice as "Priesterbetrug".

The subjects which were submitted to the god for oracular decision show clear signs of historical evolution. In the first half of the New Kingdom, such matters as accession to the throne and prospects for military expeditions were decided by the oracle; in the Amarna Period, the oracle broadened its focus to include decisions touching on life in general, and also in particular judicial matters, whereby the oracle adhered closely to the practices of ordinary civil law. In the Greco-Roman period, we find ostraca which were submitted for divine decision on all topics of ordinary life.[1]

A feature which should perhaps be remarked on at this point is that ancient Egyptian oracle-giving produced no oracle-specialist that we know of: it was and remained strictly a function of the usual temple priests. As such, however, it was integrated into the national theology in unmistakable fashion.

It is sometimes maintained that the Egyptians never systematically collected omens, as the specialists in Mesopotamia did.[2] This is very obviously true, with only one exception: dream omina. In 1935, A.H. Gardiner published a study of a Middle Egyptian collection of dream omens which derive from the 19th dynasty (ca.1309-1080), and which Gardiner felt go back to a much older original, perhaps as early as the 12th dynasty (ca.1971-1786).[3] This publication was shortly followed by A. Volten's publication of a demotic "dream-book" which was composed around the 2nd century AD, but which reveals obvious links with Gardiner's text, and with the few other published Egyptian works

---

[1] Cf. *Lexicon der Ägyptologie*, IV, p. 601.

[2] Cf. e.g. J. Leclant, *La Divination*, p. 19.

[3] A.H. Gardiner: *Hieratic Papyri in the British Museum*, Third Series, (London, 1935). Vol. 1 contains the text of Papyrus Beatty Nr. III, while Vol. 2 contains the plates of the text, and is for the specialist alone. The dates mentioned for the dynasties in question are, of course, only very approximate (they are derived from *Die altorientalischen Reiche*, Vols. 1-2, and employ the so-called "long chronology", which is today being increasingly called into question. The *Lexicon der Ägyptologie*, I, 970, offers 1991-1785 for the 12th dynasty and 1320/1306-1200/1185 for the 19th.

on dreams.[1] Gardiner's Chester Beatty Papyrus Nr.III is famously divided into dreams experienced by the "Sons of Seth" and the "Sons of Horus", an apparently ethico-theological analysis of mankind (unfortunately only very little of the material pertaining to the "Sons of Horus"—the presumptive paradigms of virtue—is preserved). The omina in Volten's demotic collection are, by way of contrast, organised topically according to such objective features of the dreams as sitting, placing, having sexual intercourse with various animals or classes of men (said of women's dreams, the reference to women being altogether unusual in a Near Eastern context), speaking, and so forth. A.L. Oppenheim is inclined in his study of dream divination in the ancient Near East to regard the demotic papyri published by Volten as having arisen under Mesopotamian influence, whereas he sees Gardiner's document as an independent Egyptian production which arose more or less simultaneously with its Mesopotamian counterpart.[2] Of the correctness of Oppenheim's first conclusion, I think, there can be no doubt; of the second, however, there is reason for deliberation. In the first place, the Egyptians collected no other omens, that is, no casuistically phrased protases linked with appropriate "predictions". As we have seen, the Mesopotamians did, extensively so. In the second place, Oppenheim himself calls attention to the fact that in the Chester Beatty papyrus the words "good" or "bad" have been inserted between protasis and apodosis to explain the relevant apodosis, e.g.: "(If a man see himself in a dream) eating donkey-flesh: good; it means his promotion".[3] It was noted in the previous section that Mesopotamian omen apodoses, however picturesque, were generally understood as positive or negative by the diviners. No explanatory rubrics were generally thought to be necessary, as the apodoses were assumed to be

---

[1] A. Volten, *Demotische Traumdeutung (Pap.Carlsberg XIII und XIV Verso)* (Copenhagen, 1942). It should be noted that Volten did not see an omen collection in his texts: "It is out of the question to regard our papyri as the usual sort of omen texts, not only because of the physical impossibility of this interpretation. . . but rather because of their trivial and quotidien contents. . . ."(pp. 4-5). From the point of view of form, topics, and similarity with the *Assyrian Dream Book*, however, there is no doubt at all.

[2] Oppenheim, *Dreams*, p. 245.

[3] *Dreams*, p. 244.

intelligible without further ado. The fact that the Egyptian tradents of Chester Beatty Papyrus Nr.III found it necessary to explain the apodoses in question to their readers seems to me an obvious sign of the adoption of a foreign, in this case Mesopotamian, tradition. However, I am willing to concede that the subdivision of humanity into two opposed camps (Seth vs. Horus) was probably a feature of the Egyptian adaptation of the tradition.[1]

Whether my conjectures on this issue are correct or not, it is clear from the extreme rarity of dream omens in Egypt that they never competed seriously with the all-pervasive oracle as a means of knowing the divine will.

As I mentioned previously, there are indications that the Egyptians also practised oil or water divination in some form *lecanomancy*); however, the only indications of this are, to the best of my knowledge, very late (Coptic).[2] It is accordingly clear that in this case we have to do with the secondary adoption of a foreign tradition. The same can be said of the Egyptian knowledge of *astrology*. The earliest texts from this tradition in our possession date from the 3rd century BC at the earliest, and the most detailed of them presuppose knowledge of the zodiac, which was a late-blooming conception in Mesopotamia (late 5th century).[3] Thus already F. Cumont correctly held that, "Astrology was unknown in ancient Egypt; it was not until the Persian period. . . that it

---

[1] Yet even this conclusion is not completely certain. The followers of the god Seth are characterised as red-haired, rowdy, licientious, woman-chasing, and so forth (11,6-13); this is introduced by a fragmentary section on the physical characteristics of such men (11,3-5). This is reminiscent of the union of physiognomical and behavioural omens in Kraus' famous *Sittenkanon*. If this is correct, then the only Egyptian novelty was in making explicit the theological assignments of the two moral "types" in the received tradition. Perhaps one ought in passing to mention that it is frequently held by Biblical scholars that some varieties of dualism were introduced into the ancient Near East by the Persians in the 6th century and later. As we see, however, there is some evidence that the idea was nascent from an early date.

[2] See Leclant, *La Divination*, p. 20.

[3] Cf. Leclant, *La Divination*, pp. 21-22; and esp. P. Derchain, "Essai de classement chronologique des influences Babyloniennes et Hellénistiques", in *DM*, pp. 146-58.

began to be cultivated there".[1]

In sum, a variety of forms of technical divination were practised in ancient Egypt. However, the few distinctively Mesopotamian genres in use there were either very late arrivals on the scene (oil divination, astrology) or played at best only a modest part compared with the single domestic practice, the oracle. This impression fully agrees with the usual perception of ancient Egyptian society as a society so exclusive that it verged on the xenophobic; a trait which only began to give way after Egypt had been repeatedly subjected to foreign rule.

Divination among the Hittites

Hittitology is a considerably younger discipline than is Assyriology, her sister study, as we note from the simple facts that even an only approximate sketch of Hittite grammar first appeared in 1915,[2] and that serious progress—at least in the understanding of hieroglyphic Hittite—was first made possible by the discovery of the Karatepe bilingual inscription in 1947.[3] Nevertheless, it was recognised already at a relatively early date not only that the Hittites practised divination, but also that some forms of divination were specific to the ambit of Hittite language and social institutions. Thus, for example, in 1935 A. Boissier noted that the Hittites had employed such methods as the omen sacrifice, augury, a home-grown variety of oracle designated KIN, and a fourth method which he took to be a variety of extispicy.[4] By the time of the publication of the second edition of A. Goetze's *Kulturgeschichte Kleinasiens*,[5] this list had been expanded to include 1) the ravings of extatics 2) dream revelations (mainly through incubation) 3) extispicy 4) augury 5) the KIN-oracle, which Goetze took to be a form of lot-casting.[6] Unfortunately, Goetze maintained the then-current

---

[1] *Astrology and Religion Among the Greeks and Romans* (New York, 1960 [1912]), p. 43.

[2] Cf. B. Hrozny, "Die Lösung des hethitischen Problems", *MDOG* 56 (1915), pp. 17-50.

[3] Cf. O.R. Gurney, *The Hittites* (Harmondsworth, 1969 [1952], p. 13).

[4] *Mantique Babylonienne et Mantique Hittite*, p. 26, and see further pp. 27-38.

[5] (Munich, 1957).

[6] *Kulturgeschichte Kleinasiens*, pp. 149-51.

Assyriological perception of divination as a proto-scientific undertaking, and one which he accordingly strongly distinguished from other Hittite magical acts.[1] Purely *en passant*, one notes that this approach was being pursued twenty years after the publication of Evans-Pritchard's *Witchcraft, Oracles and Magic Among the Azande*. It is unfortunate that neither the Hittitologists nor their Assyriological brethren were at this time concerned to keep abreast of developments in social anthropology, for their attempts to characterise the forms of divination used in the societies they studied lack all resemblance to a social perspective on the phenomena.[2]

The years since Goetze's publication have seen the production of numerous fairly detailed studies of Hittite divination. Thus, in 1958 E. Laroche studied the evidence for Hittite *oil divination*; Laroche returned to the subject of Hittite divination with an examination of the Hittite language pertaining to the *omen sacrifice* in 1970.[3] Also in 1970 appeared the late K.K. Riemschneider's investigation of Hittite misbirth (*izbu*) omens.[4] The fine Italian scholar A. Archi turned his attention to the *KIN oracle* in 1974, and to Hittite *augury* in 1975; both articles cover what is even today virtually all that is known of the respective practices.[5] Archi has since followed these studies up with numerous

---

[1] In *Kulturgeschichte Kleinasiens*, p. 149, divination is explicitly referred to as a "Wissenschaft"; an entirely separate subsection, called "Die Magie", is devoted to the practices of defensive magic. See also Gurney, *The Hittites*, pp. 158-59, and note that Gurney, too, detaches divination from magic (pp. 160-63).

[2] Boissier, *Mantique Babylonienne et Mantique Hittite*, pp. 49-79, calls attention to the divinatory practices of the Arabs, various African peoples, the Malaysians, Mongols, Chinese, and even among the ancient Etruscans. Unfortunately, he does so in the best tell-all-you-know spirit so despised by M. Finley and, in a social anthropologicl context, already lampooned by B. Malinowski. One is reminded of Dylan Thomas' wonderful remark, in his famous *A Child's Christmas in Wales*, about receiving as a Christmas present a book "that tells you everything about the wasp, except why".

[3] "Lécanomancie hittite", *RA* 52 (1958), pp. 150-62 and "Sur le vocabulaire de l'haruspicine hittite", *RA* 64 (1970), pp. 127-39.

[4] *Babylonische Geburtsomina in hethitischer Übersetzung* (Wiesbaden, 1970) (= *Studien zu den Bogazköy-Texten* 9).

[5] "Il sistema KIN della divinazione ittita", *OA* 13 (1974), pp. 113-44; "L'Ornitomanzia ittita", *Studi micenei ed egeo-anatolici* 16 (1975), pp. 119-80.

publications of handmade copies of the originals,[1] which, however, as such are solely useful for the professional Hittitologist.

This phase of the study of Hittite divination may be compared with what I above termed the first phase of the study of Mesopotamian divination: many texts have been published, and some detailed studies have also appeared; though, thankfully, without the speculative bent that characterised so much of early Assyriological research. This phase may be said to have been completed in 1976 by the publication of A.-L. Kammenhuber's *Orakelpraxis, Träume und Vorzeichenschau bei den Hethitern.*[2]

Kammenhuber's work is unfortunately not merely badly, but terribly written; both Assyriologists and Hittitologists seem on occasion to forget that their researches are, ideally, supposed to convey information also to scholars working outside of their narrow disciplines. If scholarship is not a dialogue, it is nothing at all. Nevertheless, by virtue of its all-round references to the literature and its attempt to summarise what is known of Hittite divination in general, Kammenhuber's study will remain the point of departure for investigations for some time to come. This makes it all the more regrettable that the author has not troubled to describe the procedures in question—not even provisionally—at any length.[3]

Briefly, then: Kammenhuber notes that the Hittites practised five different types of oracle-divination (i.e., procedures for provoking an omen), namely the KIN, MUŠEN, KUŠ, MUŠEN-HURRI, and MUŠ

---

[1] In the series *Keilschrifturkunden aus Boghazköi*, Deutsche Akademie der Wissenschaften, Nrs 49 (1979), 50 (1979), 52 (1983), Berlin; under the common title *Hethitische Orakeltexte.*

[2] (Heidelberg, 1976).

[3] A step in the right direction has been taken by A. Ünal in his *Ein Orakeltext über die Intrigen am hethitischen Hof* (Heidelberg, 1978), which details the lengthy sequences of oracles which were undertaken in the course of a series of intrigues occasioned by the royal spouse while her husband (presumably Tuthaliya IV) was ill (for the "real" date and subjects of the work in question, see pp. 36-52; but note that Ünal himself admits (p. 42) that "A cool regard reveals that practically all the themes which occur in this text. . . could have manifested themselves in conjunction with any Hittite king".

oracles. She characterises the KIN-oracle as a variety of lot-casting;[1] a description which can be allowed to stand once one has qualified it by noting that according to Archi this oracle was quite complex and apparently utilised many different counters or appropriate symbols for the subjects of the enquiry, and that some of the answers returned indicate movement of some kind on the part of these counters (they may even have been animals, for all we know).[2] The KIN-oracle is far and away the most frequently-attested of the Hittite oracles, with over 500 attestations. It was performed by the [SAL] ŠU.GI, "old woman" (or "female elder"), a cultic functionary who is attested among the Hittites, Luwians, and the Hurrians, but nowhere else. The prominence of such a female cultic functionary shows perhaps better than any other social fact except the Indo-European structures of the Hittite language itself that we have to do with a non-Semitic social realm.[3] Kammenhuber describes the practice of the KIN-oracle as "bodenständig zentralanatolisch".

The next most popular type of oracle (184 by Kammenhuber's count) was the MUŠEN, based on the observation of the flights, movements, and behaviour of birds. The MUŠEN-oracle was performed by the [LÚ] IGI.MUŠEN or [LÚ] MUŠEN.DU.[4]

Of far lower popularity but nevertheless significantly attested was the KUŠ-oracle, of which the MUŠEN-ḪURRI may simply have been a variant.[5] The KUŠ (variants SU and TE) oracle was the specifically Hittite version of the omen sacrifice, which the Hittites adopted from the Babylonians under Hurrian mediation.[6] Both oracle types were

---

[1] *Orakelpraxis*, p. 10.

[2] Cf. "Il sistema KIN della divinazione ittita", pp. 113-44, esp. p. 131.

[3] For extensive references to the various cultic activities of the [SAL] ŠU.GI, see Kammenhuber, *Orakelpraxis, Träume und Vorzeichenschau* , pp. 119-28.

[4] Cf. Kammenhuber, *Orakelpraxis, Träume und Vorzeichenschau*, pp. 10 and 130.

[5] Kammenhuber, *Orakelpraxis, Träume und Vorzeichenschau*, p. 11 and n. 14.

[6] Kammenhuber, *Orakelpraxis, Träume und Vorzeichenschau*, pp. 11-12. Unfortunately, Kammenhüber is so determined to prove her thesis that the Hittites learned Mesopotamian divination indirectly, that is, through Hurrian mediation, that her study devotes a disproportionate amount of space to this peripheral concern. On the thesis itself, see the critical remarks of S.R. Bin-Nun, "Some Remarks on Hittite

performed by the ^{LÚ} ḪAL (= Akk. *bārû*), as was a nameless specialty based on the observation of the sacrificial animal prior to sacrifice.[1] The MUŠ, the last and relatively rare form of divination employed by the Hittites, was apparently based on the movements of a water-snake, or perhaps an eel, across the surface of a container of water.[2] Kammenhuber also notes that the Hittites knew of many different sorts of spontaneous omens, not in the Mesopotamian sense of whole classes of natural phenomena which might yield a message from the divine, but more the result of a sort of rough and ready sense that a sudden rainfall, lightning, storm, dream, or whatever might happen to portend something (usually unfavourable, but not always) which required to be investigated systematically by a sequence of oracular enquiries. Moreover, in spite of the apparent popularity of the KIN-oracle, there was no single oracle-of-last-resort; the results of any one oracle were apt to be investigated further by some other oracle. Furthermore, the personnel involved were by no means as stable as the brief listing above might seem to imply; both the terminology characterising them and their cultic functions seem to have changed considerably over the centuries. These observations agree well with the long-standing perception of Hittite society as more composite than integrated, a fact which may well have contributed to its relatively speedy disintegration.

Summary

This all too cursory control investigation of the status of divination in Egypt and the Hittite empire cannot do justice to the respective phenomena, but then, it was not meant to. It was merely intended to show that the influence of the Mesopotamian tradition was mainly at the literary level: the various types of Mesopotamian practices are primarily attested at the level of *Übersetzungs-literatur*, although it seems to me obvious that they must also have been employed in their "pure" form, if only experimentally. The preferred means of divination, both in Egypt

Oracles, Dreams and Omina", *Or* N.S. 48 (1979), pp. 118-27, esp. pp. 124-26.

[1] Cf. Kammenhuber, *Orakelpraxis, Träume und Vorzeichenschau*, pp. 11-12 and, on the ^{LÚ} ḪAL, pp. 134-36.

[2] Kammenhuber, *Orakelpraxis, Träume und Vorzeichenschau*, p. 27 and n. 50; cf. also H. Berman, critical review in *JCS* 34 (1982), p. 119.

and in the Hittite empire, remained the (more or less) indigenous oracle practices (i.e., the "bark of the god" in Egypt and the KIN-oracle in Boghazkeui and elsewhere). Moreover, even in cases in which significant borrowing actually took place, as with the KUŠ-oracle, that is, the Hittite version of the omen sacrifice, the practice diverged significantly from its Mesopotamian model. We do not have to do with some naively undifferentiated "pattern", as was assumed by the scholars of the "myth and ritual school" a generation or so ago, but with the sophisticated absorption of those features of a foreign tradition which could safely be incorporated into domestic practice.

CHAPTER 5

DIVINATION IN ANCIENT ISRAEL

There has never been any doubt among students of the Old Testament that the ancient Israelites utilised a variety of forms of divination. After all, there is direct reference to some form of consultation already in the "patriarchal age",[1] where we are informed that Isaac's wife Rebekah ("went to enquire of the Lord", Gen 25.22), as to the commotion in her innards which, or so we are told, portended the birth of quarrelsome twins. Lot-casting, a form of divination, appears to have decided the guilt of Achan, during the "conquest" (Jos 7.14-18), just as it later decided the apportionment of the land (Jos 13-19, esp. 19.51).

A rather corrupt context in Deuteronomy (33.8) seems to refer to the Urim and Thummim (in reverse order), which, we are told in Priestly contexts (Exod 28.30; Lev 8.8; Num 27.21), were contained in the high priest's "breastpiece of judgement", and which, if the LXX reading of 1 Sam 14.41ff. is correct, may have been oracular lots or counters. A very few contexts suggest that the Teraphim, possibly some sort of divine images, were employed in Israelite divination (cf. Hos 3.4; Zech 10.2). Another few contexts (e.g., Judg 17.5; 18.14-20; 1 Sam 14.3ff.; 23.9; 30.7) suggest the oracular use of the mysterious *ephod*, while a great number imply that the goral-lot also served oracular functions.

En route to his kingship, the youthful David is invariably assisted by reliable oracles from Yahweh (e.g., 1 Sam 22.13-15; 23.2-4, 9-12; 30.7-8, 2 Sam 2.1). By way of contrast, the hapless king Saul, having earlier been made king by some oracular procedure (1 Sam 10.17-27), but now desperate for divine advice, receives no counsel ("whether from dreams, Urim, or prophets", 1 Sam 28.6, cf. v 15), and hence "enquires"

---

[1] In what follows, the terms "patriarchal age", "wilderness wanderings", "conquest" and "age of the Judges" will be set off by inverted commas to indicate that they are literary, but not necessarily historical, quantities.

of a necromanceress. Also, figures as disparate as Jacob (Gen 28.10-17) and Solomon (1 Kgs 3.5-15) receive reliable and portentous dreams.

Furthermore, it is obvious that certain types of divination were regarded as unacceptable in ancient Israel, as is evident from the tale of Saul's consultation with the "witch"of Endor (1 Sam 28),[1] from the repeated prophetic references (e.g., Jer 10.2; Isa 8.19; Micah 5.11; Zech 10.2, etc.), and from the express prohibitions in the Israelite legal corpora (e.g., Lev 19.26,31; 20.6; Deut 13.1-5; 18.10-11,14).

Finally, the Israelites were well aware of the fact that the surrounding countries also practised various forms of divination. For example, a Philistine procedure for determining whether a catastrophe was visited upon them by Yahweh is extensively described in 1 Sam 6.1-12, and a fleeting reference in 2 Kgs 1.2 seems to imply that the Philistines retained their oracular practices for some time to come. Later, Ezekiel announces that ". . . the King of Babylon stands at the parting of the way, at the head of the two ways, to use divination; he shakes the arrows, he consults the teraphim, he looks at the liver. . . " (Ezek 21.21; Heb 21.26). Similarly, Deutero-Isaiah rails at the Babylonians to

> Stand fast in your enchantments
> and your many sorceries,
> with which you have labored
> from your youth. . .
> You are wearied with your many counsels;
> let them stand forth and save you,
> those who divide the heavens,
> who gaze at the stars,
> who at the new moons predict
> what shall befall you.
> (Isa 47.12-13, RSV)

Nor should we neglect the fact that such figures as Joseph and Daniel are on record (see, e.g., Gen 41.8-32 and Dan 4.18-27, Aram 4.16-24) as having been able to beat the foreign specialists in divination at their own game and on their own ground (which, of course, already Deutero-Isaiah was claiming to be able to do).

---

[1] I write "witch" here in inverted commas, as the concept of witch as "oracle" differs significantly from the meaning of the term as employed in social anthropology. Witches are malefactors in a community, whether real or imagined, a description which hardly fits the woman in question here.

All this makes it more than passingly noteworthy that early Jewish tradition expressed negligible interest in the phenomenon of divination. In point of fact, none of the above passages, or the phenomena they refer to, including the references in the legal corpora, is even mentioned in the Mishnah, with the sole exception of the Urim and Thummim (see Yoma 7.5; Sota 9.12; Shebuoth 2.2). This is very curious, when we consider that it is now well known that many forms of magic and divination flourished in Palestine in the intertestamental period and later, that is, when the Mishnah was in the process of being compiled. The Talmud proper, of course, is another matter, but that brings us to quite a remove from the historical Israel.[1]

One Biblical passage in particular deserves our attention; this is Deut 18.9-14:

> 9 When you come into the land which the Lord your God gives you, you shall not learn to follow the abominable practices of those nations. 10 There shall not be found among you any one who burns his son or his daughter as an offering, any one who practices divination, a soothsayer, or an augur, or a sorcerer, 11 or a charmer, or a medium, or a wizard, or a necromancer. 12 For whoevever does these things is an abomination to the Lord; and because of these abominable practices the Lord your God is driving them out before you. 13 You shall be blameless before the Lord your God. 14 For these nations which you are about to dispossess give heed to soothsayers and to diviners; but as for you, the Lord your God has not allowed you so to do (RSV).

What is particularly interesting about this passage is that it is the only one in the legal corpora which regards certain forms of divination as essentially foreign practices. The Priestly legislation in Leviticus (Lev

---

[1] See already L. Blau, *Das altjüdische Zauberwesen* (Westmead, England, 1970 [1898]), pp. 16-167; more recently, see e.g. J. Hull, *Hellenistic Magic and the Synoptic Tradition* (Napierville IL, 1974) (= *SBT* Second Series 28); further, M. Smith, *Jesus the Magician* (New York and Toronto, 1978), pp. 68-152, for Jesus as a Jewish-Hellenistic "wonder worker". For more on the theme of such wonder workers, see G. Vermes, *Jesus the Jew. A Historian's Reading of the Gospels* (London, 1976 [1973]), pp. 58-83; and B.M. Bokser, "Wonder-Working and the Rabbinic Tradition: the Case of Hanina ben Dosa", *JSJ* 16 (1985), pp. 42-92. See also D. Sperber, "Some Rabbinic Themes in Magical Papyri", *JSJ* 16 (1985), pp. 93-103.

19.26,31; 20.6) makes no such distinction, although, of course, given the time-honoured view that D preceded P, it may well presuppose it. Furthermore, this understanding of divination is *historicistic*, which is to say that it presupposes a certain understanding of the process whereby Israel came into being, namely 1) outside of Israel, 2) as a religious community, 3) with its entire cult firmly established. On the Deuteronomic-Deuteronomistic view, as is well known, Israel's fate subsequent to the "conquest"was to be unable to eradicate fully the original inhabitants of the land, so that the various beliefs and cultic usages of the "Canaanites" remained as permanent temptations and sources of apostasy, for which reason first Israel, and then Judah succumbed to foreign conquest.[1]

This "historicising" interpretation of the phenomenon of divination seems to have underlain the rabbinical strictures against it and other forms of magic.[2] Moreover, the classical study of Jewish magic by L. Blau regards the phenomenon "as a remnant, in part as foreign influence in the lap of the monotheistic people. . . ",[3] which indicates the persistence of the Deuteronomic-Deuteronomistic interpretation. In fact, for Blau, the magical practices of Jews in Talmudic times produce an eerie resonance with the situation in Old Testament times:

> after the Babylonian exile, the Jews had completely vanquished idol-worship and regarded the Law of Moses as the sacred norm of life; they were nevertheless unable. . . to free themselves from the thrall of demons, spirits and ghosts; in fact, in spite of all their respect for and sacred observance of the revealed Law they practised magic arts, against both the clear word of the law and the oral tradition which

---

[1] Still fundamental on this point is M. Noth's famous *Überlieferungs-geschichtliche Studien. Die sammelnden und bearbeitenden Geschichtswerke im Alten Testament* (Darmstadt, 1957 [Halle, 1943]). Any doubts that Deut 18.9-14 is Deuteronomistic should be dispelled by a glance at 2 Kgs 17.17. In v 15 we are told that the great sin of the inhabitants of the northern kingdom had consisted in the fact that they, "went after false idols, and became false, and they followed the nations that were round about them. . . .", after which we read, "And they burned their sons and their daughters as offerings, and used divination and sorcery. . . ." (v 17).

[2] Cf. Blau, *Zauberwesen*, pp. 19-23.

[3] Blau, *Zauberwesen*, p. 6.

flowed from it.[1]

Blau's study was to prove trend-setting for the modern Jewish understanding of Israelite divination. Y. Kaufmann's famous study of Israelite religion is symptomatic:

> Deuteronomy 18:9-22 bans nahash as a custom of the nations, not as a form of seeking oracles from YHWH (whom the nations do not know). . . while diviners and astrologers are time and again named among the courtiers of foreign kings, Israelite kings. . . inquire of YHWH only through Urim and prophets. Just as they have no court magicians, so they have no professional diviners. . .
> Corresponding to this fact is the absence of any struggle between Israelite soothsayers and prophets, let alone between prophets and soothsayers of YHWH. . . On the other hand, no pagan is ever spoken of as divining by means of the ephod or Urim. Dreams, prophets, teraphim, and lots are common to Israel and the nations; the ephod and Urim are peculiarly Israelite.[2]

In fact, the only difference between Blau's view and Kaufmann's is that, in the interests of apologetic, Blau completely underplays the significance of divination. Thus, on no evidence whatever he simply affirms that, according to Jewish tradition, divination does not belong to the realm of magic.[3] He is right, of course, in the sense that if the Israelites rejected all forms of magic, as he claims, it is nevertheless demonstrable that they did not reject the Urim and Thummim, the ephod, prophecy, and so forth: hence on these lines, Israelite divination cannot be magical. Blau accordingly refers to divinatory phenomena only three times in his entire work.[4]

As we saw above, Kaufmann is too realistic to invent a pseudo-category for divination so as to differentiate it from magic. Thus,

[1] Blau, *Zauberwesen*, p. 19; it might be added that M. Jastrow, *A Dictionary of the Targumim, the Talmud Babli and Yerushalmi, and the Midrashic Literature*, Vols. I-II (New York, 1967), lists ample references in the Targums and in both Talmuds on the topics pertaining to Jewish magic and divination.

[2] *The Religion of Israel. From its Beginnings to the Babylonian Exile* (ET [abridged vers.] M. Greenberg) (Chicago and London, 1963 [1960]), p. 89.

[3] Blau, *Zauberwesen*, p. 3.

[4] Blau, *Zauberwesen*, p. 26 (Rab's determination of the cause of an illness which had filled an entire cemetery, which Blau does not call divination, although anyone else would), p. 45, pp. 166-67.

if he wants to insist on the exclusiveness of the specifically Israelite
practices (and his work is nothing if not a fine exercise in theological
apologetic), he has no alternative but to distinguish sharply between
(purportedly foreign) nahash-divination and (avowedly Israelite) ephod
and Urim-and-Thummim divination. As we shall see presently, this
distinction is both overly artificial and also fails adequately to account
for the passages in which Israelites make use of nahash-divination.
Moreover, it has the problematical consequence, which may be
mentioned already in this context, that it leaves all forms of Israelite
divination without a single verb to characterise them. As far as magic
is concerned, and divination in particular, modern Western Old
Testament study has also tended to follow the lead of the
Deuteronomist(s). So, for example, J. Spencer published a study of the
Urim and Thummim in 1670 in which he found the Urim and Thummim
to have been divinely accorded means of revelation, in contrast to the
Teraphim, which he saw as used by the nations. He also held the
employment of the Urim and Thummim by the priesthood to have been
a special grace which shielded the credulous populace from constantly
seeking oracles.[1] In the same vein, in 1854 the *Kirchen-Lexikon oder
Encyklopädie der Katholischen Theologie* spoke of a "close connexion
between magic and idol-worship", and polemicised rationalistically
against belief in the phenomenon.[2] Almost a century later, the *Lexikon
für Theologie und Kirche* claimed that "The revelation in the Old and
New Testaments expels all heathen divination, which it repeatedly traces
back to demons".[3] Of course, this purported connexion between magic
and the worship of foreign (false) gods merely reiterates the
Deuteronomic-Deuteronomistic understanding. Indeed, this was the basis
of the late medieval and renaissance view which held magic and religion
to be opposed quantities, a view which, as we have seen, is still
influential today.

---

[1] *Dissertatio de Urim et Thummim in Deuteron. c. 33. v. 8 "In qua Eorum
natura et origo, Non paucorum rituum Mosaicorum rationes, et Obscuriora
quaedam Scripturae loca"*, with the modest addendum, *"probabiliter explicantur"*
(Cambridge, 1670), pp. 229-319.

[2] H.J. Wetzer and B. Welte (eds.), Vol.1 (Freiburg im Breisgau, 1854), sub
Zauberei (magia).

[3] M. Buchberger (ed.), (Freiburg im Breisgau, 1938).

A symptom of the adherence of Old Testament scholars to this view is the pronounced lack of interest any of them have shown in ancient Israelite magical practices. In actual fact, only two facets of Israelite divination have occasioned studies in any sort of depth, namely *the priestly oracle* and *the interpretation of dreams*. Already in 1865, G. Klaiber published an obscure booklet in which he amplified some few previous observations by J.D. Michaelis and H. Ewald. Essentially, according to Klaiber, the Israelites practised divination by means of the Urim and Thummim, which he etymologised, following Ewald, as "revelation" and "truth", respectively, and which he held to have been lots.[1] Klaiber's method is simplicity itself: he observes that Exod 28.30, Lev 8.8, Num 27.15-21 and Deut 33.8 refer to Urim and Thummim in conjunction with "bearing the judgement of the people of Israel" before Yahweh (Exod 28.30) as a high-priestly activity. These passages also show that Eleazar's task after Moses' demise was to "inquire for him (Joshua) by the judgement of the Urim before Yahweh" (Num 27.21). Klaiber then proceeds to analyse all passages in the Old Testament chronographic literature where oracles are sought, but clearly not from prophets, as if the priestly oracle by means of Urim and Thummim were the means in question.[2]

Concern with the priestly oracle to the exclusion of all other Israelite magical practices (except, of course, prophecy) also characterised the views of J. Wellhausen,[3] W.W. Baudissin,[4] and, more recently, F. Küchler,[5] J. Begrich,[6] E. Sellin,[7] J. Lindblom,[8] and L.

---

[1] "Das priesterliche Orakel der Israeliten", in: *Programm des Königlichen Gymnasiums in Stuttgart zum Schluss des Schuljahrs 1864-65*, (Stuttgart, 1865), pp. 1-19; here pp. 5-6; and see p.15: "We may imagine them as three different-coloured pebbles, one of which confirmed matters, one negated, while the third refused to answer".

[2] With the reservation that he maintains, in the event the priest in question was not of Levitical descent, that he could not have used the high-priestly Urim and Thummim, but only lesser copies of them (*Program*, p. 9).

[3] *Prolegomena zur Geschichte Israels* (Berlin, 1905 [1883]), pp. 128-29.

[4] *Die Geschichte des Alttestamentlichen Priestertums* (Leipzig, 1889), pp. 58-60, 64, 186-87, 205-7, 268-71.

[5] "Das priesterliche Orakel in Israel und Juda", (eds W. Frankenberg and F. Küchler) *ZAW* Beiheft 33 (Giessen, 1918), pp. 285-301.

Delekat.[1] In recent introductions to the Old Testament, if any form of Israelite divination is mentioned, reference is made only to the priestly oracle, and that either dismissively or with a profound lack of interest.[2]

Nor is the situation significantly different with respect to the study of Israelite dreams and dream interpretation, although in this connexion Old Testament scholars have been reasonably well served by the publication of studies by E.L. Ehrlich,[3] A. Resch,[4] W. Richter,[5] B.

---

[6] "Das priesterliche Heilsorakel", *ZAW* 52 (1934), pp. 81-92.

[7] *Einleitung in das Alte Testament* (Leipzig, 1935), pp. 54-6; the same, *Alttestamentliche Theologie auf religionsgeschichtlicher Grundlage*, Pt. 1 (Leipzig, 1933), p. 25: "But Moses had apparently brought about a change in the nature of the priesthood...the communication of oracles and law-saying, as well as the giving of the Law in Yahweh's name, cf. Deut 33.8 and Exod 18".

[8] *Israels Religion*, (Stockholm, 1967 [1936]), pp. 102-3: "The main tasks of the priesthood were threefold: delivering oracles, teaching, and offering sacrifice (cf. the clear formulation in Deut.33:8-10)...one would be much mistaken if one did not claim that from the beginning it was insight in the art of delivering oracles which gave the members of the tribe of Levi their great authority with respect to ordinary priests" (trans. by the writer). See also pp. 104-6; 135-36.

[1] *Asylie und Schutzorakel am Zionheiligtum. Eine Untersuchung zu den privaten Feindpsalmen* (Leiden, 1967). Although largely a spokesman for the rôle of the cult prophet, S. Mowinckel also accepted that the priestly oracle had a part to play in ancient Israel: "Ancient Israel saw no contradiction between the spontaneous free oracle and pronouncement of inspiration and the oracle which was secured by technical means...Also the priest's technical oracle which was derived, for example, by means of lot-casting, had to be given form and style, be expressed in sensible, intelligible words; that, too, was an expression of 'wisdom' and 'inspiration'" (*Offersang og sangoffer. Salmediktningen i Bibelen* [Oslo, Bergen, Tromsø, 1971], pp. 311-12). Trans. by the writer.

[2] Cf. B.S.Childs, *Introduction to the Old Testament as Scripture* (London, 1979), p. 518; O. Kaiser, *Einleitung in das Alte Testament* (Gütersloh, 1984), p. 338; R. Rendtorff, *Das Alte Testament. Eine Einführung* (Neukirchen, 1988), pp. 108 and 129.

[3] *Der Traum im Alten Testament* (Berlin, 1953) (= *BZAW* 73).

[4] *Der Traum im Heilsplan Gottes. Deutung und Bedeutung des Traums im Alten Testament* (Freiburg im Breisgau, 1964).

[5] "Traum und Traumdeutung im AT. Ihre Form und Verwendung", *BZ* (NF) 7 (1963), pp. 202-20.

Stemberger,[1] and R. Gnuse,[2] among others.

Now this demonstrable lack of interest shown by Old Testament scholars in Israelite divination stands in the starkest conceivable contrast to the Old Testament texts which, as we have seen, insist that Israel parcelled out her lands, removed apostates from her midst, was guided in the desert, initiated her battles, sanctified her holy places, and confirmed the election of her first king by means of one or another form of non-prophetic divination. One is forced to ask why this should be so, that is, why practices which the Old Testament so self-evidently regards as characteristic of ancient Israelite society seem to have so little import for the understanding of the Hebrew Bible today.

At least one answer to this question, I feel, has to do with the way scholars approached the question of magic in the Old Testament, and indeed in ancient religion in general. In the first edition of *Die Religion in Geschichte und Gegenwart*, H. Gressmann noted that then-contemporary students of the history of religions understood magic as the primitive origin of religious activity, whereas, "historians, whose objects are mainly the great religions of world-historical import, ascribe by contrast a much lesser significance to magic".[3] In spite of some well-founded hesitation about various views of the sociologists of his time, Gressmann went on to affirm that there exists "a sharp opposition between religion and magic", a view which is by now familiar to us; moreover, he noted that "In most religions. . . magic remains on the periphery. . . it is mainly popular superstition. . . and is only characteristic of the lowest social strata".[4] This was a curious remark

---

[1] "Der Traum in der rabbinischen Literatur", *Kairos* 18 (1976), pp. 1-42.

[2] "A Reconsideration of the Form-Critical Structure in I Samuel 3: An Ancient Near Eastern Dream Theophany", *ZAW* 94 (1982), pp. 379-90; the same, *The Dream Theophany of Samuel: Its Structure in Relation to Ancient Near Eastern Dreams and its Theological Significance* (Lanham [Maryland], 1984).

[3] *RGG*[1], (Tübingen, 1913), Vol.4, sub "Mantik, Magie, Astrologie", Col. 125.

[4] Same place, Col. 127. That this view of the marginality of divination was not peculiar to Gressmann is evidenced by the fact that the great W. Robertson Smith had only a few years previously managed to write an extensive study of Semitic religious practices in which divinatory phenomena are scarcely mentioned (*The Religion of the Semites. The Fundamental Institutions* (New York, 1959 [1889]), pp. 133, 177-78, 194. He was slightly more forthcoming in his *The Old Testament in*

to make for a man who was almost notorious in his own time for his adherence to history-of-religions approaches which sometimes scandalised other Old Testament scholars; in addition to which, as the study presented above has shown, it is dead wrong. Nevertheless, the view led Gressmann to observe, on the one hand, that numerous magical practices in ancient Israel enjoyed both wide usage and considerable respect, while on the other he concluded that the technical oracle was originally of considerable importance, but that it was eventually replaced by the "inspiration-based oracle of the prophets".[1] In short, the evolutionistically-orientated sociology of the 19th century, coupled with the apparent historical development in ancient Israel, led to the view that magical contact with the deity was a stage in social development which the Israelites eventually sloughed off in favour of the "immediate" and "personal" contact conferred by Israelite prophecy.

The article by A. Bertholet in the next edition of *Die Religion in Geschichte und Gegenwart* is symptomatic of the development of the times. Bertholet, too, registers the priority of prophecy over technical divination in the Old Testament.[2] Still inspired by evolutionistic thought, Bertholet maintains that both the Israelite divining-priest and the prophet derived from the earlier "seer"; he then merely presents a thumbnail-sketch of the phenomenology of the many types of divination which are attested in the Old Testament, and concludes, much as Gressmann had done, that "The prophets were in a higher sense the victors over that which was non-spiritual in the mantic arts".[3] This was much the style of the approaches to divination which figured in the

---

the Jewish Church. A Course of Lectures on Biblical Criticism (New York, 1892), pp. 286-91, where he adopts the familiar understanding of the superiority of prophecy as a "spiritual" undertaking, whereas divination is supposed to be a merely "technical" one.

[1] The same, Col. 132.

[2] *RGG*² (Tübingen, 1927), Vol.3, Col. 1979.

[3] The same, Cols. 1980-1981.

standard handbooks around the first third of the 20th century.[1]

There have been only two really sizable studies of Israelite divination in modern times, T. Witton Davies' *Magic, Divination, and Demonology Among the Hebrews and their Neighbours*,[2] and A. Guillaume's *Prophecy and Divination.*[3] Witton Davies' work openly acknowledges its debt to the sociological approach of E.B. Tylor, which, as we saw in the second chapter of this work, has definite deficiencies, although it was praiseworthy of Witton Davies to take account of the most informed opinion of his day. The author's dependence on Tylor is immediately obvious in his assumption that numerous magical and divinatory phenomena are "survivals"of more primitive stages of social development.[4] However, Witton Davies was by no means as contemptuous of his subject matter as Tylor was. Thus he maintained both that "it is hard to say when exactly the magician resigns, and the priest enters upon office",[5] and, moreover, that "all magic is a sort of religion".[6] He also recognised that "It is exceedingly difficult, if indeed possible, to indicate the boundary line between divination and

---

[1] For a comparable English-language approach, see the article entitled "Divination" by M. Gaster in J. Hastings and J.A. Selbie (eds.), *Encyclopaedia of Religion and Ethics* (Edinburgh, 1911), Vol. IV, pp. 806-13. For a similar approach in French, see "Divination" by A. Lesêtre in J. Vigouroux (ed.), *Dictionaire de la Bible* (Paris, 1899), Vol.2, Cols. 1443-1448, and "Oracle", in the same, Vol. 4, Cols. 1846-1848.

[2] (London and Leipzig, 1898).

[3] (London, 1938). R. Cambell Thompson's *Semitic Magic* (London, 1908) is only obliquely concerned with divination as such. A. Jirku, *Mantik in Altisrael. Inaugural Dissertation* (Rostock, 1913), examined only the ephod, the teraphim, Urim and Thummim, divination by means of arrows (the attestation of which is, incidentally, highly questionable), and lecanomancy; as in his earlier study of Israelite demonology (the same, *Die Dämonen und ihre Abwehr im Alten Testament* [Leipzig, 1912]), Jirku found Israelite magical practices to have been "spiritualised" (cf. *Mantik*, pp. 51-54). For E.A. Wallis Budge, *Amulets and Superstitions* (New York, 1978 [1930]), pp. 443-67, divination was apriori written off as "superstition".

[4] Witton Davies, *Magic, Divination and Demonology*, pp. 30-40, 95-100.

[5] *Magic, Divination and Demonology*, p. 3.

[6] *Magic, Divination and Demonology*, same place.

prophecy".[1] Unfortunately, the author's definition of divination as "the attempt on man's part to obtain from the spiritual world supernormal or superhuman knowledge"[2]. mistakes the manifest content (that is, what is affirmed or is apparently maintained) concerning the social use of divination for its latent content (i.e., what the phenomenon actually does). Moreover, Witton Davies' work is a surprisingly slipshod study, when one considers that it was a doctoral dissertion of the university of Leipzig; its author devotes precisely one page to "Babylonian and Assyrian Divination",[3] two and a half pages to Arabic divination,[4] a single page to Egyptian divination,[5] and, astonishingly, only four pages to Old Testament divination.[6] He does, however, devote six pages to a philological discussion of the terminology of Israelite divination, reflecting the perennial philological concerns of the faculty at Leipzig.[7] Those who came to Witton Davies' study convinced that Israelite divination was only a peripheral activity in comparison with the panorama of Israelite prophecy cannot have found any reason in this examination to change their minds.

The same cannot, however, be said of Guillaume's study, among other things because it was a full-length monograph which at least touched the bounds of what was known at the time of Semitic mantic practices, but also because its author was a well-known Orientalist and Arabist. Guillaume's approach was, however, relentlessly evolutionistic, in that it embraced the notion that pagan divinatory practices are motivated by fear, which primitive peoples attempt to overcome by taking the future in their own hands, as it were, in acts of technical divination and manipulative magic, whereas the Judeo-Christian tradition is motivated by secure faith in the divinely once-and-for-all conferred revelation of God. Thus he was able to hold, with Sir James Frazer, that "the progress of a religion. . . is in proportion to its success in freeing

---

[1] *Magic, Divination and Demonology*, p. 73.

[2] *Magic, Divination and Demonology*, p. 6.

[3] *Magic, Divination and Demonology*, p. 93.

[4] *Magic, Divination and Demonology*, pp. 90-92.

[5] *Magic, Divination and Demonology*, p. 94.

[6] *Magic, Divination and Demonology*, pp. 74-78.

[7] *Magic, Divination and Demonology*, pp. 78-84.

itself from the legacy of the medicine man and the magician until it attains to a living communion with the object of its worship".[1] By the same token, however, Guillaume was too sophisticated a scholar to content himself with easy answers. Hence on the question of the *genesis* of religion he was well aware that the rise of religion did not simply attend on the decline of magic, but that the two coexist throughout the Near East.[2]

Drawing on his impressive knowledge of Arabic literature, Guillaume pointed to dozens of parallels between Mesopotamian and Arabic divinatory phenomena, a procedure which has the interesting consequence of making the former seem rather less and the latter rather more sophisticated, than either in reality was.[3] But, of course, this is an unavoidable pitfall of indiscriminate comparative analysis without a functional standard of comparison.

In the years since Guillaume's study, there has been a gradual dawning of awareness among Old Testament scholars that Israelite divination ought perhaps to be taken more seriously than has hitherto been the case, as a considerable number of lesser publications indicates, and as is also indicated by fresh approaches in at least two of the major scholarly handbooks.[4]

Methodological Evaluation

Before we press on, I think it would be wise to point to the problems which I feel have plagued the study of divination in ancient Israel up to

---

[1] *Prophecy and Divination*, p. 390.

[2] *Prophecy and Divination*, p. 387. At the same time, however, Guillaume maintained that there *is* a perceptible evolutionary trend whereby "magical" cults led by "inspired" prophets tend to give way to the governance of priests, and for religious rites to supplant "mana" (*Prophecy and Divination*, pp. 37-38).

[3] *Prophecy and Divination*, pp. 117-33; 167-68; 197-213; 300-12.

[4] See A. Barucq's excellent study in *DBSup*, Vol. 6, Cols. 752-87, which shows a much greater sympathy for the phenomenon as such than previous writers have demonstrated; and note the conclusion of B.O. Long in *IDBSup*, p. 242: "Certain segments in Israelite society prohibited divination...Yet the practices seem to have been diverse and rather more widespread than many earlier scholars would have admitted". For further references to recent studies, see below.

the present. The first of these is obviously that scholars have been attempting to understand the socio-historical situation vis à vis divination on Deuteronomistic premisses. This manifests itself in extreme form in the works of Blau and Kaufmann, but certainly applies also to the works of other students of the Old Testament. Of course, it was not until comparatively recently that it was realised the extent to which the combined Pentateuchal-Deuteronomistic history represents a powerful idealisation of Israel's past, one which in many respects need have no necessary resemblance to what actually went on. By adhering to this idealisation, scholars have limited their focus largely to the priestly oracle and to the study of the dreams recounted in the Old Testament, that is, to the means of consultation of which the Old Testament itself manifestly approves.

Secondly, in embracing the evolutionary schemes of 19th century social science, scholars automatically ceased to focus on divination, as they were concerned to focus on the evolutionary stage which, "as everyone knew", had replaced it, namely prophecy.

Thirdly, in attempting to deal with divination on the basis of isolated phenomena like the Urim and Thummim, the ephod, dreams, or whatever, scholars committed themselves to a historical-critical phenomenological approach. They forgot, if they ever knew, that divination is, at least in primitive societies, indicative of an entire pattern of behaviour which entails a number of corollaries for the ways such societies understand cause and effect, deal with illness, uncertainties, social tensions, and so on.

The phenomenological approach was, however, in part very realistically motivated by a chronic problem facing anyone who attempts to understand ancient Israel, and which I shall designate the fourth problem of research into Israelite divination. This is the fact that certain social behaviours may be well attested in the Israelite chronographic literature, but such behavioural features seem to scholars to pale to insignificance when compared with the relatively enormous corpora of prophecies, Wisdom literature, psalms, legal materials, and so on. The literature has been allowed to overshadow the social reality of which the literature is merely one of many expressions. This has led to the almost perverse oddity in this case that a behaviour which the Israelite literature insists was absolutely central to Israelite social, cultic, and political life has received very little attention. Consider, for example, the simple fact that the Old Testament implies that divination persisted in Israelite society from "patriarchal" times cf.(Gen 25.22) until after the exile (Zech 10.2). Only the few studies I have indicated above have appeared in approximately a century's worth of research, whereas the last ten years have seen the publication of numerous major monographs on the Israelite prophets who, despite their undoubted merits, and quite apart from the questions concerning their historicity which have been raised by recent scholarship (see below), are not claimed by the OT to have influenced Israelite society for its entire history, but only for a relatively limited span of years.

The Problems of Prophecy and History

Before proceeding to a discussion of Israelite divination per se, it will first be necessary to address two important limitations which, I believe, confront anyone attempting to deal with detailed socio-historical issues in connexion with ancient Israel. The first of these has to do with the relationship between divination and prophecy; the second has to do with the historical tradition.

As far as the first problem is concerned, it is related to a pseudo-alternative for which the heritage of Max Weber is in part responsible, namely the distinction between "office" (German "Amt") and "calling" (German "Berufung", which, however, is often expressed in Weberian terms as "Charisma"). The school of Wellhausen and his followers accustomed us to think of the Law as secondary to prophecy, and not the other way round, as the Bible insists.[1] This powerful emphasis on the priority of prophecy (which is, incidentally, no longer shared, at least in its simplest form, by most Old Testament scholars)[2]

---

[1] Cf. e.g. J. Wellhausen, *Prolegomena*, and, for a broad overview, see S. Loersch, *Das Deuteronomium und seine Deutungen* (Stuttgart, 1967), pp. 14-24; and H.F. Hahn and H.D. Hummel, *The Old Testament in Modern Research. With a Survey of Recent Literature* (Philadelphia, 1966 [1954]), pp. 1-26.

[2] See, in brief A.G. Auld, "Prophets through the Looking Glass: Between Writings and Moses", *JSOT* 27 (1983), pp. 3-23 and, more recently, H.M. Barstad, "No Prophets? Recent Developments in Biblical Prophetic Research and Ancient Near Eastern Prophecy", *JSOT* 57 (1993), pp. 39-60. In general, the historical existence of prophets in pre-exilic Israel has been strongly questioned from a

led, understandably enough, to an emphasis on the ethical rôle of the prophets, and to attempts to depict their activities as critics and reformers of the Israelite society and cult.[1] It received psychological underpinning from G. Hölscher's famous—and controversial—concept of ecstatic prophecy.[2] The prophet was thereby in danger of becoming totally romanticised into a Promethean figure of implacable rectitude, the sole righteous individual in a society in which both cult and people had fallen into an abyss of Canaanite depravity. Naturally, his opponents, as we might expect, were the priests of the local sanctuaries. Each had his own characteristic mode of legitimation; the priest by his (Levitical or Aaronic) descent, the prophet by his "call", a psycho-social event which some Old Testament scholars seem to invest with the same significance Protestant church historians ordinarily award to Luther's

---

number of vantage-points. It is also clear that as long as there was an Israel, it must had a cult, and hence also a cultic tradition of sorts. Cf. N.P. Lemche ([trans. F.H. Cryer] *Ancient Israel: A New History of Israelite Society* (Sheffield, 1988): "The occurrence of the large collections (of laws) in which many different types of legislation are contained reveals that some individual regulations may be much older than their present literary situation would suggest. It is therefore clear that on this point it would be wise to modify Wellhausen's view and to radicalize it at the same time, and thus to conclude that it is not the letter of the law that is later than the prophets, but its 'spirit'" (p. 210). See also the apposite remarks of J. Day, "Prophecy", in D.A. Carson and H.G.M. Williamson (eds.), *It is Written: Scripture Citing Scripture. Essays in Honour of Barnabas Lindars* (Cambridge, 1988), pp. 39-55; here pp. 39-41.

[1] Cf. e.g. J. Lindblom, *Prophecy in Ancient Israel* (Oxford, 1967 [1962]); this somewhat romantic impression of OT prophecy is wonderfully reflected in E.W. Heaton's popular study, *The Old Testament Prophets* (Harmondsworth, 1969 [1958]). The classical German-language statement of this position was already developed by e.g. E. Sellin in his *Alttestamentliche Theologie auf religionsgeschichtlicher Grundlage* (Leipzig, 1933), pp. 67-99; see also R. Kittel, *Geschichte des Volkes Israel*, Vol.I: *Palästina in der Urzeit: Das Werden des Volkes*, (Gotha, 1912), pp. 550-51.

[2] *Die Propheten* (Leipzig, 1914), esp. pp. 129-57. A. Guillaume, too, *Prophecy and Divination*, pp. 290-333, saw the basis of prophecy to be ecstatic phenomena; see also Lindblom, *Prophecy in Ancient Israel*, pp. 1-64, 122-37.

Turmerlebnis.[1]

Seen against this background, it is clear that divination could not be taken seriously. Studying the entrails of a sheep, or whatever, requires skill and knowledge, but no "calling"; so the diviner was *per definitionem* on the other side of the divide from the prophet, and as such, suspect.[2]

Happily, fairly early on in this century, some scholars noted that the prophets themselves had a close attachment to the cult, and that the Old Testament even seems to presuppose that some prophets were cult functionaries.[3] After all, the prophet Ezekiel was "the priest, the son of Buzi" (Ezek 1.3), and Jeremiah was "the son of Hilkiah, of the priests

---

[1] It might be better not to mention any names in this connexion, but see in any case F.M.T. de Liagre Böhl's "Priester und Prophet" in *Opera Minora* (Antwerp, 1939), pp. 50-62. Astonishingly, at a time when Old Testament studies are devoting increasing attention to the purely literary, formal characteristics of the prophetic literature, O. Kaiser (*Einleitung in das Alte Testament* (Gutersloh, 1984), pp. 212-18) has returned to a psychologising understanding of prophecy which takes its point of departure in the twin roots of "nomadisches Sehertum" and "altorientalisches extatisches Prophetentum". Since, as will be evident from my remarks in what follows below on the historical tradition, I do not believe we possess much in the way of useful information about the early phases of Israelite society, I find this concern to pursue semi-mythical "origins" into later periods less than helpful.

[2] In his *Sacrifices and Offerings in Ancient Israel. Studies in their Social and Political Importance* (Atlanta, 1987), pp. 4-14 G.A. Anderson has accused Old Testament scholars of falsely distinguishing between a "Canaanite" cult based on "magical" practices and an elevated Israelite one, whose cult was largely "ethically" orientated. I could not agree more.

[3] The breakthrough in this respect may be said to have come about with the publication of S. Mowinckel's *Psalmenstudien III: Die Kultprophetie und prophetische Psalmen* (Kristiana, 1923). In Germany, A. Jepsen designated the *nabi* as the archetypical "prophet of weal" against whom such figures as Amos, Micaiah ben-Imlah, and Jeremiah had to contend (*Nabi: Soziologische Studien zur alttestamentlichen Literatur und Religionsgeschichte* [Munich, 1934]). In Sweden, A. Haldar pointed to the widespread practice of ecstatic prophecy in the ancient Near East (*Associations of Cult Prophets among the Ancient Semites* [Uppsala, 1945]), while in Wales A.R. Johnson argued, cogently and very learnedly, for the participation of Israelite prophets in the cult, though largely in vain (*The Cultic Prophet in Ancient Israel* [Cardiff, 1962] [1944]). A.S. Kapelrud (*Profetene i det gamle Israel og Juda* [Oslo, et al., 1966], pp. 10-20) accepted the distinction between prophet and "nabi" without hesitation.

who were in Anathoth in the land of Benjamin" (Jer 1.1), where Solomon is said to have banished his father's quondam high priest, Abiathar (1 Kgs 2.26-27), and who, incidentally, is supposed to have divined on David's behalf during the latter's career as a condottiere. There is, then, no necessarily hard and fast dividing-line between priest and prophet,[1] and a few hardy souls have occasionally been willing to risk the claim that the prophets themselves made use of "technical" oracular procedures, i.e., divination.[2]

Actually, in social terms, this was entirely to be expected. In a highly differentiated society, discrete institutional rôles are usually assigned to a variety of actors. By way of contrast, where there is little distinction between social actors in terms of income, status, political power, and so on there is little reason to diversify rôle assignments.[3] Now ancient Israelite society was a primitive agricultural society in

---

[1] I affirm this in spite of the influence of Noth's well-known study, *Amt und Berufung* (Bonn, 1958) (= *BAR* 19), which, it seems to me, almost perfectly incorporates the misunderstanding I have been addressing. G. Fohrer ("Priester und Prophet — Amt und Charisma?", *KuD* 17 (1971), pp. 15-27), while adhering to Jepsen's understanding of the distinction between "real" prophets and "Berufspropheten", nevertheless acknowledges that the polarity between "office" and "calling" seriously oversimplifies the relations between priest and prophet: "The difference between them and the priests consisted mainly in the fact that the prophets acted to a greater degree spontaneously, often in an ecstatic state, whereas the priests to a higher degree made use of technical prerequisites (e.g., the lot-oracle)" (p. 25).

[2] Cf. e.g. M.Bič, "Der Prophet Amos — ein Haepatoskopos", *VT* 1 (1951), pp. 293-96 (rebutted by A. Murtonen, "The Prophet Amos — A Hepatoscoper?", *VT* 2 [1952], pp. 170-71); for further discussion see J. Wright, "Did Amos Inspect Livers?", *Australian Biblical Review* 23 (1975), pp. 3-11; P.G. Craigie, "Amos the noqed in the light of Ugaritic", *Science Religieuse/Studies in Religion* 11 (1982), pp. 29-33.

[3] For more detailed argumentation on this point, see my article, "Der Prophet und der Magier. Bemerkungen anhand einer überholten Diskussion" in R. Liwak and S. Wagner (eds.), *Prophetie und geschichtliche Wirklichkeit im alten Israel. Festschrift für Siegfried Herrmann* (Stuttgart, 1991), pp. 79-88.

which the vast majority of actors made their living from the soil,[1] and in which their was little difference between the rural and urban populations in terms of housing and material possessions.[2] Moreover, the majority of cultic installations point to a cult which mainly took place in private houses,[3] with, of course, the exception of the central national shrine and perhaps a few others in peripheral regions.[4] Furthermore, social organisation, at least just prior to the national period, was segmentary, based on the units of family, lineage, clan, and tribe. There will thus have been little difference between individuals at comparable levels of the social structure.[5] Thus a highly differentiated class of cultic personnel, that is, one consisting of "seers", "nabis", "prophets", "priests", "divining priests", "temple servants", "Levites", temple scribes, "qodešot" (whatever they were),[6] Nazirites and so on seems most unlikely: this would reflect a social organisation of a much more evolved type than Israel was to possess for the first several

[1] See D.C. Hopkins, *The Highlands of Canaan: Agricultural Life in the Early Iron Age* (Sheffield, 1985); and O. Borowski, *Agriculture in Iron Age Israel: the Evidence from Archaeology and the Bible* (Winona Lake [IN], 1987). In their exploitation of agricultural resources, the Israelites no doubt employed a variety of "risk spreading" strategems to lessen the impact of the failure of one or another link in their economic chain; see J.W. Flanagan, *David's Social Drama. A Hologram of Israel's Early Iron Age* (Sheffield, 1988) (= *The Social World of Biblical Antiquity Series* 7), pp. 171-83.

[2] This appears to be true for both Iron I and II; see H. Weippert, *Palästina in vorhellenistischer Zeit* (Munich, 1988), pp. 393-406, 449, 510, 594, etc.

[3] *Palästina in vorhellenistischer Zeit*, pp. 407, 447-49, 628.

[4] *Palästina in vorhellenistischer Zeit*, p. 621.

[5] Cf. Lemche, *Ancient Israel*, pp. 92-104.

[6] Certainly not "sacral prostitutes", as argued by H.W. Wolff on the dubious analogy of the Sumerian "sacred marriage" texts and a snippet or two of Herodotus (in: *Dodekapropheton*, Vol. I [Neukirchen-Vluyn, 1961]); cf. W. Rudolph, "Präparierte Jungfrauen?" *ZAW* 75 (1963), pp. 65-73; H.M. Barstad, *The Religious Polemics of Amos* (Leiden, 1984), pp. 21-32.

centuries of her existence.[1] After all, one must consider that in the "secular" realm of the royal administration during the period of the monarchy, Israelite society apparently knew only an incompletely-drawn distinction between the *'bdym* and the *śrym*, to whom a wide variety of functions were more or less ad hoc assigned.[2]

Since, as I have suggested, there was most probably not a great deal of differentiation within Israelite society, it is likely that one and the same figure exercised more than one function. The plethora of terminology for various cultic and magical personnel we encounter in the Old Testament, then, probably describes functional, rather than

---

[1] By this I mean to signify that ancient Israel was by no means an "urbanised" or rural-urban society in which social life was dictated by the tensions between the cities and the rural population. Scholars since the last century have greatly overestimated the extent of Israelite urbanisation. The characteristic presupposition of this view is that the introduction of the monarchy in Israel, which is supposed to have resulted in the growth of such urban centres as Jerusalem, Megiddo, Hazor, and so forth, represented a decisive innovation, as the Biblical text states (1 Sam 8.1ff.). Among historians of Palestinian society a typical representative of this view is W. Thiel (*Die soziale Entwicklung Israels in vorstaatlicher Zeit* [Neukirchen- Vluyn, 2. Aufl., 1985], esp. pp. 92-118). Among Palestinian archaeologists, a typical representative of this view is V. Fritz; see his recent *Die Stadt im alten Israel* [München, 1990], esp. pp. 135-53. Actually, the monarchy must be understood as an internal development within Palestinian society, one which resulted from the consolidation of regional power by local chieftains, as R.B. Coote & K.W. Whitelam (*The Emergence of Early Israel in Historical Perspective* [Sheffield, 1987] (= *The Social World of Biblical Antiquity Series*, 5) have maintained (although Coote and Whitelam in general place too much emphasis on the rôle of material factors in determining the process of settlement in Palestine at the expense of social factors). For a convincing and well informed study, both from an archaeological and from a socio-historical point of view, see the recent investigation by H.M. Niemann, *Herrschaft, Königtum und Staat. Skizzen zur soziokulturellen Entwicklung im monarchischen Israel* (Tübingen, 1993). On Niemann's view, ancient Israel may first be accurately characterised as an "urban" society from the close of the 9th century, while Judah may be described as urbanised first from the end of the 8th century and the beginning of the 7th century. Niemann's conclusions tie in very well with the wonderful study, undertaken from a completely different viewpoint and applicable only to ancient Judah, by D. Jamieson-Drake, *Scribes and Schools in Monarchic Judah: A Socio-Archaeological Approach* (Sheffield, 1991).

[2] See U. Rütersworden, *Die Beamten der israelitischen Königszeit. Eine Studie zu śr und vergleichbaren Begriffen* (Stuttgart, Berlin, et al., 1985).

institutional rôles; that is, the terms used are not mutually exclusive titles, pertaining to distinct institutional "offices" (although they may have been interpreted as such by later, archaising traditionalists). As R.R. Wilson has noted, paraphrasing the Weber school,

> the title 'priest' can be applied to any specialist who participates in the regular maintenance of a cult. Thus, prophets, shamans, witches, mediums, and diviners can also be priests if they have regular cultic roles in their societies. In turn, priests can on occasion function as diviners, prophets, or mediums. . . the fact that priests sometimes have other religious functions prevents sharply distinguishing the priest from other religious specialists.[1]

It is accordingly hardly surprising that we find such figures as Ezekiel and Jeremiah doubling in the rôles of priest and prophet; Israelites may not necessarily have seen any important distinction between them.[2] In this connexion it is important to remember that many of the functions

---

[1] *Prophecy and Society in Ancient Israel* (Philadelphia, 1980), p. 27. Recently, D.L. Petersen has also attempted an analysis of prophetic behaviour based on Weberian rôle theory; cf. *The Roles of Israel's Prophets* (Sheffield, 1981). Although aware of Petersen's study, and superficially willing to acknowledge that institutional "offices" were indistinct in early periods of Israel's history, G. Wallis has recently nevertheless restated the classical Amt-Charisma dialectic; cf. Wallis (ed.), *Zwischen Gericht und Heil. Studien zur alttestamentlichen Prophetie im 7. und 6. Jahrhundert v. Chr.* (Berlin, 1987), pp. 14-25.

[2] The sharp Old Testament emphasis on Levitical descent, as well as the distinction between a higher priestly class and a lower, Levitical one, was a very late ideological development, as already Wellhausen (*Prolegomena*, pp. 112-39) recognised. See further A.H.J. Gunneweg, *Leviten und Priester. Forschungen zur Religion und Literatur des Alten und Neuen Testaments* (Göttingen, 1965) (= (*FRLANT* 89), who denies emphatically that there ever was a secular tribe of Levi. The difficulties are, of course, legion. Illustrative is the observation of J.A. Soggin, in connexion with the "Levitical cities" and "cities of refuge" mentioned in Josh 21.1-42 and Num 35.1-8 (cf. 1 Chron 6.39-66), that "It is not in fact easy to find a precise historical or sociological setting for these two institutions, not just in the context of the conquest but even in the history of Israel generally" (*A History of Israel. From the Beginnings to the Bar Kochba Revolt, A.D.135*, trans. J. Bowden [Philadelphia, 1984], p. 150). Predictably, Israeli scholars tend to affirm the historical basis of the Old Testament understanding of the Levites; cf. e.g. M. Haran, *Temples and Temple-Service in Ancient Israel. An Inquiry into the Character of Cult Phenomena and the Historical Setting of the Priestly School* (Oxford, 1978), esp. pp. 58-131.

which were performed by the Assyro-Babylonian *bārû* in the second millennium were performed by the mašmašu/ašîpu in Assyria, at least, in the first millennium. Similarly, we have seen that the names applied to the Hittite divining professionals changed bewilderingly over the centuries, although the functions performed by them remained more or less constant. We may therefore permit ourselves to suppose that there were also prophets who performed the "priestly" function of "technical" divination, without the Israelites having thereby noted either incongruity or heterodoxy.[1]

The Problem of the Historical Tradition

So far, I have been careful to parenthesise references to Israel's distant past with inverted commas or with such circumlocutions as "is said to have (taken place)", or the like, as the attentive reader will surely have noticed. My reasons for this are in part theoretical, motivated by the considerations offered in the introduction to this study. However, they are also in part motivated by the concrete results of recent research into Israel's earliest history. The "conquest", as related in the Bible, never took place, and no serious scholar since A. Alt has maintained otherwise.[2] As I indicated in the introduction to this work, as far as the pre-national period is concerned we are faced with a number of more or less plausible hypotheses as to how Israel came into being, but of concrete knowledge we possess only a little.

I have also claimed that we do not really know much more about the monarchical period. What we possess in the Books of Kings are

---

[1] For a recent study which agrees largely with the conclusions arrived at independently here, see T.W. Overholt, *The Channels of Prophecy. The Social Dynamics of Prophetic Activity* (Minneapolis, 1989), pp. 117-48. I should like to stress, against Overholt, that this does *not* mean that any of the Israelite "writing prophets" were actual historical personnages. All we are entitled to conclude is that comparative data allow us to surmise that the social features which we derive from the prophetic texts reflect a society in which prophecy played a significant part. Historically, this society could as easily be post-exilic, Persian period or even hellenistic as pre-exilic.

[2] Admittedly, there was some disagreement about this on the other side of the Atlantic for some time, but adherents of Albright's, Bright's and Wright's version of the Conquest are thin on the ground these days.

numerous statements whose "ontological commitment", as linguists say, remains to be demonstrated,[1] coupled with a chronology which defies simple resolution into the time-scheme of the ancient Near East.[2] This is not the stuff of which history is made.[3]

At the literary level, I have recently delivered an address at a Society of Biblical Literature congress in Copenhagen in which I discussed the difficulties M. Noth's concept of a Deuteronomistic history encounters when it is seriously confronted with the contents of the Books of Samuel.[4] In all brevity, I pointed out that Noth thought to

---

[1] By this I mean that the texts themselves do not distinguish between, for example, prophetic legends and "historical" narratives about various kings of Israel and Judah: we, however appropriately or inappropriately, do. The anachronism consists in trying to supply such texts with a descriptive precision (= ontological commitment) which would have been foreign to their original authors and readers. See the fine and thoughtful article published some years ago by N. Wyatt, "The Old Testament Historiography of the Exilic Period", *ST* 33 (1979), pp. 45-67.

[2] See F.H. Cryer, "To the One of Fictive Music: Old Testament Chronology and History", in *SJOT* 2 (1987), pp. 1-27. To take a simple example: the sum of the regnal years listed in the Old Testament for the Israelite kings from Jehu's accession to the fall of Israel is 143 years, whereas ancient Near Eastern sources suggest about 120 years as the "actual" interval; similarly, the sum of the Judaean regnal years from the accession of Athaliah to the fall of Jerusalem is 287 years, although our external sources tell us that no more than 245 years can have elapsed (see for this example J.M. Miller, *The Old Testament and the Historian* [Philadelphia, 1976], p. 75). As I have shown in my article, scholars have produced a number of more or less plausible number-juggling systems to "explain" these and other discrepancies. But in so doing they have neglected the fact that chronology is a system of measurement, and that the simple and inflexible rule of all such systems, as shown already by the great German mathematician C.F. Gauß (1777-1855), is that no system is any more reliable than its worst measurement. Therefore, unless one or another of the explanations for the inaccuracies of the Israelite chronological data should be empirically demonstrated (and not merely argued), we are stuck with a chronology whose best-case accuracy is about 23 years, and whose worse-case is about 43 years. The reader is invited to consider the adequacy of a "history" of the 20th century which posits the close of the Second World War in either 1902 or 1998, i.e., plus or minus 43 years.

[3] The reader is again referred to my remarks in the introduction to this work, pp.17-22.

[4] "Die Samuelbücher als Hindernis für die Annahme eines deuteronomistischen Geschichtswerkes", delivered at Moltkes Palæ, Copenhagen, 8 August 1989.

have based his notion of a unified work on the literary critical observations of earlier scholars. As he held, the unity of the "work" in question can be asserted on the basis of 1) the cohesive theology of history which links the whole structure 2) the forward- and backward-looking speeches placed in the mouths of various actors (Moses, Joshua, Samuel, Solomon), plus the notices framing the careers of various figures 3) the chronology which runs through the entire composition, giving it a unified time-frame. Of these points, the first can be left out of account, as virtually any given theological "telos" can be asserted no matter what the state of the texts. I did not address myself to the chronology, but it should be obvious from my previous remarks that the unificatory tendency which Noth thought to demonstrate is far from evident in what can be held to be the Deuteronomistic chronological notices.[1] As far as the speeches are concerned, I pointed out that every one of the "Deuteronomistic" speeches cited by Noth contains information which contradicts or fits only very badly indeed together with statements in other of the "Deuteronomistic" speeches or framework passages. We are thus left with a framework which does not cohere with the passages it purportedly frames. This observation leaves us with only one obvious conclusion: that there once was a "Deuteronomistic" collection which attempted to present a unified history of Israel, but that this collection is no longer extant. It has been so much reworked that its framework passages now refer to nothing we know of. This means, in literary terms, that large sections of the Books of Samuel, and, by implication, other works within the compass of the Deuteronomistic history, are necessarily post-Deuteronomistic.

The historical consequences of this argument should be clear: if the balance of the materials in the Books of Samuel are post-Deuteronomistic, then they are separated from the events they purport to describe by at least four or five centuries. This means that they are not primary sources for the history of an Israelite united monarchy and the foundation of an Israelite state; rather, they are legendary sources roughly as far removed in time from their object as Sir Walter Scot's

---

[1] This view now finds welcome support in the recent study by J. Hughes, *Secrets of the Times. Myth and History in Biblical Chronology* (Sheffield, 1990) (= *JSOTSup* 66), pp. 55-96, which shows, if nothing else, the state of disorder in the Deuteronomistic chronology.

Ivanhoe is from the High Middle Ages it represents. It is a topic to which I intend to return in an extensive monograph.[1]

This observation, coupled with the recent arguments of J. Van Seters, R. Rendtorff, H.H. Schmid, E. Blum, R.N. Whybray and others for the lateness of the Yahwistic materials in the Pentateuch leads me to the conclusion that we really have very little written evidence as to the earliest phases of Israel's history, and, as I suggested above, the materials in Kings are problematical as well. For the purposes of this work, this means that it is impossible simply to claim that one or another form of divination was practised in ancient Israel in such and such a period, only to disappear in the following one, which lasted from

---

[1] As is well known, a very extensive tradition of Old Testament interpretation insists that the Deuteronomistic collection suffered at least a single redaction subsequent to its compilation. See A. Kuenen, *De Boeken des Ouden Verbonds*, Part 1: *De Thora en de historische Boeken des Ouden Verbonds* (Amsterdam, 2nd rev. edn, 1884), pp. 418-33; A. Jepsen, *Die Quellen des Königbuches* (Halle [Saale], 1956); R. Smend, "Das Gesetz und die Völker. Ein Beitrag zur deuteronomistischen Redaktionsgeschichte", in: H.W.Wolff (ed.), *Probleme biblischer Theologie. Gerhard von Rad zum 70.Geburtstag* (Munich, 1971), pp. 494-509; the same, *Die Entstehung des Alten Testaments* (Stuttgart, Berlin, et al., 1978), pp. 110-25; W. Dietrich, *Prophetie und Geschichte* (Göttingen, 1972) (= *FRLANT* 108); the same, *David, Saul und die Propheten. Das Verhältnis von Religion und Politik nach den prophetischen Überlieferungen vom frühesten Königtum in Israel* (Stuttgart, Berlin, et al., 1987); T. Veijola, *Die ewige Dynastie. David und die Entstehung seiner Dynastie nach der deuteronomistischen Darstellung* (Helsinki, 1975); the same, *Das Königtum in der Beurteilung der Deuteronomistischen Historiographie. Eine redaktionsgeschichtliche Untersuchung* (Helsinki, 1977); the same, *Verheissung in der Krise. Studien zur Literatur und Theologie der Exilszeit anhand des 89.Psalms* (Helsinki, 1982); R.D. Nelson, *The Double Redaction of the Deuteronomistic History* (Sheffield, 1981) (= *JSOT Sup* 18); A.D.H. Mayes, *The Story of Israel between Settlement and Exile. A Redactional Study of the Deuteronomistic History* (London, 1983); I.W. Provan, *Hezekiah and the Books of Kings* (Berlin and New York, 1988); H. Schnabel, *Die 'Thronfolgeerzählung David's'. Untersuchungen zur literarischen Eigenständigkeit, literarkritischen Abgrenzung u. Intention von 2 Sam 21,1-14; 9-20 1 Kön 1-2* (Regensburg, 1988); and M.A. O'Brien, *The Deuteronomistic History Hypothesis: A Reassessment* (Göttingen, 1989) (= *OBO* 92). One notes that the point of departure of most of these studies is the Books of Kings, or else Joshua-Samuel are understood from the vantage of Kings. I intend to show that such approaches cannot show what they have been held to show. At stake is our understanding of Deuteronomism as a literary-historical process.

A to B. Rather, it seems to me that virtually all of the references to Israelite divination in the Old Testament prose materials are rather late, which means Deuteronomistic at the earliest. Many, if not most, are surely post-Deuteronomistic, and hence exilic or post-exilic, which makes it intelligible that even late texts such as Zech 10.2 and Lev 19.26,31[1] find it meaningful to condemn divination: it was no doubt after the demise of the monarchy, which had been its strongest pillar of support, that the religious hierarchy experienced difficulties maintaining its traditional monopoly on the means of revelation.

But what, then, are we to make of Deut 18.9-14, which condemns divination and other magical practices as usages of the "inhabitants of the land" whom the Israelites are held to be displacing? It was long ago noted that Israelite knowledge of the distant past of the ancient Near East is by no means as accurate as we should expect, if the Israelite chronographic literature really is as old as scholars have thought it to be. Gen 14.1-17, with its amazing mishmash of garbled names deriving from all manner of periods was merely the first major case in point.[2] Van Seters cut to the heart of the matter in 1975 when he wrote that,

> There seems to be no clear distinction in Genesis among the terms Canaanite, Hittite, and Amorite, though a preference may be seen in the use of any one term by a particular literary source, and in this respect the term Hittite is usually assigned to the Priestly source. . . .

However, as he proceeded to observe, already with the Neo-Assyrian empire, in Assyro-Babylonian literature

> the term Hatti (had) lost any specific ethnic or cultural connotation. It simply became an archaic designation for the political states of the

---

[1] The lateness of Lev 19.26,37 is obvious, given its derivation from P (concerning which date of composition only Israeli scholars are still trying to argue for a pre-exilic date); for the context of Zech 10.2, see B. Otzen, *Studien über Deuterosacharja* (Copenhagen, 1964), pp. 216-25.

[2] Cf. e.g. J. Van Seters, *Abraham in History and Tradition* (New Haven and London, 1975), pp. 296-308; A. Dillmann, *Die Genesis* (Leipzig, 6th edn, 1892), observed that "the narrative (makes) the impression on the reader of being more 'historical' in a strict sense than do the other Abraham narratives"; however, as he goes on to note, already then such scholars as Bohlen, Hitzig, Nöldeke, Kuenen and Wellhausen had held Gen 14 to be "an invention for the glorification of Abraham" (p. 234).

West, frequently corresponding to Amurru.[1]

It is therefore reasonable to suppose, as scholars increasingly tend to do today, that the various designations of "the peoples" inhabiting Palestine at the time of the Biblical "conquest" are archaising expressions, features in an imaginative reconstruction of an ancient Palestine that never was. N.P. Lemche has recently published in English a correlative study of the concept of "the Canaanites", as used in the Old Testament. In brief, Lemche shows that the term "Canaanite" in ancient Near Eastern documents was never an ethnic expression, but either 1) a broad designation for the inhabitants of a very indistinct region, or 2) an occupational designation suggesting something like "trader" or "merchant".[2] Thus the Old Testament polemic against learning the practices of the Canaanites, Amorites, Hittites, and so on makes meaningless distinctions between "peoples" who never existed, and Israel. Conversely, the many lists of the autochthonous population of Palestine in the Pentateuch (including the Hivites, Girgashites, Perizzites,[3] etc.) consistently name peoples who did not exist. By the same token, they studiously avoid mentioning the one people resident in Palestine who actually *did* exist, namely the Philistines.[4]

One does not have to be a structuralist anthropologist to arrive at the conclusion that this sort of polarity has nothing to do with an attempt to describe an actual historical situation; rather, its force is ideological, and its goal is to assist in the definition of what is "Israelite" and what is not.

A Control Investigation

A brief check on the correctness of the above-mentioned assumption

---

[1] Van Seters, *Abraham in History and Tradition*, p. 45; see also pp. 44 and 46.

[2] *The Canaanites and Their Land* (Sheffield, 1991).

[3] There is also no reason to believe that the Perizzites existed; see H.M. Niemann, "Das Ende des Volkes der Perizziter", *ZAW* 105 (1993), pp. 233-57.

[4] This is an insight arising out of discussions with Michael Niemann, of the universities of Rostock and Hamburg. This cannot be explained away by reference to the tradents' desire to depict Palestine in the time prior to the immigration of the Philistines. All indications suggest that the Biblical authors had no such well-developed chronological understanding of Israel's past.

may be made in the form of an etymological investigation of the terms which Deuteronomy 18.9-14 specifically prohibits as characteristic of "the peoples", and hence not of Israel. As mentioned above, the Deuteronomic-Deuteronomistic fiction of Israel's origins has the Israelites succumbing to partial assimilation to the indigenous culture. There is no question but that Hebrew belongs to the group of "Canaanite" languages.[1] Hence, if the fiction had some truth to it, we should expect to find the Israelite-Jewish terms for magic and divination reflected in the languages of the peoples around Israel from, shall we say, the close of the second millennium to the first half of the first millennium. The terms in question are: מכשף, מנחש, מעגן, קסם קסמים, שאל אוב, חבר חבר, דרש המתים and ידעני. Now of these, the first derives from the root קסם, which is well attested in Palmyrene Aramaic, Syriac, Ethiopic, Mishnaic Hebrew, the Talmud, and the Aramaic of the Targums in the meaning "to conjure", or the like, and in Arabic in the meaning "to cut (in pieces)".[2] On the other hand, the word is unattested in this or any other meaning in Ugaritic,[3] Phoenician-Punic,[4] or Old or Imperial Aramaic.[5] If the art of divining by קסמים was truly a phenomenon Israel had learnt from her neighbours, it is curious that

---

[1] See R.M. Voigt, "The Classification of Central Semitic", *JSS* 32 (1987), pp. 1-21; E.A. Knauf, *Midian. Untersuchungen zur Geschichte Palästinas und Nordarabiens am Ende des 2. Jahrtausends v. Chr.* (Wiesbaden, 1988), pp. 64-77.

[2] Cf. L. Koehler and W. Baumgartner, *Hebräisches und Aramäisches Lexicon zum Alten Testament* (Leiden, 1967-1983), sub קסם; see also H. Zimmern, W. Max Müller, O. Weber (eds.), *Wilhelm Gesenius' Hebräisches und Aramäisches Handwörterbuch über das Alte Testament* (17th edn, Berlin, Göttingsen, Heidelberg, 1962 [1917]); M. Jastrow, *A Dictionary of the Targumim, the Talmud Babli and Yerushalmi, and the Midrashic Literature*, Vols. I-II, (New York, 1967).

[3] Cf. J. Aistleitner (O. Eißfeldt [ed.]), *Wörterbuch der ugaritischen Sprache* (Berlin, 1963).

[4] I have consulted R.S. Tomback, *A Comparative Semitic Lexicon of the Phoenician and Punic Languages* (New York, 1978); J.C.L. Gibson, *Textbook of Syrian Semitic Inscriptions.* Vol. 3; C.-F. Jean and J. Hoftijzer, *DISO,* (Leiden, 1965).

[5] See the glossaries of F. Rosenthal, *An Aramaic Handbook*, Pt. I/2 (Wiesbaden, 1967); S. Segert, *Altaramäische Grammatik* (Leipzig, 1983 [1975]) and H. Donner and W. Röllig, *Kanaanäische und aramäische Inschriften*, Vol. III (Wiesbaden, 1976); J.C.L. Gibson, Vol. 2, *Aramaic Inscriptions* (Oxford, 1985).

they have left no record of it.

The מעֹנן, clearly, divined by ענן, a verbum mediae geminatae (ayin " ayin) which offers no particular grammatical difficulties; the problem is, however, that the lexica and glossaries offer no examples of it in Ugaritic, Phoenician, Punic or Old Aramaic; on the other hand, it is attested in a single Aramaic-Middle Persian glossary.[1] Already Gesenius characterised the verb as "zweifelhaft". Once again, the Old Testament itself is the oldest certain attestation.

With the efforts of the מנחש, we come to the root נחש, which, as we have seen, is regarded by Jewish traditionalists as the *foreign* divinatory term par excellence. We should note that the root is attested in the meaning "to divine" only in Mishnaic and Talmudic Hebrew, Late Aramaic, Syriac, and Mandaic.[2] The Arabic cognate *nahuša* means "to be unlucky" (Gesenius) or "calamitous" (Koehler-Barmgartner), though the corresponding substantive *nihšat* means "evil" or "omen" (Koehler-Baumgartner). The root may have its "mantic" significance in two attestations from Hatra and Palmyra.[3] It is again unattested in Phoenician or Punic,[4] Ugaritic,[5] and Old and Imperial Aramaic.[6] In short, in order to find non-Jews using this term at all in the sense required by Y. Kaufmann, one has again to seek in texts which are younger than the Old Testament and which may have been influenced by it.[7] The Akkadian cognate, *nahāsu*, means "to be abundant", and

---

[1] Cf. Jean-Hoftijzer, *DISO*, p. 219.

[2] See Koehler-Baumgartner, *HAL*, on the root; see also Jastrow, *Dictionary*, for a wealth of Talmudic references.

[3] Cf. Jean-Hoftijzer, *DISO*, p. 177.

[4] Cf. Tomback, *Comparative Semitic Lexicon*.

[5] Cf. Aistleitner, *Wörterbuch*.

[6] Cf. Segert, *Grammatik*, Donner-Röllig, *KAI*, and Gibson, *SSI* Vol. 2.

[7] On the other hand, of course, it is not inconceivable that the root n/l-h-š ultimately derives from Arabic, as we have seen, and E.A. Knauf has in fact argued that Israel's southern neighbours, the Midianites and the Ishmaelites, were "proto-Arabic" speakers who had established themselves to the south of Judah in the 10th century and the 7th-6th century, respectively — although "proto-Arabs" are hardly the "neighbours" the Deuteronomists have in mind. See E.A. Knauf, *Ismael. Untersuchungen zur Geschichte Palästinas und Nordarabiens im 1. Jahrtausend v. Chr.* 2nd rev. edn (Wiesbaden, 1989); and the same, *Midian. Untersuchungen zur*

provides no point of contact with the Hebrew mantic usage. On the other hand, the verb *nhš* has a sister form, *lhš*, which is widely attested: in Ugaritic in the meaning "whisper";[1] in the Phoenician of Arslan Tash in the meaning "to conjure";[2] and, again, in Jewish Palestinian Aramaic and other late sources, including Mandaic and Ethiopic, in the meanings "to divine" and "to charm".[3] This root may, then, have been a substrate root which the Israelites might have acquired from their environment at an early date, rather than a late one. Von Soden, however, it might be mentioned, denies that *nhš* and *lhš* are "missible" forms of the same root.[4]

The next form, מכשף, derives from the Akkadian root *kašāpu*, noun *kišpu*. It is unattested in Ugaritic, Phoenician, Punic, and Old Aramaic. In Mesopotamia, however, it was quite at home as a designation for the practice of black magic.[5] One has the suspicion that if the Israelites had wanted to ban the practice of *kešef* at the time of the "conquest", they would have had to go to Babylonia to do it.[6] The root is richly attested in rabbinical literature in the meaning "to conjure, cast a spell".[7]

The חבר בבר is problematical, not for the thesis under

Geschichte Palästinas und Nordarabiens am Ende des 2. Jahrtausends v. Chr. (Wiesbaden, 1988). "Proto-Arabic" influence is also not to be ruled out in the case of some features present in 9th-century Moabite (private communication from Prof. Knauf).

[1] See Aistleitner, *Wörterbuch*, p. 170 (but only as a noun, *lhst*).

[2] Cf. Tomback, *Comparative Semitic Lexicon*, p. 157.

[3] Tomback, *Comparative Semitic Lexicon*; see also Jastrow, *Dictionary*, for references in late Jewish literature.

[4] Cited in Koehler-Baumgartner, *HAL*, sub .

[5] Cf. e.g. G.Meier, *Die assyrische Beschwörungssammlung Maqlu*, *AfO*, Beiheft 2, (Berlin, 1937), p. 7, Tablet 1, obv. line 4: aš-šu kaššaptu u-kaš-šip-an-ni: "since the witch has bewitched me". See further the CAD, AHw, sub *kašpu*.

[6] Perhaps more to the point: had they done so, it would have been a little belated, as already in Hammurabi's time the practice of black magic was punishable by death; cf. *ANET*, p. 163, 2 (and note that Hammurabi built some safeguards into his codex against frivolous accusations). There is nothing unusual in the Israelite attacks on *kešef*, seen from the point of view of the ancient Near East.

[7] Cf. M. Jastrow, *Dictionary*, sub כשף.

examination here, but for its very meaning. The root חבר is well attested in the meanings "to bind together," "to form a community" (Koehler-Baumgartner).[1] It means "conjure" or "charm" only in Middle Hebrew.[2] A Punic text from Spain has been translated "the conjurers of TNT".[3] Some Hasmonaean coins bear the legend *hbr*, which most assuredly does not refer to enchantment, but to "community" or the like.[4] It is attested in Ugaritic, but only in the meanings "companion" or "vessel".[5] Nor does Old Aramaic offer any useful parallels.[6] Thus the meaning "to conjure", "to charm" is purely inner-Hebrew, derivable only with difficulty from Deut 18.11, Ps 58.5 (Heb v 6: obscure), Isa 47.9,12 (where, in both cases, only the proximity of *kešef* seems to imply "conjuring").

The twin expressions שאל אוב and דרש המתים would seem to be synonyms; the verbs *šā'al* and *dāraš* are regularly used in Hebrew of consultations with Yahweh or even other gods (cf. 2 Kgs 1.2). If the dead were regarded in ancient Israel as divine,[7] then the use of these two verbs in this sense would be completely intelligible. Hebrew *'ôb*,

---

[1] References in Jean-Hoftijzer, *DISO*, p. 81.

[2] Cf. Jastrow, *Dictionary*, sub חבר.

[3] Cf. Tomback, *Comparative Semitic Lexicon*, p. 97. However, the expression could as easily derive from the main sense of the root, hence: "the intimates/companions/congregation of TNT" (probably the Punic form of the goddess Anath; cf. F.O.Hvidberg-Hansen, *La Déesse TNT. Une étude sur la religion canaanéo-punique*, Vols. 1-2 [Copenhagen, 1979]).

[4] Cf. Jean-Hoftijzer, *DISO*, p. 82.

[5] Cf. Aistleitner, *Wörterbuch*, p. 99.

[6] Cf. Segert, *Grammatik*; Gibson, *SSI* Vol. 2; Rosenthal, *Aramaic Handbook*; Donner-Röllig, *KAI*.

[7] One thinks, for example, of the "famous dead", like the Rephaim; analogous to the shadowy survivals of the heroes in the Elysian fields in classical literature; if such a concept was embraced by the Israelites (analogous to the Moslem practice of requesting oracles at the graves of the weli's, the "Schutzheilige"; cf. A. Jirku, "Zu den altisraelitischen Vorstellungen von Toten- und Ahnengeistern", *BZ* 5 (1961), pp. 30-38; here p. 38; and see R. Liwak's forthcoming very judicious contribution on the Rephaim in *TWANT*), then 1 Sam 28.13 is virtually the only strong witness for such a notion. See also J. Tropper, *Nekromantie. Totenbefragung im Alten Orient und im Alten Testament* (Neukirchen-Vluyn, 1989) (= *AOAT* 223), pp. 125, 283.

is, of course, a famous puzzle: one for which no Syro-Palestinian (but extra-Israelite) etymology has ever been convincingly demonstrated.[1] The practice itself, as I mentioned previously, is attested sparsely for Assyria, and otherwise extensively in Talmudic sources. Again, the practice was either acquired by the Israelites directly from Mesopotamia, or developed independently by themselves. There are no extra-Biblical Syro-Palestinian references from the Biblical period.

The last term referring to forbidden magic/divination is יִדְּעֹנִי. The word itself must be derived from NW Semitic y/w-d-ʿ, as the lexica agree. The dagesh forte in the d suggests an intensive stem; the ending ôn is a reflex of Semitic â > ô. The ôn theme occurs in abstract nouns and diminutives; the î (iy) suffix expresses "belongingness" (pertaining

---

[1]   See the lexica and additionally   H.A. Hoffner, "Second Millennium Antecedents to the Hebrew 'ob", *JBL* 86 (1967), pp. 385-401; F. Schmidtke, "Träume, Orakel und Totengeister als Künder der Zukunft in Israel und Babylonien", *BZ* 11 (1967), pp. 240-46; the earlier article by H. Wohlstein in *BZ* 5 (1961), pp. 30-38; further, J. Lust, "On Wizards and Prophets", *VT* 26 (1974), pp. 133-42; H.R. (Chaim) Cohen, *Biblical Hapax Legomena in the Light of Akkadian and Ugaritic* (Missoula [Montana], 1978) (= *SBL Diss. Series* 37), pp. 73-74, n. 144 (on the interesting question of the relation of the *'ôb* to Ugaritic *'ib*). To be cheerfully ignored is the two-part study by J. Ebach and U. Rüterswörden, "Unterweltsbeschwörung im Alten Testament", *UF* 9 (1977), pp. 57-70 and 12 (1980), pp. 205-20, which ultimately merely amplifies the conclusions of Hoffner (see above), without stopping to consider that the Hitittite [SAL] ŠU.GI, evinced as a parallel to the "witch" of Endor (1 Sam 28), is otherwise only attested in non-Semitic contexts (i.e., Hurrian and Hittite). A Hittite > NW Semitic loan is dubious historical philology which is not improved by even more dubious socio-historical assumptions. Since A. Kammenhuber's study of Hittite divination had appeared already in 1976, they ought to have known better, at least as far as the latter point is concerned. See also J. Tropper, *Nekromantie*, pp. 189-316, esp. pp. 312-16. Tropper opts for the solution that Heb. *'ôb* and *'âb* are essentially identical, the former being merely a theologically motivated revocalisation of the latter. The interpretation seems forced; Tropper tends to see ancestor worship on every high hill and under every green tree. The crux of the matter is that, in addition to considering the *'ôb* to be a spirit, some Biblical passages suggest that one can "make" an *'ôb*, or even "have" or "burn" one. Thus suggestions from as far afield as Sumerian and Hittite have been advanced to resolve the conundrum. Even if one of these should prove to be adequate, we are far indeed from the world of Israel's "neighbours".

to?).[1] Obviously, the figure in question has something to do with knowledge (literally: "pertaining/belonging, to one who makes known"), but of what sort it is impossible to say. RSV's "wizard" is as good a guess as any. The word is unattested anywhere outside of the Old Testament and rabbinical literature.[2]

This short review of the categories of magical and mantic practices which were outlawed in the Deuteronomic-Deuteronomistic literature should be sufficient to show that the language which describes these practices is virtually without exception either first derivable from Hebrew itself or from Mesopotamia; but not, however, from Israel's "neighbours". This fact suggests that the surmise offered above is correct. The traditional critical notion that Israelite magic and divination were borrowed from Israel's neighbours is yet another example of the extent to which we have understood ancient Israel on the lines laid down by the Deuteronomists and their successors. An almost entirely domestic vocabulary means an almost entirely domestic praxis.[3] The best analogy to this is presented by the Hittites who, as we have seen, borrowed a considerable amount of mantic usage from Mesopotamia, but did so either at the level of literary loans, or else (e.g., the KUŠ oracle) completely adapted the phenomenon in question to their own needs, and correspondingly, to their own language. However, we should note that the parallels to these terms almost without exception are found

---

[1] Cf. S. Moscati (ed.), *An Introduction to the Comparative Grammar of the Semitic Languages. Phonology and Morphology* (3rd edn, Wiesbaden, 1980), pp. 82, section 12.21 a) and 83, section 12.23 c), respectively.

[2] See Tropper, *Nekromantie*, pp. 200-1; 205-319, esp. pp. 317-19. Tropper's philological analysis of *yidde'ônî* agrees almost completely with mine, but he additionally points out that "Noun formations of this type are extremely rare in Hebrew and mainly occur in younger strata of the language" (p. 317). He regards the intensive aspect of the form as signifying "someone who is especially knowledgeable" (p. 318), and holds it to be an epithet applied to the "wise" spirit of the dead whom the necromancer interrogates (p. 319). On every high hill. . . .

[3] Naturally, some theological conservative *might* object that the very lack of early attestations of these terms in Israel's environment could be taken to suggest that the Israelites had in fact brought these forms of divination with them during their wanderings and the subsequent "Conquest" or "settlement" of Palestine. Of course, such a view would fail to take account of the fact that Deuteronomy patently regards these "abominations" as practices of the "neighbours".

only in late sources.

Moreover, as far as the thesis of characteristic Israelite prophecy versus imported Israelite magic and divination is concerned, one has only to consider that the root *hzh*, "to see", is richly attested in Israel's surroundings.[1] Thus, the only conclusion historical linguistics permits is that prophetic terminology, if not the phenomenon itself, was derived from Israel's "neighbours", whereas Israel's various forms of magic were in all likelihood domestic.

Historical Conclusion

The acknowledgement of this fact re-emphasises the fundamental problem of Old Testament historical research, a problem which few scholars are as yet willing to tackle face to face. In terms of the classical historiography of the 19th century, there is only one way we can be sure of the dates, and hence (in part, but only in part) the source-value, of our sources. Obviously, this is when a source is quoted in another source which we can date in a more or less absolute fashion. It is, for example, unacceptable to suppose, as Noth and von Rad did, that the Yahwistic history is based on an (indemonstrable) *Grundschrift*, one which "must" be old because the Yahwistic "history" reflects the intellectual activity which is presumed to have taken place at Solomon's court because the Old Testament tells us that Solomon's court represented the flower of Israelite intellectual life. One cannot read a document of indeterminate origins, extract a "history" from it, and then proceed to use this "history" to elucidate other documents, on the basis of which further conclusions can be drawn. The circularity of this process is obvious. As a method, it had something in its favour back when there was a fair presumption that the Old Testament literature was an adequate source for the history of Israel. Now that we are increasingly becoming aware the extent to which the Old Testament is a very late, ideologically coloured,[2] and largely inaccurate source for

[1] See H.F. Fuchs, *Sehen und Schauen. Die Wurzel hzh im Alten Orient und im Alten Testament. Ein Beitrag zum prophetischen Offenbarungsempfang* (Würzburg, 1978), esp. pp. 30-57.

[2] Again, see G. Garbini, *Storia e Ideologia nell'Israele Antico* (Brescia, 1986); Eng. trans. (J. Bowden) *History and Ideology in Ancient Israel* (New York, 1988).

Israel's history, this method has to be discontinued by those who intend to pursue historical research.

For historians doing research into the Old Testament chronographic literature, this insight limits the certainties which can be derived from the use of other sources within the Old Testament. For scholars conducting research into Israelite prophecy it has profound implications, since the historical situation of the individual prophet and his society has traditionally played a major rôle in the interpretation of the prophetic literature. And since the "historical background" against which we have up to the present attempted to understand the prophets derives in large measure from Deuteronomistic and post-Deuteronomistic sources, that "background" provides only the shakiest of foundations. If we face the fact that we do not actually know very much about the history of the monarchical period, then exegetes dealing with the prophetic literature would be better advised to reconsider their approach. But, and I say this in the teeth of a burgeoning tendency in Old Testament scholarship to try to do without history and historical insights altogether, history is the fundamental category of Western experience and reflection. We can no more dispense with it than we can do without drinking-water.[1]

Descriptive Survey of Israelite Divination:
Dreams

As we have seen, Y. Kaufmann was forced to acknowledge that "Dreams, prophets, teraphim and lots are common to Israel and the nations; the ephod and Urim are peculiarly Israelite".[2] We shall not deal

---

[1] This has been vividly acknowledged from a philosophical point of view by P. Ricoeur, *Temps et récit*, Vol.1 (Paris, 1983); and by H.N. Schneidau, *Sacred Discontent: The Bible & Western Tradition* (Berkeley, Los Angeles and London, 1976), from the point of view of Biblical studies and Western culture. It is worth considering that the very effort simply to *read* an ancient text written in one of the so-called "dead languages" is itself an undertaking that cannot be accomplished without constant recourse to the tools and methodologies of the historical philologist and linguist.

[2] *The Religion of Israel. From its Beginnings to the Babylonian Exile*; trans. (abridged) M. Greenberg (Chicago and London, 1963 [1937-56]), p. 89.

here with the question of Old Testament prophecy as a means of social-ly-sanctioned divination; the reader is instead referred to the study by E. Noort on prophecy in Israel's environment, and R.R. Wilson and D.L. Petersen, for Israel.[1] But any review of Israelite divination must take the Old Testament references to the teraphim, lots, and dreams into account. We shall begin with dreams because, as I have shown previous-ly, there was a fairly extensive Mesopotamian tradition of dream divin-ation which seems to have reached as far as Egypt at a reasonably early date. It is therefore likely that the Israelites participated in the reception of this tradition. But first it will be essential to examine how dreams are employed in the Old Testament literature.

In Gen 15, the promise of progeny comes to Abram in a "vision" (מחזה, v 1). The term used occurs only four times in the entire Hebrew Bible; here it most likely signifies a dream-incident. Note that the event takes place at night (or Abram would not be able to see the stars, v 5). "Night vision" or "dream by night" are otherwise terms used to describe nocturnal dream revelations (cf. חלום הלילה, Gen 20.3; 31.24; חזיון לילה, Job 4.13; 28.8; 33.15; note especially the related מראת הלילה, Gen 46.2); Micah 3.6 may well be the only pre-exilic passage which presupposes the term (cp. לילה לכם מחזון)—assuming, and it is an "if", that the passage actually is from Micah's hand. Moreover, the covenant ceremony which Abram witnesses takes place after he has fallen into a תרדמה or "deep sleep" (v 12). The "night vision"was a staple of Akkadian dream revelations, as was noted already by E.L. Ehrlich[2] and by A.L. Oppenheim.[3]

In Gen 28, Jacob spends the night at Luz/Bethel and dreams of the famous ladder between earth and heaven; this provides the etiology for the renaming of the site, and hence for its future relationship to Israel. Later, during his stay in Aram Naharaim, Jacob again dreams (Gen 31.10-13), and is ordered to return to the land of his birth. We should note that in the rest of Genesis outside of Gen 28.12, the verb

---

[1] E. Noort, *Untersuchungen zum Gottesbescheid in Mari. Die 'Mariprophetie'in der alttestamentlichen Forschung*, (Neukirchen-Vluyn, 1977); R.R. Wilson, *Prophecy and Society in Ancient Israel*, (Philadelphia, 1980); D.L. Petersen, *The Roles of Israel's Prophets*.

[2] E.L. Ehrlich, *Der Traum im Alten Testament*, (Berlin, 1935), p. 1, n. 5.

[3] A.L. Oppenheim, *Dreams*, p. 225: Akk. *tabrit muši*; Sum. *MAŠ.GE*.

חלם occurs only in the Joseph story. In fact, in the rest of the Old Testament it occurs three times in Deuteronomy (13.2,4,6), where its practitioner is condemned, twice in the prose sections of Jeremiah (23.25; 29.8: also condemnatory), twice in an apocalyptic context in Isaiah (29.8), and once in Isaiah 38.16 (unclear).

Dreams from Yahweh intervene on behalf on Abraham and his wife Sarah (Gen 20.3-7), and a dream prevents Laban from revenging himself on his renegade son-in-law, Jacob (Gen 31.24). Moreover, the entire Joseph story is prefigured in Gen 37 by two dreams which portend Joseph's future greatness (Gen 37.5-7,9-10), just as the two dreams of Pharaoh's baker and butler lead to his release from prison (Gen 40.8-19), and Pharaoh's own two dreams (Gen 41.1-4,5-7) give Joseph the opportunity to rise to great heights. Joseph himself notes that "the doubling of Pharaoh's dream means that the thing is fixed by God" (Gen 41.32), an interpretive principle which applies to the previous dreams in Joseph's career as well. Finally, near the close of the story, Jacob is assured by Yahweh in "visions of the night" (מראת הלילה, Gen 46.2) that his projected sojourn in Egypt is only a continuation of an earlier covenant (v 3).

In short, in the Old Testament narrative materials, dreams serve either to legitimate important cultic (e.g., the sanctuary at Bethel) or theological (the covenant with Abraham) themes, or else they are simply narrative instruments which illustrate Yahweh's protection (e.g., from Abimelech of Gerar, Gen 20; Laban, Gen 31) of and care for his chosen people (Jacob and Joseph). All of these passages presuppose that dreams provide accurate and reliable information. Conversely, 1 Samuel 28.6,15 illustrate what happens to the king who has fallen from Yahweh's favour (cf. 1 Sam 15.24-29): he is denied access to the divine, including through the agency of dreams. Since it is a standard *topos* of ancient Near Eastern dream reports that kings receive clear and unambiguous "message" dreams, while the hoi polloi receive dreams which require to be interpreted (i.e. "symbolic" dreams),[1] the denial of dream revelation to Saul powerfully underlines the fact of his abandonment by Yahweh, and hence prepares for his ironic last confrontation with the ghost of Samuel. By way of contrast, in the previously-mentioned passage in

---

[1] Cf. Oppenheim, *Dreams*, pp. 185-92; Stemberger, "Der Traum in der rabbinischen Literatur", p. 2.

Isaiah (Isa 29.8) the prophet compares the attacks of Israel's foes with the dreams of a hungry man who dreams that he is eating, but awakens empty. Dreams need not, then, necessarily convey a divine message; a variation on this point is brought out in Numbers 12, where Yahweh's direct revelation to Moses is contrasted with that vouchsafed to a prophet, who receives a mere dream or a vision (v 6). The word "vision", incidentally, Hebrew מראה, occurs only eleven times in the Old Testament: four times in Ezekiel, four in Daniel, 1 Sam 3.15, Gen 46.2, and here. The distribution reveals it to be quite late.

The famous *crux* in Deuteronomy 13 (v 2-6) mentions the prophet and "dreamer of dreams" as if they were synonyms, and warns against accepting their "signs", even if they should come true, if they happen to counsel apostasy. This is one of the major "proof texts" in the traditional discussion of the problem of "true and false prophecy".[1] It is also, incidentally, yet another case in which the question of empiricism, that is, whether the predictions of the "dreamer" should happen to come true, is shown to be absolutely irrelevant for the purposes of those who are concerned with God's revelation. As I pointed out in my survey of Mesopotamian divination, empiricism is not a concern of the diviner: he has weightier interests than mere "correspondence with the facts". The parallel passage is Jeremiah 23.27, where we are told that some prophets are attempting to make the people forget the name of Yahweh "by their dreams". Their activity is contrasted, in terms we have never succeeded in interpreting adequately, with the prophet who has Yahweh's "word" (v 28).

Qoheleth (5.2,6) re-echoes Isaiah's low evaluation of dreams, which may, in fact, underly the remarks in the Deuteronomistic and Priestly contexts. The prophet Joel, however, enthuses that, after the Day of Yahweh, "your sons and daughters will prophesy, your old ones will dream dreams, and your young men will see visions" (3.1). The apocalypticists, as it seems, preserved a generally higher estimate of mantic behaviour than did other streams of Israelite tradition (cf. Isa 29.7-8).

Generally speaking, then, it appears that Israel acknowledged the validity of dreams as a means of communication with the divine, even if people were also aware that some dreams were without mantic

---

[1] See e.g. R.R. Wilson, *Sociological Approaches to the Old Testament* (Philadelphia, 1984), pp. 67-80.

significance.

Mesopotamian Dreaming in Israel

A proper understanding of the Mesopotamian dream tradition must begin with the realisation that dreams were regarded as divine communication borne to the dreamer by a spirit messenger from the divine world. He was known by a wide variety of titles, ranging from Sumerian ᵈMa.mu, ᵈSIG.SIG, ᵈAN.SAG.GAR, to Akkadian Zaqiqu, and like most gods of the Mesopotamian pantheon even had a female manifestation, DUMU.SAL.ᵈUtu.ke4 = daughter of Shamash.[1] Zaqiqu means, in non-hypostatised contexts, simply "soft, blowing wind, zephyr",[2] and in Assyrian royal inscriptions, "storm wind".[3] The verb zâqu is frequently used to designate the swift attack of sickness demons, who can seep through the smallest aperture in a house to attack a man who is undefended by his personal god[4]. The parallelism of blowing wind with demonic attack explains to some extent the dual nature of the dream god as a demonic threat as well as a bearer of communication. Zaqiqu is also used in some contexts signifying "to become, turn into wind", that is, "nothingness".[5] This is immediately reminiscent of the scornful dismissal of certain senseless dreams by Isaiah and Qoheleth. There is also considerable parallelism between the semantic ranges of Akkadian *zaqîqu* and Hebrew *rûah*; the Hebrew has, however, the additional sense of "soul/life" not encompassed by Akk. *zaqîqu*.

In Akkadian, the verbs *patāru* and *pašāru* are used in the sense of to tell a dream and to interpret it, respectively.[6] Hebrew usage, by way of contrast, employs *šāpar* of the notion of telling a dream, and *pātar*, with its parallel, *pāšar*, of its interpretation (cf. Gen 37.9,10; 40.8,9; 41.8,12; Judg 7.13, etc.). The noun formed from *pātar* is *pitrôn*. Use of the twin verbs *pātar* and *pāšar* is detectable in Israelite literature

---

[1] Oppenheim, *Dreams*, p. 232.

[2] Oppenheim, *Dreams,* p. 232.

[3] Oppenheim, *Dreams*, p. 233.

[4] Oppenheim, *Dreams*, p. 234.

[5] Oppenheim, *Dreams*, p. 234.

[6] Oppenheim, *Dreams*, pp. 218-19.

mainly in relatively late literature.[1]

There are a number of phenomenological parallels between the Hebrew and Akkadian dream literatures which it would be most appropriate simply to state: 1) Both literatures knew, as we have seen, an immediately intelligible "message" dream, which is bequeathed by a deity to royalty in order to legitimate some important activity. Thus, in Mesopotamia, the dream of Gudea of Lagaš legitimates temple construction, while in Gen 28 Jacob's dream legitimates the cult site at Bethel. Similarly, the dream of Gilgamesh at the Cedar Mountain warns Gilgamesh not to anger the gods by doing battle with Humbaba; in Gen 20.3, Abimelech of Gerar is warned not to antagonise Yahweh by impiety. Further, a dream sent by Ishtar of Arbela informs Aššurbanipal's army that it is safe to cross the river Idid'e.[2] In Gen 46.3ff., Jacob's journey to Egypt is approved by Yahweh. 2) Both traditions also know the "symbolic" dream, which requires interpretation before it can be understood. In a dream dialogue between Nabonidus and Nebuchadnezzar, the former mentions that "In my dream I saw with joy the Great Star, the Moon, and the planet Marduk high up in the sky and it (the Great Star) called me by name".[3] Oppenheim points out that the purpose of this dream report is to legitimate the accession of Nabonidus to the throne of Nebuchadnezzar.[4] Nabonidus'chief astrologer, Šamaš Šumukin, records that "in a dream I saw the Great Star, Venus, Sirius, the moon and the sun. . . I shall (now) investigate (it) with regard to a favourable interpretation for my Lord Nabonidus. . . and for Belshazzar, the crown prince".[5] These two passages show that in Mesopotamian dream divination the configuration of sun, moon and stars seen in a dream was a portent bearing on the royal succession. This casts some light on Joseph's previously-mentioned dream in Gen 37.9: "See, I have dreamed another dream, and see, the sun, the moon and eleven stars

---

[1] E.g., Dan 2.9,45; 4.15; 5.16; 7.16; Sir 38.14; Qoh 8.1.

[2] Trans. by Oppenheim in *Dreams*, p. 249.

[3] Cited by Oppenheim in *Dreams*, p. 250, nr. 13.

[4] Oppenheim, *Dreams*, p. 204.

[5] Oppenheim, *Dreams*, p. 205; for a rigorous form critical analysis of the dreams of the Joseph narrative, the Jacob cycle, and in Judges, see W. Richter, "Traum und Traumdeutung im AT. Ihre Form und Verwendung", *BZ* 7 (1963), pp. 202-20.

were bowing down to me". Commentators have frequently understood this dream just as Jacob does in the text, as presupposing that he stands for the sun, Rachel for the moon, and so on. Rachel, however, was long dead by this time, so many have assumed that the passage owes its present inconsistency to a somewhat mindless process of redaction. But if sun-moon-stars dreams simply mean "inheritance", then there is no inconsistency: Jacob is simply being represented as having misunderstood the significance of the dream. Of course, this also implies that the narrator knew the Mesopotamian tradition of astronomical dreams rather well.

Similar observations can be made of the dreams of Pharaoh's butler and baker. The butler's dream in Gen 40.9-11 contains a number of stylised elements, such as the three shoots of the grapevine (v 10), his holding the cup in his hand, squeezing the grapes, and giving the cup to Pharaoh, and so forth. Commentators have generally understood the incident, and Joseph's interpretation, in the light of the seeming bias against divination in the Old Testament. Thus, for example, von Rad:

> There were men who had learned the technique of dream interpretation, and, indeed, there was quite a literature on the subject. . . Joseph's reply, that 'Dream interpretations come from God' is directed polemically against this. . . The interpretation of Dreams is not a human art, but a gift of grace (Ger. *Charisma*) which it is in God's power to bestow.[1]

In actual fact, however, as I mentioned previously in my review of the dream tradition in Mesopotamia, Mesopotamian dream lore concentrates exclusively on certain very specific characteristic activities which may occur in a dream, while other features, such as whether a dream was pleasant or no, were held to be meaningless.[2] The omen series represented by the Assyrian Dream Book published by A.L. Oppenheim is an incomplete collection of just such features, with their accompanying prognostics. It is therefore important to recognise that the

---

[1] G. von Rad, *Das erste Buch Mose. Genesis*, (Göttingen, 1976 [1972]), pp. 303-4.

[2] This means that the psychological aspects of dreaming were of little account in the ancient Near East; a point which makes the psychological approach of A. Rösch, *Der Traum im Heilsplan Gottes. Deutung und Bedeutung des Traums im Alten Testament* (Freiburg et al., 1964) both irrelevant and anachronistic.

stylisation of the dream in question (Gen 40.9-11) contains numerous features that were held to be significant in Mesopotamia.

For example, one of the primary tasks of the diviner, as we have seen, was to establish the *adannu*, or time period during which a portent was held to be applicable.[1] Specific *adannu's* were frequently arrived at by the feature of the division of an object, as in Gen 40.10; cf. the following extispicy: "if the head of the plain, left, of the 'finger' is cracked once, the sixth day is its adannu".[2] Thus when Joseph predicts the time in question on the basis of the division of the grapevine, he is simply following routine Mesopotamian practice.

Furthermore, in Gen 40.11 the Butler notes that "Pharaoh's cup was in my hand, and I took the grapes and pressed them. . . and placed the cup in Pharaoh's hand". In the Dream-Book, there are a number of dreams dealing with cups, such as: "If one gives him a full goblet, he will have a name and offspring".[3]

The baker's dream (Gen 40.16-17) offers a fully analogous procedure for working out the *adannu* in question. In v 16 the baker reports that in his dream he had three cake-baskets on his head; this is to be compared with the fact that the Dream-Book happens to contain a fragmentary list of portents accompanying things that one has on one's head, such as: "If he carries dates on his head: sorrow".[4]

The theme of Joseph outperforming Pharaoh's court diviners has so impressed the commentators that none (to my knowledge) has recognised the real point of the story: Pharaoh, the godking of Egypt, has received a *symbolic* dream, which is otherwise only the lot of commoners (compare the "message" dream of Thutmoses IV). Pharaoh's "symbolic" dreams (Gen 41.1-7) offer again the simple device of a

---

[1] On the *adannu* established by extispicy, see Gadd in *DM*, pp. 31-4; in šumma ālu: Or 39-42 (1929) 26-7, line 20; pp. 34-5; line 19; pp. 102-3, lines 24,27; etc.; in the Dream-Book: Oppenheim, *Dreams*, p. 267, lines x+5, x+6; p. 268, line x+2; p. 277, line x+15 (all *adannus* of one year). See further the CAD, sub *adannu*; J.J.M. Roberts, "Of Signs, Prophets, and Time Limits: A Note on Psalm 74:9", *CBQ* 39 (1977) pp. 474-81.

[2] Cited by Gadd in *DM*, p. 32.

[3] 85-5-22, 538, rev. I: x + 8. Trans. in Oppenheim, *Dreams*, p. 279.

[4] Oppenheim, *Dreams*, p. 288, line x+1; see p. 289, lines x+12, x+14, x+15, x+16.

replication or division of things as a key to deriving an *adannu*. But note that the first dream (v 1-4) includes among its circumstantial detail the fact that it takes place on the banks of the Nile. This is to be compared with the fact that the Dream-Book offers at least twenty-seven omens connected with events seen, performed, or experienced in a river or from its banks.[1]

No parallels are to be found in the Dream-Book to Pharaoh's second dream, but there is the interesting feature of Joseph's analysis, to which I have alluded before, that he stresses that the repetition of a dream means that its outcome is certain. In Mesopotamia, as noted by Oppenheim, Gilgamesh receives a three-fold dream experience of a troubling dream which comes true; similarly, in the "Poem of the Righteous Sufferer" (*Ludlul bel nemeqi*), the sufferer dreams three times of his restoration to health—and again is proved right.

Finally, it is the achievement of R. Gnuse to have demonstrated that the account of Samuel's dream in 1 Sam 3.1-18 is heavily dependent for its contents and structure on the ancient Near Eastern "message" dream identified by Oppenheim.[2] Whether this entitles us to term the passage in question a "dream theophany" is, however, debateable,[3] but the distinction is in any case inessential for our purposes, which are simply to show the extent of Israelite familiarity with the Mesopotamian tradition.

In short, there are a great many points of contact between the dreams of the Joseph story and the Mesopotamian tradition. This tradition, as I have said previously, seems to have become popularised

---

[1] See Oppenheim, *Dreams*, pp. 287-8.

[2] R.K. Gnuse, *The Dream Theophany of Samuel: It Structure in Relation to Ancient Near Eastern Dreams and Its Theological Significance* (Lanham [Maryland], 1984); cf. Gnuse's earlier article, "A reconsideration of the Form-Critical Structure in I Samuel 3; An Ancient Near Eastern Dream Theophany", *ZAW* 94 (1982), pp. 379-90, which is almost as informative as his book.

[3] See D. Pardee's critical remarks in his review in *JNES* 48 (1989), p. 145: "it appears likely that rather than imitating the pattern in order to imply a dream, the narrator made use of auditory dream motifs, but without the explicit references to sleeping, dreaming, and awakening in oder to heighten the similarity with the Moses stories. . . for Moses was reputed to have dealt with Yahweh face-to-face and in a waking state (Exod 33)".

in Mesopotamia, and was of little account in the "official" tradition. How the Israelites came into contact with it must remain mysterious. It is interesting, though, that while the Joseph novella superficially emphasises the superiority of the Yahweh-inspired Israelite to the court diviner, it does so in a manner explicitly derived from the tradition of that very diviner. And, in fact, if we examine the rabbinical attitude towards "technical" dream interpretation, we discover that it was by no means as dismissive as one might have been led to expect; one early rabbi was even a professional dream interpreter![1]

The Teraphim

The teraphim are unquestionably problematical. The lexica provide no useful etymology for the root *t-r-p*.[2] The word occurs only fifteen times in the Hebrew Bible;[3] the various references seem to fall into two categories: those which envision the teraphim as an *idol* (e.g., Gen 31.19,34,35; 1 Sam 19.13,16; Judg 17.5; 18.14,17,18,20), and those which mention it/them as an *instrument of divination* (Hos 3.4, Ezek 21.21, Zech 10.2). In the light of my previous remarks about the source-value of the Israelite chronographic literature, the references in the prophetic literature would seem to be the more reliable source. However, the two categories need not necessarily exclude one another.

---

[1] See, again, B. Stemberger, "Der Traum in der rabbinischen Literatur", p. 7.

[2] Jastrow, *A Dictionary of the Targumim*, Vol.2, sub תרפים , illustrates a number of Talmudic usages; Koehler-Baumgartner suggest "decay, perish", which is clearly derived from the theological usage of the term in the Old Testament and rabbinical literature, but gives no inkling of the meaning of the root. As we might expect, it is not found in Ugaritic (Aistleitner), Phoenician, Punic (Tomback), or NW Semitic generally (Jean-Hoftijzer, Donner-Röllig, Gibson). H.A. Hoffner has pointed to the inadequacy of traditional attempts to find a Semitic basis for the root t-r-p(f), and instead designates the Hittite root tarpi*, which recent Hittite lexical discoveries identify as an "evil demon", often paired with Hittite *anaris*, corresponding to Akk. *šedu* and *lamassu*, respectively (see "Hittite Tarpis and Hebrew Teraphim", *JNES* 27 [1968], pp. 61-68). Like most such outré suggestions, the Hittite etymology is interesting, except that it is nowhere implied in the Old Testament that the teraphim are evil; moreover, one wonders why the word would have crept into Hebrew alone and have left no trace on the neighbouring languages.

[3] Gen 31.19,34,35; Judg 17.5; 18.14,17,18,20; 1 Sam 15.23; 19.13,16; Ezek 21.26; Hos 3.4; Zech 10.2.

Symbols of the presence of the deity were usually employed in Mesopotamian magic and divination, above all in connexion with extispicy, so it is conceivable that the Old Testament conjunction of teraphim=idol and teraphim=oracle-instrument are merely two sides of the same coin.[1]

Lots: Or Were They? The Problem of the Urim and Thummim

With the question of lots we arrive at the ancient discussion of the significance of the Urim and Thummim. In a way, it is odd that these quantities have excited so much curiosity as they have done historically, when we consider that they are actually only attested in the Old Testament seven times. In part, however, this is because, amid the extensive description of the cult and its appurtenances in Exod 25.1-31.11 we are told that "in the breastpiece of judgment you shall put the Urim and the Thummim, and they shall be upon Aaron's heart, when he goes in before the Lord; thus Aaron shall bear the judgment of the people of Israel upon his heart continuously" (Exod 28.30). Likewise, in Num 27.19-21 Moses is told that Joshua is to be made "to stand before Eleazar the priest. . . who shall inquire for him 'through the judgement of the Urim' (במשפט האורים) before the Lord". Thus, in an age when Old Testament scholars were inclined to lend considerable credence to the narratives of Israel's desert wanderings, the Urim and Thummim were seen as the primeval Yahwistic means of priestly divination. Unsurprisingly, a considerable number of studies have attempted to determine a bit more about their use, appearance, and so forth.[2] The most recent thorough discussion, namely that of E. Noort,

---

[1] Cf. e.g. A. Goetze, "An Old Babylonian Prayer of the Divination Priest", *JCS* 22 (1968) pp. 25-29, where we learn (obv. lines 29-30, 39, and 49) that the gods who are envisioned as "seated on golden thrones" in the heavens are expected "to descend" to render judgement on the oracle consultation, in the course of which they will be "seated on the chair". Thus some sort of (empty?) throne was made available to the gods. Note that in Gen 31 Rachel sits on the teraphim (v 34): the "sitters", sat upon, perhaps?

[2] Cf. e.g., G. Klaiber, "Der Priesterliche Orakel der Israeliten"; A. Jirku, *Mantik in Altisrael.* Inaugural- Dissertation (Rostock, 1913), pp. 29-40; I. Friedrich, *Ephod und Chosen im Lichte des Alten Orients* (Wien, 1968); J. Maier, "Urim und Tummim", *Kairos* 11 (1969), pp. 22-38; E. Noort, *Gottesbescheid in Mari*, pp.

assumes the oldest and most reliable attestion of the Urim and Thummim to be Deut 33.9 (Heb. v 8). Here, one notes, the Thummim are mentioned first, and then the Urim; Noort accordingly maintains that,"The sequence in the quotation about Levi which puts the oracular enquiry in the first rank and sacrificial service in the second may in fact reflect an historical development".[1] Precisely the assumption of some sort of historical development has, however, been assumed by all of the scholars who have been concerned with the Urim and Thummim.[2] The difficulty, as I have previously maintained, is that we cannot date our sources, and hence have no idea as to the relation-ship of the various attestations to one another.

The remaining four attestations are: Lev 8.8, Ezra 2.63, Neh 7.65 and 1 Sam 28.6. There is no sign whatever that an Israelite prophet had so much as heard of the Urim and Thummim. Even more interesting is the fact that, although Old Testament commentators generally pair the Urim and Thummim together, the Israelites did not. In actual fact, only the Urim is mentioned in 1 Sam 28.6 and Num 27.21; Urim and Thummim occur toge ther in the Ezra and Nehemiah passages (where, in Neh 7.65 we note the presence of an almost unintelligible mater lectionis (*Wāw*) in the spelling of Thummim (the *mater lectionis* in what must be a closed, unstressed syllable is odd indeed for "Biblical Hebrew", but unremarkable for Middle Hebrew;[3] Deut 33.8, as we have seen, gets the order backwards. Further, if one accepts the view of many commentators that the הבה תמים in 1 Sam 14.41 is to be understood as "(give) tûmmîm",[4] we get an eighth attestation which, however, mentions the Thummim alone, unless one follows Wellhausen's course

94-101, and see in particular his extensive note on p. 94.

[1] Noort, *Gottesbescheid in Mari*, p. 96.

[2] Particularly spectacular in this respect is I. Friedrich who, in his previously-mentioned work, not only manages to follow the development of the ephod and chosen all the way "back" to Egypt, but details their inter-relationships with the Urim and Thummim!

[3] Cf. M.H. Segal, *A Grammar of Mishnaic Hebrew* (Oxford, 1958 [1927]), p. 25.

[4] As already J. Wellhausen was the first to do; see *Der Text der Bücher Samuelis* (Göttingen, 1871), pp. 93-94.

and adopts the radically divergent text of the LXX.[1]

So much variation within a mere seven or eight attestations necessarily raises the question whether the Urim and Thummim could possibly have been the ancient oracle instruments they have been claimed to be. Had they been ancient, the pair would surely have formed an invariable parallel expression like English "back and forth", German "hin und zu", Scandinavian "frem og tilbage"/"fram och tilbaka" (cf. Heb. "heaven and earth", "from least to greatest", "good and evil", etc.), and so on. Moreover, the lack of witness in the prophetic literature is no less compromising for the idea of the antiquity of the Urim and Thummim.

A third point has yet to be made concerning the nature of the Urim and Thummim, which is a) that, according to the Old Testament witness itself, no one in the post-exilic period knew how to administer the Urim and Thummim (cf. Ezra 2.63 and Neh 7.65). This is made even more clear when we examine the various translations offered by the LXX of the Urim and Thummim, for if we do so, we speedily note that Urim and Thummim are sometimes translated as "lights and perfections", sometimes as "clarity" (Urim); indeed, on one occasion the Urim are taken to be a weird Hiphil of the root *'wr* (Neh 7.65 = Esdras II 17.65 : "a priest to shed light" [on the matter]). When one notes that such details as which ear and which thumb of the high priest were to be dipped in the blood of the sacrificial ram of ordination (Exod 29.19-20) managed to be perfectly preserved in the tradition, one wonders just how a small detail like Israel's pre-eminent oracle managed to be forgotten. There is, then, no evidence that the Urim and Thummim were part of an ancient Israelite mantic institution.

This insight does not, however, mean that the references to the Urim and Thummim are without value for the study of Israelite divination. It only means that there is no point in trying to reconstruct a

---

[1] Against the reading *haba tamim*, "give a perfect" (elliptical: "answer"; suggested by J. Lindblom) is Albrektson's observation that, "in spite of the fact that the word (i.e., tamim) occurs about 80 times in the Hebrew Bible" such a usage is not attested (B. Albrektson, "Some Observations on Two Oracular Passages in 1 Sam.", *ASTI* 11 [1977/1978], pp. 1-10). On the other hand, Yahweh is not otherwise asked to choose between a reigning king and his heir-presumptive, either, so the request for a "perfect" verdict may have special point here.

"history" of them which many strata in the Old Testament do not even know, or cannot be shown to have known. The first observation that presents itself here is that the "judgement of the Urim" is subordinated to the usual juridical metaphor which otherwise governed ancient Near Eastern divination. The second is that at least the concept of the Urim and Thummim, however and by whom they may have been conceived, presupposes that they delivered simple binary answers. This, as we have seen, characterises every ancient Near Eastern form of divination, ranging from the Mesopotamian omen sacrifice to the ancient Egyptian "bark of the god" oracle. They may or may not have been conceived as lots of some sort,[1] but this fact is actually inessential to understanding their rôle in the texts.

The Gôrāl-lot

A glance at the concordance reveals that the *goral*-lot is attested 78 times in the Old Testament; it is accordingly the best-witnessed of all ancient Israelite oracular tools. However, as far as I can see, it is also the *latest* of all the means attested, as we note from the simple fact that it is totally absent from Samuel and Kings, and is only present in Joshua and Judges in passages which already M. Noth had dismissed from the Deuteronomistic corpus as being secondary accretions.[2] There are, however, all of five references to the *goral*-lot in the works which bear the names of some of the pre-exilic prophets: Isa 17.14; 34.17; and 57.6; Jer 13.25; and Micah 2.5. Of these, Isa 17.14, 57.6 and Jer 13.25 merely have the meaning "portion, lot in life". The other two seem to refer to an actual act of deciding something by lot-casting; indeed, Micah 2.5 says to the wicked, "you will have none to cast the line by lot in the assembly of the Lord". In addition to this is one reference to an

---

[1] See E. Noort's reckoning on the possibilities connected with this eventuality, *Gottesbescheid in Mari*, pp. 93-94.

[2] I.e., Jos 14-19; Judg 1.3 and 20.9; cf. Noth, *Überlieferungsgeschichtliche Studien*, p. 8: "Now as is generally acknowledged, Judg 1 shows no signs of Deuteronomistic reworking". See also pp. 182-89 on Jos 13-19. H.H. Schmid, art. "goral" in (eds.) E. Jenni and C. Westermann, *Theologisches Handwörterbuch zum Alten Testament* (Munich, 1971), Col. 414, tries to explain the absence of the *goral* from Deuteronomy by the notion that the Deuteronomist was not interested in the apportionment of the land, but only in the land as a whole.

undoubtedly cultic lot-casting procedure in Ezek 24.1-6; here the besieged Jerusalem is described as a sacrifice stewing in the pot. The king of Babylon is then encouraged to "Take out of it piece after piece, no lot (*gôrāl*) has fallen upon it (v 6)". This implies, one supposes, that the sacrificial meal was ordinarily apportioned by lot-casting, much as the rota of temple service was established in the post-exilic community by a similar lot (cf. 1 Chron 24.7; 25.9; 26.14, etc.). These uses agree well with the context of Jona 1.7, where the unfortunate prophet is singled out by the *gôrāl* as the cause of the sailors' peril. Clearly, there is no question of a "secular" procedure of lot-casting here; the references to sacrifice and temple service show that casting the *gôrāl* took place under divine auspices. It is tempting to see in the *gôrāl* the model for the oracle that was used to decide such matters as Achan's guilt (Jos 7) and Saul's election (1 Sam 10.17-22), but the means employed in the latter cases are not stated; moreover, the verb employed in both cases is the Niphal of *lkd*, which never occurs in conjunction with any of the 78 attestations of the *gôrāl*.

In passing, one notes again that there is no useful extra-Israelite etymology for the *goral*-lot from the early pre-exilic period: it seems that almost all of Israel's magical terminology, licit and "illicit", was home-grown.[1]

The Ephod and the Ark

In reality, the ephod does not deserve a chapter to itself, although some have devoted sizable studies to the phenomenon.[2] Unlike the Urim and Thummim, the ephod is relatively well attested in the Old Testament; all of 49 occurrences are recorded. The distribution, however, is

---

[1] Of course, as already Gesenius noted, the Arabic *grl/grwl*, "pebble" (= lot) offers not a bad parallel at all, which forces us once again to consider the possibility that the "neighbours" from whom Israel had learnt so much divination were in fact the Arab peoples who settled along the fringes of Palestinian society in the course of the first millennium. But naturally, they would first have been demographically significant from about the end of the 7th century at the earliest (cf. E.A. Knauf: *Ismael*, passim, and *Midian*, passim).

[2] See I. Friedrich, *Ephod und Chosen*.

interesting, as we note that 29 of these fall in the Book of Exodus (chs. 25; 28; 29; 35; and 39); 2 in Lev (8.7 (2X)); 7 in Judges (8.27; 17.5; 18.14,17,18,20, and 27; and 10 in Sam (1 Sam 2.18(2X),28; 14.3; 21.10; 22.18; 23.6,9; 30.7; 2 Sam 6.14. There is a single reference to the ephod in Hos 3.4, where, interestingly, it is mentioned together with the teraphim. Again the distribution is calamitous for the notion of an ancient cultic implement, particularly if my surmise is correct that the Books of Samuel mainly preserve post-Deuteronomistic literary materials.[1] Why, one wonders, are there so few references to these priestly oracular instruments in the prophetic books? This lack is especially pointed when we recall, as mentioned previously, that the Old Testament itself claims that both Jeremiah and Ezekiel were of priestly lineage.

But never mind; what is important is that the various references to the priestly ephod fall into several categories, as was noticed by

---

[1] For example, on the assumption that the Deuteronomistic speeches tell us something about what was in the original Deuteronomistic collection, note that 2 Sam 7.6 knows nothing about the "house of God" in Shiloh, 1 Sam 1.7,24; 3:15. Note further that 1 Chron 17.5 contains the same remark. As with textual criticism, so with literary criticism: it is legitimate to postulate one thoughtless scribe who did not consider the narrative context of the passage he was working on, but not, I think, two of them. The implication is that Samuel's birth-and-youth legend was not added to the Books of Samuel until after the composition of 1 Chronicles 17.1ff. This conclusion recommends itself anyway, as the birth legend is one of the two parentheses which enclose the Samuel materials (the other is 1 Sam 28, the lateness of which has been argued by numerous scholars; see J. Tropper, *Nekromantie*, pp. 208-23.)

The Deuteronomistic origin of 2 Sam 7 was not originally acknowledged by scholars, but see already D.J. McCarthy, "2 Sam 7 and the Structure of the Deuteronomic History", *JBL* 84 (1965), pp. 131-38, plus the remarks of F.M. Cross, *Canaanite Myth and Hebrew Epic. Essays in the History of the Religion of Israel* (Cambridge [MA] and London, 1973), pp. 241-61. S. Herrmann has argued for the substantial unity of 2 Sam 7 on the form critical grounds of its resemblance to the Egyptian "Königsnovelle" ("Die Königsnovelle in Ägypten und in Israel. Ein Beitrag zur Gattungsgeschichte in den Geschichtsbüchern des Alten Testaments", *Wissenschaftliche Zeitschrift Universität Leipzig*, 3 (1953/1954), *Gesellschafts- und sprachwissenschaftliche Reihe* 1,51-62, im Selbstvertrag der Universität = the same, *Gesammelte Studien zur Geschichte und Theologie des Alten Testaments* (Munich, 1986), pp. 120-44, esp. pp. 135-44). I do not think this judgement can hold against the intensive literary critical scrutiny which the chapter has experienced in recent years (see, for example, the many analyses of 2 Sam 7 in the several admirably thorough studies of T. Veijola and others).

scholars at an early date: 1) those which suggest that the ephod was a priestly or high-priestly garment (e.g., Exod 28.5-10; 1 Sam 2.18,28; 14.3); 2) those which insist that it had to do with oracular consultation (e.g., 1 Sam 23.6-9; 30.7; 3) the single passage which informs us that David, of all Israelite kings, wore an ephod on a single occasion (2 Sam 6.14), and 4) those which imply that the ephod was a cult object of some sort, perhaps an image (e.g., 1 Sam 21.9 (Heb 10); Judg 8.27; 17.5, etc.).[1] A brave attempt has been made to unify all these references by H. Thiersch,[2] who holds that the ephod was a sort of *ependytes*, that is, a sacred vestment which, in ancient Greece, clothed both statues of various (particularly) oracle-giving deities and the priests who served them. Thiersch's view has received some support from Johs. Lindblom,[3] who holds that the term signified the garment in question, but then was expanded by a (for students of Oriental languages) familiar process of *pars pro toto* to designate the deity in question.[4]

Not all scholars have been persuaded by the Thiersch-Lindblom approach; Barucq, for example, points out that the translators of the LXX, who knew pretty fair Greek, actually reserved the word *ependytes* for the translation of the priestly *me'il* (tunic).[5] To maintain Thiersch-Lindblom's argument then, one would also have to postulate that the precise character of the ephod, too, like that of the Urim and Thummim, had been forgotten in the century or two that separated the LXX translation from the composition or compilation of the Priestly Document.

It may sound surprising, as I am generally inclined to discount the historical nature of many of the texts in question, but I am willing to

---

[1] See already A. Jirku, "Mantik", pp. 7-12; K. Budde, "Ephod und Lade", *ZAW* 39 (1921), pp. 1-42; Barucq, *DB Sup*, Cols. 779-781; I. Friedrich, *Ephod und Chosen*, passim (who, as I mentioned above, attempts to solve the difficulties by tradition historical means—and, one might add, by some extremely speculative Egyptian etymologies). The brief review by Noort, *Gottesbescheid in Mari*, pp. 101-4, is sensibly and soberly presented.

[2] H. Thiersch, *Ependytes und Ephod. Gottesbild und Priesterkleid im alten Vorderasien* (Stuttgart, 1936).

[3] "Lot-casting in the Old Testament", *VT* 12 (1962), pp. 164-78.

[4] Lindblom, "Lot-Casting", p. 171.

[5] Barucq, *DB Sup*, Col. 780.

attempt to buttress the argument of Thiersch and Lindblom from another angle. It seems to me that the discussion has got mired down because of the association of the ephod with the Greek *ependytes*. There is no need to go so far afield for adequate parallels. In 1949, A.L. Oppenheim published a fascinating study in which he described various types of ornate festal garments which were used in ancient Mesopotamia to clothe a) divine statues (which in Mesopotamia were life-sized) b) priests and c) kings.[1] These garments were very costly, as they were studded quite thickly with rosettes of pure gold. In one text cited by Oppenheim, Akkadian *nalbašu* translates both the Sumerian expressions for "garment of the gods" and "garment of the king".[2] Another Akkadian term is *têdiqu*, "a ceremonial piece of apparel belonging to the wardrobe of gods and kings".[3] An interesting parallel to the Akkadian *nalbašu*-garment of god and king is offered by 2 Kgs 10.22, where we are told that the devotees of Ba'al were clad in a special *lebuš/malbuš*; and by Isa 63.1, where we read that Yahweh is "he that is glorious in his apparel (bilbušo)", a term that recurs in v 2 (lilbušeka, "your apparel"). Naturally, this sort of reference is usually dismissed as mere metaphor by those who maintain that the Israelite religion was imageless from its inception. But, if Akkadian diviners could place an empty throne or chair to symbolise the presence of the gods at their consultations, could the Israelites not have done the same thing with an (empty) costume, to which corresponded the rich garments of the priesthood?

To the possible objection that some of the Israelite references to the ephod presuppose that a considerable amount of precious metal went into its construction,[4] it is possible to reply that the smallest amount mentioned by Oppenheim for one of the "golden garments of the gods" is 8 minas 52 shekels (= 532 shekels) of gold, while the largest amount

---

[1] A.L. Oppenheim, "The Golden Garments of the Gods", *JNES* 8 (1949), pp. 172-93.

[2] Oppenheim, "Golden Garments", p. 174 and n. 6.

[3] Oppenheim, "Golden Garments", p. 178.

[4] Cf. e.g. Judg 17.3-5 which seems to presuppose that 200 pieces of silver went into making an ephod and a teraphim; and Judg 8.26-27, where 1700 shekels of gold go into the making of a single ephod.

is four whole talents of gold for the garments of Marduk and Sarpan-itum.[1] It might be mentioned in passing that rosettes of the type in question, perforated to enable sewing onto garments, have been excavated at Megiddo.[2]

But what connects the ephod with the *nalbašu*-garment? It should be noted that the verb *sph*, which is a biradical parallel to *'pd*, means "to cover with metal", and in this connexion is so used in connexion with Israelite cultic implements (cf. Num 17.3-4; Exod 38.17,19). The verb *'pd* itself is rare, but is used to designate the donning of the chosen of the ephod (Exod 29.5; Lev 8.7). Both verbs figure together in Isa 30.22:, "you shall defile your silver-wrapped images (כספך צפוי פסילים) and your gold-covered idols (מסכת זהבך אפדת)".[3] I think this use of the verb *'pd* brings us very close to a gold-studded garment, intended for a divine statue, a priest, or a king. The latter, incidentally, might help to explain why David is depicted as wearing an ephod in 2 Sam 6.14.

Of course, none of this is to say that the Israelites in pre-exilic times actually used an ephod studded with rosettes of gold to symbolise the presence of the deity, and to clothe their priests and kings. But it does provide a possible frame of reference for understanding the conception. As I remarked in connexion with the teraphim, there is nothing remarkable in symbols of the deity being present during acts of oracular consultation or other magics; this was quite standard in Mesopotamia and, as we have seen, such symbolisation was entirely literal in Egypt, as it was the statue of the god itself to which the enquirers addressed their questions. As for the method of oracular consultation that the ancient writers considered appropriate to the ephod, I can only agree with E. Noort that,

> It is hardly coincidental that in connexion with the depiction of these consultations the techical description of the process retreats into the background. Neither priestly personnel nor the means of consultation are described. Everything is concentrated around YHWH's assurance

---

[1] Oppenheim, "Golden Garments", pp. 172-73.

[2] Oppenheim, "Golden Garments", p. 188.

[3] Trans. by the writer.

of victory. . . Thus the concrete consultation is scarcely tangible.[1]

The Ark

There is no room here for a discussion of the manifold theories about the origin of the Ark of God. Suffice it to say that its most important use in the various contexts of the Old Testament is as a symbol of the divine presence.[2] Since, as I have argued, such symbols were commonly used in the ancient Near East in conjunction with oracular consultations, it is no surprise that Samuel is sleeping in front of the Ark when he receives a dream visitation from Yahweh (1 Sam 3.3-4), nor that the Ark is stored in the "ancient" Tent of Meeting in the desert where Moses receives his revelations "face to face" (cf. Num 12.4-6, esp. v 4), nor that Saul calls for the Ark of God when he wishes to undertake a consultation as to whether to attack the Philistines (1 Sam 14.18-19).[3] As for the type of oracle that was considered appropriate to the presence of the Ark the texts are sublimely uninformative. However,

[1] Noort, *Gottesbescheid in Mari*, p. 104.

[2] The reader is referred to M. Haran, "The Nature of the 'Ohel Mo'edh in Pentateuchal Sources", *JSS* 5 (1960), pp. 50-65; J. Maier, *Das Altisraelitische Ladeheiligtum* (Berlin, 1965), and to T.N.D. Mettinger, (trans. F.H. Cryer) *The Dethronement of Sabaoth. Studies in the Shem and Kabod Theologies* (Lund, 1982), pp. 19-24. Naturally, I differ fundamentally from these scholars in that I decline to see "history" where we have in fact only relatively late, but still undatable, texts. Certain phrases, such as "jošeb hak-kerubbim" (like the analogous "Aaronite blessing formula" from Kuntillat 'Ajrud and Ketef Hinnom, cf. G. Barkay, *Ketef Hinnom. A Treasure Facing Jerusalem's Walls* [Jerusalem, 1986], pp. 29-30), may indeed go back to pre-exilic times (Meier, p. 53; Mettinger, p. 24 and n. 18), but whether they then had anything to do with the storied "Ark" remains to be demonstrated.

[3] The passage is clearly Deuteronomistic, in my sense of the word; or else it is dependent on the very beginnings of the Deuteronomistic collection. We have seen that 2 Sam 7.6, which plays a massive structuring rôle in the Deuteronomistic history, does not know of the "house of God" or "temple" at Shiloh. This text, too, assumes blithely that the Ark is with the Israelites, rather than at Shiloh, or secure in the house of Eleazar ben Abinadab at Kiriath-jearim (1 Sam 7.1-2). This fact points to an immediate linkage with 2 Sam 11.11.

when Saul tells his attending priest, Ahijah, to "withdraw your hand" (1 Sam 14.19), this in fact rules out the possibility of a lot-casting procedure.[1] The converse of this expression, "to stretch out the hand", was, as we have seen, the standard Sumerian expression for the omen sacrifice (*šu.gíd.gíd*), rendered by Akkadian *lipit qāti*, "the touch of the hand"; it has many well-attested parallels in the Old Testament (e.g., Exod 29.10,15,19; Lev 1.4; 3.2,8,13, etc.) in conjunction with sacrifice. Hence, it is conceivable that the reference here is to an omen sacrifice. We shall return to this possibility presently.

Other Forms of Israelite Divination

Signs

There was an area of overlap between the Mesopotamian and Israelite understanding of "signs". One of the more obvious evidences of this is the practice, repeatedly attested in Mesopotamia, of pairing one sort of divination with yet another; thus, confirmation by one means of consultation signified confirmation of the other "prediction" as well.[2] In Israelite literature, as is well known, we find a variant on this theme: a secondary prophecy accompanies the "primary" one, so that when the secondary prophecy is "fulfilled", one has reason for faith in the "primary" one.[3] As I mentioned previously, in Mesopotamia this behaviour was linked, at least in part, to attempts by the crown to limit frivolous "prophecies"; this may in fact have been the case in Israel as

---

[1] If the priest was groping manually after lots in a bag or jar, as is often assumed, it would have been very difficult for him to avoid pulling just one out, i.e., "yes" or "no". The notion that there were three lots, one reading "maybe, ask again", or the like still rhymes only poorly with the fact that Ahijah fails to get an answer in an entire day of trying (cf. 1 Sam 14.37). It makes better sense with my suggestion (below) that we have to do with an omen sacrifice, as the rite, as we have seen, was performed at most only twice a day.

[2] Cf. e.g., W.L. Moran, "New Evidence from Mari on the History of Prophecy", *Bib* 50 (1969), pp. 15-56, esp. pp. 18-19.

[3] Cf. above all 1 Sam 2.34; 10.2-7, 9-10; 2 Kgs 19.29; 2 Kgs 20.10 (where, by a bit of prophetic folklore, the "sign" in question is a miracle); Isa 7.11-17.

well; note that the offers of "signs" referred to in the previous note are all made to kings, prospective kings, or religious leaders of Israel. In addition to this type of "sign" is another, represented above all by Deut 28.45-46, where we are told that concerning the curses of the covenant enumerated at such great length in ch. 28, they (v 46), "will be on you for signs and wonders and on your seed for ever". This implies that the physical manifestations of the curses can be interpreted as "signs" of divine displeasure and can be understood as such in isolation from a prophetic "word". A list of such "signs of blessing" are also enumerated in Deut 28.1-14, most of which have to do with fertility and material well-being, though v 7 represents a "sign" of military success, and is answered by a corresponding curse in v 25. In Josh 7.6-7 we see at least one literary context where precisely this conclusion is drawn: defeat is a "sign" of the divine displeasure, which then has to be further explored by subsequent technical oracles (v 14-18) until the guilty party has been found. The resemblance to the similar Hittite procedure is unmistakable. Another example is offered by 2 Sam 6.6-7, where Uzzah puts out his hand to steady the Ark, only to be struck down by Yahweh for his impiety. That this was a sign of Yahweh's displeasure is explicitly acknowledged by David (v 9); more interestingly, the Ark could not be moved until Yahweh had blessed the house of Obed Edom, in whose house it was lodged. Clearly, "signs of blessing" (though the term is not used) were necessary to nullify the previous bad portent.

Excursus: The Israelite Verb "to Divine"

There is an obvious reluctance in the Old Testament to designate this class of portent as a "sign", probably because this variety was well known in the Mesopotamian cultural sphere. Divination by all manner of unexpected "signs" was probably designated by the verb נחשׁ, in spite of Y. Kaufmann's denials. Evidence of this is based on one common-sense observation and a number of textual references. We have seen that the terminology employed by the Deuteronomists to designate "forbidden" divination was entirely of Israelite origin and cannot be traced back to the practices of Israel's "neighbours" at the beginning of the first millennium; therefore the practices in question were instead

Israelite practices[1] which were forbidden at a very late point in Israel's social development. This fact should be obvious, as the only materials forbidding such practices are in Priestly and Deuteronomic-Deuteron-omistic contexts.[2] Accordingly, we should note that Joseph, the paragon of the late collection in Genesis, claims (falsely in this case) to have discovered the "theft" of his divining-cup by divination: "Do you not know that such a man as I can indeed divine?" (Gen 44.15); and, since his cup is in his brother's bags, he obviously does not mean them to think that lecanomancy was the means in question available to him in this instance. A similar case occurs in 1 Kgs 20.32-33 where messengers from the defeated Ben-Hadad to Ahab hear him say, "Does he still live? He is my brother." To this remark we are told: "Now the men were watching for an omen (האנשים ינחשו) and they hurried to take it up from him" (וימהרו ויחלטוה ממנו, v. 33, reading with the Qere). Since within the fiction of the narrative Ahab is depicted as accepting the validity of the messengers' omen we must assume that the text represents generally accepted ideas about the speech omen (*egirru*). In this connexion it is important to observe that the verb נחש clearly means "to divine", as it is used of Joseph's divining cup (Gen 44.5), of the nameless means implied by him (Gen 44.15), of Laban's unspecified revelation (Gen 30.27) and of the speech omen, here. Further, on the previously-mentioned assumption that the terms employed to describe various acts of divination in reality reflect purely Israelite praxis, there is the interesting remark in Numbers 24, where we are told that "When Balaam saw that it pleased the Lord to bless Israel, לא הלך כפעם לקראת נחשים "he did not go, as at other times, to encounter omens" (v 1; trans. by the writer). Obviously, this use of נחש by the narrator was assumed to be intelligible to his readers, which leads directly to the conclusion that the root and its derived nouns was a broad term, simply signifying "to divine" by unspecified means. But the variety of contexts in which the root appears shows that divination by the interpretation of random "signs" was an established and well-understood phenomenon in Israel. This gives especial poignancy to the Psalmist's much-discussed lament in Ps 74.9, in which he says, "we do not see our signs (אותתינו),

[1] Many of which no doubt *were* the common property of the ancient Near East.

[2] See already Witton-Davies, *Magic, Divination and Demonology*, pp. 37-38.

nor even a prophet (נביא), and no one is with us who knows how long"
(לא אתנו ידע עד מה).[1] Now establishing the "how long" (Akk. *adannu*)
of a portent was, as we have seen, one of the primary goals of the
Mesopotamian diviner, as it presumably also was of his Israelite
colleague.

Furthermore, there is the point that I mentioned earlier, namely,
that if the verb נחש is to be assigned to "the nations" (which, as we
have seen, is unlikely in terms of historical linguistics), then the
Israelites are left with only circumlocutions like "to seek the face of
Yahweh", "to enquire of Yahweh", and the like to designate a behaviour
they self-evidently engaged in. The broad range of נחש indicates that it
was probably the all-purpose verb in question, however unwilling the
late redaction of our sources may be to admit the fact.

The Priestly Oracle

We have seen above that, at least in earlier times, Old Testament
scholars have, generally been prepared to accept that the Israelite
priesthood knew some procedures for deriving oracles from Yahweh.
Fundamental to this understanding of the rôle of priestly divination was
W.W. Baudissin's distinction between the Israelite "tent of meeting" as
described in JE, which Baudissin saw as an "oracle-tent"/ "Orakelzelt",
in contradistinction to P's (consciously anti-"magical") "sacrificial tent"/
"Opferzelt".[2] The first extensive study of the alleged phenomenon of
priestly divination was by F. Küchler, in 1918. Küchler assumed that
there had once been many ways of consulting Yahweh in ancient Israel,
and held that the uniformity implied by the Urim and Thummim texts
in the Old Testament was the result of late redaction.[3] Following the
Deuteronomistic line, Küchler believed that such oracular implements
as the ephod had been adopted by the Israelites from the "Canaanites",

---

[1] For a different interpretation of this meaning of Heb. אות see O. Loretz, *Leberschau, Sündenbock, Asasel in Ugarit und Israel* (Altenberge, 1985), pp. 96-101, and see the discussion below.

[2] W.W. Baudissin, *Die Geschichte des alttestamentliche Priestertums* (Leipzig, 1889), p. 60; explicitly cited by F. Küchler, "Das priesterliche Orakel in Israel und Juda", *ZAW* Beiheft 33, 26 Sept. 1917, W. Frankenberg and F. Küchler (eds.) (Giessen, 1918), pp. 285-301.

[3] Küchler, "Das priesterliche Orakel", pp. 286-87.

whereas the Urim and Thummim were of Mosaic origin; he assumed, following the leading "Bibel und Babel" enthusiasts of his day, that there was some sort of connexion to the Mesopotamian oracular institutions.[1] Küchler perceptively allowed himself to wonder whether Ezek 21.21(26) really means that the Babylonians knew the Teraphim, or whether the prophet is not simply supplying the corresponding Israelite term.[2] Somewhat surprisingly, he rejected the notion that priestly divination included the interpretation of dreams, whereas he held it to be probable that the priesthood had interpreted random "signs"; on the other hand, Küchler found it to be entirely possible that the Israelites had known and used the omen sacrifice, although he admitted that the evidence, above all in P, was negligible.[3] Küchler further noted that most of the oracular enquiries in the Books of Samuel presuppose a simple yes- or-no, that is, binary, answer, whereas in cultic contexts, as in prophetic ones, it was phrased in poetic form.[4] Formal analysis of "oracular" passages in Numbers, Judges, Samuel, and elsewhere revealed to him that the primary verbs used to describe consultations were שאל and דרש, while the answers returned were generally expressed with either ענה or אמר.[5] But Küchler's major influence on the research tradition lay in his contention that the reason for the sudden change of mood from despondency to complete confidence which is manifested in several of the "individual psalms of lamentation" (e.g., 6.8-9; 20.6-7; 30.11-12) was an oracle which had been pronounced in the cult in favour of the supplicant.[6] Of especial interest for our purposes is the fact that Küchler maintained that the priestly oracle must have continued to play a rôle in the post-exilic period, as the mood-change in question is clearly present in numerous psalms whose post-exilic date he held to be unchallengable.[7]

Küchler's insights were further developed—though without

---

[1] Küchler, "Das priesterliche Orakel", p. 288.

[2] Küchler, "Das priesterliche Orakel", p. 290.

[3] Küchler, "Das priesterliche Orakel", pp. 293, 294-95, respectively.

[4] Küchler, "Das priesterliche Orakel", p. 297.

[5] Küchler, "Das priesterliche Orakel", p. 297.

[6] Küchler, "Das priesterliche Orakel", pp. 299-301.

[7] Küchler, "Das priesterliche Orakel", p. 300.

attribution to Küchler—by J. Begrich in an article which appeared in 1934.[1] Begrich's article attempts to demonstrate that the change of mood characteristic of the moodswings in the individual psalms of lamentation is also demonstrable in the poetic contexts of Deutero-Isaiah; he interpreted this phenomenon as "imitations of the priestly salvation oracle".[2] The rest of Begrich's article is a form-critical sketch of the extent to which various passages in Deutero-Isaiah really do reflect the language of the psalms in question. Of special interest is Begrich's conclusion, apropos of the priestly oracle, that the original priestly oracle must have been executed by the priest in connexion with the sacrifice (he does not say omen sacrifice in so many words).[3] This is an interesting conclusion. We have already seen that the traditional sharp distinction between priest and prophet which Old Testament scholars have attempted to maintain has no necessary sociological basis. By adhering to this distinction, Begrich could offer no better reason for Deutero-Isaiah's use of an "imitation" of the priestly oracle than to point to the rootedness of both the prophet and his audience in the Jerusalemite psalmic tradition.[4] A more obvious answer is that Deutero-Isaiah was so intimately familiar with the priestly oracle because he himself was accustomed to proclaiming it, that is, in priestly fashion. But this problem is, as we shall see, a recurrent one in Old Testament research. Since, as we have seen, most Old Testament scholars have not been persuaded that the priestly oracle really existed (or if they have been, they have found it of little significance), Begrich's article has nevertheless been influential in pointing to the extent to which the poetry of Deutero-Isaiah derives from the cult.

The last major study of the priestly oracle is L. Delekat's work,

---

[1] "Das priesterliche Heilsorakel", *ZAW* 52 (1934), pp. 81-92.

[2] Begrich, "Das priesterliche Heilsorakel", p. 82.

[3] Begrich, "Das priesterliche Heilsorakel", p. 91: "(what the supplicant needs to know is solely) whether Yahweh accepts or rejects the prayer. . . But if the announcement of the salvation oracle has to do with the sacrifice, then only the priest may be considered as the giver of the oracle".

[4] Begrich was in fact to go on to develop the idea of prophetic "imitations" ("Nachahmungen") of the priestly torah; cf. idem, "Die priesterliche Tora", *BZAW* 66 (1936) pp. 63-88 = *Gesammelte Studien zum Alten Testament* (Munich, 1964), pp. 232-60.

which appeared in 1967.[1] In many ways, Delekat's work is a throwback to the days when Old Testament scholars, under the influence of form criticism's incessant demand for a social *Sitz im Leben* for the genres it studies, suddenly discovered the cultic dimension of Israelite texts. Briefly, Delekat notes that a number of psalms, above all (once again) those of individual lamentation, especially those in which the sufferer speaks of his persecution by nameless "enemies", also contain references to the sufferer's request for "asylum".[2] Battening on Küchler's observations as a point of departure, the author maintains that the sufferer in such circumstances was actually seeking asylum in the sanctuary, and that his right to such asylum was granted by the deity if one of a number of priestly oracular procedures decided in his favour.[3] Oddly, he finds—on virtually no evidence—that the behaviour of the sacrificial fire provided one such omen (as we have seen, this sort of oracle disappeared from Mesopotamian tradition already in the Old Babylonian period); and that the other possibilities were the judgement of the Urim and Thummim (oddly and very loosely determined to have been sacred "arrows"), and, on the dim analogy of some bedouin practices, a priestly incubation oracle.[4] Not to leave anything out, Delekat also admitted the possibility of oracles being communicated via cultic prophecy.[5] The author's main evidence for the priestly oracle undertaken on behalf of an applicant for asylum is Ps 91.1-5,14-16.[6] Being built on so loose a foundation, Delekat's study could not convince the majority of scholars in its own time, and is today a monument to the wild and wooly days when the leap from text to cultic practice, and from cultic practice to social institution was, if not fully accepted procedure, then at least a viable one for scholars with imagination and social insight. What is surprising is that a scholar of Delekat's calibre did not invest more effort in the exploration of what was, even in 1967,

---

[1] *Asylie und Schutzorakel am Zionheiligtum. Eine Untersuchung zu den privaten Feindpsalmen* (Leiden, 1967).

[2] Delekat, *Asylie und Schutzorakel*, pp. 11-39.

[3] Delekat, *Asylie und Schutzorakel*, p. 17.

[4] Delekat, *Asylie und Schutzorakel*, pp. 57-73.

[5] Delekat, *Asylie und Schutzorakel*, p. 71.

[6] Delekat, *Asylie und Schutzorakel*, pp. 235-41.

already known of the procedures of Israelite (not to mention other ancient Near Eastern forms of) divination.

In this connexion, it is worth calling attention to a perceptive article by B.O. Long which appeared some years ago.[1] In his article, Long offers, to begin with, the simple observation that Israelite prophecy is merely one of many forms of divination which were practised in both Israel and the Israelite environment. He distinguishes, perhaps too sharply, between שׁאל (priestly)-divination, based on the analogy of Num 27.21 (as already Klaiber had done), and דרשׁ (prophetic)-divination, following such examples as Gen 25.22; Exod 18.15; 1 Sam 9.9, etc.[2] Since he adheres to the usual historicistic scheme of Israel's development, Long holds that the priestly oracle declined just as the popularity of prophetic divination waxed; thus, by the time of Jeremiah and Ezekiel, "Men apparently still went to the prophets for a 'word from Yahweh'. . . but the procedure was most akin to seeking political advice and religious comfort".[3] Long sees the further development of the prophets' oracle as a transformation into intercessory prayer; he notes that this variety of prophetic enquiry ceased with the exile. The author then offers a surprisingly informative (given its brevity) thumbnail-sketch of Mesopotamian divination,[4] the purpose of which is to point to some formal characteristics of the extispicy enquiry. This leads to a similar formal analysis of some passages in which priestly divination is practised in the Old Testament, but, since the passages he has chosen (1 Sam 14.36-37; 23.2-4; 2 Sam 2.1; 5.19,22) are the mere *en passant* references to the phenomenon which had been examined already—without notable success—by Klaiber, Küchler, and others, the scheme he arrives at consists of a mere two elements: 1) report of an enquiry, and 2) the oracle itself.[5] By way of contrast, Long finds the prophetic enquiry to have consisted of 1) the setting 2) the request for an oracle 3) the delivery of the oracle 4) a note

---

[1] B.O. Long, "The Effect of Divination Upon Israelite Literature", *JBL* 92 (1973), pp. 489-97.

[2] Long, "The Effect of Divination", pp. 489-90.

[3] Long, "The Effect of Divination", p. 491.

[4] Long, "The Effect of Divination", pp. 492-93.

[5] Long, "The Effect of Divination", p. 493.

as to the fulfilment of the oracle.[1] Long concludes that this prophetic-consultation pattern seems to have left its marks on the preaching of both Ezekiel and Jeremiah:

> The schema (sic) is of course no longer directly related to that early setting (i.e., of the original prophetic oracle); it now is quite free of genuine narrative, and divinatory contexts, for that matter. It simply is a pattern of Jeremianic word, and in Ezekiel it merges essentially unaltered with reports of symbolic action.[2]

Thus an originally prophetic, highly formalised style of consultation has been held to have left its impress on subsequent genres of prophetic speech.

In reaction to Long, and in fact to the whole "historicising" tendency of which he is one of the better representatives, I would say that his study is based part and parcel on the Deuteronomic-Deuteronomistic evaluation of the chronological relationship between priestly and prophetic divination. Apparently, up to the present only A. Weiser has had a sharp enough eye to discern the fact that the priestly oracles which accompany David throughout the story of his rise are in fact merely narrative conventions illustrating Yahweh's concern for his chosen king:

> The frequent use of this (oracular) motif, which may have been occasioned by the tradition immediately preceding, is 'no accident', but rather a conscious theme intended to legitimate David as the effectuator of the divine will who, always obedient to Yahweh's command, is led by him in all his attempts to escape.[3]

After Jerusalem is captured, the priestly oracle ceases, and, indeed, it is a subsidiary theme of the so-called Succession Narrative that God is no longer in his heaven, as it were, but in Jerusalem, never to leave it again.[4] Neither in priestly word nor in priest-borne symbol does Yahweh again abandon Jerusalem, until, of course, Ezekiel's famous

---

[1] Long, "The Effect of Divination", pp. 494-96.

[2] Long, "The Effect of Divination", p. 496.

[3] A. Weiser, "Die Legitimation des Königs David" *VT* 16 (1966), pp. 325-54; here p. 335.

[4] Cf. 2 Sam 15.24-29, where Abiathar and Zadok attempt to remove the Ark from the city in the face of Absalom's approach, only to be ordered back by David.

vision in Ezek 11.23 in which he sees the divine כבוד leave the city and stand upon the mountain to the east of the city, thus denying it his protection.[1] This means that the "cessation of the oracle" in the Old Testament chronographic tradition is not intended to be an historical reminiscence; it makes a theological statement about the lack of need for further revelation, once God (and Zadok) are installed in the temple in the holy city of David. It also implies, as I have suggested all along, that this tradition is very late indeed.[2]

As far as the thesis of Israelite priestly divination as a whole is concerned, my major criticism of it is that no one has taken the trouble to prove that it was at all "priestly"; from F. Küchler to the present (and even already from G. Klaiber, in 1865), scholars have followed the Deuteronomic-Deuteronomistic line. Even when J. Begrich succeeded in identifying texts similar to the psalmic priestly oracle texts in the corpus attributed to Deutero-Isaiah, this led to no consternation about the supposed sharp divide between priests and prophets. But then, no other Old Testament scholar who has concerned himself with these texts has rethought the matter, either; at most, one sees the alternative suggestion that such oracles were "prophetic", that is, pronounced by a cult prophet. As I have suggested earlier, the distinction between priest and prophet, as traditionally maintained in Old Testament scholarship,

---

[1] Cf. T.N.D. Mettinger (trans. F.H. Cryer), *The Dethronement of Sabaoth. Studies in the Shem and Kabod Theologies* (Lund, 1982), pp. 97-114.

[2] In this connexion it is interesting to note that the literature of antiquity provides precisely one parallel to the theme of the pious hero who is everywhere led by successful divination en route to establishing his empire, namely the Alexander narratives, although scholars have not been inclined to take the parallelism with David's career seriously, as the original Alexander narratives no longer survive. What reminiscences we have of them are preserved in Diodorus Siculus, Curtius Rufus, and so forth. But it is no doubt the case that the historical Alexander prided himself on the gods' favour as manifested in their oracles to him, and as borne out by his worldly triumphs. This provides some food for thought as to the dating of this motif in the Davidic corpus. See my forthcoming monograph, *David und Alexander: Die Saul-Davidgeschichten als Beispiele hellenistischer Geschichtsschreibung*; and, on the silence of the OT on the theme of divination from Exodus until Joshua, see my article, "Der Prophet und der Magier. Bemerkungen anhand einer überholten Diskussion" in: R. Liwak and S. Wagner (eds.), *Prophetie und geschichtliche Wirklichkeit im alten Israel* (= Festschrift Siegfried Herrmann) (Stuttgart, 1991), pp. 79-88.

is illegitimate, as there was no question of discrete "offices" in Israel for most of her history, but only of fairly loosely defined functional rôles.

Perhaps the best evidence on offer as to the "priestly" capacity of Israelite prophets is provided, not by the obviously stylised theological portraits in which figures like Moses, Joshua or Samuel seemingly preside over sacrifices or the like (such features are all too easily explained away as the result of a late "pro-prophetic" redaction of the texts which understood the prophets as Israel's mediators and saviours), but by incidental features present in the works of the canonical prophets which point to the performance by the prophet in question of decidedly "priestly" functions. In connexion with divination, the most clear association of this kind is provided by the numerous passages in which various prophets assign time-limits to their prognostics, for this, as we have seen, was one of the principle functions of the Mesopotamian diviner. Predictions of the prophets of Mari in the Old Babylonian period and of the priests and priestesses of Ishtar whose "prophecies" were relayed to the great king in the Neo-Assyrian period never contained what we have called *adannus*, as far as I am aware, whereas the prognostics of the divining priests usually did. Thus we note that Isaiah stipulates a time-limit already in the famous prophecy in Isa 7.8 ("within 65 years Ephraim will be broken to pieces so that it will no longer be a people").[1] A similar *adannu*, although less concretely expressed, is also present in the prose account in 7.16 ("before the child knows how to refuse the evil and choose the good, the land before whose two kings you are in dread will be deserted"), in the prose prophecy in 8.4 ("before the child knows how to cry 'my father' or 'my mother', the wealth of Damascus and the spoil of Samaria will be carried away before the king of Assyria"). Furthermore, the tradition of prophetic *adannus* seems to have been so well established in the Isaianic corpus that late redactors also continued it, although in a very prosaic manner, as in Isa 16.14 ("In three years, like the years of the

---

[1] Admittedly, this *adannu* is so badly placed in the present form of the text that it is invariably dismissed as an addition by commentators (cf. e.g. O. Kaiser, *Der Prophet Jesaja. Kapitel 1-12* [Göttingen, 1978] [= *ATD* 17]), p. 74: "We apparently have to do with a later intrusion which reveals itself as such by its thoughtless interruption of the train of thought".); it is also already parenthesised in the RSV and other translations.

wage-earner,[1] the glory of Moab will be brought into contempt") and 21.16 ("Within a year, according to the wage-earner's year, all the glory of Kedar will come to an end"). In fact, the late additions Isa 16.14 and 21.16 reveal such formal similarity and conciseness of expression that it is conceivable that they represent the sort of "technical" oracle from which extensive poetic oracles were normally derived.[2] The famous prose narrative of the healing of Hezekiah (Isa 38.1-6; cf. 2 Kgs 20.1-6) also presupposes that pronouncing the *adannu* of the life of the king was a not-unusual prophetic undertaking (Isa 38.6; 2 Kgs 20.6: 15 years). One of the prose passages in Jeremiah (28.1-4) reflects what might be termed a "diviner's protocoll" (for the concept, see below) containing 1) the name of the diviner in question (Hananiah ben Azzur) 2) the date 3) the place (in the house of Yahweh) 4) the prediction 5) the enquirers (v 1: the priests and all the people) 6) the *adannu* of the prediction (v 3: within 2 years). We shall see shortly that precisely this form of record was characteristic of Israelite priestly divination, as it also was in Babylonia and Assyria, at least from the 7th century onwards. This observation alone is sufficient to bring into question the separate status of at least some of the Israelite prophets from their priestly colleagues.

---

[1] On the "wage-earner's year", see F.H. Cryer, "To the One of Fictive Music: OT Chronology and History", *SJOT* 2 (1987), pp. 21-24.

[2] It was once axiomatic in form criticism that short forms develop prior to longer ones, and indeed both Gunkel and Gressmann thought it possible to write the history of the development of Israelite literature as a history of the evolution of the forms it employed. Like most evolutionary schemes, this was a bit naive, as J. Van Seters has shown (*In Search of History*, [New Haven and London, 1983], pp. 209-13). Nevertheless, the question of how prophets developed their oracles has never been satisfactorily explained; in particular, the notion of extatic prophecy has complicated the discussion. It is conceivable that originally short, one-line responses to the enquirer's questions were subsequently developed into extensive literary (whether oral or no is unimportant) productions. A parallel example is offered by the Greek "prophetic" oracles at shrines such as the famous one at Delphi. These can be traced as far back as the 7th century BC and have been thought to have been mainly in verse; however, J. Fontenrose has shown in a careful historical and form-critical study that the original oracles were invariably simple yes or no answers, and that the poetic versions were later developments (*The Delphic Oracle. Its Responses. With a Catalogue of Responses* [Berkeley, Los Angeles, London, 1978]).

To return to the question of Israelite priestly divination and the omen sacrifice, there is one obvious point to make, from a comparative perspective: that none of the forms of ancient Near Eastern divination which were examined in the previous section happened to be employed, as far as we know, in the course of other liturgical actions. The omen sacrifice was itself a very involved cultic-ritual act which required extensive preparations and had its own specific prayer. Moreover, as we have also seen, the evidence that the omen sacrifice took place in temples is only modest at best. Of course, this is not a decisive argument against the Israelite priestly oracle, since, as we have seen, both the Hittites and the Egyptians were judicious in their reception and adaptation of the Mesopotamian inheritance. Moreover, it could be argued that such oracular consultations were performed in the forecourt of the temple, or in a "tent sanctuary"[1] separate from the temple precincts, although both suggestions would clash with the usual conception of the way the Israelite psalms were performed in connexion with temple worship. But it probably does mean that we should require more evidence than the mere "certainty of a hearing" passages in the individual psalms before we accept the thesis of temple-divination in Israel.

Excursus: Did the Israelites Use the Omen Sacrifice?

I have hinted previously that it is conceivable that the Israelites utilised the omen sacrifice (extispicy), among their several forms of divination. This is not a new suggestion; already Gunkel was prepared to accept the idea in connexion with the story of Cain and Abel,[2] as was the great S. Mowinckel in connexion with several psalms.[3] Recently, O. Loretz has

---

[1] Cf. 2 Sam 6.17, where David erects a tent for the Ark; 1 Chron 21.29, where we learn that the אהל מועד of Moses resided at Gibeon, although Solomon (and presumably, the Ark) dwelled in Jerusalem before the temple was built; and recall Baudissin's theory of the "Orakelzelt" of JE.

[2] Cf. H. Gunkel, *Genesis. Übersetzt und erklärt* (5th edn, Göttingen, 1922), p. 43: "How did Cain recognise the divine disfavour? The text clearly has some sign proper to the omen sacrifice in mind, as this was everywhere respected in antiquity".

[3] S. Mowinckel, *Psalmenstudien I. Åwän und die individuellen Klagepsalmen* (Kristiania, 1921), pp. 145-46.

returned to the question and added new impetus to the discussion on the basis of some Ugaritic evidence.[1] The Ugaritic evidence includes the liver and lung models from Ugarit labelled KTU 1.143, KTU 1.141 and KTU 1.142; two other models have been recovered, but in such a bad state of preservation that we cannot interpret them. The previously-mentioned models concern such topics as the purchase of a slave and the success of a sacrifice for the dead. The important model KTU 1.78 apparently represents an extispicy which was undertaken to explore the significance of a particular astronomical/astrological conjunction of the new moon and the planet Mars. Here line 5 is of crucial importance: *kbdm tbqrn*: a liver you investigate(d).[2] Already in 1921, Mowinckel had suggested, on the basis of its use in Ps 5.4 and 2 Kgs 16.15, that the verb בקר, the basic meaning of which is "to cleave", means in this case "to examine closely", which he explained as a *technicus terminus* of the omen sacrifice.[3]

As Loretz points out, the liver and lung models which were discovered in Ugarit were found in the house of a private individual, that is, one who did not live in the palace compound; moreover, some of the topics he treated pertained to the crown, while others clearly had to do with the private sphere. There is thus good reason to believe that the omen sacrifice was established at Ugarit on the same sort of broad basis it enjoyed in Mesopotamia.[4] A careful analysis of the few passages in which the verb *bqr* (in the Pi'el) figures in the Old Testament leads to the partial elimination of its use in Ps 5.4, the total elimination of its relevance in Ps 27.4, confirmation of Mowinckel's hypothesis in 2 Kgs 16.15, disconfirmation in connexion with Lev 19.20, and to the rejection of the meaning "hepatoscoper" suggested by M. Biç in connexion with Amos 7.14.[5] Loretz then proceeds to an examination of the terminology for "liver" in Israelite legal literature on

---

[1] O. Loretz, *Leberschau, Sündenbock, Asasel in Ugarit und Israel* (Altenberge, 1985), pp. 9-34; 58-80; 81-112.

[2] Loretz, *Leberschau*, p. 11.

[3] Mowinckel, *Psalmenstudien I*, p. 146.

[4] Loretz, *Leberschau*, p. 12.

[5] Loretz, *Leberschau*, pp. 13-24.

the basis of L. Rost's well-known study;[1] this leads Loretz to conclude that,

> From the treatment of the lobe of the liver in the sacrificial laws we
> can deduce with certainty that hepatoscopy once was known in Israel
> and was presumably also favoured.[2]

I would not question Loretz' conclusion on this point, as it seems clear to me that Israel must have been familiar with the omen sacrifice. However, it should be noted that several of his assumptions—including those he adopts from Rost—are dead wrong. For example, Rost held that only the caudate lobe of the liver was of interest for the purposes of extispicy. It was possible to hold this on the basis of earlier Assyriological literature, but the numerous protocolls of the diviner which have been published in the last twenty-five years have made it clear that there was never, in the ancient Near East, a practice of "hepatoscopy", that is, in isolation from the study of the rest of the exta (extispicy) of the sacrificial animal. Roman and Greek divination concentrated almost exclusively on the liver, which is why we have inherited such terms as "haruspex" and "haruspicy" from the classical world; but this was not true of the practice as it was known in Assyro-Babylonian divination. This poses difficulties for the notion of Israelite extispicy: either the references to the other parts of the exta which the Israelites studied have been censored entirely, or else the type of omen sacrifice practised in Israel was more akin to that bequeatheed by the Etruscans to Greece and Rome, the exact tradition-pathway of which is not known.

Furthermore, Loretz builds a case that the references to "signs" in Ps 74.4,9 are to the ominous "signs" that were discovered in the animal in the course of an ominous consultation.[3] But, in fact, a "sign" is a "sign", and the Babylonian series of random omens known as *šumma ālu* contained, as we have seen, 120-odd tablets of them. Since the Israelites, as I have argued, were also familiar with the genre of

---

[1] L. Rost, "Der Leberlappen", *ZAW* 79 (1967), pp. 35-41.

[2] Loretz, *Leberschau*, p. 26.

[3] Loretz, *Leberschau*, pp. 81-107, esp. pp. 96-101; more precisely, he accepts the reference in 74.9, and specifies 74.4 as very late, pertaining to the events in Israel ca. 168 BC.

šumma ālu-like omens, it seems remarkable to take this one word in so very specific a meaning as Loretz proposes to do here.

Nevertheless, I think it is possible to support Loretz' case by a close examination of some Biblical texts which refer to a clearly defined omen consultation. These texts, which have been examined by commentators from Klaiber and Küchler to B.O. Long (with varying results), are as follows: 1) Judg 18.2-24 2) Judg 20.18-28 3) 1 Sam 9.22-24; cf. v 15-18 4) 1 Sam 14.2-19 5) 1 Sam 14.35-37 6) 1 Sam 21.2ff.; cf. 1 Sam 22.10-17 7) 1 Sam 23.1-12 8) 1 Sam 30.7-8 9) 2 Sam 2.1 10) 2 Sam 21.1 11) 2 Sam 24.11-15. Of these, the last two are only of passing interest: 2 Sam 21.1 because it is so tersely formulated as to be unhelpful, except for the use of the verb בקשׁ, which does not otherwise figure in "technical" consultations, and 2 Sam 24.11-15. The latter is couched in the guise of a "prophetic" consultation, although the Hebrew shows a revealing display of archaism (גד הנביא חזה דוד v 11). The various punishments "offered" to David all derive the time-periods mentioned in v 13 from the number three in v 12; this, as we have seen, is the standard device of a diviner in arriving at the *adannu* of a "prediction", and the "prophet" in question simply varies the number according to the sequence year-month-day.[1] The year-month-day scheme was the basis of the final chronological notices in the Deuteronomistic history (cf. e.g., 2 Kgs 25.1,3, etc.), so we need have no fear that the account here actually relates to the time of David.

1 Sam 9.22-24 also offers some interesting features, in particular because the figure of Samuel has been reworked so many times that it is always difficult to tell with which "Samuel" we have to do: with the military hero of 1 Sam 7, the "Judge" of 1 Sam 8 and 12, the anonymous "man of God" of parts of 1 Sam 9.6-8, the "seer" of 1 Sam 9.9,11,18-19, the "priestly" Samuel of 1 Sam 10.17-27, and so on. In 1 Sam 9.15-16 we are told that Yahweh had informed Samuel "on the day before this" of the destined arrival of Saul. On the day in question, Samuel had not yet "blessed the sacrifice" (v 13); he is nevertheless able to tell the cook to "bring the portion of which I said to you, 'put

---

[1] The "seven years of famine" of MT v 13 are contradicted by both the parallel reading in 1 Chron 21.12 and the LXX, and was no doubt motivated by a clumsy attempt to connect this passage with the famine years of the Joseph story (cf. Gen 41.27 and 30: רעב שׁבע שׁני).

it aside' (v 23). Therefore the piece which had been put aside was from the sacrifice of the previous day. This tells us that the sacrifice in question was a sacrifice of שלמים, as it was only the flesh of this sacrifice which it was customary to save, as seems to be preserved in Lev 7.16. This prompts the question as to whether the שלמים-sacrifice was in some way related to Yahweh's message to Samuel on the previous day. In other words: had Samuel undertaken an oracular consultation in the form of an omen sacrifice to determine whether Yahweh would send Israel a saviour? Naturally, the answer to this question would tell us nothing about what any "actual" Samuel did or did not do; it would merely tell us what the author or redactor of the narrative in 1 Sam 9 wanted to imply by his guarded remarks about the sacrifice.

The data pertaining to the remaining passages are perhaps best displayed in list form:

1) *Location*: Judg 18.2-24; cf. v 2,3,5: Micah's house shrine in the hill country of Ephraim; Judg 20.18-28; cf. v 18,(23, presumably),26: the sanctuary at Bethel; 1 Sam 14.2-19; cf. v 2: "in the outskirts of Gibeah under the pomegranate tree which is at Migron"; 1 Sam 14.35-37; cf. v 31: Aijalon; 1 Sam 21.2ff. cf. 1 Sam 22.10-17: Nob; 1 Sam 23.1-12; cf. v 1-2: Keilah; 1 Sam 30.7-8; cf. v 1: ruins of Ziklag; 2 Sam 2.1; cf. 1.1: Ziklag.

2) *Time*: Judg 20.18: evening (cf. v 19); Judg 20.23: evening; Judg 20.26: evening; 1 Sam 14.35-37: evening (cf. v 36: the attack is planned for nightfall); 1 Sam 30.7-8: evening (the attack takes place at twilight, v 17).

3) *Cultic equipment* mentioned: Judg 18.2-24: (presumably) the ephod and teraphim; cf. v 3 and 5; Judg 20.18-28: the Ark of the covenant (v 27); 1 Sam 14.2-19: the Ark of God (v 18); 1 Sam 14.35-37: an altar (v 35); 1 Sam 21.2ff./ 1 Sam 22.10-17: the ephod; cf. 1 Sam 21.10; 1 Sam 23.1-12: the ephod (v 6 and 9); 1 Sam 30.7-8: the ephod (v 7); 2 Sam 2.1: ? (presumably the ephod).

4) *Procedure mentioned*: Judg 20.26: whole burnt offerings and šelamim; 1 Sam 14.19: "stretching out the hand"= sacrifice; 1 Sam

14.35-37: possible sacrifice.[1]

5) *Technical language*: Judg 18.5; 20.18,23,27; 1 Sam 14.37; 1 Sam 22.10,13,15; 1 Sam 23.2,4; 1 Sam 30.8; 2 Sam 2.1: שאל.

6) *Personnel*: Judg 18.3: "a young Levite"(= v 30 "Jonathan the son of Gershom, son of Moses"); Judg 20.28: "Phineas, the son of Eleazar, the son of Aaron"; 1 Sam 14.3: "Ahijah, the son of Ahitub"; 1 Sam 14.35-37: presumably the same as previous example; 1 Sam 22.15: Abimelech, priest of Nob; 1 Sam 30.7: Abiathar, the son of Abimelech; 2 Sam 2.1: presumably the same as previous.

7) *Enquirers*: Judg 18.2: "five able men"; Judg 20.18,23,26,27: the Israelites; 1 Sam 14.18: Saul; 1 Sam 14.37: Saul; 1 Sam 22.14: David; 1 Sam 23.2,4,9,12: David; 1 Sam 30.7: David; 2 Sam 2.1: David.

In short, when examined in their narrative totality, the passages in question reveal an impressive array of formal similarities. The tradents were concerned to note the location, the time, the cultic inventory (ephod, Ark, altar), a few technical expressions such as קרב and שאל, a few oblique and almost shy references to sacrifice (the 'ôlā and šᵉlamim, as well as such circumlocutions as the implied "stretching out the hand"), very consistent—and totally artificial—references to the practitioner in question, plus no less artificial mentions of the enquirers in question, which are either "all Israel"or designated leaders of anything from a tribe (the Danites) to the army (David) and the monarchy itself (Saul). Moreover, the *purpose* of the consultations in question is invariably quite clear: success of an expedition (the Danites; David's pursuit of the Amalekites), engagement in battle (Israel against Benjamin, Saul and Israel against the Philistines, David against the Philistines), personal danger (David in Keilah), direction of a journey (David to Hebron).

The consistency described above exceeds what we would expect if there were a single narrative *Vorlage* which was then repeatedly modified so as to give the impression of a number of distinct events; rather, it should be clear that this rigidity is traceable back to a single

---

[1] An altar is constructed in v 35, and the priest's injunction to "let us draw near there to God" (נקרבה, v.36) employs the cohort. Qal of the root קרב. Among other passages, the root in the Qal, plus an altar, occur together in Exod 40.32; Lev 9.7,8; Num 18.3; and 2 Kgs 16.12-13 in immediate connexion with sacrifice.

literary *Gattung* (genre), which has been variously adapted for the purposes of narrative. To find the source or "original" of this Gattung, I suggest that we examine some diviner's protocols from the ancient Near East.

The first group which presents itself is a sample of fifteen Old Babylonian reports which was published by J. Nougayrol in 1967.[1] The formal elements of these reports are quite simple: usually a remark at the beginning, "a sheep for sacrifice to the god X", the purpose of the extispicy (usually ana šulmi(m): "for the well-being of"), the time-period (*adannu*) pertaining to the sacrifice, then a list of the features of the organs inspected, the positive or negative result of the enquiry (if positive: šalmat), followed by the date. Fairly frequently (e.g., Nougayrol's texts A:21; B:2; C:10; K:1; L:1; M:1; N:1) we are told on whose behalf (i.e., the *enquirer*) the consultation has taken place. Nougayrol's texts L, M and N allow us to infer the *site* at which the extispicy was performed, as the reports in question are the main parts of letters sent by a diviner (Sin-Ašared) to his sovereign, and hence mention the region which the former was sent to investigate. In other words, outside of the technical details of the omen sacrifice, the god in question, the *location, purpose, time* (both *date* and *adannu*), *result, officiant* and *enquirer* were considered to be important and were duly recorded.

The Middle-Babylonian "protocols" treated by F.R. Kraus[2] (some of which are redated "Old Babylonian" texts previously treated by Nougayrol and Goetze) contain largely the same elements, although the purpose (well-being: *šulmum*),[3] the location (e.g., Nr.1:28: Dur-Kurigalzu; Nr.3:38: Nippur; Nr.4:72: Nippur, etc.) and time (date and *adannu*) are completely regular components of the reports; on occasion, the practitioner himself is also named.[4]

The Neo-Assyrian "query" texts are, as we have seen in the previous section, quite extensive, as they include prayers, *ezib* ("disregard")-lines, and extensive lists of omens appropriate to the exta

[1] "Rapports paléo-Babyloniennes d'haruspices", *JCS* 21 (1967), pp. 219-35.

[2] "Mittelbabylonische Opferschauprotokolle", *JCS* 37 (1985), pp. 127-203.

[3] Kraus, "Mittelbabylonische Opferschauprotokolle", pp. 154-55.

[4] Kraus, "Mittelbabylonische Opferschaufprotokolle", p. 156.

of the sacrificial animal instead of a simple yes or no answer (although a diviner probably recognised their "sum" at a glance). Important for our purposes is the fact that J.A. Knudtzon, who first edited and translated the "queries", was tempted to call them "Befragungen des Sonnengottes".[1] This he did for the simple reason that their first line is almost invariably introduced by the initial statement, "*šamaš bēlu rabû ša ašallūka anna kīna apalanni*", that is, "Shamash, great lord, that which I ask you answer me with a reliable 'yes'".[2] In other words, their most marked single feature is their use of Akkadian *šālu(m) / ša'ālu(m)*, "to enquire" (cf. Heb. שאל). The tablets on which the "queries"were written were frequently inscribed (on the left edge) with the names of one or more of the diviners who were responsible for the performance of the relevant extispicy; these "subscripts" are sometimes also dated and include the name of the city in question.[3] It has been pointed out that the tendency to add dates and names to the "queries" accelerated from the reign of Esarhaddon to that of Assurbanipal.[4] The Akkadian verb *qarābu*, "to draw near" (cf. Heb. קרב; and see 1 Sam 14.36) is rare in the "query" texts, but note Knudtzon's Nr. 114, rev. 9, which speaks of an appointee of Assurbanipal whose name is "brought before" Shamash' face in the course of the extispicy, for approval or disapproval.

To be brief, if we seek a model of a divinatory report from the ancient Near East in which such features as the location, the time, the deity (on the assumption that the Ark, the ephod and the teraphim serve, as I have suggested, as symbols of the presence of the deity), the enquirer, the officiant, and even the technical terms "to enquire" (Heb. שאל) and "to draw near" (Heb. קרב) are attested, the Neo-Assyrian "query" texts provide good subjects for comparison. Since the texts from Samuel and Judges which we have been considering are narrative, rather than ritual materials, we should hardly expect to find extensive prayers, *ezib*-lines, or descriptions of the various details of the exta of the

---

[1] Cf. J.A. Knudtzon, *Gebete an den Sonnengott für Staat und königliches Haus aus der Zeit Asarhaddons und Asurbanipals*, Vol. 2 (Leipzig, 1893), p. 63.

[2] Knutzon, *Gebete*, p. 8.

[3] See the list in Knutzon, *Gebete*, pp. 58-60.

[4] Cf. J. Aro in *DM*, p. 113.

animals in them; nor do we. More to the point, although it seems to me clear that the formal model for the Israelite accounts under consideration here was one of the late Assyro-Babylonian types of extispicy report.[1] our texts are, as I have suggested, reluctant to affirm that we actually have to do with extispicy. This suggests that they derive from a late date, meaning from as "early"as the composition of the Deuteronomistic history or as late as the attacks on divination in the Priestly materials. But the many similarities suggest that the authors of the "priestly divination" texts in the Old Testament were as familiar with the tradition of the omen sacrifice as were the tradents of the dreams in the Joseph narrative with the Mesopotamian tradition of dream interpretation.

To clinch this impression, let us examine the few statements which are actually delivered by the priests officiating at the Israelite omen consultations in question. In Judg 18.6 the Danites' representatives are told to, "Go in peace. The journey on which you go is before the (sight of the) Lord". This may be compared with the following standard omen apodosis for the omen sacrifice: "the favourable eyes of the god will be on the enquirer".[2] In Judg 20.28, the Israelites ask whether they should renew their battle with the Benjaminites and are told to "Go up; for tomorrow I will give them into your hand". A standard apodosis again provides a more or less precise parallel: "the enquirer: his hands will attain the desire of his heart".[3] In 1 Sam 23.1-4, David and his men "enquire" of Yahweh twice as to whether they should attempt to relieve the town of Keilah from a Philistine assault; the first positive

---

[1] We cannot say with certainty which; the Neo-Assyrian "reports" published by E. Klauber (*Politisch-religiöse Texte aus der Sargonidenzeit* [Leipzig, 1913], passim) all contain notices as to the purpose, officiants, date, and sometimes the enquirer, in conjunction with an ominous consultation. Moreover, it is certain that reports similar to those used in Assyria at this time had their parallels in then-contemporary Babylon, although texts from this period in Babylon are lacking: more than half of the exiting "query" texts are in fact written in Babylonian, rather than Assyrian, as was noted already by Knudtzon, *Gebete*, p. 64.

[2] Akk.: i-ni-in i-lim da-am-qa-tum e-li a-wi-li-im ib-ba-aš-ši-a; AO 9066 18ss; text and trans. in: J. Nougayrol, "Textes hépatoscopiques d'époque ancienne", *RA* 44 (1950), p. 25; duplicates (the same, p. 25) K 7929,5; YBT X,17,19; KAR 423,I, 41.

[3] Akk. a-wi-lum i-zi-im-ti li-ib-bi-šu qa-ta-šu i-ka-aš-ša-da-a; cited in *RA* 44, p. 26, 29ss, with parallels.

answer merely repeats the verbs used in David's question, and hence signifies simply "yes" (v 1-2); the second time, however, they not only receive a "yes" (i.e., "go down to Keilah"), but the added conventional response, "I will give the Philistines into your hand" (v 4). In v 10-12, David asks Yahweh a double question: ". . . Saul seeks to come to Keilah to destroy the city on my account. (11) Will the men of Keilah surrender me into his hand? Will Saul come down. . . ?" He receives affirmative answers on both counts, and accordingly withdraws from the town. This might seem like so unusual a situation that a parallel to it could not be found in the omen apodoses; in fact, a parallel was published long ago by Nougayrol: "the enemy will surround the town; the town will revolt and kill its lord".[1]

These parallels should suffice to show that the late first-millennium Assyro-Babylonian "queries / reports" tradition provided the formal background for the descriptions in Judges and Samuel of the various ominous consultations which there take place. Similarly, apodoses from the so-called "canonical" omens of the omen sacrifice (extispicy) seem to have provided some of the concrete "prognostics" which are occasionally, if rarely, cited in these passages. Once again I should like to emphasise that this does not prove that the Israelites were actually employing extispicy in the "period of the Judges" or the time of Saul and David. The texts in which these various models were used have, as I have argued, a theological, not an historical, thrust. Judg 18, the chapter which contains the first of the so-called "priestly oracle" texts (Judg 18.5-6), begins with the statement that, "In those days there was no king in Israel" (v 1). Furthermore, the story of the destruction and salvation of the Benjaminites (Judg 19-21), which contains the second of them (Judg 20.18,23,26-28), likewise begins on the remark that, ". . . there was no king in Israel" (Judg 19.1), and concludes on the famous statement that, "In those days there was no king in Israel; every man did what was right in his own eyes" (Judg 21.25). It is no accident that, as I have remarked, the oracle ceases

---

[1] AO 7030 [II], obv. 33-35 (Nougayrol, *RA* 40 [1942-1946] 91-92): na-ak-ru-um a-la-am i-la-a-wi a-lum i-ba-la-ka-al-ma bi-el-šu i-da-ak.

completely when Israel got her ideal king, David,[1] which is another
way of saying that the theme of successful divination in fact links these
late additions to the DtrH in Judges with the Saul-David narratives.

An intriguing question, but one which cannot be answered here,
is whether the developmental history of the Syro-Palestinian šelamim-
sacrifice[2] can be traced back to a time when it may have doubled as an
omen sacrifice. The references to which I have pointed above may be
taken as more than suggestive.

[1] I do not intend to steal my own thunder, as it were, with respect to my next
work, but it should in any case be clear that the "priestly oracle" texts I have
examined here are, without exception, post-Deuteronomistic. When the
Deuteronomist wanted to introduce Solomon's career with a divinely-appointed
charisma, he was unable to provide it through the priestly oracle and the agency of
either Abiathar or Zadok, because Dtr had never heard of the oracle in question.
Solomon had instead to trudge off to Gibeon, as is related in 1 Kgs 3.3-15.

[2] Concerning which, see the thorough study by B. Janowski, "Erwägungen zur
Vorgeschichte des israelitischen Selamim-Opfers", *UF* 12 (1980), pp. 231-59; and
G.A. Anderson, *Sacrifices and Offerings in Ancient Israel. Studies in their Social
and Political Importance* (Atlanta, Georgia, 1987) (= *HSM* 41), pp. 36-55.

CHAPTER 6

THE LITERARY USES OF DIVINATION

We have already seen, in the sections dealing with Israelite knowledge
of the Mesopotamian tradition of dream interpretation and with Israelite
knowledge of the omen sacrifice, that Old Testament references to
divination tend to be used in literary contexts to endow certain figures
with divine authority (e.g., Joseph and David), to illustrate Yahweh's
benevolent concern for his chosen leaders (Jacob, David), or, as in the
case of Saul (1 Sam 28.6,15), we have seen that its lack demonstrates
the loss or absence of such *charisma* (cf. also Num 17.1-10 = Heb.
17.16-26).[1]

The "Philistine"[2] procedure mentioned in 1 Sam 6.2-9 is of a

---

[1] Jonathan's use of a speech omen in 1 Sam 14.6-12, confirmed by an
earthquake in v 15, is problematical. That Jonathan's procedure explicitly impetrates
a binary omen is obvious, and was acknowledged already by Witton-Davies, *Magic,
Divination and Demonology*, pp. 75-76, though he had no name for the
phenomenon; and by A. Guillaume, *Prophecy and Divination* (along with many
other examples), pp. 164-170, under the Greek designation, *kledon*; and by
Oppenheim in *AfO* 17 (1954-56), p. 52, who recognised the omen as the ancient
Sumerian *enim.gar*, Akkadian *egirru*-omen. The problem in this context is that
Jonathan's success with the omen in contrast to his father's failure to consult the
oracle (1 Sam 14.19) and its subsequent refusal to answer him (v 37) identifies
Jonathan as pleasing to God; this "legitimates" him, just as the "priestly oracle" later
legitimates David, as we have seen. Perhaps this lends point to the story of David's
rise: the divinely-sanctioned Saulide transfers his authority to his father's rival (cf.
1 Sam 23.15-18).

[2] I write "Philistine" here in inverted commas as there is no earthly reason to
suppose that the rite in question was actually practised by the Philistines. The
procedure is carefully described, complete with casuistically phrased alternatives in
v 9 for the divinatory procedure and a wealth of detail as to the defensive-magical
precautions to be taken (v 4-5). Whatever the state of Israelite "science" in the 11th
century BC, I think we can rule out *apriori* an interest in the "antiquities of the
Philistines". An interest in the highly literate and internationally famous traditions
of Mesopotamia and Egypt, however, is both intelligible and, to some extent,

piece with this general tendency. The rite is explicitly one of divination, as it is proposed by the "priests" and "diviners" (קֹסְמִים, v 2); moreover, the decision expected is binary, being decided by which of the two possible routes (towards Israel / not towards Israel, v 9) the cart bearing the Ark actually pursues. The phenomenology of the proposed method transpar-ently reflects that of the Egyptian "bark of the God" oracle, with the difference that, since the Ark cannot tilt forwards or backwards like the divine statues in Egypt, here the *route* chosen has to substitute for this behaviour.[1] It is evident that the Ark plays the part of a divine statue in this narrative from the simple fact that the statue of Dagon has already done obeisance to it (1 Sam 5.3). Thus Dagon's statue answers the *implicit* question, made pertinent by Israel's loss of the battle at Ebenezer (1 Sam 4.1ff.), as to which was the greater god; and the Ark of Yahweh itself answers the *explicit* question (1 Sam 6.9) as to which god had sent the various plagues upon the Philistines. As in the dreams of Joseph, one does not need to know the background in the relevant mantic tradition in order to understand its use in the present context, but the preceding reflections should serve to show that the author of the passage was, as in other cases we have examined, well-versed in the divinatory tradition he was manipulating.

Dreams, signs, the "bark of the god", the omen sacrifice, the speech omen: there can be no doubt but that the Israelite tradents of the Old Testament chronographic texts were both knowledgeable about div-ination and able to adapt it in literary contexts in a sophisticated manner (see, for example, the beautiful example of a speech omen concealed within a dream omen in Judg 7.10-15). Since they were clearly so knowledgeable, it is justifiable to point to a few other passages in which various mantic traditions seem to be at work.

One interesting example of divination by "signs" in a narrative context which has not, to my knowledge, been detected previously is 2

---

demonstrable—and was shared by everyone else in the ancient Near East.

[1] Naturally, the acknowledgement of the Egyptian parallel offers no point of contact for a possible date for this narrative, as the Egyptian procedure extends back into the mists of time and forwards into the Christian period.

Kgs 3.22-23. The larger context of the passage is the fable[1] of the

[1] I do not use the term "fable" here lightly. The Old Testament claims that the joint Israelite-Judaean-Edomite invasion of Moab in reaction to Moab's bid for independence took place on the death of Ahab (2 Kgs 1.1; 3.1,5). This cannot have been the case, since Ahab was immediately succeeded by his son Ahaziah, who reigned for two years (1 Kgs 22.40,51), whereas the account of the Moabite campaign relates that it took place under Joram/Jehoram (cf.3.1,6, etc.). Also, Mesha himself claims that Israelite hegemony over the east Jordanian territory lasted for Omri's days plus "half his son's days" (see below), which locates the event to Ahab's 11th year (cf.1 Kgs 16.29), rather than after his death. Then again, the route chosen, that is, through Judah all the way around the Dead Sea through the "wilderness of Edom" (v 8), is plain silly, given that Israel must still have held the fords of the Jordan at the time—or else the counterattack took place some years after Joram/Jehoram's accession to the throne, rather than immediately, as the text implies. Furthermore, the idea—suggested by some—that the route chosen owed to the necessity to ensure that the Edomite king also participated in the campaign (cf. 2 Kgs 3.9,26) encounters the difficulty that the Old Testament acknowledges that *"there was no king in Edom"* (1 Kgs 22.47a; 47b, which claims that *"a deputy was king"*, has clearly been added to erase the contradiction with the narrative in 2 Kgs 3). Also, the Israelite chronology—as usual—leaves no room for the event. Mesha of Moab says that Omri's regime of domination over the east Jordanian territory lasted his own reign, plus "half of his son's days" taken together were about 40 years (cf. J.C.L. Gibson, *Textbook of Syrian Semitic Inscriptions. Vol.1. Hebrew and Moabite* [Oxford, 1971], pp. 74-76, lines 7-8. Note that Gibson attempts to avoid the chronological problem by rendering חצי as "much of"), while the Old Testament gives us to believe that the combined rules of Omri, Ahab, Ahaziah and Jehoram totalled about 37 years (cf. e.g. the revised Jepsen-Hanhart chronology reprinted in G. Fohrer, *Geschichte Israels* [Heidelberg, 1979], p. 80). Most commentators attempt to dismiss Mesha's "40 years" as "a round number" signifying "a long time", but to do so is pure arbitrariness: why should Mesha be inaccurate about this and the Old Testament not be, for example, in the cases of the similar 40-year reigns of David, Solomon, and Joash? (For more on the chronological problems of this period, see J. Strange's interesting article, "Joram, King of Israel and Judah", *VT* 25 (1975), pp. 191-201; Strange tries to solve the difficulties by hypothecating a single king Joram, instead of two, one Israelite and one Judaean, of the OT tradition. While this is merely a plausible hypothesis, its very plausibility indicates the actual state of our ignorance of this period.).There is also the further problem that Mesha seems to have got the Israelite *king* wrong as well: he claims that the opponent in question was Omri's son ("Joram, King of Israel and Judah", line 8), rather than his grandson Jehoram, as the Old Testament states. If it really *was* Ahab, rather than Jehoram, note that the Assyrians claim that he was able to field 2,000 chariots and 10,000 foot-soldiers (both absurdly large numbers, given the demographic situation in the then Northern Kingdom) against them in Qarqar in 853, so that Moab would not have had a prayer of success (cf. the so-called "monolith-inscription of Shalmanasser

Israelite-Judaean-Edomite invasion of Moab to prevent Moab's bid for independence. In the passage in question, the Moabites see the landscape flooded by the waters summoned by Elisha's miracle (v 20) which reflect the morning sun "as red as blood" (v 22). This leads them to conclude, "This is blood; the kings have surely fought together, and slain one another. Now then, Moab, to the spoil!" The question is, of course, just why such a sight should have prompted precisely this conclusion, which led the Moabites to charge recklessly to their deaths (v 24-25). In this connexion we should observe that what actually flooded the region was water seeping into a "dry stream-bed" (v 16), and compare with the following omen from *šumma ālu:* "If a river carries blood: country with country will fight, house with house will be hostile, brother will devour the flesh of brother, armies will reduce (themselves)".[1] If the blood-coloured water was a popularly-known omen—and we have seen that omens of the *šumma ālu* type are generally assumed to reflect popular conceptions—then the thrust of the story is the familiar Old Testament point of the foolishness of foreign divination compared with the might of Yahweh as mediated through his prophets.

In the chronographic literature, we have already seen a fair sampling of references to highly formalised "techniques" of divination. The question presents itself whether the Israelites also knew of such facets of the Mesopotamian tradition as are preserved in the tablets of *physiognomic and diagnostic* omens. The answer to this seems to be an unqualified affirmative; the chronographic literature, as is well known, singles out certain features of prominent individuals for comment,

---

III", *TUAT* I, p. 360, l.91-92; ANET, p. 279) even in the event that he launched a less ambitious campaign. See further the remarks of K.A.D. Smelik (trans. H. Weippert), *Historische Dokumente aus dem alten Israel* [Göttingen, 1987], pp. 47-48, who does his best to "save the appearances". What historical information we possess invalidates the narrative in 2 Kgs 3 as historical reminiscence; on the other hand, its theological significance is not unimpressive.

[1] Šumma nāru dāmu u-bil mātu itti māti i-taq-rib bitu itti biti ittakir[ir] ahu šir ahi (and cf. the וִיכּוּ אִישׁ אֶת־רֵעֵהוּ of 2 Kgs 3.23) ikkal sabe[meš] isahiru[meš]: cf. F. Nötscher, Šumma Ālu ina mele šakin, *Or* 51-54 (1930), pp. 2-243; here pp. 136-137 (text and Ger. trans.) = CT 39.14ff.= Tab. 61 A, Nr. 132; and note that Nrs. 1, 2, 3, 22, 79, 127, and 61B = CT 39.22; 40.47, Nr. 6 are all omens dealing with blood-coloured water.

although the reasons for these comments are not always immediately clear, for which reason they have also occasioned a variety of interpretations from scholars.

An obvious case in point is the repeated description of Saul in which we are told that "from his shoulders upward he was taller than any of the people" (1 Sam 9.2; cf. 10.23). As many commentators have noted, this characterisation seems to be almost explicitly countered by the Deuteronomist, who observes, in the description of the choosing of David as Saul's successor, that "man looks on the outward appearance, but Yahweh looks on the heart" (1 Sam 16.7).[1] Given the fact that the ancient Near East knew of an ancient tradition of mantic interpretation of physical characteristics, and that this tradition is attested as far afield

---

[1] More precisely, they have noted that the passage aims at the earlier description of Saul, and not, as it appears, at Samuel's perception of Eliab (v 6). Far from all scholars accept that the section of which v 7 is a part is Deuteronomistic. The problem of 1 Sam 16.1-13 seems to have been first acutely perceived by Wellhausen, who saw in it clear signs of a late text (*Die Composition des Hexateuchs und der Historischen Bücher des Alten Testaments* [Berlin, 1899], p. 247). Numerous commentators, however, have attempted to see in it a continuation of the preceding section (cf. e.g., already H.P. Smith, *A Critical and Exegetical Commentary on the Books of Samuel* [Edinburgh, 1899], p. 143; and, most recently, M.A. O'Brien, *The Deuteronomistic History Hypothesis: A Reassessment* [Göttingen, 1989], p. 102, n. 72). Noth, however, acknowledged that the section is a "Zusatz" to a presumed ancient "Saul-Überlieferung" (*Überlieferungsgeschichtliche Studien*, I, p. 62, and n. 1). A. Weiser, "Die Legitimation des Königs David", *VT* 16 (1966), pp. 326-27, recognised the theological *Tendenz* of the passage, but held this to be original to the story of David's rise, of which he saw 1 Sam 16.1-13 as the beginning. It was J. Van Seters who first pointed out that 1) all the signs of lateness which virtually all commentators have observed point directly to Dtr; that 2) 1 Sam 16.1-13 is indeed part of the story of David's rise and hence 3) the story of David's rise must be a Deuteronomistic composition (*In Search of History*, pp. 260-64). On the specific linguistic and textual features of v 7 see Wellhausen, *Der Text der Bücher Samuelis* (Göttingen, 1871), p. 101; H.J. Stoebe, *Das erste Buch Samuelis* (Gütersloh, 1973), p. 301, 7)a); P.K. McCarter, *1 Samuel. A New Translation with Introduction and Commentary*, (Garden City [NY]), 1980, pp. 274-77, who, however, does not acknowledge the force of Wellhausen's observation that *'ynym* simply means "appearance" (concerning which, see also E. Dhorme, *L'emploi métaphorique des noms de parties du corps en hébreu et en akkadien* [Paris, 1963], pp. 49-50).

as ancient Egypt, and, later, at Qumran,[1] it is hard to understand this remark as anything but a rebuff to those who claimed to be able to "read" human destinies on the basis of physical characteristics. At all events, a parallel to the Biblical description of Saul seems to be provided by the Babylonian physiognomical omen, "If his head is long: he will get riches: he will get children; (variant): he will die alone".[2] Without putting too fine a point on the matter, one notes that all of these characteristics apply to Saul as related in the Biblical narrative. Remarks similar to that characterising Saul are included in the Old Testament text with respect to both David (1 Sam 16.12) and his son Absalom (2 Sam 14.25-26). I know of no parallels to the description of David in the omen literature, but even commentators with no knowledge of the omen tradition have wondered about the significance of the reference to Absalom's hair which, when it was cut annually, weighed "two hundred shekels by the king's weight" (2 Sam 14.26).[3] The

---

[1] See 4 Q 186, originally published by J. Allegro, republished in P. Benoit, J.T. Milik, et al. (eds.), *Discoveries in the Judaean Desert*, Vol. 5 (Oxford, 1968). The text has been recently understood by M.R. Lehman as an "astrological" text ("New Light on Astrology in Qumran and the Talmud", *RevQ* 32 [1975], pp. 599-602), which is patently silly, as it consists almost entirely of lists of various physiognomical features of the "types" in question, with only two references to horoscope-like phenomena; it has been correctly seen as a fragment of the physiognomical-omen genre by J.C. Greenfield and M. Sokoloff, "Astrological and Related Omen Texts in Jewish Palestinian Aramaic", *JNES* 48 (1989), p. 210 and n. 25-26.

[2] šumma SAG.DU GID.DA NIG.TUK DUMU.MEŠ TUK^{si} var.: AS.A BA.BAD; text and translation in F.R. Kraus, "Weitere Texte zur babylonischen Physiognomatik", *Or* N.S. 16 (1947), p. 174: $18' + 4' = $ CXLII.

[3] H.P. Smith, *Samuel*, p. 337, calls the passage a "panegyric to Absalom's personal beauty"; this is an odd remark, since Smith was well aware that the reference to shekels "by the king's weight" points to a late period. Why would someone writing centuries later care to describe as being beautiful the instigator of a bloody civil war which had challenged the authority of the revered David? I hold this to be unlikely, and that instead the ominous sense of the description provides literary foreshadowing of the dire events to come. This point differs absolutely from the conclusion of moralising scholars, who have decided that the verse refers to Absalom's vanity, on the (always assumed, but never demonstrated) assumption that such vanity indicates Absalom's unfitness to rule and his (ultimately rebellious)

remark seems odd, and may well derive from some such tradition as the physiognomic-diagnostic tradition which has been preserved in part in Kraus' "Sittenkanon" and, to some extent, in *šumma ālu*. One Old Babylonian omen text from this tradition offers not a bad parallel: "If a man is distinguished by beautiful hair: (the end of) his days is near".[1] One aspect of the characterisation of Absalom has usually been understood rationalistically, namely his seduction of the Israelites in the city gate with the remark, "Oh that I were judge in the land! Then every man with a suit or cause might come to me, and I would give him justice" (2 Sam 15.4). In searching for an appropriate Assyro-Babylonian parallel, one has to recall that justice was the express province of Shamash, the sungod, and that already Hammurabi was aware that he could not *give* justice: as a divine quality, he could at best *administer* it.[2] It is therefore interesting to note, concerning Absalom's claim that the physiognomic tradition says, "If he continually takes Shamash in his mouth, Shamash will requite it /variant: defeat him".[3] Thus Absalom's claim to being able to dispense justice may actually be a harbinger of the evils to follow.

Further texts of interest from the "physiognomic" point of view

egotism. They seem to have Milton's Satan in mind, rather than a figure in an early Semitic narrative. The "ominous" interpretation at least has the virtue of being based on then-contemporary literature (the omen collections), whereas the moralising view is anachronistic.

[1] F. Köcher and A.L. Oppenheim, "The OB Omen Text VAT 7525", *AfO* 18 (1957-58), pp. 62-80; here obv. col. I, lines 17-18 (text and trans. p.63); Akk.: DIŠ LU sar-tam da-mi-iq-tam su-uk-lu-ul / UD-ma-tu-šu qi-ir-ba.

[2] Although he naturally attributes the origins of justice to Marduk, the city-god of Babylon: inuma Marduk ana sutesur nisi, matim usim suhuzim uwaeranni, kittam u mišaram ana pi matim aškun. . . : "when Marduk sent me in order to lead the people rightly and to teach the country proper behaviour, (and) I established truth and justice in the mouth of the country. . . "; following the text in G. Bergsträßer, *Einführung in die semitischen Sprachen* (repr. Darmstadt, 1977 [1928]), p. 30. Note also the remark of W.G. Lambert ("Nebuchadnezzar King of Justice", *Iraq* 27 (1965), pp. 1-11; here p. 4): "Long before the time of Nebuchadnezzar II royal inscriptions had extolled the virtues of the reigning monarch, and quite often it is said that the king was appointed by the gods to uphold justice in the land".

[3] Text and translation in Kraus, "Weitere Texte", p. 201 7´and p. 202.

are such as Prov 6.12-15, 16.30 and Isa 58.9. These have been ably studied by G.E. Bryce in an investigation which calls our attention to the fact that such gestures as pointing with the finger, winking the eye, and dragging the foot are well established in the Mesopotamian literature of physiognomic omens as emblematic of the individual whom the gods will presently destroy.[1] Bryce also attempts to depict a period of secondary moralisation within this tradition,[2] which, or so he holds, developed into a conflated style of "omen wisdom". As I have pointed out previously, however, the moralising slant of the physiognomic omen texts was characteristic already of the Neo-Sumerian (Wisdom) and Old Babylonian (omen) texts. In fact, in so intensely ethically polarised a social sphere as that of Babylonia and Assyria, it would be remarkable if any aspect of human endeavour was ever divorced from religio-ethical considerations.

A case in point is the idiom "to change face". In his ground-breaking study of the earliest of Sumerian proverb collections, B. Alster points to the Sumerian expression *igi.bal*, which he understands to have the nuances "to squint, wink", "to change face", and, in a single text, "to change a word". The writer concludes that *igi.bal* "is always used in contexts which describe the unreliability of a person. . . it covers the same semantic range as the English 'turncoat'".[3] In reality, the idioms "to change one's word, face, mind" recur literally countless times in the Mesopotamian omen literature, and also in other contexts which mantically characterise those to whom it is applied. In the "Sittenkanon" we read, "If he habitually changes his face (zi-mi-šu ittanak-karu^{ru}) his days have drawn near/end of days".[4] A first millennium tablet which bears a recognisable relationship to the "Sittenkanon" offers the following: "if someone continually changes his words (di-ib-bi uš-ten-

[1] "Omen Wisdom in Ancient Israel", *JBL* 94 (1975), pp. 19-37.

[2] Bryce, "Omen Wisdom", pp. 21-22.

[3] B. Alster, *The Instructions of Shuruppak* (Copenhagen, 1974), p. 90 and cf. p. 89.

[4] Kraus, "Sittenkanon", p. 98, nr. 34.

ni), he will go constantly in unhappiness of heart".[1] Further, the Cassite-period series of conjurations known as *Šurpu* lists extensive series of transgressions against divine norms of which the sufferer may (wittingly or unwittingly) be guilty. The pedantic zeal of the composers of the series was such that we may be reasonably certain that no significant cultic or moral transgression was left out. In our connexion it is interesting to note that the series speaks of the "mamitu (tabu) to fix a boundary, but change it (nu-uk-ku-ru) / the tabu (mamitu) to promise, but change (e-ni-e). . . ."[2] I suspect that the concrete referent of this concept is the notion of not changing the wording of a contract, since contracts were entered upon under oath in Babylonia and Assyria; thus, changing one's "word" was equivalent to blasphemy, and consequently was severely punished.[3] But, since most Mesopotamian contracts were actually oral agreements in which the important element was the presence of witnesses (the written report was useful only in the absence of the witnesses),[4] this emphasis on keeping one's word obviously had extensive significance also in non-juridical contexts. Most business and practical relationships will have been governed by oral practices; hence the importance of the tabus in question.

I propose that this understanding of the significance of "change" underlies a considerable number of Old Testament passages. The contractual sense of the concept is attested in, for example, Ps. 89.35, where Yahweh assures Israel that "I will not breach my covenant or

---

[1] S.M. Moren, "A 'Lost' Omen Tablet", *JCS* 29 (1977), pp. 65-72; here p. 66 line 20 (text); p. 68 line 20 (trans.).

[2] E. Reiner, *Šurpu* (Graz, 1958) (= *AfO* Beiheft 11), III.54-55; and see also VIII.73.

[3] Cf. e.g. M. Schorr, *Urkunden des altbabylonsichen Zivil- und Prozessrechts* (Leipzig, 1913), nr. 28-29: *niš ᵈšamaš u šu-mu-la-ilum ša a-wa-at duppim an-ni-im u-na-ka-ru*: "(they have sworn) the oath of Shamash and Shumulailu that they will not *change* the contents of this tablet". See further nrs. 13A 15-16; 33 rev.1-3; 310 36-40, etc.

[4] Cf. e.g. M. San Nicolo, *Die Schlussklauseln der altbabylonischen Kauf- und Tauschverträge. Ein Beitrag zur Geschichte des Barkaufes* (Munich, 1922), pp. 23-24; R. Haase, *Einführung in das Studium keilschriftlicher Rechtsquellen* (Wiesbaden, 1965), pp. 119-27, esp. p. 123.

change the word that went forth from my lips" (cf. לֹא אֲשַׁנֶּה, Mal 3.6). The juridical sense of the idiom recurs, probably in its original *Sitz im Leben*, in Prov. 24.21: "Fear Yahweh, my son, and the king: with 'changers' you shall not exchange pledges" (v 21: יְרָא אֶת יהוה בְּנִי וּמֶלֶךְ עִם שׁוֹנִים אַל־תִּתְעָרָב).[1] "God and the king" was the standard oath closing contracts in the sphere of Babylonian business dealings;[2] that it was also practised in Israel has long been known.[3] Hence, to "fear" the oath means not to join in business dealings with partners who "change" their obligations, the consequences of which could be, in civil cases, lethal (cf. 1 Kgs 21.10,13)[4], not to speak of what Yahweh would do to one. The ominous sense of "change" signifying someone who has

---

[1] Admittedly, the Hithp. of עָרַב can mean "to make a wager" (cf. e.g. 2 Kgs 18.23); but the meaning of the root has to do with mortgaging, leaving something in security, giving sureties, and so forth (see Koehler-Baumgartner, Gesenius-Buhl, sub עָרַב). Here the sense of the Hithp. implies the (expected) reciprocity of business dealings.

[2] For example, virtually all the contracts in Schorr, *Rechtsurkunden*, were completed by swearing this oath. The oath continued to be sworn at least through the Neo-Babylonian period; cf. e.g. M. San Nicolo and H. Petschow, *Babylonische Rechtsurkunden aus dem 6.Jahrhundert vor Chr.;* Bayerische Akademie der Wissenschaften Philosophisch-historische Klasse, Abhandlungen, N.F. 51 (1960), pp. 1-122, Nrs.2, lines 6-14 (with the "change clause" in lines 7 and 14); Nr. 4,lines 30-33; Nr. 16, lines 16-19, etc.

[3] See e.g. F. Horst, "Der Eid im Alten Testament", *EvT* 17 (1957) 378 = the same, *Gottes Recht* (Munich, 1961); p. 307.

[4] As was originally recognised, as far as I am aware, by F.I. Andersen, "The Socio-Juridical Background of the Naboth Incident", *JBL* 85 (1966), p. 55. Scholars seem to have expended undue energy, though, in trying to puzzle out the accusation against Naboth, namely the fact that he is said to have "blessed" God and king. No one has noticed that scribal euphemism was actually the *language* of this particular oath: at Mari, the accused was said to have "eaten the *ašakku*" of god and king (cf. *ARM* 8,7,9´-10´; the same, 8,11,29-31, with sar(meš) for asakku; and note that in juridical contexts Akk. *akālum* does *not* mean "to eat", but "to expropriate, steal", etc.); at OB Susa there was a "command" (awātum) of g. and k. (cf. P. Koschaker,"Göttliches und weltliches Recht nach den Urkunden aus Susa", *Or* 4 (1935), pp. 38-80; here p. 44 and n. 1), a "crime" (ḫattum) of g. and k. (same place, p. 46, n. 1), an "oath/curse" (mamitum) of g. and k. (p. 54, n 2) ; in Israel one either "blessed" (b-r-k) or "cursed" (q-l-l) god and king. What is significant is that in Mari, Susa, and, apparently, Israel, *violation* of "god and king" was a capital crime.

secured divine disapproval is fully reflected in Jer 2.35b-36: "See, I will bring you to judgement for saying 'I have not sinned'; oh, how lightly you wander about, changing your way" (לשנות את דרכך). Virtually imitating a Sittenkanon-like omen, the poet of Job laments to Yahweh about the futility of man's situation (Job 14.20): "you prevail forever against him, and he passes; if he changes his face (משנה פניו), you send him away". This brings us back to our original idiom, "to change face". We have seen that it figures in the physiognomic omens to signify someone the gods (above all Shamash) are sure to destroy; however, it also figures in the *diagnostic* omens to describe an epileptoid attack: "if the whole character of a man's face changes,[1] a gallu-demon has possessed him".[2]

Also this variety of "omen" has at least one self-evident parallel in the Old Testament chronographic literature: feigning madness in Achish's court to avoid retribution, David is said to have "changed his discernment (וישנו טעמו) before their eyes, and became mad in their hands. . . ." (1 Sam 21.13).

The category of diagnostic omens and Israelite familiarity with them leads us further to the vexing question of the relationship between the Israelite purity laws and the Mesopotamian tradition. We have seen above Lemche's observation that individual laws and conceptions which are enshrined in the Israelite legal corpora may prove to have a very ancient paternity, although the literary context which now surrounds them represents a very late stage of the tradition. It is accordingly likely that, however highly "theologised" some elements of the purity laws are in their present context, they may on examination be shown to have derived from a quite different sphere of ideas. Although we cannot go into this matter more extensively here, it should be noted that a certain relationship has already been established between some features of the Israelite sin-offering (אשם) and the Cassite series of defensive-magical

---

[1] The phonetic complement -ir shows that this verb is certainly *nakāru*.

[2] ND 4368 obv., col. i, line 10; pub. by J.V. Kinnier Wilson in "Two Medical Texts from Nimrud", *Iraq* 19 (1957), pp. 40-49, here pp. 40-41 (text and Eng. trans.).

incantations called *Šurpu*.[1]

A parallel question to that of sin and its atonement is the notion of uncleanness, specifically as manifested in the laws concerning leprosy in Lev 13-14. Even a cursory reading of this section suffices to show that certain objective features, such as "white spots" (13.3) or "reddish-white spots" are cited as providing decisive clues as to the cultic state of the enquirer/sufferer, which is to say, they tell the priest whether the patient is "clean" or not. Any attempt to dismiss the idea that the section in question is based on "magical" conceptions immediately founders on the simple fact that analogous spots on both garments (Lev 13.47-52) and the walls of houses (Lev 14.34-45) are sufficient to get them, too, declared "leprous". Noth thinks that the latter two passages represent the transference by analogy of conceptions pertaining to human skin diseases onto inanimate objects.[2] However, he makes no attempt to explain just what could be intended by such a transference. Admittedly, skin diseases are harmful to the individual, and some may infect other people.[3] It therefore follows that such infected individuals are to be excluded from society until they are well. But does Noth really imagine the Israelites thought that an Israelite would contract "leprosy" from a house or garment, or the reverse? What was implied by such a transference? For that matter, K. Elliger is no more helpful, although he does allow—in guarded circumlocutions—for the possibility of magical conceptions underlying the phenomenon, which, however, he assumes were not necessarily shared by the leaders of the official, as opposed to the popular, cult—a view which leaves one wondering why there was

---

[1] Cf. e.g. M.J. Geller, "The Šurpu Incantations and Lev. V.1-5", *JSS* 25 (1980), pp. 181-92.

[2] M. Noth, *Das 3.Buch Mose: Leviticus* (Göttingen, 1973) (= *ATD* 6), p. 91.

[3] Though it must be acknowledged that true leprosy, or "Hansen's disease", was unknown in the ancient Near East; cf. J.V. Kinnier-Wilson, "Leprosy in Ancient Mesopotamia", *RA* 60 (1966), pp. 47-58.

priestly legislation about the phenomena at all.[1] Both scholars very practically acknowledge that the phenomena in question (i.e., in garments and houses) must be some sort of fungus, mildew, or whatever.[2]

The notion of the transference of the illness conception from the animate (man) to the inanimate (e.g., houses), as I pointed out above, solves nothing and explains nothing. It might be more useful to point out the essential *difference* between these phenomena: the one represents the invasion of the living (man) by something else that is living, if inappropriate (whatever fungus or bacterium is devouring his skin); while the other examples are cases in which the *artificial* (woven garments, whether made of animal or vegetable fibres; house walls) is invaded by the *natural*. Thus, what seems to be resented is not the possibility of say, catching "leprosy" from a house, but the inappropriateness of "wild flesh" (בשׂר חי, 13.14-16) assaulting normal flesh, disordered life (fungus) attacking the structured products which man has made. The occurrence of any of these things tells the priest that the world is no longer in balance, that its fundamental categories have been violated, which naturally represents a threat to Israel.[3]

This awareness of the symbolic potential of such phenomena was not restricted to Israel. An Old Babylonian omen text containing a mixture of physiognomic and diagnostic omens informs us that, "If the

---

[1] K. Elliger, *Leviticus* (Tübingen, 1966) (= *HAT* 4), p. 186. This notion of "official" vs. "popular" cult and cultic practices has long been a convenient rabbit which Old Testament scholars like to whisk out of the hat whenever Yahwistic usages do not seem sophisticated enough to suit their taste; frequently, it has been made to dovetail with the Deuteronomist's "Canaanite hypothesis" (i.e., the people's popular practices in reality simply consist in their embracing "the way of the peoples"). The whole notion requires more careful analysis than it has so far received. Certainly, we can no longer speak, as scholars used to do, of Israelite "syncretism" in the sense of a decline from a once-pristine Yahwism. See already G. Ahlström, *Syncretism in Israelite Religion* (Lund, 1963), pp. 12-13.

[2] See Noth, *Das Dritte Buch Mose*, pp. 91 and 94; Elliger, *Leviticus*, pp. 185 and 189.

[3] I acknowledge my debt to M. Douglas and C. Lévi-Strauss for the preceding.

skin of a man exhibits white *pusu*-areas, or is dotted with *nuqdu*-dots, such a man has been rejected by his god and is (to be) rejected by mankind".[1] A Neo-Assyrian text offers a convincing parallel to this, which shows that this sort of diagnostic omen was a persistent element in the omen tradition: "If a man has the surface of his flesh covered with black and white spots, the disease is the mamitu *(curse/tabu)*.[2]

In Israel, in connexion with a case of "leprosy" which was discovered in a house, the procedure called for the attending priest to scrape off the offending patch, along with the plaster beneath it, to dispose of the removed material, and then to replaster the surface (Lev 14.41-42). As the reader may recall, the Assyrian *namburbi* incantations were defensive-magical rituals dating from the first millennium for repelling the threat of a bad portent, usually of the omens contained in the *šumma ālu* series. Several of these offer fairly precise parallels to Lev 14.41-42:

> To avert the evil portended by *katarru*-fungus, that it may not approach a man: you make seven knives of tamarisk. . . (another reads): To avert the evil portended by fungus, with a copper knife: You *plaster* with. . . (yet another quotes the omen itself before proceeding to prescribe the appropriate treatment): If there is fungus in a man's house, on the outer north wall, the lord of the house will die and his house will be scattered. To avert the evil you. . . (finally): If there is fungus on the outer east wall, the lady of the house will die, and that house will be scattered. To avert its evil, you *scrape off the fungus* with an axe of poplar. . . .[3]

These examples should suffice to indicate that both physiognomic and diagnostic omens were well known in ancient Israel, sufficiently so in fact as to have left their mark in the chronographic, Wisdom, and legal corpora.

Finally, there are two classes of omens which, as we have seen, were staples of the Mesopotamian tradition and yet which are only

---

[1] F. Köcher and A.L. Oppenheim, "The OB Omen Text VAT 7525"; here obv. col.II, lines 42-45; text and trans. p .66.

[2] AMT 15,3:16; cited in the *CAD*, sub *mamitu*.

[3] Published by R. Caplice in *Or* N.S. 40 (1971), pp. 144-46; the examples offered here are not exhaustive: this was a common sort of portent with a common sort of remedy.

marginally attested in the Israelite-Jewish literature. These are the classes of *misbirth*-omens (*izbus*) and, more importantly, *astrology*. As far as the former class of omens is concerned, it is significant that most *izbus* are, biologically considered, simply spontaneous abortions caused by defective fetus-formation.[1] This means that the corresponding Hebrew term for *izbu* could have been מַשְׁכֵּלָה, "misbirth"; the term, however, does not occur in significant contexts in the Old Testament. Of perhaps more interest is Rebekah's consultation with the diviner in Gen 25.22. Here the text informs us that, "The children struggled together within her" (וַיִּתְרֹצְצוּ הַבָּנִים בְּקִרְבָּהּ). The phenomenology should be clear in this instance; Rebekah has felt or heard some inexplicable "sign" in her innards, and accordingly visits the appropriate specialist to secure its interpretation. In this connexion it might be interesting to discover that the first four omens in the omen series *šumma siništu arratma*, the counterpart of *šumma izbu* (it deals mainly with monstrous human births, rather than animal births, as in *šumma izbu*) have to do with portents experienced in the course of pregnancy, rather than with monstrous births as such.[2] In addition to this observation we can adduce the results arrived at by P.A. Porter in a recent study of the various extraordinary monsters envisioned in Daniel 7-8.[3] Porter's brief study enquires into the significance of the teratological metaphors in these chapters, in part on the basis of M. Black's now-famous contributions to the study of the concept of metaphor. Porter determines that the chapters in question, as well as visionary sequences in Ethiopic Enoch, the Testament of Joseph and, of course, Revelation reveal an extraordinary parallelism between the monsters described and the political situations to which they correspond, on the one hand, and various portents recorded in *šumma izbu* with their (largely political) prognostics, on the other. There is, then, a body of

---

[1] Cf. e.g. R. Passmore and J.S. Robson (eds.), *A Companion to Medical Studies* (Oxford, London et al., 1979), Vol.II, section 42.2: "There is. . . a close affinity between abortion, defective embryogenesis, and teratogenesis". See further E. Leichty, *The Omen Series Šumma Izbu*, pp. 16-18.

[2] Cf. Leichty, *Šumma Izbu*, p. 32 = Tablet I, 1-4.

[3] P.A. Porter, *Metaphors and Monsters. A Literary-Critical Study of Daniel 7 and 8* (Uppsala, 1983) (= *Coniectanea Biblica*. Old Testament Series 20).

evidence to the effect that the Israelites also knew of portents of the *šumma izbu* (misbirth) type, although the bulk of the evidence in question is very late indeed.

As far as *astrology* is concerned, there is not much room for doubt that the Israelites neither practised it, nor, more to the point, did they have the resources to pursue astrological endeavours in a serious way. As the studies of Oppenheim, Parpola, and Sachs-Hunger referred to previously have shown, the first-millennium practice of astrology in Mesopotamia (and particularly in Assyria, from which most of our records have come) required an extensive apparatus of specialists reporting on the various astronomical and meteorological phenomena for the benefit of the crown. Moreover, in spite of the protests of those scholars who would prefer to see in ancient astronomy the predecessor of the modern study of the heavens, and who accordingly would like to see ancient astronomy and astrology kept separate, in actual fact at least the Assyrian astrologers were versed in the astronomical lore of their day, as an aid to observation. It is doubtful whether ancient Israel possessed at any time in her history the resources to support a class of specialists devoted to this sort of specialty. Convincing evidence of this fact is provided by the modern studies on the ancient Israelite calendar, as these have shown that the Israelites utilised calendars of 360 days, 365 days, and 364 days, and that the community at Qumran was prepared to argue for the adequacy of the 364-day calendar as late as the first century AD.[1] This would not have been possible in a society in which astronomical observation was undertaken on a systematic basis. In Mesopotamia, observational astronomers had discovered the actual length of the year already in the second millennium. Thus, attempts were made, though on an unsystematic basis, to correct the lunar calendar normally in use so as to harmonise with the solar calendar,

---

[1] See, once again, my previously-mentioned articles in *SJOT* (1 [1987], pp. 116-22; 2 [1987], pp. 18-23), and my article in *Bib* 66 (1985), pp. 241-61. For extra-Biblical evidence, see the fine, though regrettably unpublished study by J. Rook, *Studies in the Book of Jubilees: The Themes of Calendar, Genealogy and Chronology*, thesis presented for the degree of Doctor of Philosophy at the University of Oxford, 1984, esp. pp. 34-38 and 70-72, and see already Rook's brief but useful article, "A Twenty-eight-day Month Tradition in the Book of Jubilees", *VT* 31 (1981), pp. 83-87.

though the task was not settled satisfactorily before around the fifth century BC. It would only have been possible for the Israelites to reject the Mesopotamian calendrical reckonings if they were acquainted with them solely as abstract numbers, rather than as the results of reliable observations. And since they very clearly *did* reject them, it is evident that the Israelites had no astronomers, and hence no astrologers, except perhaps on a very primitive and *ad hoc* basis. I am accordingly prepared to agree with J. McKay, who concludes that, "the Israelites. . . had their own astral lore, and venerated the stars in a fairly popular and superstitious manner. . . ."[1]

This insight into the lack of an Israelite astrology perhaps explains the repeated and explicit prophetic jibes and attacks on Assyro-Babylonian astrology (e.g., Isa 47.12-13; Jer 10.2), although the other forms of Mesopotamian divination receive only indirect comment (notably Ezekiel's reference to Nebuchadnezzar's extispicy in 21.21 [Heb. 21.26] contains not a hint of *criticism* of the "liver examination" he mentions; in fact, the text presupposes that the king receives a valid answer, as he is about Yahweh's business of punishing Israel).

By way of summary, then, we may conclude that Israelite literature makes conscious use of various features of all of the major genres of Mesopotamian divination literature, with the single exception of literature on astrology; references to these traditions, either oblique or virtually verbatim, recur across the spectrum of Israelite literature. Their function is in many cases to legitimate or enhance the authority of one or another Israelite figure or practice. In others, as in the "physiognomic" references to Saul and Absalom, it serves to foreshadow ironically the coming developments in the narratives in question. In the Wisdom materials, divination is linked to moralising guidelines for

---

[1] J. McKay, *Religion in Judah under the Assyrians* (London, 1973), p. 48; H. Spieckermann, *Juda unter Assur in der Sargonidenzeit* (Göttingen, 1982), p. 271 claims that the Israelite worship of "the son, the moon and the host of heaven", so often criticised by the Deuteronomist, and which is supposed to have been halted by Josiah (2 Kgs 23.5), whose reform "Points in its individual elements to an Assyrian origin, in which connexion the corresponding cult practised in the Jerusalem temple, not unlike that in Assyria, implies the observation of the stars for the purposes of divination". Spieckermann has simply not considered the amount of resources necessary to the task.

ordering one's life. Finally, in such "legal" contexts as Lev 13-14 a widely-disseminated tradition as to the import of certain diagnostic signs has simply been adopted and *ad hoc* assimilated to Israelite conceptions of purity. The depth and breadth of Israelite knowledge about divination is everywhere evident, even if the Israelite literature only betrays the extent of such knowledge when it is examined closely.

CONCLUSION

The first conclusion that the study presented in these pages compels us to draw is that *ancient Israel was a "magic society"*, like those around her, and similar in many respects to any number of magic-using "savage" societies which modern social anthropology has studied.

The texts presuppose that divination was used to enquire in cases of illness, to determine whether or not to undertake a venture (often a military campaign, but the idea is presumably a generalisation of more prosaic usage), to determine whether or not it was safe to undertake a journey, to enquire as to certain features of a pregnancy, to allay fears in pressing situations, to determine the cause of present misery, and so on. In short, Israelite divination corresponded broadly in the range of its uses to the utilisation of divination in Mesopotamia and elsewhere in the Near Eastern environment.

We have no indication that divination was normally performed in extended sequences of oracular enquiries, as in the Hittite kingdom; on the other hand, a few passages, such as the Achan narrative in Joshua 7, suggest that Israelite divination could be used in a juridical fashion. This procedure was common in Egypt, whereas in Mesopotamia it was solely the province of the *ordeal*, a practice which is only rarely attested. Precisely in Joshua 7, however, and in its companion-piece, 1 Sam 10.17-27, we find juridical divination wedded to extended sequences of enquiries. Whether this is purely a literary invention which answers to the needs of the respective narrative situations (i.e., the need to separate a single individual from the masses of Israel), or whether it actually reflects some hybrid, originally Israelite institution, is impossible to say, given the state of the evidence.

It was noted in conjunction with the examination of the "Urim and Thummim", which I regard as a late catch-all invention designed to symbolise the entire practice of cultic divination, that the practice is explicitly subordinated to the juridical metaphor which was the common ideological foundation of ancient Near Eastern divination in general. This will no doubt also have been true of earlier practices. In Israel, as I have mentioned, this conception was wedded to the notion of the

"Divine Council", and it is therefore unsurprising that we find (prophetic) divination conjoined with the idea of the "council" in the famous Micaiah ben-Imlah narrative in 1 Kgs 22. However late this narrative may ultimately prove to be, there is no reason to doubt that it faithfully reflects at least this traditional understanding of the juridico-theistic basis of Israelite divination.

As far as the *actors* are concerned who engaged in Israelite divination, the texts in their present state attempt sharply to distinguish between priestly and prophetic divination. However, as I have pointed out, there is no reason to suppose that this distinction was anywhere near as sharply drawn in ancient Israelite society as the Old Testament will have us believe. Prophets, too, will certainly have practised "technical" divination, as a considerable number of passages allow us to infer (mainly those referring to prophetic *adannus*). But in addition to the assumption that divination was practised by both priests and prophets, I have pointed to considerable knowledge on the part of Israelite narrators and their audience of various features deriving from the traditions of dream interpretation, signs of the *šumma ālu* type, physiognomic and diagnostic omens, as well as the speech omen (*egirru*). References to all these phenomena occur in all genres of Israelite literature, from Wisdom to legal materials, and also in the chronographic literature. This implies that many of these practices will have been practised at the popular level, which allows us to suppose that there was a broad base of magical usage in Israelite society. It is against this background that the references to priestly and prophetic divination must be understood.

It was shown in my cursory presentation of the Azande that the upper echelons of Zande society were openly contemptuous of much of the magic that was embraced by their social inferiours, and that far less magic was practised at the top than at the bottom of society. By the same token, those magics which were embraced by Azande leaders were assumed *apriori* to be highly efficacious, with the prince's poison oracle as the ultimate symbol. Thus we may conclude that the omen sacrifice, which appears to lie behind the descriptions of priestly usage in the Books of Samuel and Judges, was such an "élite" oracle. Contrariwise, the "popular" varieties, knowledge of which is everywhere presupposed in the narrative literature and elsewhere, reflect the broad stream of popular usage.

As far as the *historical development of Israelite divination* is concerned, we have very little precise information. The Deuteronomist and the Priestly Writer will have us believe that Israel banned all forms of divination except for the priestly oracle and prophecy at an early date. We have seen that this cannot possibly have been the case, as even the relatively late Deuteronomistic and post-Deuteronomistic chronographic literature contains a plethora of references to the main genres of the Mesopotamian tradition. We have also seen that there is no reason to believe that the various phenomena which the Israelites banned as "practices of the peoples" were actually derived from Israel's neighbours. The terminology employed, at least, almost without exception has to be regarded as domestic, originally Israelite; hence, the practices in question no doubt were, too. How are these facts to be reconciled with one another? I should like to emphasise that on this point we are at the level of historical conjecture pure and simple, even if it is to some extent informed by historical and social anthropological analogy.

We have seen that it commonly occurs in magic-using societies that there is an "oracle of last resort", that is, one which validates or invalidates the results of other methods. This is no doubt much more frequently the case in hierarchically, centrally organised societies than in "akephalous" ones, to use a bit of jargon that has crept into the sociological discussion of state-formation. After all, a hierarchy has need of sanction to undergird its authority, and a single determining oracle would eliminate ambiguity and the possibility of dissatisfaction.

Since, as I have pointed out previously, divination is always assumed to *work* in magic-using societies, it is regarded as generating real *knowledge*. Moreover, access to knowledge is restricted in all societies, whether primitive or no, as knowledge is a scarce commodity. Access to it therefore accords with the power and status relationships in society. That this was true in ancient Mesopotamia I have already shown; both the ancient Marians and, a millennium later, the Assyrians seem to have been most insistent on reserving a virtual monopoly on mantic knowledge to the crown. The Old Testament informs us that this was also the case in ancient Israel: Saul is not only said to have driven out the diviners and necromancers, but also to have slaughtered the priests who had dared to provide his rival, David, with mantic information. It is interesting that the text in question, 1 Sam 22.17-19, makes no comment on the massacre in question; it simply records that, "Nob, the city of the priests, he put to the sword; both men and women, children and sucklings, oxen, asses and sheep, he put to the sword". Modern commentators, unable to imagine that the Bible can refer uncensoriously to such slaughter, have often provided the censure themselves.[1] This is uncalled-for, however; Saul is merely doing what the narrator assumes should be done to anyone practising illicit, that is, unsanctioned, divination. And the further history of the priestly oracle attaches it firmly, as we have seen, to the centre of political power in Israel. Moreover, as far as the type of divination known as prophecy is concerned, the Old Testament records that attempts were made to muzzle it either by priests (Amaziah vs. Amos in Amos 7.10-17; Jeremiah versus the "priests and prophets", Jer 26.11) or by the crown (Jehoiachim versus Uriah, Jer 26.20-23; Zedekiah versus Jeremiah, Jer 36.20-26, etc.). All this is consonant with the practice in every society which uses divination, from the Azande to ancient Assyria: divination is invariably brought into line with existing authority structures.

It is in this light, then, that we must understand the Deuteronomistic and Priestly strictures against certain forms of divination: not, as scholarship has traditionally assumed, as a blanket prohibition of the practice of divination, but as a means of restricting the practice to those who were "entitled" to employ it, that is, to the central cult figures who enjoyed the warrants of power, prestige and, not least, education, as at least the "élite" forms of divination were very much the privilege of the tiny literate stratum in ancient Near Eastern societies. I suspect that historically these must have been the religious leaders who were responsible for transforming Israelite religion into the early Judaism of the post-exilic period.

This conjecture has some inherent plausibility. We have seen that already Blau lamented that after the exile the Jews speedily "declined" to the practice of divination, in spite of the bitter lessons that their experience prior to the exile "should" have taught them. In fact, as we have seen, the Talmuds, particularly the *Talmud Babili*, are full of references to rabbinical magic and divination. As I have mentioned

---

[1] Cf. e.g. H.W. Hertzberg, *Die Samuelbücher* (Göttingen, 1973) (= *ATD* 10), p. 152: "This is open war against the servants of the Lord, that is, against God himself. . . ."

previously, at least one of the early rabbis actually practised the interpretation of dreams for a living, and did not seem to find this to clash with his understanding of scripture. Recent studies have brought a number of indications to light that the post-exilic tradition in fact continued to practise divination and other magics in many forms. Indeed, P. Schäfer has recently spoken of the surviving documents of Jewish magic from antiquity and the early middle ages as "an immense quantity, tremendous both in number and variety, of fragments in the Hebrew, Aramaic, Arabic, Judeo-Arabic, Judeo-Spanish, Judeo-Persian and Syrian languages".[1] Moreover, it was at this time that Babylonian astrology finally made some converts in Israel.[2] Indeed, it was also at this time that the diviner's techniques of interpreting the "signs" of the phenomenal world were transferred to the interpretation of scripture itself within mainstream Jewish exegesis.[3] Since, as is widely acknowledged, not everyone in post-exilic Judaism was convinced that God had ceased to utter revelation to his people, divination persisted, although not to the extent that it had before the canon began to take shape. Furthermore, since the main tradition continued to consult oracles, at least on occasion, the sectarian movements did so as well; indeed, as I have mentioned, the early apocalypticists seem to have had a somewhat higher evaluation of divination than did the mainstream of early Judaism.[4] Nothing testifies more eloquently to the fact that the Priestly and Deuteronomistic prohibitions were *not* regarded as total

---

[1] Cf. P.Schäfer, "Jewish Magic Literature in Late Antiquity and Early Middle Ages", *JJS* 41 (1990), pp. 75-91, here p.76.

[2] Cf. D.C. Duling, "The Eleazar Miracle and Solomon's Magical Wisdom in Flavius Josephus's *Antiquitates Judaicae* 8.42-49", *HTR* 78 (1985), pp. 1-25; J.C. Greenfield and M. Sokoloff, "Astrological and Related Omen Texts in Jewish Palestinian Aramaic", *JNES* 48 (1989), pp. 201-204. P.Kuhn's *Offenbarungsstimmen im Antiken Judentum. Untersuchungen zur* bat qol *und verwandten Phänomenen (= Texte und Studien zum Antiken Judentum 20)* (Tübingen, 1989), pp. 281-85, points to the survival of the speech omen (Akk. *egirru,* Greek *kledon*) in rabbinical tradition.

[3] See J. Tigay, "Aggadic Exegesis", in H. Tadmor and M. Weinfeld (eds.), *History, Historiography and Interpretation. Studies in Biblical and Cuneiform Literatures* (Leiden/Jerusalem, 1984), pp. 169-190, esp. p.173.

[4] See J.C. Vanderkam, *Enoch and the Growth of an Apocalyptic Tradition* (Washington, 1984), pp. 62-76.

than the discovery of texts dealing with divination among the extreme legalists of Qumran. Taken together, these facts very much suggest that the Pentateuchal prohibitions on the practice of divination and other magics were not aimed, or were not construed to be aimed, at the cult leaders.

These observations allow us to conclude that Israelite divination was traditionally hierarchically organised, with many competing forms of divination of varying authority at low levels of society, and a few central instances of officially sanctioned and hence authoritative divination at the centres of power. Anti-divination legislation in the law codes represents an attempt at a late date to ensure that, ultimately, communication with the divine remained a privilege of the religious leadership. This may have been necessitated by the demise of the monarchy; with no unquestioned central authority, it must have become a pressing concern to preserve the religious hierarchy's traditional grasp on the means of revelation. This may serve to account for the disappearance of the omen sacrifice in Israel. Elsewhere in the ancient Near East, at least in the first millennium, extispicy had become an almost exclusively royal undertaking: a fact that must have been as much economically as ideologically motivated (sheep are expensive). Thus, without the need to make "enquiries" on behalf of the crown (we should recall that extispicy figured very largely in conjunction with the military projects of the crown, which will naturally have been an irrelevancy in post-exilic Israel), it must have been difficult, as well as pointless, to maintain the apparatus that served it.

At the *conceptual* level, the brief study offered previously of the popular Israelite understanding of the "changer" as someone destined for destruction points to the central conceptual problem which was addressed by the practice of divination in the ancient Near East. This is the problem of *change* in the phenomenal world. We noted in our all-too cursory examination of the Assyriological study of the omen sacrifice that what the diviner presupposed was a sort of "ideal" set of viscera in his sheep. Thus, any sort of deviation, that is, *change*, was understood as a message which had been inscribed in the sheep by the gods in answer to the enquirer's question. This insight can be extended to cover most other forms of so-called "technical" divination: even the random signs recorded in *šumma ālu* represent unexpected and unusual phenomena: three snakes intertwined on the path, a wild animal entering a town, and so on. And it equally clearly applies to astrology and its preoccupation with "changes"in the "signs"in the heavens—or, more precisely, only the changes were in fact "signs".

Ancient Near Eastern divination presupposed, then, a sort of standard "world" in which a certain set of expectations obtained. If one encountered some variation on these expectations, this was by definition a "change", and hence was susceptible of interpretation as a divine message of some sort. In this connexion it is significant that various Akkadian verbs for "change" frequently figure in the apodoses of omen texts, where they invariably signify something unpleasant.[1] It was through the device of the *pars familiaris—pars hostilis* system of "transformations", as the structuralists would call them, that it became possible to interpret such "changes" as applying either to the enquirer or to his opponent. This perception of the world did not descend from heaven like Sumerian kingship; it evolved through time, like other historical manifestations. We have seen, for example, that it was eventually realised that illness represents a diametrically opposite "sign" from health; therefore an apodosis which was normally positive for a healthy man became an unfortunate portent for a sick one, and so on, in the Cassite period and later.

Seen against this background, it is hardly surprising that a man who "changes" was understood in Israel and elsewhere in the ancient Near East to be doomed; he was the very incarnation of that mutability of the world which the ominous tradition found so threatening. In their attempts to deal with the problem of change in the phenomenal world, the Near Eastern diviners anticipated the preoccupation of the pre-socratic philosophers with the same problem. However, as I have repeatedly stressed, the approach to such problems in the realm of Semitic thought was piecemeal and pragmatic, rather than systematic;

---

[1] For example, *šumma ālu* offers some thirty-odd examples, such as "if a god approaches a wolf (sexually), the lord of the field will change (išanni^{ni}), this city (presumably, 'will be destroyed', or the like). . ." (Nötscher, *Or* 51-54 [1930], p. 162); "if a palmtree has two 'crowns' and these are bowned down, change of plans (nu-kur milki), change of mind/report/plan (šan^e temi)" (the same, p. 103); for extispicy, see e.g., "if the 'palace gate' is twice present, and if they press upon each other, the vizir will change (iš-te-ne-e) the throne of his lord" (YOS 10.24.2); "if the 'neck' of the lung has turned about, the plan (te$_4$-e-em) of the country will continually change (iš-ta-na-an-ni)(YOS 10.36. IV.25f.)".

there was never any idea of generalising the observations in the omen literature to a universal understanding of world processes or underlying principles.

It is vital that we acknowledge that the "world" which the ancient Near Eastern diviner, including, naturally, the Israelite diviner, presupposed was not *our* world; rather, it was the world as presented to him in his socially mediated network of symbolisations. The juridical metaphor mentioned above was only *one* of the principles which served to order and categorise this symbol system; there were many, and the investigation of these is in its infancy, both in Assyriological and in Old Testament research. But it is a fact that the diviner's world differed immensely from ours. His was, after all, a world in which it was meaningful to claim that a sheep could have survived and grown to maturity, and hence could be available for the omen sacrifice without a heart, a liver, kidneys, or whatever; or that a sow could bear a litter of sixteen; or that a woman could give birth to eight or nine children at one go; or, in Israel, that the sun could stand still, or go backwards, or that an axehead could float.

These observations mean that the attempt to reconstruct the conceptual framework within which ancient Israelite divination took place entails the recognition that ancient Israel was a far more "primitive" society than modern western theology has so far been inclined to acknowledge. No society in which divination and other magics are prominent practices has arrived at a stringent understanding of cause and effect which in any way corresponds to the understanding(s) of causation adhered to in "empirically" orientated societies. Rather, cause and effect blur together in many instances; so, for example, it was possible in ancient Mesopotamia to confuse an *egirru*-omen, which we would be inclined to regard as a simple prediction, with a *curse* which was held to *cause* the effect it mentions. Or, there are multiple "causes", one human and one divine, or diabolical, or whatever: in any case, a variant of philosophical over-determination, which is simply nonsense within our framework of thought. Or, what we should regard as the "empirical" cause receives scant attention, if any, as the phenomenon in question is entirely subjectively defined (one thinks of Castaneda's man-who-flies-like-a-man-who-has-been-turned-into-a-bird). If, at the beginning of this study, I was rather critical of attempts to characterise Israelite and other writing in the ancient world about the past as "historical" writing, it is partially because of this very fact. Scholars who maintain that the difference between such a world-view and a "modern" one is only a question of degree or a matter of precision, or whatever, have simply not understood the epistemological issues involved. The difference is absolute, and it is a prime goal of the ancient historian to seek to determine in each case the *mode* of relationship to the past evinced by the ancient text under study. Failure to acknowledge the different modalities of concern with the past which may be present in ancient texts forces the scholar to substitute, often unconsciously, the assumptions of his own time, or some derivation of them, for the phenomenon under study.

In the domain of the history of ideas, it is interesting to recall that the version of Ptolemaic astronomy-astrology which was embraced in Western Europe in the late Middle Ages and the Renaissance repre-sented a marriage of Aristotelianism with astronomy. This view main-tained that the heavens above the orbit of the moon were unalterable, sublime and perfect in the repetition of their courses, whereas the sublunary realm, where man resides, was the precinct of "mutability".[1] By that time, however, mutability had acquired the sense of bewildering, self-contradictory and senseless multiplicity, ultimately without significance, which is why men looked for divine guidance, not on earth, but in the serene realm of the upper sphere. As is well known, it took the appearance of Tycho Brahe's "nova stella" in 1572—*above* the orbit of the moon—to prove that the heavens were not exempt from change,[2] and that change had accordingly to be taken seriously, as the diviners had all along insisted. But that is another story.

[1] See T.S. Kuhn, *The Copernican Revolution. Planetary Astronomy in the Development of Western Thought* (New York and Toronto, 1959 [1957]), pp. 82-84 (on the sublunary realm).

[2] Kuhn, *The Copernican Revolution*, pp. 206-7 (on the "new star").

SELECTED LITERATURE

Adorno, T. W., et al., *Der Positivismusstreit in der deutschen Soziologie*. Darmstadt and Neuwied, 1969; repr. 1972

Ahern, E.M., "The Problem of Efficacy: Strong and Weak Illocutionary Acts", *Man* 14 (1979), pp. 1-17.

— "Rules in Oracles and Games", *Man* NS 17 (1982), pp. 302-313.

Ahlström, G., *Syncretism in Israelite Religion*. Lund, 1963.

Aistleitner, J., *Wörterbuch der ugaritischen Sprache*. Berlin, 1963.

Alster, B. (ed.), *Dumuzi's Dream. Aspects of Oral Poetry in a Sumerian Myth*. Copenhagen, 1972 (= Mesopotamia 1).

— *The Instructions of Suruppak. A Sumerian Proverb Collection*. Copenhagen, 1974.

— *Studies in Sumerian Proverbs*. Copenhagen, 1975.

— *Death in Mesopotamia. XXVIe Rencontre assyriologique internationale*. Copenhagen, 1980.

Anatolian Studies Presented to Hans Gustav Güterbock on the Occasion of his 65th Birthday. Istanbul, 1974.

Anderson, G.A., *Sacrifices and Offerings in Ancient Israel. Studies in their Social and Political Importance*. Atlanta, 1987.

Archi, A., "Il sistema KIN della divinazione ittita", *OA* 13 (1974), pp. 113-144.

— "L'Ornitomanzia ittita", *Studi micenei ed egeo-anatolici* 16 (1975), pp. 119-180.

— "Hethitische Orakeltexte", in *Keilschrifturkunden aus Boghazköi*, (pub.) *Deutsche Akademie der Wissenschaften*, Nrs. 49 (1979), 50 (1979), 52 (1983), Berlin.

Artzi, P., (and Mrs.Warda Lask), "'The King and the Evil Portending, Ominous Sign in His House' (EA 358)", in Nissen, H.-J. and Renger, J. (eds.), *Mesopotamien und seine Nachbarn*, Teil 1, pp. 317-20.

Assmann, J., *Ägypten. Theologie und Frömmigkeit einer frühen Hochkultur*. Stuttgart, Berlin et al., 1984.

Baines, J., "Literacy and Ancient Egyptian Society", *Man*, 18 (1983), pp. 572-99.

Barkay, G., *Ketef Hinnom. A Treasure Facing Jerusalem's Walls*. Jerusalem, 1986.

Barnes, H.E., *A History of Historical Writing*. Toronto and London, 1963.

Barstad, H.M., *The Religious Polemics of Amos*. Leiden, 1984.

Barta, W., "Zur Entwicklung des ägyptischen Kalenderwesens", *ZÄS* 110 (1983), pp. 16-26.

— "No Prophets? Recent Developments in Biblical Prophetic Research and Ancient Near Eastern Prophecy", *JSOT* 57 (1993), pp. 39-60.

Bartlett, J.R., *Edom and the Edomites*. Sheffield, 1989.

Bascom, W., *Ifa Divination. Communication Between Gods and Men in West Africa*. Bloomington and London, 1969.

Baudissen, W.W., *Die Geschichte des Alttestamentlichen Priestertums*. Leipzig, 1889.

Beard, M., (and J. North), *Pagan Priests. Religion and Power in the Ancient World*. London, 1990.

Beatty, J., "Sorcery in Bunyoro", in Middleton, J. and Winter, E.H. (eds.), *Witchcraft and Sorcery in East Africa*, pp. 29-30.

Beckman, G., "Mesopotamians and Mesopotamian Learning at Hattusa", *JCS* 35 (1983), pp. 97-114.

Begrich, J., "Das priesterliche Heilsorakel", *ZAW* 52 (1934), pp. 81-92.

— "Die priesterliche Tora", *BZAW* 66 (1936), pp. 63-88 = *Gesammelte Studien zum Alten Testament*. Munich, 1964, pp. 232-60.

Bengtson, H., *Einführung in die Alte Geschichte*. 8. Aufl., 1979.

Bennett, G., *Traditions of Belief. Women and the Supernatural*. London and Harmondsworth, 1987.

Berger, P. (and Luckmann, T.) *The Social Construction of Reality*. New York, 1967.

— "Sociology of Religion and Sociology of Knowledge", in R. Robertson (ed.) *Sociology of Religion*. Harmondsworth, 1976, pp. 61-73.

Bergman, J., *Die Metallzeitliche Revolution: Zur Ensteheung von Herrschaft, Krieg und Umweltzerstörung*. Berlin, 1987.

Bergsträßer, G., *Einführung in die semitischen Sprachen*. 3rd. ed., Munich, 1928; repr. Darmstadt, 1977.

Berthelot, R., *La Pensée de l'Asie et l'Astrobiologie. Les origines des sciences et des religions supérieures...*. Paris, 1949.

Biggs, R.D., *ša.zi.ga: Ancient Mesopotamian Potency Incantations*. Locust Valley, 1967 (*TCS* Vol. 2).

— "More Babylonian 'Prophecies'", *Iraq* 29 (1967), pp. 117-132.

— "A propos des textes de libanomancie", *RA* 63 (1969), pp. 73-74.

— "Qutnu, masrahu and related terms in Babylonian extispicy", *RA* 63 (1969), pp. 159-167.

— "A Babylonian Extispicy Text Concerning Holes", *JNES* 33 (1974), pp. 351-58.

— "The Babylonian Prophecies and the Astrological Traditions of Mesopotamia", *JCS* 37 (1985), pp. 86-90.

Binford, L., "Contemporary Model-Building: Paradigms and the Current State of Palaeolithic Research", in Clarke, D. (ed.), *Models in Archaeology*. London, 1972, pp. 109-66.

—and Binford, S.R., *New Perspectives in Archaeology*. Aldine, 1968.

Bin-Nun, S.R., "Some Remarks on Hittite Oracles, Dreams and Omina", *Or* N.S. 48 (1979), pp. 118-27.

Biç, M., "Der Prophet Amos—ein Haepatoskopos", *VT* 1 (1951), pp. 293-96.

Black, M.B., "Belief Systems", in Honigmann, J.J. (ed.), *Handbook of Social and Cultural Anthropology*, pp. 509-77.

Blau, L., *Das altjüdische Zauberwesen*. Budapest, 1898 (repr. Westmead, England, 1970).

Boissier, A., *Mantique Babylonienne et Mantique Hittite*. Paris, 1935.

Bokser, B.M., "Wonder-Working and the Rabbinic Tradition: the Case of Hanina ben Dosa", *JSJ*, 16 (1985), pp. 42-92.

Borger, R., "Gott Marduk and Gott-König Sulgi als Propheten", *BO* 28 (1971), pp. 3-24.

Borowski, O., *Agriculture in Iron Age Israel: the Evidence from Archaeology and the Bible*. Winona Lake (Indiana), 1987.

Braudel, F., "History and Sociology" in the same, *On History*. Chicago, 1980, pp. 64-82.

Bruck, A., "Neue Überlegungen zum Konzept der Funktion", *ZfE* 113 (1988), pp. 1-20.

Brunner, H., *Altägyptische Religion. Grundzüge*. 2nd edn Darmstadt, 1989.

Bryce, G.E., "Omen Wisdom in Ancient Israel", *JBL* 94 (1975), pp. 19-37.

Budge, E.A.W., *Egyptian Magic*. London, 1901; repr. New York, 1971.
—*Amulets and Superstitions*. Oxford, 1930, repr. New York, 1978.

Burstein, S.M., *The Babyloniaca of Berossus*. Malibu (Calif.), 1978 (= Sources and Monographs. Sources from the Ancient Near East, Vol.1, Fasc.5).

Campanile, E., et al. *Bilinguismo e biculturalismo nel mondo antico*. Atti del colloquio interdisciplinare tenuto a Pisa il 28 e 29 settembre. Pisa, 1988.

Caplice, R., "Namburbi Texts in the British Museum", *Or* N.S. 34 (1965), pp. 105-31; 36 (1967), pp. 1-38; pp. 273-98; 39 (1970), pp. 111-51; 40 (1971), pp. 133-83; 42 (1973), pp. 508-17.

— *The Akkadian Namburbi Texts: An Introduction*. Los Angeles, 1974 (=Sources and Monographs. Sources from the Ancient Near East, Vol.1, fasc.1).

Caquot, A. (and Leibovici, M., eds.), *La Divination*. Vol.1, Paris, 1968.

Cassin, E., Bottéro, J., Vercoutter, J. (eds.), *Die Altorientalischen Reiche*, I-III. Frankfurt am Main, 1965-1967 (repr.1980-1984).

Castaneda, C., *The Teachings of Don Juan: A Yaqui Way of Knowledge*, (orig.pub. 1972), repr. Harmondsworth, 1973.

Centre d'Etudes Supérieures Spécialisé d'Histoire des Religions de Strasbourg (ed.), *La Divination en Mésopotamie Ancienne et dansles Régions Voisines (= DM)* (=XIVe Rencontre Assyriologique Internationale). Paris, 1966.

Charpin, D., "Les Archives du Devin Asqudum dans la Résidence du 'Chantier A'", *M.A.R.I.* 4 (1985), pp. 453-62.

— et al., *Archives Epistolaires de Mari* I/1-2. Paris, 1988.

Childe, V.G., *Social Evolution*. London, 1951.

—*What Happened in History*. orig. pub. 1945, repr. Harmondsworth, 1982.

Childs, B.S., *Introduction to the Old Testament as Scripture*. London, 1979.

Cicero, Marcus Tullius, *De Divinatione*. text and Eng. trans. by W.A. Falconer, London and Cambridge, (MA), 1964.

Cicourel, A.V., *Cognitive Sociology. Language and Meaning in Social Interaction*. New York, 1974.

Codrington, R.H., *The Melanesians*. Oxford, 1891.

Cogan, M., "Omens and Ideology in the Babylon Inscription of Esarhaddon", in: (eds.) Tadmor, H. and Weinfeld, M., *History, Historiography and Interpretation*, pp. 72-83.

Cohen, H.R. ("Chaim"), *Biblical Hapax Legomena in the Light of Akkadian and Ugaritic*. Missoula (Montana), 1978 (= *SBL Diss. Series* 37).

Collingwood, R.G., *The Idea of History*. 1946, repr. Oxford, 1970.

Conrad, D., "An Introduction to the Archaeology of Syria and Palestine on the Basis of the Israelite Settlement"; Appendix 1 in J.A.Soggin, *A History of Ancient Israel*, Philadelphia, 1984, pp. 357-367.

Contenau, G., *La Divination chez les Assyriens et les Babyloniens*. Paris, 1940.

Cooper, D.E., "Alternative Logic in 'Primitive Thought'", *Man* 10 (1975), pp. 238-256.

Cooper, J., "Apodictic Death and the Historicity of 'Historical' Omens", in Alster, B. (ed.), *Death in Mesopotamia*, pp. 99-105.

Coote, R.B., (and Whitelam, K.W.), *The Emergence of Early Israel in Historical Perspective*. Sheffield, 1987 (The Social World of Biblical Antiquity Series, 5).

Craigie, P.G., "Amos the noqed in the light of Ugaritic", *Science Religieuse/Studies in Religion* 11 (1982), pp. 29-33.

Crenshaw, J.L., "Method in Determining Wisdom Influence upon 'Historical' Literature", *JBL* 88 (1969), pp. 129-42.

Cross, F.M., *Canaanite Myth and Hebrew Epic*. London and Cambridge (Mass.), 1973.

Cryer, F.H., "On the Relationship Between the Yahwistic and the Deuteronomistic Histories", *BN* 29 (1985), pp. 58-73.

— "The Interrelationships of Gen 5,32; 11,10-11 and the Chronology of the Flood", *Bib* 66 (1985), pp. 241-61.

—"The 360-Day Calendar Year and Early Judaic Sectarianism", *SJOT* 1 (1987), pp. 116-22.

—"To the One of Fictive Music: OT Chronology and History", *SJOT* 2 (1987), pp. 1-27.

—"Der Prophet und der Magier. Bemerkungen anhand einer überholten Diskussion" in: (eds.) R. Liwak and S. Wagner, Festschrift Siegfried Herrmann, pp. 79-88.

Cumont, F., *Astrology and Religion Among the Greeks and Romans*. (orig.pub. 1912), repr. New York, 1960.

Çig, M., (and Kizilyay, H.), *Zwei altbabylonische Schulbücher aus Nippur*. Ankara, 1959.

Dalley, S., *Myths from Mesopotamia. Creation, The Flood, Gilgamesh and Others*, Oxford and New York, 1991.

Dandamayev, M.A., "About Life Expectancy in the First Millennium B.C.", in Alster, B., *Death in Mesopotamia*. Copenhagen, 1980, pp. 183-87.

Danto, A.C., *Narration and Knowledge. Including the Integral Text of Analytical Philosophy of History*. New York, 1985.

Davies, T. Witton, *Magic, Divination, and Demonology Among the Hebrews and their Neighbours*. London and Leipzig, 1898.

Day, J., "Prophecy", in Carson, D.A., and Williamson, H.G.M., *It is Written: Scripture Citing Scripture. Essays in Honour of Barnabas Lindars*, Cambridge, 1988, pp. 39-55.

Delekat, L., *Asylie und Schutzorakel am Zionheiligtum. Eine Untersuchung zu den privaten Feindpsalmen*. Leiden, 1967.

Denner, J., "Der assyrische Eingeweideschautext II R.43", in *WZKM* 41 (1934), pp. 180-220.

Derchain, Ph., "Essai de classement chronologique des influences Babyloniennes et Hellénistiques", in DM, pp. 146-58.

Dhorme, E., *Les Religions de Babylone et d'Assyrie*. Paris, 1949.

— *L'emploi métaphorique des noms de parties du corps en hébreu et en akkadien*. Paris, 1963.

Dietrich, M., (and Loretz, O.),"Sonnenfinsternis in Ugarit. PRU 2,162 (=RS 12.61),

Das älteste Dokument über eine Totaleklipse", in *UF* 6 (1974), pp. 464-65.

— (plus Loretz, O. and Sanmartin, J.) "Der keilalphabetische šumma izbu-text RS 24.247+265+268+328", in *UF* 7 (1979), pp. 134-40.

— (plus Hecker, K., Hoftijzer, J., Kammerzell, F., Loretz, O., Müller, W.W.), *Deutungen der Zukunft in Briefen, Orakeln und Omina*, Gütersloh, 1986 = Texte aus der Umwelt des Alten Testaments II.1).

Dietrich, W., *Prophetie und Geschichte*. Göttingen, 1972 (= *FRLANT* 108).

— *David, Saul und die Propheten. Das Verhältnis von Religion und Politik nach den prophetischen Überlieferungen vom frühesten Königtum in Israel.* Stuttgart, Berlin, et al., 1987.

Dillmann, A., *Die Genesis*, 6th ed. Leipzig, 1892.

Donner, H., (and Röllig, W.), *Kanaanäische und aramäische Inschriften*, Vol.III, Wiesbaden, 1976.

Dossin, G., "Prières aux 'Dieux de la Nuit' (AO 6769)", *RA* 32 (1935), pp. 179-87

Dover, K.J., *The Greeks and Their Legacy*. Oxford, 1988.

Dray, W.H., *On History and Philosophers of History*. Leiden, New York et al., 1989.

Driel, G. van, et al. (eds.), *Zikir Šumim. Assyriological Studies Presented to F.R. Kraus on the Occasion of his Seventieth Birthday*. Leiden, 1982.

Droysen, J.G., (ed. R. Hübner) *Historik. Vorlesungen über Enzyklopädie und Methodologie der Geschichte*, 8. Aufl., Munich, 1977.

Duling, D.C., "The Eleazar Miracle and Solomon's Magical Wisdom in Flavius Josephus's Antiquitates Judaicae 8.42-49", *HTR* 78 (1985), pp. 1-25.

Durkheim, E., *Les formes élémentaires de la vie religieuse*, Paris, 1912 (= trans. J. Swain (R. Nisbet, ed.), *The Elementary Forms of the Religious Life*. (2nd edn London, 1976).

Ebach, J., (and U. Rüterswörden), "Unterweltsbeschwörung im Alten Testament", *UF* 9 (1977), pp. 57-70 and 12 (1980), pp. 205-20.

Ehrlich, E.L., *Der Traum im Alten Testament*. Berlin, 1953 (*BZAW* 73).

Eliade, M., *The Sacred and the Profane*. New York, 1961.

Elliger, K., *Leviticus*. Tübingen, 1966 (= *HKAT* 4).

Ellis, M. de Jong (ed.), *Ancient Near Eastern Studies in Memory of J.J. Finkelstein*. Hamden (Connecticut), 1977.

— "Observations on Mesopotamian Oracles and Prophetic Texts: Literary and Historiographic Considerations", *JCS* 41/2 (1989), pp. 127-86.

Eucharisterion. Festschrift Herrmann Gunkel dargebracht. Vol. 1, Göttingen, 1923. (= *FRLANT* 19).

Evans-Pritchard, E.E., *Witchcraft, Oracles and Magic among the Azande*. Oxford,

1937; abridged edition, Oxford, 1976, repr. 1980.

— *Nuer Religion*. New York and Oxford (orig. pub. 1956), 1974.

— "Anthropology and History". 'A lecture delivered in the University of Manchester with the support of the Simon Fund for the Social Sciences'. Manchester, 1961, repr. 1971.

— *Social Anthropology and Other Essays*. Oxford, 1962; repr. New York, 1966.

— *Theories of Primitive Religion*. Oxford, 1965.

— *The Azande: History and Political Institutions*. Oxford, 1971.

Fales, F.M., *Assyrian Royal Inscriptions: New Horizons in Literary, Ideological, and Historical Analysis*. Rome, 1981.

Falkenstein, A., and von Soden, W. (eds.), *Sumerische und akkadische Hymnen und Gebete*. Zurich and Stuttgart, 1953.

Falkowitz, R.S., "Round Old Babylonian School Tablets", *AfO* 29 (1983/84), pp. 18-45.

Feeley-Harnik, G., "Is Historical Anthropology Possible?" in Knight, D.A. (ed.), *Humanizing America's Iconic Book. Society of Biblical Literature Centennial Addresses*. Chico (CA), 1980; repr. 1982, pp. 95-126.

Finet, A., "Un cas de clédonomancie à Mari", in: van Driel, G. et al. (eds.), *Zikir Šumim...*, pp. 48-56.

— "La place du devin dans la société de Mari", in: *DM*, pp. 87-94.

Finkel, I.L., "A New Piece of Libanomancy", *AfO* 29 (1983), pp. 50-57.

— "Necromancy in Ancient Mesopotamia", *AfO* 29-30 (1983-84), pp. 1-17.

Finkelstein, I., *The Archaeology of the Israelite Settlement*. Jerusalem, 1988.

Finkelstein, J.J., "Mesopotamian Historiography". *PAPS* 107 (1963), pp. 461-72.

Finley, M.I., *Ancient History. Evidence and Models*. New York, 1986.

— *Aspects of Antiquity*. 2nd edn Harmondsworth, 1977.

— *The World of Odysseus*. 2nd rev. edn Harmondsworth, 1978.

Finnegan, R., "How to do things with words: performative utterances among the Limba of Sierra Leone", *Man* 4 (1969), pp. 537-53.

— "Literacy versus Non-literacy: The Great Divide?", in: Horton, R. and Finnegan, R. (eds.), *Modes of Thought*. pp. 112-44.

Fischer, D.H., *Historians' Fallacies. Toward a Logic of Historical Thought*. New York, 1970.

Flanagan, J.W., *David's Social Drama. A Hologram of Israel's Early Iron Age*. Sheffield, 1988 (= The Social World of Biblical Antiquity Series 7).

Foget, F.W., "The History of Cultural Anthropology", in Honigman, J.J. (ed.), *Handbook of Social and Cultural Anthropology*. Chicago, 1973.

Fohrer, G., "Priester und Prophet—Amt und Charisma?", *KuD* 17 (1971), pp. 15-27.

— *Geschichte Israels*. Heidelberg, 1979.

Fontenrose, J., *The Delphic Oracle. Its Responses. With a Catalogue of Responses*. Berkeley, Los Angeles, London, 1978.

Fornara, C.W., *The Nature of History in Ancient Greece and Rome*. Berkeley, Los Angeles and London, 1988.

Fossey, C., *Textes assyriens et babyloniens relatifs à la Divination*. Paris, 1905.

Fox, R.L., *Pagans and Christians in the Mediterranean World from the Second Century AD to the Conversion of Constantine*. London, 1988.

Frake, C.O., "Cognitive Maps of Time and Tide Among Medieval Seafarers", *Man* N.S. 20 (1985), pp. 254-70.

Frankfort, H., Mrs.H.A. Frankfort, J.A. Wilson, T. Jakobsen (eds.), *Before Philosophy. The Intellectual Adventure of Ancient Man*, Chicago, 1946; repr. Harmondsworth, 1971.

Frazer, J.G., *The Golden Bough. A Study in Magic and Religion*. 3rd edn, Vols. 1-2, London, 1911.

Friedrich, I., *Ephod und Chosen im Lichte des Alten Orients*. Wien, 1968.

Friis, H., "Eksilet og den israelitiske historieopfattelse", *DTT* 38 (1975), pp. 1-16 = (Ger. trans. B.J.Diebner) "Das Exil und die Geschichte", in *DBAT* 18 (1984), pp. 63-84.

Fuchs, H.F., *Sehen und Schauen. Die Wurzel hzh im Alten Orient und im Alten Testament. Ein Beitrag zum prophetischen Offenbarungsempfang*, Würzburg, 1978.

Gadd, C.J., *Teachers and Students in the Oldest Schools*. London, 1956.

Gamper, A., *Gott als Richter in Mesopotamien und im Alten Testament. Zum Verständnis einer Gebetsbitte*, Innsbruck, 1966.

Garbini, G., *Storia e Ideologia Nell'Israele Antico*. Brescia, 1986 (= trans. John Bowden, *History and Ideology in Ancient Israel*. New York, 1988).

Gardiner, A.H., *Hieratic Papyri in the British Museum*. Third Series, London, 1935. Vols. 1-2.

Garelli, P., "La conception de la royauté en Assyrie", in Fales, F.M. (ed.), *Assyrian Royal Inscriptions: New Horizons.*, pp. 1-11.

Gell, A., "How to Read a Map: Remarks on the Practical Logic of Navigation", *Man* N.S. 20 (1985), pp. 271-86.

Geller, M.J., "The Šurpu Incantations and Lev. V.1-5", *JSS* 25 (1980), pp. 181-92.

Gibson, J.C.L, *Textbook of Syrian Semitic Inscriptions*. Vol.1. *Hebrew and Moabite*. Oxford, 1971.

— Vol.2, *Aramaic Inscriptions.* Oxford, 1975, repr.1985.

Gnuse, R., "A Reconsideration of the Form-Critical Structure in I Samuel 3: An Ancient Near Eastern Dream Theophany", *ZAW* 94 (1982), pp. 379-90.

— *The Dream Theophany of Samuel: Its Structure in Relation to Ancient Near Eastern Dreams and its Theological Significance.* Lanham (Maryland), 1984.

Goetze, A., *Kulturgeschichte Kleinasiens.* Munich (orig.pub.1933) 1957, 2nd rev. edn 1974.

— "Historical Allusions in Old Babylonian Omen Texts", *JCS* 1 (1947), pp. 253-66.

— *Old Babylonian Omen Texts.* New Haven, 1957 (= *YOS* 10).

— "Reports on Acts of Extispicy From Old Babylonian and Kassite Times", *JCS* 11 (1957), pp. 89-105.

— "An Old Babylonian Prayer of the Divination Priest", *JCS* 22 (1968), pp. 25-29.

Golka, F.W., "Die israelitische Weisheitsschule oder 'Des Kaisers neue Kleider'", *VT* 33 (1983), pp. 257-71.

Goody, J., *The Domestication of the Savage Mind.* Cambridge, 1977.

— *Literacy in Traditional Societies.* Cambridge, 1968.

Gordon, E.I., *Sumerian Proverbs.* Philadelphia, 1959.

— "A New Look at the Wisdom of Sumer and Akkad", *BO* 17 (1960), pp. 122-52.

Grayson, A.K. (with W.G. Lambert), "Akkadian Prophecies", *JCS* 18 (1964), pp. 7-23.

— *Assyrian and Babylonian Chronicles.* Locust Valley (New York), 1975.

— *Babylonian Historical-Literary Texts.* Toronto and Buffalo, 1975.

— "Histories and Historians of the Ancient Near East: Assyria and Babylonia", *Or* 49 (1980), pp. 140-94.

— (and D.B. Redford), *Papyrus and Tablet.* Englewood Cliffs (New Jersey), 1973.

Greenfield, J.C. (and Sokoloff, M.), "Astrological and Related Omen Texts in Jewish Palestinian Aramaic", *JNES* 48 (1989), pp. 201-214.

Gunneweg, A.H.J., *Leviten und Priester.* Göttingen, 1965 = (*FRLANT*) 89.

Güterbock, H.G., "Die historische Tradition bei Babyloniern und Hethitern", *ZA* 42 (1934), pp. 79-86.

Guillaume, A., *Prophecy and Divination.* London, 1938.

Gunkel, H., *Genesis. Übersetzt und erklärt.* 5th edn, Göttingen, 1922.

Gurney, O.R., *The Hittites.* orig.pub.1952; 2nd ed. Harmondsworth 1954, repr.1969.

— "The Sultantepe Tablets (continued)" IV. 'The Cuthaean Legend of Naram-Sin', *Anatolian Studies* 5 (1955), pp. 93-113.

Haase, R., *Einführung in das Studium keilschriftlicher Rechtsquellen.* Wiesbaden, 1965.

Hahn, H.F., *The Old Testament in Modern Research. With a Survey of Recent*

Literature (H.D. Hummel). Philadelphia, 1966.

Haldar, A., *Associations of Cult Prophets among the Ancient Semites*. Uppsala, 1945.

Halifax, J., *Shamanic Voices. The Shaman as Seer, Poet and Healer*. Harmondsworth, 1979.

Hallo, W.W., "Akkadian Apocalypses", *IEJ* 16 (1966), pp. 231-42.

Hallpike, C.R., "Is there a Primitive Mentality?" *Man* 11 (1976), pp. 253-70.

— *The Foundations of Primitive Thought*. Oxford, 1979.

Hanson, F.A., *Meaning in Culture*. London and Boston, 1975.

Haran, M., "The Nature of the 'Ohel Mo'edh in Pentateuchal Sources", *JSS* 5 (1960), pp. 50-65.

— *Temples and Temple-Service in Ancient Israel. An Inquiry into the Character of Cult Phenomena and the Historical Setting of the Priestly School*. Oxford, 1978.

Harrak, A., "Historical Statements in Middle Assyrian Archival Sources", *JAOS* 109 (1989), pp. 205-09.

Heaton, E.W., *The Old Testament Prophets*. Harmondsworth, 1958, 2nd edn 1961, repr. 1969.

Heidel, A., *The Gilgamesh Epic and Old Testament Parallels*. Chicago and London, 1946, 6th edn 1967.

Helms, M.W., *Ulysses' Sail. An Ethnographic Odyssey of Power, Knowledge, and Geographical Distance*. Princeton, 1988.

Hempel, C.G., "The Logic of Functional Analysis", in L. Gross (ed.), *Symposium on Sociological Theory*, Evanston (Illinois), 1959, pp. 271-307.

— "The Function of General Laws in History", *The Journal of Philosophy* 39 (1942) 35-48 = *Aspects of Scientific Explanation. And Other Essays in the Philosphy of Science*. New York, 1965, pp. 231-43.

— *Aspects of Scientific Explanation and Other Essays in the Philosophy of Science*. New York,1965.

— *The Philosophy of Natural Science*. Englewood Cliffs (N.J.), 1966.

Herrmann, S., "Die Königsnovelle in Ägypten und in Israel. Ein Beitrag zur Gattungsgeschichte in den Geschichtsbüchern des Alten Testaments", *Wissenschaftliche Zeitschrift Universität Leipzig*, 3 (1953/1954), *Gesellschafts-und sprachwissenschaftliche Reihe 1,51-62, im Selbstvertrag der Universität* = idem, *Gesammelte Studien zur Geschichte und Theologie des Alten Testaments*. Munich, 1986, pp. 120-44.

— *Zeit und Geschichte*. Stuttgart, et al., 1977.

— Review of A. Lemaire's *Les écoles et la formation de la bible...*, in: *OLZ* 80/3

(1985), pp. 255-58.

— "Israels Frühgeschichte im Spannungsfeld neuer Hypothesen", *Rheinisch-Westfälische Akademie der Wissenschaften, Abh.78, "Studien zur Ethnogenese"*, Bd. 2, 1988, pp. 43-95.

Hertzberg, H.W., *Die Samuelbücher*. Göttingen, 1973 (= *ATD* 10).

Hölscher, G., *Die Propheten*. Leipzig, 1914.

Hoffner, H.A., "Second Millennium Antecedents to the Hebrew 'ob", *JBL* 86 (1967), pp. 385-401.

— "Hittite Tarpiš and Hebrew Teraphim", *JNES* 27 (1968), pp. 61-68.

Homans, G.C., "Bringing Men Back in", in Ryan, A. (ed.), *The Philosophy of Social Explanation*, pp. 50-65.

Honigmann, J.J. (ed.), *Handbook of Social and Cultural Anthropology*. Chicago, 1973.

Hopkins, D.C., *The Highlands of Canaan: Agricultural Life in the Early Iron Age*. Sheffield, 1985.

Horton, R., and Finnegan, R., *Modes of Thought. Essays on Thinking in Western and Non-Western Societies*. London, 1973.

Horton, R., "African Traditional Thought and Western Science", *Africa* 37 (1967), pp. 50-71; pp. 155-87.

Hughes, J., *Secrets of the Times. Myth and History in Biblical Chronology*. Sheffield, 1990.

Hull, J., *Hellenistic Magic and the Synoptic Tradition*. Napierville (Illinois), 1974 (= *SBT* Second Series 28).

Hunger, H. — see Sachs, A.J.

Hunger, J., *Becherwahrsagung bei den Babyloniern*. Leipzig, 1903. (= *LSS* I,1).

Hussey, M.I.,"Anatomical Nomenclature in an Akkadian Omen Text", *JCS* 2 (1948), pp. 21-32.

Hvidberg-Hansen, F.O., *La Déesse TNT. Une étude sur la religion canaanéo-punique*. Vols.1-2, Copenhagen, 1979.

Jacobs, R.A. (and Rosenbaum, P.S.), *Readings in English Transformational Grammar*. Waltham (MA), 1979.

Jacobsen, T., *The Treasures of Darkness. A History of Mesopotamian Religion*, London, 1976, repr. 1978.

Jacoby, F., "Ueber die Entwicklung der griechischen Historiographie und den Plan einer neuen Sammlung der griechischen Historikerfragmente", *Klio* 9 (1909), pp. 80-123.

Jamieson-Drake, D., *Scribes and Schools in Monarchic Judah: A*

Socio-Archeological Approach. Sheffield, 1991.

Janowski, B., "Erwägungen zur Vorgeschichte des israelitischen "Šelamim-Opfers", *UF* 12 (1980), pp. 231-59.

Jarvie, I.C., and Agassi, J., "The Problem of the Rationality of Magic", in : Wilson, B.R. (ed.) *Rationality*, pp. 172-93.

Jastrow, M., *Die Religion Babyloniens und Assyriens.* rev. edn, Vol. 2-3, Gießen, 1912.

— *Aspects of Religious Belief and Practice in Babylonia and Assyria.* orig. pub. 1911, repr. New York, 1971.

— *A Dictionary of the Targumim, the Talmud Babli and Yerushalmi, and the Midrashic Literature.* Vols.I-II, New York, 1967.

Jean, C.-F., (and Hoftijzer, J.), *Dictionnaire des Inscriptions Sémitiques de l'Ouest.* Leiden, 1965.

Jenni, E., (and Westermann, C.), *Theologisches Handwörterbuch zum Alten Testament.* Munich, 1971.

Jeppesen, K. (and Otzen, B.), *The Productions of Time. Tradition History in Old Testament Scholarship.* Sheffield, 1984 (trans. F.H. Cryer).

Jepsen, A., *Nabi: Soziologische Studien zur alttestamentlichen Literatur und Religionsgeschichte.* Munich, 1934.

— *Die Quellen des Königbuches.* Halle (Saale), 1956.

Jeyes, U., "The 'Palace Gate' of the Liver. A Study of Terminology and Methods in Babylonian Extispicy", *JCS* 30/4 (1978), pp. 209-33.

— "The Act of Extispicy in Ancient Mesopotamia: An Outline", in (ed.) B. Alster, *Assyriological Miscellanies* 1 (1980), pp. 13-32.

— "Death and Divination in the Old Babylonian Period", in (ed. B.Alster) *Death in Mesopotamia*, pp. 107-21.

Jirku, A., *Mantik in Altisrael. Inaugural Dissertation.* Rostock, 1913.

— "Zu den altisraelitischen Vorstellungen von Toten- und Ahnengeistern", *BZ* 5 (1961), pp. 30-38.

Johnson, A.R., *The Cultic Prophet in Ancient Israel.* Cardiff, 1944, repr. 1962.

Kaiser, O., "Das Orakel als Mittel der Rechtsfindung im alten Ägypten", *ZRG* 10/3 (1958), pp. 193-208.

Der Prophet Jesaja. Kapitel 1-12. Göttingen, 1978 (= *ATD* 17).

— *Einleitung in das Alte Testament.* 5th rev. edn, Gütersloh, 1984.

Kapelrud, A.S., *Profetene i det gamle Israel og Juda.* Oslo, et al., 1966.

Kaufmann, Y., *The Religion of Israel. From its Beginnings to the Babylonian Exile.* orig. pub. 1937-1956; trans. (abridged) M. Greenberg, Chicago and London, 1960, repr. 1963.

Kammenhuber, A., *Orakelpraxis, Träume und Vorzeichenschau bei den Hethitern*, Heidelberg, 1976.

Kenyon, K., *Archaeology in the Holy Land*. orig. pub. 1960, 4th rev. edn, New York and London, 1979.

Kiekhofer, R., *European Witch Trials: Their Foundations in Popular and Learned Culture*. 1300-1500, London, 1976.

— *Magic in the Middle Ages*. Cambridge, 1990 [1989].

Kinnier-Wilson, J.V., "The Nimrud Catalogue of Medical and Physiognomical Omina", *Iraq* 24 (1962), pp. 52-63.

— "Two Medical Texts from Nimrud" in *Iraq* 19 (1957), pp. 40-49.

— "Leprosy in Ancient Mesopotamia", *RA* 60 (1966), pp. 47-58.

Kippenberg, H.G., *Magie. Die sozialwissenschaftliche Kontroverse über das Verstehen fremden Denkens*. Frankfurt am Main, 1978, repr. 1987.

Kirk, G.S., *Myth. Its Meaning and Functions*. London, Berkeley and Los Angeles, 1970.

Kittel, R., *Geschichte des Volkes Israel*, I: *Palästina in der Urzeit: Das Werden des Volkes*, rev. edn Gotha, 1912.

Klaiber, G., "Das priesterliche Orakel der Israeliten", in: *Programm des Königlichen Gymnasiums in Stuttgart zum Schluss des Schuljahrs 1864-65*, Stuttgart, 1865, pp. 1-19.

Klauber, G., *Politisch-Religiöse Texte aus der Sargonidenzeit*. Leipzig, 1913.

Kluckhohn, C., *Navaho Witchcraft*. Cambridge (MA), 1944.

— Kluckhohn, C. and Leighton, D., *The Navaho*. rev. edn, Cambridge (MA) and London, 1946, 1974.

Knauf, E.A., *Ismael. Untersuchungen zur Geschichte Palästinas und Nordarabiens im 1. Jahrtausend v. Chr.*, 2. erw. Aufl., Wiesbaden, 1989.

— *Midian. Untersuchungen zur Geschichte Palästinas und Nordarabiens am Ende des 2. Jahrtausends v. Chr.*, Wiesbaden, 1988.

Knudtzon, J.A., *Assyrische Gebete an den Sonnengott*. Leipzig, 1893.

Köcher, F., (and A.L. Oppenheim), "The Old Babylonian Omen Text VAT 7525" in *AfO* 18 (1957-1958), pp. 62-80.

— *Die babylonisch-assyrische Medizin in Texten und Untersuchungen*. Vols. 1-3, Berlin, 1963-64.

Koehler, L., (and Baumgartner, W.), *Hebräisches und Aramäisches Lexicon zum Alten Testament*. Leiden, 1967-1983.

Koschaker, P., "Göttliches und weltliches Recht nach den Urkunden aus Susa", *Or* 4 (1935), pp. 38-80.

Koselleck, R. (et al., eds.), *Objektivität und Parteilichkeit*. München, 1977.

— *Vergangene Zukunft. Zur Semantik geschichtlicher Zeiten.* Frankfurt am Main, 1979.

Kramer, S.N., *The Sumerians. Their History, Culture and Character.* Chicago and London, 1963.

Kraus, F.R., "Ein Sittenkanon in Omenform" , *ZA* 43 (1936), pp. 77-113.

— "Babylonische Omina mit Ausdeutung der Begleiterscheinungen des Sprechens", in *AfO* 11 (1936-1937), pp. 219-30.

— *Texte zur babylonischen Physiognomatik,* in: *AfO Beiheft* 3, Berlin, 1939.

— "Weitere Texte zur babylonischen Physiognomatik", in *Or* N.S. 16 (1947), pp. 172-206.

— "Mittelbabylonische Opferschauprotokolle", *JCS* 37 (1985), pp. 127-203.

Kroeber, A.L. (and Kluckhohn, C.), *Culture: A Critical Review of the Concepts and Definitions,* in: Papers of the Peabody Museum of American Anthropology and Ethnology 47 (1952), pp. 1-223.

Küchler, F., "Das priesterliche Orakel in Israel und Juda", (W. Frankenberg and F. Küchler, eds.) *ZAW Beiheft* 33, 1917, pub. Giessen, 1918, pp. 285-301.

Kuenen, A., *De Boeken des Ouden Verbonds.* 2nd rev. edn, Part 1: *De Thora en de historische Boeken des Ouden Verbonds.* Amsterdam, 1884.

Kuhn, P., *Offenbarungsstimmen im Antiken Judentum. Untersuchungen zur bat qol und verwandten Phänomenen* = Texte und Studien zum Antiken Judentum 20), Tübingen, 1989.

Kuhn, T.S., *The Copernican Revolution. Planetary Astronomy in the Development of Western Thought.* New York, 1957.

Kuhrt, A., "Nabonidus and the Babylonian Priesthood", in M. Beard and J. North (eds.), *Pagan Priests,* pp. 117-56.

Labat, R., "Un traité médical Akkadien", *RA* 40 (1945-1946), pp. 27-49.

— *Traité akkadien de diagnostics et prognostics médicaux.* Vols. 1-2, Paris and Leiden, 1951.

— *Un Calendrier Babylonien des Travaux, des Signes, et des Mois (Séries iqqur ipuš),* Paris, 1965.

— "Medecins, devins et prêtres-guerisseurs en Mésopotamie ancienne" in *Archeologia* 8-13 (1966), pp. 11-15.

Lambert, W.G., "Nebuchadnezzar King of Justice", *Iraq* 27 (1965), pp. 1-11.

— "The Tamitu Texts", in *DM,* pp. 119-23.

— *Babylonian Wisdom Literature.* Oxford, 1967, repr.1975.

— "Enmeduranki and Related Matters," *JCS* 21 (1967), pp. 126-38.

— "History and the Gods: A Review Article", *Or* N.S. 39 (1970), pp. 170-77.

— *The Background of Jewish Apocalyptic. The Ethel M. Wood Lecture delivered before the University of London on 22 February 1977*. London, 1978.

Landsberger, B., (and H. Tadmor), "Fragments of Clay Liver Models from Hazor", *IEJ* 14 (1964), pp. 201-18.

Lang, B., *Anthropological Approaches to the Old Testament*. Philadelphia and London, 1985.

Laroche, E., "Lécanomancie hittite", *RA* 52 (1958), pp. 150-62.

— "Sur le vocabulaire de l'haruspicine hittite", *RA* 64 (1970), pp. 127-39.

Larsen, M.T., *The Old Assyrian City-State and its Colonies*. Copenhagen, 1976.

— (ed.) *Power and Propaganda. A Symposium on Ancient Empires*. Copenhagen, 1979.

Leach, E.R., Claude Lévi-Strauss, New York, 1970.

— "Two Essays Concerning the Symbolic Representation of Time", in Leach, E.R. (ed.), *Rethinking Anthropology*. London, 1961, pp. 124-36.

Leech, G., *Semantics*. 2nd edn, Harmondsworth, 1987.

Lehman, M.R.,"New Light on Astrology in Qumran and the Talmud", *RevQ* 32 (1975), pp. 599-602.

Leichty, E., *The Omen Series Šumma Izbu*. Locust Valley (N.Y.), 1970 (= *TCS* 4).

— Leichty in "Literary Notes", in M. de Jong Ellis (ed.), *Ancient Near Eastern Studies in Memory of J.J.Finkelstein*. pp. 143-44

Lemaire, A., *Les écoles et la formation de la bible dans l'ancien Israël*. Göttingen, 1981.

Lemche, N.P., "'Hebrew' as a National Name for Israel'", in *StTh* 33 (1979), pp. 1-23.

— *Ancient Israel*. Sheffield, 1988 (trans. F.H. Cryer).

— *Early Israel. Anthropological and Historical Studies on the Israelite Society Before the Monarchy*. Leiden, 1985.

Lenormant, F., *La Divination et la science des présages chez les Chaldéens*, Paris, 1875.

Lévi-Strauss, C., *La pensée Sauvage*. Paris, 1962.

Lewis, I.L., *Ecstatic Religion*. Harmondsworth, 1971, repr. 1975.

— *Social Anthropology in Perspective*. Harmondsworth, 1976.

— *Religion in Context. Cults and Charisma*. Cambridge, 1986, repr. 1987.

Lienhardt, G., *Divinity and Experience: the Religion of the Dinka*. Oxford, 1961.

Lindblom, Johs., *Israels Religion*. orig. pub. 1936, repr. Stockholm, 1967.

— *Prophecy in Ancient Israel*. Oxford, 1962.

— "Lot-casting in the Old Testament", *VT* 12 (1962), pp. 164-78.

Lindstrom, L., "Doctor, Lawyer, Wise Man,Priest: Big-Men and Knowledge in Melanesia", in *Man* (N.S.) 19 (1984), pp. 291-309.

Livingstone, A., *Mystical and Mythological Explanatory Works of Assyrian and Babylonian Scholars*. Oxford, 1986.

Liwak, R., "Die Rettung Jerusalems im Jahr 701 v. Chr. Zum Verhältnis und Verständnis historischer und theologischer Aussagen", *ZThK* 83 (1986), pp. 137-66.

— *Der Prophet und die Geschichte. Eine literar-historische Untersuchung zum Jeremiabuch*. Stuttgart, Berlin, Köln, Mainz, 1987.

— "Literary Individuality as a Problem of Hermeneutics in the Hebrew Bible", in H.G. Reventlow (ed.), *Creative Biblical Exegesis*. Sheffield, 1988 (*JSOT Sup* 59), pp. 89-101.

— (with S. Wagner, eds.), *Prophetie und geschichtliche Wirklichkeit im alten Israel*. Stuttgart, 1991 (= Festschrift Siegfried Herrmann).

Liverani, M., *Antico Oriente. Storia - Società - Economia*. Roma-Bari, 1988.

Loersch, S., *Das Deuteronomium und seine Deutungen*. Stuttgart, 1967.

Long, B.O., "The Effect of Divination Upon Israelite Literature", *JBL* 92 (1973), pp. 489-97.

Loretz, O., *Habiru - Hebräer. Eine sozio-linguistische Studie über die Herkunft des Gentiliziums 'ibrî vom Appelativum habiru*. Berlin and New York, 1984.

— *Leberschau, Sündenbock, Asasel in Ugarit und Israel*. Altenberge, 1985.

Luck, G., *Arcana Mundi. Magic and the Occult in the Greek and Roman Worlds*. Baltimore, 1985; repr. Aquarius Press, England, 1987.

— *Magie und andere Geheimlehren in der Antike*. Stuttgart, 1990.

Lukes, S., "Political Ritual and Social Integration", *Sociology* 9 (1975), pp. 289-308.

Lust, J., "On Wizards and Prophets", *VT* 26 (1974), pp. 133-42.

Lyons, J., *Introduction to Theoretical Linguistics*. Cambridge, 1971.

— *Language and Linguistics*. London, New York, et al., 1981.

Læssø, J., *Studies on the Assyrian Ritual and Series bit rimki*. Copenhagen, 1955.

McCarter, P.K., *1 Samuel. A New Translation with Introduction and Commentary*. Garden City (New York), 1980.

McCarthy, D.J., "2 Sam 7 and the Structure of the Deuteronomic History", *JBL* 84 (1965), pp. 131-38.

McEwan, G.J.P., *Priest and Temple in Hellenistic Babylonia*. Wiesbaden, 1981 (= *Freiburger Altorientalischen Studien*, Vol.4).

McKay, J., *Religion in Judah under the Assyrians*. London, 1973.

Maier, G., *Die assyrische Beschwörungssammlung Maqlu*. Berlin, 1937.

Maier, J., *Das Altisraelitische Ladeheiligtum*. Berlin, 1965.

— "Urim und Tummim", *Kairos* 11 (1969), pp. 22-38.

Malamat, A., "Die Frühgeschichte Israels - eine methodologische Studie", *ThZ* 39 (1983), pp. 1-16.

Malinowski, B., *Magic, Science and Religion and Other Essays.* London, 1974.

Mann, M., *The Sources of Social Power, Vol.1. A History of Power from the Beginning to A.D.176*, Cambridge, New York, et al., 1986, 3rd edn 1988.

Mauss, M., and Hubert, H., *Esquisse d'une théorie générale de la magie.* Repr. from *L'Année Sociologique* 1902-1903 in C. Lévi-Strauss/Presses Universitaires de France (eds.), Paris, 1966.

Mayes, A.D.H., *The Story of Israel between Settlement and Exile. A Redactional Study of the Deuteronomistic History.* London, 1983.

Mettinger, T.N.D., *Solomonic State Officials.* Lund, 1971.

— *The Dethronement of Sabaoth. Studies in the Shem and Kabod Theologies* (trans. F.H. Cryer), Lund, 1982.

Meyer, J.-W., *Untersuchungen zu den Tonlebermodellen aus dem Alten Orient.* Neukirchen-Vluyn, 1987 (= *AOAT* 39).

Meyer, L. de, "Deux prières ikribu du temps d'Amisaduqa", in: G. van Driel, et al. (eds.), *Zikir Sumim*, pp. 271-79.

Middleton, J., *Lugbara Religion.* Oxford, 1960.

— and Winter, E.H., *Witchcraft and Sorcery in East Africa.* London, 1963; repr. 1978.

— "Secrecy Among the Lugbara", in K.W. Bolle (ed.), *Secrecy in Religions.* Leiden, New York, et.al., 1987, pp. 25-43.

Miller, P.D., Jr., *The Divine Warrior in Early Israel.* Cambridge (MA), 1973.

Moran, W.L., "New Evidence from Mari on the History of Prophecy", *Bib* 50 (1969), pp. 15-56.

Moren, S.M., "A Lost 'Omen' Tablet", *JCS* 29 (1977), pp. 65-72.

—"Šumma Izbu XIX : New Light on the Animal Omens", in *AfO* 27 (1980), pp. 53-70.

Moscati, S., *An Introduction to the Comparative Grammar of the Semitic Languages. Phonology and Morphology.* 3rd edn, Wiesbaden, 1980.

Mowinckel, S., "Die vorderasiatischen Königs- und Fürsteninschriften: eine stilistische Studie", in: *Eucharisterion... Festschrift Herrmann Gunkel dargebracht*, pp. 278-322.

— *Psalmenstudien I. Åwän und die individuellen Klagepsalmen.* Kristiania, 1921.

— *Psalmenstudien III: Die Kultprophetie und prophetische Psalmen.* Kristiana, 1923.

— *Offersang og sangoffer. Salmediktningen i Bibelen.* Oslo, Bergen, Tromsø, 2nd edn, 1971.

Munn, N.D., "Symbolism in a Ritual Context" in J.J. Honigmann (ed.) *Handbook of Social and Cultural Anthropology*, pp. 579-612.

Murray, M., *The God of the Witches*. London, 1952.

Murtonen, A., "The Prophet Amos — A Hepatoscoper?", *VT* 2 (1952), pp. 170-71.

Na'aman, N., "Historical and Chronological Notes on the Kingdoms of Israel and Judah in the Eighth Century B.C.", *VT* 36 (1986), pp. 71-92.

Nadel, S.F., *Nupe Religion*. London, 1954, repr. 1970.

Nagel, E., *The Structure of Science*. New York, 1961.

Nelson, R.D., *The Double Redaction of the Deuteronomistic History*. Sheffield, 1981 (= *JSOT Sup* 18).

Neugebauer, O., "Some Atypical Cuneiform Texts.I", *JCS* 21 (1967), pp. 183-218.

— *A History of Ancient Mathematical Astronomy*, Pt.1. Berlin, Heidelberg, New York, 1975.

— *Astronomy and History. Selected Essays*. New York, Berlin, Heidelberg, Tokyo, 1983.

Nicholson, E.W., *God and His People: Covenant and Theology in the Old Testament*. Oxford, 1986.

Niemann, H.M., *Herrschaft, Königtum und Staat. Skizzen zur soziokulturellen Entwicklung im monarchischen Israel*. Tübingen, 1993.

— "Das Ende des Volkes der Perizziter", *ZAW* 105 (1993), pp. 233-57.

Nissen, H.-J. (and J. Renger) *Mesopotamien und seine Nachbarn (=XXV. Rencontre Assyriologique Internationale Berlin, 3. bis 7. Juli 1978)*, Berlin, 1978.

Nötscher, F., "Haus- und Stadtomina der Serie šumma âlu ina mêlê šakin", *Or* N.S. 31 (1928), pp. 1-78; 39-42 (1929), pp. 1-247; 51-54 (1930), pp. 1-243.

Noort, E., *Untersuchungen zum Gottesbescheid in Mari. Die 'Mariprophetie' in der alttestamentlichen Forschung*, Neukirchen-Vluyn, 1977.

— *Biblisch-archäologische Hermeneutik und alttestamentliche Exegese*. Kampen, 1979.

North, J., "Diviners and Divination at Rome", in M. Beard and J. North (eds.), *Pagan Priests*, pp. 51-71.

Noth, M., *Das System der zwölf Stämme Israels*. BWANT IV/1, Stuttgart, 1930.

— *Überlieferungsgeschichtliche Studien. Die sammelnden und bearbeitenden Geschichtswerke im Alten Testament*. repr. Darmstadt, 1957.

— *Geschichte Israels*. Göttingen, 1950.

— *Amt und Berufung*. Bonn, 1958 (= *Bonner Akademische Reden* 19).

— *Das 3.Buch Mose: Leviticus*. Göttingen, 1973 (= *ATD* 6).

Nougayrol, J., "Textes hépatoscopiques d'époque ancienne conservés au musée du Louvre", *RA* 38 (1939-1941), pp. 67-88.

— "Note sur la place des présages historiques dans l'extispicine babylonienne", in *Ecole Pratique des Hautes Etudes , Section des Sciences Religieuses, Annuaire* (1944-1945), pp. 5-41.

— "Textes hépatoscopiques d'époque ancienne au musée du Louvre", *RA* 40 (1945-1946), pp. 56-97.

— "Textes hépatoscopiques d'époque ancienne au musée du Louvre", *RA* 44 (1950), pp. 1-44.

— "Présages médicaux de l'haruspicine babylonienne", *Semitica* 6 (1956), pp. 5-14.

— "Rapports paléo-babyloniennes d'haruspices", *JCS* 21 (1967), pp. 219-35.

—"Le foie d'orientation BM 50494", *RA* 62(1968), pp. 31-50.

— (with J. Aro) "Trois Nouveaux Recueils d'haruspicine Ancienne", *RA* 67 (1973), pp. 41-56.

— "Les 'silhouettes de référence' de l'haruspicine", in: B.L. Eichler, et al. (eds.), *Kramer Anniversary Volume. Cuneiform Studies in Honor of Samuel Noah Kramer*. Neukirchen-Vluyn, 1976, pp. 343-50.

O'Brien, M.A., *The Deuteronomistic History Hypothesis: A Reassessment*. Göttingen, 1989 (= *OBO* 92).

Oden, R.A., Jr., "Hermeneutics and Historiography: Germany and America", *SBLSP*, 1980, pp. 135-57.

O'Keefe, D.L., *Stolen Lightning. The Social Theory of Magic*. Oxford, 1982.

Oppenheim, A.L., "Zur keilschriftlichen Omenliteratur", *Or*, N.S. 5 (1936) 199-228.

— "The Golden Garments of the Gods", *JNES* 8 (1949), pp. 172-93.

— *The Interpretation of Dreams in the Ancient Near East. With a Translation of an Assyrian Dream Book*. in *TAPS* N.S. 46/3 (1956), pp. 179-353.

— "A New Prayer to the Gods of the Night", *Studia Biblica et Orientalia* 3 (1959), pp. 282-301.

— *Ancient Mesopotamia*. Chicago, 1964, repr. with notes by E. Reiner, Chicago, 1977.

— "Divination and Celestial Observation in the Last Assyrian Empire", *Centaurus* 14 (1969), pp. 97-135.

— *Letters from Mesopotamia*. Chicago and London, 1967.

— "New Fragments of the Assyrian Dream-Book", in *Iraq* 31 (1969), pp. 153-65.

— "A Babylonian Diviner's Manual", in *JNES* 33 (1974), pp. 197-220.

352   *Divination in Ancient Israel*

Otzen, B., *Studien über Deuterosacharja*. Copenhagen, 1964.

Overholt, T.W., *The Channels of Prophecy. The Social Dynamics of Prophetic Activity*. Minneapolis, 1989.

Park, G.K., "Divination and its Social Contexts", *JRAI* 93 (1963), pp. 195-209.

Parker, R.A., *A Saite Oracle Papyrus from Thebes in the Brooklyn Museum*. Providence (RI), 1962.

Parpola, S., *Letters from Assyrian Scholars to the Kings Esarhaddon and Assurbanipal*, Part II, Neukirchen-Vluyn, 1970, 1983 (Vols. 1-2)(= *AOAT* 5/1 and 5/2).

— "A Letter from Šamaš-šumu-ukin to Esarhaddon", *Iraq* 34 (1972), pp. 21-34.

— "Assyrian Library Records", *JNES* 42 (1983), pp. 1-29.

Passmore, J., *A Hundred Years of Philosophy*. Harmondsworth, 1956; repr. 1968.

Pedersén, O., *Archives and Libraries in the City of Assur. A Survey of the Material from the German Excavations*, Uppsala, 1986, (= Studia Semitica Upsaliensis 6 and 8), Vols. 1-2.

Petersen, D.L., *The Roles of Israel's Prophets*. Sheffield, 1981.

Petschow, H., *Babylonische Rechtsurkunden aus dem 6. Jahrhundert vor Chr*. Bayerische Akademie der Wissenschaften Philosophisch-historische Klasse, Abhandlungen, N.F. 51 (1960), pp. 1-122.

Pettinato, G., *Die Ölwahrsagung bei den Babyloniern*. Vols. I-II, Rome, 1966.

— "Libanomanzia presso i Babilonesi", *RSO* 41 (1966), pp. 303-27.

Petzoldt, L. (ed.), *Magie und Religion*. Darmstadt, 1978.

Pickering, W.S.F. (ed.), *Durkheim on Religion. A selection of readings with bibliographies*. London, 1975.

Pingree, D., "Mesopotamian Astronomy and Astral Omens in Other Civilizations", in H.-J. Nissen and J. Renger, eds., *Mesopotamien und seine Nachbarn*, Teil 2, pp. 613-31.

Pocock, J.G.A., "The Origins of Study of the Past: A Comparative Approach", *CSSH* 4 (1961-1962), pp. 209-46.

Popper, Karl R., *Die Logik der Forschung*. Vienna, 1934.

— *The Poverty of Historicism*. London, 1957, 2nd edn, repr. 1972.

— *Conjectures and Refutations*. London, 1963.

— *Objective Knowledge*. Oxford, 1972.

— *Unended Quest*. London, 1976 (4th edn, 1978).

— *Auf der Suche nach einer besseren Welt. Vorträge und Aufsätze aus dreißig Jahren*. Munich and Zurich, 1984.

Porter, P.A., *Metaphors and Monsters. A Literary-Critical Study of Daniel 7 and 8*. Uppsala, 1983 (= Coniectanea Biblica. Old Testament Series 20).

Postgate, J.N., "The Economic Structure of the Assyrian Empire", in M.T. Larsen (ed.), *Power and Propaganda. A Symposium on Ancient Empires*, pp. 216-17.

Preisendanz, K., *Papyri Graecae Magicae*. Leipzig and Berlin, Vol.II, 1931.

Provan, I.W., *Hezekiah and the Books of Kings*. Berlin and New York, 1988.

Rad, G. von, *Das erste Buch Mose. Genesis*. Göttingen, 1972, repr. 1976.

Radcliffe-Brown, A.R., *The Andaman Islanders. An investigation of the physical characteristics, language, culture, and technology of a primitive society*, (orig. pub. 1922), Cambridge, 1964.

Rainey, A.F., "The Scribe at Ugarit: His Position and Influence", in *Proceedings of the Israel Academy of Science and the Humanities*. Jerusalem, 1969, pp. 1-22.

Ramsey, G.W., *The Quest for the Historical Israel. Reconstructing Israel's Early History*. London, 1981.

Reiner, E. (and D. Pingree), *Babylonian Planetary Omens, Part One: The Venus Tablet of Ammisaduqa*. Malibu, 1975 (= BPO 1); *Part Two: Enuma Anu Enlil. Tablets 50-51*. Malibu, 1981 (= BPO 2).

— *Šurpu. A Collection of Sumerian and Akkadian Incantations*. Graz, 1958.

— "Fortune-Telling in Mesopotamia", in *JNES* 19 (1960), pp. 23-35.

— "New Light on Some Historical Omens", in: *Anatolian Studies Presented to Hans Gustav Güterbock...*, pp. 257-61.

— "The Uses of Astrology", *JAOS* 105 (1985), pp. 589-95.

Rendtorff, R., *Das Alte Testament. Eine Einführung*. Neukirchen, 3rd edn, 1988.

Renfrew, C., *Before Civilization*. Harmondsworth, 1976.

— *Archaeology and Language. The Puzzle of Indo-European Origins*. London, 1987.

Renger, J., "Untersuchungen zum Priestertum in der altbabylonischen Zeit", 1.Teil, *ZA* 58 (1967), pp. 110-88; 2. Teil *ZA* 59 (1969), pp. 104-246.

Resch, A., *Der Traum im Heilsplan Gottes. Deutung und Bedeutung des Traums im Alten Testament*. Freiburg im Breisgau, 1964.

Reventlow, H.G., *Creative Biblical Exegesis. Christian and Jewish Hermeneutics through the Centuries*. Sheffield, 1988 (*JSOT Sup* 59).

Richter, W., "Traum und Traumdeutung im AT. Ihre Form und Verwendung", *BZ* (N.F.) 7 (1963), pp. 202-220.

Ricoeur, P., *Temps et récit*. Vol.1, Paris, 1983.

Riemschneider, K.K., *Babylonische Geburtsomina in hethitischer Übersetzung*. Wiesbaden, 1970 (= Studien zu den Bogazköy-Texten 9).

Ringgren, H., *Fatalistic Beliefs in Religion Folklore, and Literature. Papers read at* the *Symposium on Fatalistic Beliefs held at Åbo on the 7th-9th of September, 1964*, Uppsala, 1967.

Roberts, J.J.M., "Of Signs, Prophets, and Time Limits: A Note on Psalm 74:9", *CBQ* 39 (1977), pp. 474-81.

Robertson-Smith, W., *Lectures on the Religion of the Semites*. 3rd edn New York, 1956; repr. 1959.

— *The Old Testament in the Jewish Church. A Course of Lectures on Biblical Criticism*. 2nd rev. edn, New York, 1892.

Rochberg-Halton, F., "Stellar Distances in Early Babylonian Astronomy: A New Perspective on the Hilprecht Text (HS 229)", *JNES* 2 (1983), pp. 209-17.

— "Canonicity in Cuneiform Texts", *JCS* 36 (1984), pp. 127-144.

Rogerson, J.W., *Anthropology and the Old Testament*. Oxford, 1978.

— "The Hebrew Conception of Corporate Personality: A Re-examination", in B. Lang (ed.) *Anthropological Approaches to the Old Testament*. pp. 43-59.

Rosenthal, F., *An Aramaic Handbook*. Pt.I/2, Wiesbaden, 1967.

Rossi, P., *Vom Historismus zur historischen Sozialwissenschaft*. Frankfurt am Main, 1987.

Rost, L., "Der Leberlappen", *ZAW* 79 (1967), pp. 35-41.

Rowley, H.H., *The Growth of the Old Testament*. rev. edn, New York and Evanston, 1963.

Rudolph, W., "Präparierte Jungfrauen?" *ZAW* 75 (1963), pp. 65-73.

Rusen, J., "Der Historiker als Parteimann des Schicksals", in (R. Koselleck et al., eds.) *Objektivität und Parteilichkeit*, pp. 77-125.

— *Für eine erneuerte Historik. Studien zur Theorie der Geschichtswissenschaft*. Bad Canstadt, 1976.

— *Historische Vernunft. Grundzüge einer Historik. I: Die Grundlagen der Geschichtswissenschaft*. Göttingen, 1983.

— *Rekonstrutkion der Vergangenheit. Grundzüge einer Historik II: Die Prinzipien der historischen Forschung*. Göttingen, 1986.

Rüterswörden, U., see also Ebach, J. (1977, 1980).

— *Die Beamten der israelitischen Königszeit. Eine Studie zu 'îr und vergleichbaren Begriffen*. Stuttgart, Berlin, et al., 1985.

Ryan, A., *The Philosophy of Social Explanation*. Oxford, 1973, repr. 1978.

Sachs, A.J.— Hunger, H., *Astronomical Diaries and Related Texts from Babylonia. Vol.I. Diaries from 652 B.C. to 262 B.C.*. Vienna, 1988.

Sachs, A.J., "A Classification of the Babylonian Astronomical Tablets of the Seleucid Period", *JCS* 2 (1948), pp. 271-90.

Saggs, H.W.F., *The Encounter With the Divine in Mesopotamia and Israel*. London,

1978.

Salmon, M.H., "Do Azande and Nuer Use a Non-Standard Logic?", *Man* N.S. 13 (1978), pp. 444-54.

San Nicolo, M., *Die Schlussklauseln der altbabylonischen Kauf- und Tausch-verträge. Ein Beitrag zur Geschichte des Barkaufes.* Munich, 1922.

Sasson, J.M., "Some Comments on Archive Keeping at Mari", in *Iraq* 34 (1972), pp. 55-67.

— "Mari Dreams", *JAOS* 103 (1983), pp. 283-93.

— "Year: Zimri-Lim offered a Great Throne to Shamash of Mahanum". An Overview of One Year in Mari. Part I: The Presence of the King, in: *M.A.R.I.* 4 (1985), pp. 437-52.

— "Zimri-Lim Takes the Grand Tour", *BA*, Dec. 1984, pp. 246-51.

Schäfer, P., "Jewish Magic Literature in Late Antiquity and Early Middle Ages", *JJS* 41 (1990), pp. 75-91.

Scharf, J.-H., *Anfänge von systematischer Anatomie und Teratologie im alten Babylon, Sitzungsbericht der Sächsischen Akademie der Wissenschaften. Mathematisch-naturwissenschaftliche Klasse* 120 (1988) Berlin.

Schmidtke, F., "Träume, Orakel und Totengeister als Künder der Zukunft in Israel und Babylonien", *BZ* 11 (1967), pp. 240-46.

Schnabel, H., *Die 'Thronfolgeerzählung David's'. Untersuchungen zur literarischen Eigenständigkeit, literarkritischen Abgrenzung u. Intention von 2 Sam 21,1-14; 9-20; 1 Kön 1-2.* Regensburg, 1988.

Schneidau, H.N., *Sacred Discontent: The Bible and Western Tradition.* Berkeley, Los Angeles and London, 1976.

Scholte, B., "The Structural Anthropology of Claude Lévi-Strauss", in J.J. Honigmann (ed.) *Handbook of Social and Cultural Anthropology.* pp. 637-716.

Schorr, M., *Urkunden des altbabylonsichen Zivil- und Prozessrechts.* Leipzig, 1913.

Searle, J.R., *Speech Acts. An Essay in the Philosophy of Language.* London and New York, 1969.

Segal, M.H., *A Grammar of Mishnaic Hebrew.* Oxford, 1927; repr.1958.

Segert, S., *Altaramäische Grammatik.* Leipzig, 1975, repr. 1983.

Sellin, E., *Alttestamentliche Theologie auf religionsgeschichtlicher Grundlage.* Pt.1, Leipzig, 1933.

— *Einleitung in das Alte Testament.* Leipzig, 1935.

Shils, E., "Tradition", in *CSSH* 13 (1971), pp. 122-59.

Shweder, R.A., "Has Piaget Been Upstaged? A Reply to Hallpike", *AA* N.S. 87 (1985), pp. 138-44.

Singer, A., and Street, B.V., *Zande Themes*. Oxford, 1972.

Smelik, K.A.D., (trans. H. Weippert), *Historische Dokumente aus dem alten Israel*. Göttingen, 1987.

Smend, R., "Das Gesetz und die Völker. Ein Beitrag zur deuteronomistischen Redaktionsgeschichte", in: H.W. Wolff (ed.), *Probleme biblischer Theologie. Gerhard von Rad zum 70. Geburtstag*. Munich, 1971, pp. 494-509.

— *Die Entstehung des Alten Testaments*. Stuttgart, Berlin, et al., 1978.

Smith, H.P., *A Critical and Exegetical Commentary on the Books of Samuel*, Edinburgh, 1899.

Smith, M., *Jesus the Magician*. New York and Toronto, 1978.

Soggin, J.A., *A History of Israel. From the Beginnings to the Bar Kochba Revolt A.D.135*. (trans. J. Bowden), Philadelphia, 1984.

— "Probleme einer Vor- und Frühgeschichte Israels", *ZAW* (Supp.) 100 (1988), pp. 255-67.

Spencer, J., *Dissertatio de Urim et Thummim in Deuteron.c.33.v.8 In qua Eorum natura et origo, Non paucorum rituum Mosaicorum rationes, et Obscuriora quaedam Scripturae loca probabiliter explicantur*. Cambridge, 1670.

Sperber, D., "Some Rabbinic Themes in Magical Papyri", *JSJ* 16 (1985), pp. 93-103.

Spieckermann, H., *Juda unter Assur in der Sargonidenzeit*. Göttingen, 1982.

Spindler, L.S., "Witchcraft in Menomini Acculturation", *AA* 54 (1952), pp. 593-602.

Spycket, A., "Illustration d'un text hépatoscopique concernant Sargon d'Agade (?)", *RA* 40 (1945-46), pp. 151-56.

Starr, I., "In Search of Principles of Prognostication in Extispicy", *HUCA* 45 (1974), pp. 17-23.

— *The 'baru' Rituals*. Yale University Ph.D., 1974.

— "Notes on Some Technical Terms in Extispicy", *JCS* 27 (1975), pp. 241-49.

— "An Additional Note on a Technical Term in Extispicy", *JCS* 30 (1978), pp. 170-72.

— "Notes on Some Published and Unpublished Historical Omens", *JCS* 29 (1977), pp. 157-66.

— "Omen Texts Concerning Holes in the Liver", *AfO* 26 (1978/79), pp. 45-55.

— *The Rituals of the Diviner*. Malibu, 1983 (= *Bibliotheca Mesopotamica* 12 (1983)).

— "Omen Texts Concerning Lesser Known Parts of the Lungs", *JNES* 42 (1983), pp. 109-21.

— "Historical Omens Concerning Ashurbanipal's War Against Elam", *AfO* 32 (1985), pp. 60-67.

Steensgaard, P., "Time and Religion in Judaism" in A.N. Balslev and J.N. Mohanty (eds.), *Time and Religion*. Leiden, 1991.

Stemberger, B., "Der Traum in der rabbinischen Literatur", *Kairos* 18 (1976), pp. 1-42.

Stoebe, H.J., *Das erste Buch Samuelis*. Gütersloh, 1973.

Strange, J., "Joram, King of Israel and Judah", *VT* 25 (1975), pp. 191-201.

— "The Transition from the Bronze Age to the Iron Age in the Eastern Mediterranean and the Emergence of the Israelite State", *SJOT* 1 (1987), pp. 1-19.

Swoboda, H., *Propheten und Prognosen. Hellseher und Schwarzseher von Delphi bis zum Club of Rome*. Munich and Zurich, 1979.

Szalay, M. *Ethnologie und Geschichte. Zur Grundlegung einer ethnologischen Geschichtsschreibung*. Berlin, 1983.

Tadmor, H., (and M. Weinfeld) *History, Historiography and Interpretation*. Jerusalem and Leiden, 1983, repr. 1984.

Tadmor, H., "History and Ideology in the Assyrian Royal Inscriptions", in F.M. Fales (ed.), *Assyrian Royal Inscriptions: New Horizons*, pp. 13-35.

Tambiah, S.J., "Form and Meaning of Magical Acts: A Point of View", in R. Horton and R. Finnegan (eds.), *Modes of Thought....* pp. 199-229.

Taylor, L.R., *Party Politics in the Age of Caesar*. London, 6th edn, 1971.

Temple, R.K.G., "An Anatomical Verification of the Reading of a Term in Extispicy", *JCS* 34 (1982), pp. 19-27.

Thiel, W., *Die soziale Entwicklung Israels in vorstaatlicher Zeit*. 2. Aufl., Neukirchen-Vluyn, 1985.

Thiersch, H., *Ependytes und Ephod. Gottesbild und Priesterkleid im alten Vorderasien*. Stuttgart, 1936.

Thomas, K., *Religion and the Decline of Magic*. London, 1973.

Thomas, L., "On Magic in Medicine", in (author idem) *The Medusa and the Snail. More Notes of a Biology Watcher*. New York, 1979, repr. 1980.

Thompson, R.C., *The Reports of the Magicians and Astrologers of Nineveh and Babylon*. London, Vols.1-2. 1900.

— *Semitic Magic*. London, 1908.

Thomsen, M.-L., *Zauberdiagnose und Schwarze Magie in Mesopotamien*. Copenhagen, 1987 (= Carsten Niebuhr Institute of Ancient Near Eastern Studies 2).

Tigay, J., "Aggadic Exegesis", in H. Tadmor and M. Weinfeld (eds.), *History, Historiography and Interpretation*. pp. 169-90.

Tomback, R.S., *A Comparative Semitic Lexicon of the Phoenician and Punic Languages*, New York, 1978.

Toorn, K. van der, "Echoes of Judaean Necromancy in Isaiah 28,7-22", *ZAW* 100 (1988), pp. 199-217.

Trevor-Roper, H.R., *The European Witch-Craze of the Sixteenth and Seventeenth Centuries*. Harmondsworth, 1967.

Tropper, J., *Nekromantie. Totenbefragung im Alten Orient und im Alten Testament*. Neukirchen-Vluyn, 1989 (= *AOAT* Bd. 223).

Tschinkowitz, H., "Ein Opferschautext aus dem Eponymenjahr Tiglatpilesers I.", in *AfO* 22 (1968/69), pp. 59-62.

Tung Tso-Pin, *Fifty Years of Studies in Oracle Inscriptions*. Tokyo, 1964.

— "Ten Examples of Early Tortoise-shell Inscriptions", *Harvard Journal of Asiatic Studies* 11 (1948), pp. 119-29.

Turner, V., *The Forest of Symbols. Aspects of Ndembu Ritual*. Ithaca (New York), 1967.

— "Symbolic Studies", *Annual Review of Anthropology* 4 (1975), pp. 145-61.

Tylor, E.B., *The Origins of Culture. Part I of "Primitive Culture"*. New York, 1958.

Ünal, A., *Ein Orakeltext über die Intrigen am hethitischen Hof*. Heidelberg, 1978.

Unger, E., *Babylon. Die heilige Stadt nach der Beschreibung der Babylonier*. Berlin and Leipzig, 1931.

Ungnad, A., *Die Deutung der Zukunft bei den Babyloniern und Assyrern*. Leipzig, 1909.

— "Besprechungskunst und Astrologie in Babylonien", *AfO* 14 (1941-44).

Vanderkam, J.C., *Enoch and the Growth of an Apocalyptic Tradition*. Washington (D.C.), 1984.

Van Seters, J., *Abraham in History and Tradition*. New Haven and London, 1975.

— *In Search of History. Historiography in the Ancient World and the Origins of Biblical History*. New Haven and London, 1983.

Vanstiphout, H.L.J., "How Did They Learn Sumerian?", *JCS* 31 (1979), pp. 118-26.

Veijola, T., *Die ewige Dynastie. David und die Entstehung seiner Dynastie nach der deuteronomistischen Darstellung*. Helsinki, 1975.

— *Das Königtum in der Beurteilung der Deuteronomistischen Historiographie. Eine redaktionsgeschichtliche Untersuchung*. Helsinki, 1977.

— *Verheissung in der Krise. Studien zur Literatur und Theologie der Exilszeit anhand des 89. Psalms*. Helsinki, 1982.

Vermes, G., *Jesus the Jew. A Historian's Reading of the Gospels*. London, 1973, repr. 1976.

Vierhaus, R., "Rankes Begriff der historischen Objektivität", in R. Koselleck et al., *Objektivität und Partilichkeit*, pp. 63-77.

Volten, A., *Demotische Traumdeutung (Pap.Carlsberg XIII und XIV Verso)*. Copenhagen, 1942.

Waerden, B.L. van der, "History of the Zodiac", *AfO* 16 (1952/53), pp. 216-30.

Walker, C.B.F., "Notes on the Venus Tablet of Ammisaduqa", *JCS* 36 (1984), pp. 64-66.

Wallis, G., *Zwischen Gericht und Heil. Studien zur alttestamentlichen Prophetie im 7. und 6. Jahrhundert v. Chr.* Berlin, 1987.

Walters, S.D., "The Sorceress and Her Apprentice. A Case Study of an Accusation", *JCS* 23 (1970), pp. 27-38.

Weber, M., *Gesammelte Aufsätze zur Religionssoziologie*, Vols.I-III. Tübingen, 1920-1921.

Weidner, E.F., "Keilschrifttexte nach Kopien von T.G.Pinches", *AfO* 11 (1936-37), pp. 358-69.

— "Die Bibliothek Tiglatpilesers I." in *AfO* 16 (1952/53), pp. 197-215.

— "Die astrologische Serie Enuma Anu Enlil", *AfO* 14 (1944), pp. 172-95; pp. 308-18; 17 (1954-1956), pp. 71-89; 22 (1968-1969), pp. 65-75.

Weippert, H., *Palästina in Vorhellenistischer Zeit*. Munich, 1988.

Weippert, M., "Assyrische Prophetien der Zeit Asarhaddons und Assurbanipals", in F.M. Fales (ed.), *Assyrian Royal Inscriptions: New Horizons...*, pp. 71-104.

Weisberg, D.B., "An Old Babylonian Forerunner to Šumma Alu", *HUCA* 40-41 (1969-1970), pp. 87-105.

Weiser, A., "Die Legitimation des Königs David" *VT* 16 (1966), pp. 325-54.

Wellhausen, J., *Der Text der Bücher Samuelis*. Göttingen, 1871.

— *Prolegomena zur Geschichte Israels*. orig. pub. Berlin, 1883; here 6th edn, Berlin, 1905.

Westbrook, R., "Biblical and Cuneiform Law Codes", *RB* 92 (1985), pp. 247-64.

Westenholz, Aa.,"Old Akkadian School Texts. Some Goals of Sargonic Scribal Education", in *AfO* 25 (1974-1977), pp. 95-110.

White, H., "The Question of Narrative in Contemporary Historical Theory", *History and Theory* 23 (1984), pp. 1-33.

White, R.C., "Techniques in Early Dream Interpretation", in (ed. G. MacRae) *SBLSP* 1976, Missoula (Montana), pp. 323-36.

Whitelam, K.W. — see Coote, R.B.

Whitrow, G.J., *Time in History*. Oxford, 1988.

Widengren, G., *Religionsphänomenologie*. Berlin, 1969.

Wilson, B.R., *Rationality*. Oxford, 1970.

Wilson, R.R., *Prophecy and Society in Ancient Israel*. Philadelphia, 1980.

— *Sociological Approaches to the Old Testament*. Philadelphia, 1984.

Wolff, H.W., *Dodekapropheton I*. Neukirchen-Vluyn, 1961.

Wright, J., "Did Amos Inspect Livers?", *Australian Biblical Review* 23 (1975), pp. 3-11.

Wyatt, N., "The Old Testament Historiography of the Exilic Period", *ST* 33 (1979), pp. 45-67.

Xella, P., "L'influence babylonienne à ougarit, d'après les textes alphabétiques rituels et divinatoires", in: (H.-J. Nissen /J.Renger, eds.), *Mesopotamien und seine Nachbarn...*, Teil I, pp. 321-38.

Young, A., "Some Implications of Medical Beliefs and Practices for Social Anthropology", *AA* 78 (1976), pp. 4-24.

Younger, K.L., *Ancient Conquest Accounts. A Study in Ancient Near Eastern and Biblical History Writing*. Sheffield, 1991.

Zimmern, H., *Beiträge zur Kenntnis der Babylonischen Religion*. Leipzig, 1901.

— "Ein Leitfaden der Beschwörungskunst", *ZA* 30 (1915-1916), pp. 205-29.

Index of Biblical Citations